I0890858

Value Relevance of Accounting Information in Capital Markets

Marianne Ojo
George Mason University, USA

Jeanette Van Akkeren
QUT School of Accountancy, Australia

A volume in the Advances in Finance, Accounting, and Economics (AFAE) Book Series

IGI GLOBAL
DISSEMINATOR OF KNOWLEDGE
www.igi-global.com

Published in the United States of America by
IGI Global
Business Science Reference (an imprint of IGI Global)
701 E. Chocolate Avenue
Hershey PA 17033
Tel: 717-533-8845
Fax: 717-533-8661
E-mail: cust@igi-global.com
Web site: http://www.igi-global.com

Copyright © 2017 by IGI Global. All rights reserved. No part of this publication may be reproduced, stored or distributed in any form or by any means, electronic or mechanical, including photocopying, without written permission from the publisher.
Product or company names used in this set are for identification purposes only. Inclusion of the names of the products or companies does not indicate a claim of ownership by IGI Global of the trademark or registered trademark.

Library of Congress Cataloging-in-Publication Data

Names: Ojo, Marianne, editor. | Van Akkeren, Jeanette, 1960- editor.
Title: Value relevance of accounting information in capital markets / Marianne Ojo and Jeanette Van Akkeren, editors.
Description: Hershey : Business Science Reference, [2017]
Identifiers: LCCN 2016047276| ISBN 9781522519003 (hardcover) | ISBN 9781522519010 (ebook)
Subjects: LCSH: Accounting. | Stock exchanges. | Stocks--Prices.
Classification: LCC HF5636 .V35 2017 | DDC 332/.0415--dc23 LC record available at https://lccn.loc.gov/2016047276

This book is published in the IGI Global book series Advances in Finance, Accounting, and Economics (AFAE) (ISSN: 2327-5677; eISSN: 2327-5685)

British Cataloguing in Publication Data
A Cataloguing in Publication record for this book is available from the British Library.

All work contributed to this book is new, previously-unpublished material. The views expressed in this book are those of the authors, but not necessarily of the publisher.

Advances in Finance, Accounting, and Economics (AFAE) Book Series

ISSN:2327-5677
EISSN:2327-5685

Mission

In our changing economic and business environment, it is important to consider the financial changes occurring internationally as well as within individual organizations and business environments. Understanding these changes as well as the factors that influence them is crucial in preparing for our financial future and ensuring economic sustainability and growth.

The **Advances in Finance, Accounting, and Economics (AFAE)** book series aims to publish comprehensive and informative titles in all areas of economics and economic theory, finance, and accounting to assist in advancing the available knowledge and providing for further research development in these dynamic fields.

Coverage

- Environmental and Social Accounting
- Economic Theory
- Economics of Agriculture and Biotechnology
- Finance and Accounting in SMEs
- International Trade
- Banking
- Economics Geography
- Risk Analysis and Management
- Economics of Risks, Uncertainty, Ambiguity, and Insurance
- Investments and Derivatives

IGI Global is currently accepting manuscripts for publication within this series. To submit a proposal for a volume in this series, please contact our Acquisition Editors at Acquisitions@igi-global.com or visit: http://www.igi-global.com/publish/.

The Advances in Finance, Accounting, and Economics (AFAE) Book Series (ISSN 2327-5677) is published by IGI Global, 701 E. Chocolate Avenue, Hershey, PA 17033-1240, USA, www.igi-global.com. This series is composed of titles available for purchase individually; each title is edited to be contextually exclusive from any other title within the series. For pricing and ordering information please visit http://www.igi-global.com/book-series/advances-finance-accounting-economics/73685. Postmaster: Send all address changes to above address. Copyright © 2017 IGI Global. All rights, including translation in other languages reserved by the publisher. No part of this series may be reproduced or used in any form or by any means – graphics, electronic, or mechanical, including photocopying, recording, taping, or information and retrieval systems – without written permission from the publisher, except for non commercial, educational use, including classroom teaching purposes. The views expressed in this series are those of the authors, but not necessarily of IGI Global.

Titles in this Series

For a list of additional titles in this series, please visit: www.igi-global.com

Tools and Techniques for Economic Decision Analysis
Jelena Stanković (University of Niš, Serbia) Pavlos Delias (Eastern Macedonia and Thrace Institute of Technology, Greece) Srđan Marinković (University of Niš, Serbia) and Sylvie Rochhia (Université Côte d'Azur, CNRS, GREDEG, France)
Business Science Reference • copyright 2017 • 305pp • H/C (ISBN: 9781522509592) • US $205.00 (our price)

Corporate Espionage, Geopolitics, and Diplomacy Issues in International Business
Bryan Christiansen (PryMarke, LLC, USA) and Fatmanur Kasarcı (PryMarke Business Academy, Turkey)
Business Science Reference • copyright 2017 • 374pp • H/C (ISBN: 9781522510314) • US $210.00 (our price)

Handbook of Research on Globalization and the International Political Economy
Abdulkadir Isik (Namik Kemal University, Turkey)
Business Science Reference • copyright 2017 • 397pp • H/C (ISBN: 9781522508526) • US $265.00 (our price)

Handbook of Research on Global Indicators of Economic and Political Convergence
Ramesh Chandra Das (Katwa College, India)
Business Science Reference • copyright 2016 • 616pp • H/C (ISBN: 9781522502159) • US $345.00 (our price)

Global Perspectives on Trade Integration and Economies in Transition
Vasily Erokhin (Moscow University of Finance and Law, Russia)
Business Science Reference • copyright 2016 • 407pp • H/C (ISBN: 9781522504511) • US $210.00 (our price)

Handbook of Research on Social Entrepreneurship and Solidarity Economics
José Manuel Saiz-Álvarez (Tecnológico de Monterrey, Mexico)
Business Science Reference • copyright 2016 • 606pp • H/C (ISBN: 9781522500971) • US $230.00 (our price)

IGI GLOBAL
DISSEMINATOR OF KNOWLEDGE

www.igi-global.com

701 E. Chocolate Ave., Hershey, PA 17033
Order online at www.igi-global.com or call 717-533-8845 x100
To place a standing order for titles released in this series,
contact: cust@igi-global.com
Mon-Fri 8:00 am - 5:00 pm (est) or fax 24 hours a day 717-533-8661

Table of Contents

Detailed Table of Contents

values and its impact on assessing how a relationship or pattern could be established in certain jurisdictions, this chapter is aimed at contributing to the literature on how accounting information could be interpreted or conveyed in such a way as to serve as a useful and vital indicator which will enable investors to interpret financial information in such a way which mitigates information asymmetries between management and investors. It also elaborates on factors which could affect the quality of accounting information – by way of reference to contributing elements of the audit expectations gap. As a result, it recommends measures aimed at addressing issues being faced by jurisdictions which have implemented accounting and legislative reforms as a means of improving the quality of accounting information.

"The sell-off in US Treasury bonds in 2013 had global repercussions, impacting broad ranges of asset classes in both advanced and emerging market economies. The sell-off in 1994 is distinguished from 2003 and 2013 episodes in that, in 1994, not only did long-term rates surge, short-term rates also picked up significantly. By contrast, in both 2003 and 2013, bond market stress was confined mostly to longer maturities, although drivers of the 2003 event were different from those in 2013." As well as analyzing and investigating recent developments in vulnerabilities and volatility on the New York Stock Exchange, this chapter investigates the topic of the value relevance of accounting information in global capital markets as a means of contributing to the topic of value relevance – and particularly highlighting the impact of monetary policies and growth rates of certain economies at a global level. It also highlights why fundamentals presently underlying present stock market volatilities differ from those of previous crises.

In view recent developments which have resulted in the replacement of attributes of relevance and reliability with a new categorization of fundamental qualitative characteristics of accounting information and enhancing qualitative characteristics of accounting information, this chapter is aimed at highlighting why the roles of audits – and particularly accountants and auditors still serve as fundamental, vital and crucial means of verifying financial statements – such that these can be

This chapter aims to investigate the results of the value relevance of accounting information with reference to the study: "The value relevance of accounting information in the Italian and UK stock markets". Results revealed from this study are as follows: - First, evidence shows the greater value relevance of accounting information in Italy than in the UK, even if this result must be explained according to the sample's characteristics. Second, the study underlines that in Italy the most value relevant accounting data refer to earnings while in the UK the focus is mainly on cash flows. The chapter also seeks to contribute to the gap in the literature on the value relevance of accounting information in the UK and Italy. In so doing it investigates the relevance and reliability of results derived in this study, their applicability to current market developments – as well as recent fluctuations and volatility in the financial markets.

"The chief concerns of EMEs (emerging market economies) in relation to their financial systems remain developmental rather than regulatory: increasing financial savings to accelerate growth and development, and deepening their financial system to develop long term funding instruments for infrastructure financing, absorb large inflows of capital to counter the uphill backwash from EMEs to AMEs, reduce the cost of capital and reduce the leads and lags in monetary policy transmission. Advanced market economies (AMEs), on the other hand, need major regulatory changes that inoculate them more effectively against the new risks their financial systems face." As well as investigating these observations, this chapter is aimed at investigating the validity of Efficient Markets Hypothesis and Efficient Capital Markets Hypothesis in emerging economies – as contrasted with advanced market economies. In so doing, it aims to contribute to the extant literature on stock market liquidity and liquidity in capital markets.

Results appear to confirm the theory that stock market liquidity impacts and influences the ability of the market to fully reflect information. The impact of the sizes and development of capital markets on users of financial information will also be considered in this chapter – as well as other factors which could have a possible impact on the value relevance of accounting information. So will the issue of Shadow Banking and recent financial regulatory reforms which embrace the Dodd Frank legislation – as well as Liikannen, Vickers, Volcker rules and reports.

"At the early stages of its establishment the stock market is a complement rather than substitute for the banking sector. Developing the banking sector can promote stock market development as demonstrated by the experiences of many East Asian countries. However, when stock markets are sufficiently developed they tend to compete with the banking sector as shown by findings." How does commercial banking impact investment activities in capital markets – and particularly developed capital markets? Is it true then that in certain economies, the banking sector serves as a complementary component of the financial system – up till a stage where it begins to compete with the securities sector? As well as investigating these observations, this chapter is aimed at investigating the validity of Efficient Markets Hypothesis and Efficient Capital Markets Hypothesis in emerging economies – as contrasted with advanced market economies. In so doing, it aims to contribute to the extant literature on stock market liquidity and liquidity in capital markets.

Globalization is an irreversible process accounting. The global economic crisis that cross, there is need for stronger global accounting standards, to ensure a common language for each type of transaction and for each business sector. The value of intangible assets has been the main focus in the debates between consumers' evaluations about brand name and business world for many decades. Today, this concept interferes with the international process of assessment, but also is influenced by the store name and the quality of merchandise it carries.

This study belongs in the specific line of research into value relevance that aims to assess the consequences on companies' market values of the introduction of the International Accounting Standards. The specific research area concerns the role of the International Accounting Standards (IAS)/International Financial Reporting Standards (IFRS), investigating whether the adoption of the IAS/IFRS has led to a greater correlation between important financial statement values (earning, comprehensive income and equity) and stock market capitalization than in the pre-IAS/IFRS period. The study focuses on the Indian situation, analyzing a sample of 114 companies listed on the Delhi Stock Exchange. We analyze a period of eight years (2008-2015). In relation to the critique of value relevance studies by Holthausen and Watts (2001) and subsequent reactions of Barth et al. (2001), this chapter offers insights about the usefulness of value relevance especially in periods of financial crisis.

As well as illustrating wider and interrelated repercussions of plunging oil prices on the global economy – and its impact on global financial markets, this chapter also re affirms the realization that the strong form of the Efficient Market Hypothesis appears to introduce less accountability than the weak and semi strong components. Even though it appears that fundamentals underlying previous Financial Crises and recent volatilities differ, recent evidence also provides interesting information about turbulences that currently plague global stock markets. Can previous historical records be relied upon (reasonably or otherwise) to predict future outcomes? Where predictability (redictive values) and confirmatory attributes (confirming values) constitute components of relevance in financial reporting, then it appears that certain historical reports, data and information based on the age and relevance of such data, still constitute relevant and reliable data given that such information is current, relevant and reliable in the sense that it can be predicted upon, confirmed and verified.

Rising oil prices, steel prices - as well as the stronger dollar certainly impacted the financial markets during the latter part of May 2016. So also, the expected announcement of higher interest rates in June 2016 by the Federal Reserve. As well as illustrating the impact of financial shocks for emerging economies, this chapter also illustrates the impact of financial shocks for smaller – as well as more advanced economies. Having highlighted through the entire volume, the macroeconomic consequences of the changes and fluctuations of commodity prices – as reflected through the recent global financial market volatilities. This chapter will also focus on the main channels through which commodities price fluctuations affect business cycles in EMEs.

Value-relevance research is an important domain of modern capital market research. Accounting researchers have used the value-relevance research framework in many ways with the aim of measuring whether accounting information has a predicted association with equity market values. One of the most widely used models in value-relevance research is a modification of the Ohlson (1995) market valuation model in which the market value of a firm's equity is presumed to be a function of its book value of equity and abnormal earnings. Furthermore, using the Ohlson (1995) model, accounting researchers have documented the value relevance of different types of financial and non-financial information. Drawing on a selected number of recently published studies that have documented the value relevance of different types of financial and non-financial information, this chapter reviews and integrates recent findings, highlighting challenges and providing future directions for further research in this area.

This chapter presents the results of an empirical investigation on stock trading activity in the context of restatement announcements. The aim is to explore whether sophisticated investors may anticipate accounting restatements, and which factors lead their trading strategies. The empirical analysis shows that sophisticated investors sell before and buy after the announcement. Moreover sophisticated investors trade more when information asymmetry and event-related risk are higher, and do not care about stock's recent performance. In contrast, unsophisticated investors do not follow a particular trading strategy before or after the announcement, stay away from trading when the information gap (risk) is too wide (high), but trade more on stock with positive past performance. Results suggest that sophisticated investors are able to anticipate restatements and exploit their information advantage to speculate.

Whilst some valid and justified arguments have been put forward in favor of ring fencing, that is, constructing a fire-wall between consumer and investment banks, and that such activities can be achieved without restructuring banks into separate legal entities, the Liikanen Report highlights why there is need for such re-structuring. As well as considering the merits of ring fencing and the establishment of separate legal activities and entities, this chapter aims to highlight why a suitable model aimed at mitigating risks of contagion can to a large extent, be justified on a cost-benefit analysis basis. Furthermore, the chapter ultimately concludes that even though a greater degree of separation of legal entities and activities persist with the model which is referred to as "total separation", a certain degree of independence between bank activities would also be necessary under ring fencing if its purposes and objectives are to be fulfilled.

Foreword

In October 2001, the world became aware of the biggest accounting scandal in history. Enron Corporation, an American energy company, announced the restatements of its financial statements for years 1997 to 2000 in order to correct accounting violations. The restatement reduced earnings for the four-year period by $613 million (or 23 percent of reported profits during the period), increased liabilities by $628 million and reduced equity by $1.2 billion at the end of 2000 (Healy & Palepu, 2003). The Enron Scandal, as it was labeled, raised significant questions about American capitalism and its ethics, as well as about accounting regulation. An article published on The Economist on 17 January 2002, titled *Enron: The Real Scandal*, called for systemic reforms in three areas, namely auditor regulation, conflicts of interest, and accounting standards. Leading to one of the busiest enforcement periods for US regulators in all these three areas (Masters, 2011).

The Sarbanes-Oxley Act raised the bar for law enforcement significantly by requiring corporate executives to take personal responsibility for the accuracy of company accounts and by increasing auditors' responsibility in auditing financial statements. Accounting standard setters have moved towards principle-based standards, which have increased disclosure requirements. Despite introducing more discretion in financial reporting, principle-based standards claim to provide a fairer representation of companies' economic value (Hellström, 2006; Barth, Landsman, & Lang, 2008). Empirical research shows that accounting quality has been improving worldwide (Land & Lang, 2002; Barth et al., 2008), but also that the extent of such an improvement depends on other context characteristics such as law enforcement (Cairns, 1999; Street & Gray, 2001; Ball, Robin, & Wu, 2003; Burgstahler, Hail, & Leuz, 2006), regulatory and litigation environment (Bradshaw & Miller, 2008), and management and auditor incentives (Ball et al., 2003).

However, as Karl Marx noted, 'history repeats itself, first as tragedy, second as farce'. And in September 2008, Lehman Brothers Holdings Inc., the fourth largest US investment bank, declared bankruptcy formally igniting the Global Financial Crisis (GFC). Accounting practices were again the first to be in the dock. Following the Lehman collapse, the Financial Times published an article titled *Accounting is*

Dead, which quoted 'investors are once again questioning the value of the financial statements on which they spend such large sums of money' [March 15, 2010].

These major scandals have undermined investors' trust in accounting reports, despite the evident increase in accounting quality. However, accounting reports still represent the primary source of information for investors; what is changed is that investors tend integrate accounting information with other sources such as the Internet (Drake, Roulstone, & Thornock, 2012) and Social Media (Blankespoor, Miller, & White, 2014). In other words, investors tend to consider accounting information as less relevant in their decision-making than they used to.

An accounting number is described as value relevant if it has a significant association with the market value of equity (Barth, Beaver, & Landsman, 2001; Holthausen & Watts, 2001). Empirical research indicates a downward trend in accounting information value relevance (Collins, Maydew, & Weiss, 1997; Francis & Schipper, 1999; Lev & Zarowin, 1999; Core, Guay, & Van Buskirk, 2003; Dontoh, Radhakrishnan, & Ronen, 2004), but such a general trend tends to vary across countries (Hung, 2000).

Holthausen and Watts (2001) classify the extensive 'value-relevance literature' into three categories:

1. Relative association studies, which assess the variance explained in regressing stock market values on accounting measures, to determine whether one accounting standard provides more value relevant accounting information than another standard;
2. Incremental association studies, which examine the explanatory power of accounting numbers for returns or values over a long period;
3. Marginal information content studies, which determine whether the release of accounting information is related to a short-term change in equity values.

The studies reported in this volume provide useful insights on all the key aspects of accounting value relevance presented in the existing literature. In order to better prepare the ground for a deeper understanding of these significant contributions, let us consider the following questions: why is accounting information value relevance so important from a capital markets perspective? What are the effects of unreliable accounting information on capital markets participants?

The primary role of capital markets is to raise long-term funds for governments, banks, and corporations while providing a platform for securities trading. As such, capital markets provide benefit for both organizations and investors. Organizations have access to larger funding and can exploit growth opportunities while investors obtain financial growth from their investment; consequently, the development of capital markets contributes to economic growth. Harris (2002) describes trading as a 'search problem'. Buyers must find sellers, and sellers must find buyers and they both aim to trade at a fair price, which is based upon available information. A large part of the empirical research in accounting and capital markets has focused on testing market efficiency. Fama (1970, 1991) defines a market as efficient if 'security prices fully reflect all available information'. Market efficiency is of great interest to all market participants since security prices determine the allocation of wealth among firms and individuals (Kothari, 2001). Accounting information is a key source for assessing security prices since it describes the past, and provides the basis to estimate the future performance of a firm. Therefore, unreliable accounting information and poor information disclosure compromise market efficiency by enhancing the information gap between the sides of the market (i.e. information asymmetry).

Let us discuss the next question: what are the effects of unreliable accounting information on capital markets participants? In answering this question, I will refer to shares and options trading, since these are the most frequent traded instruments (Harris, 2002).

Shares are units of ownership corresponding to an equal proportion of a company's capital. Shareholders are entitled to an equal claim on the company's profits and an equal obligation for the company's debts and losses. Options are derivatives, meaning that their value is derived from the value of an underlying investment. In most of the cases the underlying investment on which an option is based is the equity shares in a publicly listed company, but they can be also based on stock indexes, exchange traded funds (ETFs), government securities, foreign currencies or commodities. Despite some important differences between shares and options, they are traded in a similar manner. Both shares and options are listed and traded on regulated marketplaces, are transacted through brokers with bids to buy and offers to sell, and can be monitored through the marketplace.

Empirical studies in accounting and finance has demonstrated that information asymmetry and uncertainty have a significant impact on market participants. In this discussion, let us focus in this discussion on three key market participants since they are the key players in capital markets, namely investors, brokers, and dealers.

Investors in capital markets are either individual or institutional (e.g. pension funds, mutual funds). They typically trade with the aim of moving wealth from the present to the future and have different levels of sophistication and risk tolerance (Harris, 2002). In case of information asymmetry, investors can be divided into two categories, namely informed and uninformed investors. Institutional investors and insiders tend to fall into first category because of their ability to process and interpret information, or to access private information. Individual investors tend to fall into the second category. When information asymmetry arises, uninformed investors tend not to trade so as to avoid losing against informed investors. As a result, information asymmetry leads uninformed investors to either give away investment opportunities or incur higher losses.

Brokers are agents who arrange trades for their clients and receive commissions for their services. They also make easier for investors to trade by solving clearing and settling problems, or by providing investment advice. Given that exchanges generally allow only their members to trade, brokers provide the only channel to exchanges that 'average investors' cannot access themselves. Information asymmetry increases the principal-agent problem, which typically exists when one party works on behalf of another party. In this case the information advantage rests on the brokers' side and may result in opportunistic behaviors aimed to increase brokers' commissions at the expense of clients' profits. When a broker takes a trading order from a client, it is a broker responsibility to obtain the best execution of that order. Opportunistic brokers typically violate such a norm for their private gain by exploiting one (or more) of the following practices:

1. **Dual Trading:** Occurs when a broker is also a dealer (broker-dealer) and it completes the orders internally instead of obtaining a better price trading against other dealers;
2. **Order Preferencing:** The routing of order flow to a preferred dealer that compensates the broker;
3. **Front Running:** Occurs when a broker improperly allows one order to trade ahead of another so that the first profits from the price impact of the following order;
4. **Fraudulent Trade Assignment:** Occurs when a broker executes orders on the same side of the market for more than one client and assigns the best prices to the favorite client;
5. **Unauthorized Trading:** Occurs when a broker trades for its clients without authorization.

It appears clear that an 'opaque' market provides higher incentives for such opportunistic behaviors, which may cause significant losses for investors.

Dealers, also known as specialists or market makers, are passive traders that provide liquidity to the market; they trade when other traders want to trade, and profit when buying from impatient traders at a low price or selling to impatient traders at a high price. Being passive traders, they cannot refuse to trade, therefore they need to carefully consider what to trade, when to trade, and at what price to trade. Dealers quote the prices at which they are willing to buy (bid) and sell (ask), the difference between these two prices is referred to as bid-ask spread. As passive traders, dealers lose when trading against informed investors therefore, when information asymmetry rises, they defend themselves by widening the bid-ask spread; in such a way they are able to recover from uninformed investors what they may have lost in trading with informed investors. This recovery from losses enables dealers to be more financially sustainable in the long run; in other words, information asymmetry increases the risk of dealer's activity and trading costs.

To summarize, value relevant accounting information provides a clear view of the economic value of companies and provides a significant contribution to capital markets development, which, in turn enables long-term economic growth.

This volume provides useful insights into the importance of value relevance of accounting information in capital markets. By addressing developed and developing countries, and theoretical and empirical studies, the volume allows the reader to explore the topic from different perspectives.

This volume is not just for academics; it is also for practitioners, accountants and regulators. The recent economic crisis has shown how interconnected the relationship between accounting, capital markets and the overall economy are, and how these relationships extend over national boundaries. In order to avoid other similar devastating crises in the future, it is essential to promote a collaborative and open approach to financial and accounting regulation. Accounting standard setters have been moving towards unified standards and market regulators around the world are working hard to increase market transparency, however further collaboration between standard setters, academics and practitioners is needed to converge upon international shared accounting and ethics standards. By proving a multidimensional view of the topic, I believe this volume is a good step in that direction.

Pierangelo Rosati
Irish Centre for Cloud Computing and Commerce (IC4), Dublin City University, Ireland

REFERENCES

Ball, R., Robin, A., & Wu, J. S. (2003). Incentives versus standards: Properties of accounting income in four East Asian countries. *Journal of Accounting and Economics*, *36*(1), 235–270. doi:10.1016/j.jacceco.2003.10.003

Barth, M. E., Beaver, W. H., & Landsman, W. R. (2001). The relevance of the value relevance literature for financial accounting standard setting: Another view. *Journal of Accounting and Economics*, *31*(1), 77–104. doi:10.1016/S0165-4101(01)00019-2

Barth, M. E., Landsman, W. R., & Lang, M. H. (2008). International accounting standards and accounting quality. *Journal of Accounting Research*, *46*(3), 467–498. doi:10.1111/j.1475-679X.2008.00287.x

Blankespoor, E., Miller, G. S., & White, H. D. (2014). The role of dissemination in market liquidity: Evidence from firms use of Twitter. *Accounting Review*, *89*(1), 79–112. doi:10.2308/accr-50576

Bradshaw, M. T., & Miller, G. S. (2008). Will harmonizing accounting standards really harmonize accounting? Evidence from non-US firms adopting US GAAP. *Journal of Accounting, Auditing & Finance*, *23*(2), 233–264.

Burgstahler, D. C., Hail, L., & Leuz, C. (2006). The importance of reporting incentives: Earnings management in European private and public firms. *Accounting Review*, *81*(5), 983–1016. doi:10.2308/accr.2006.81.5.983

Cairns, D. (1999). Degrees of compliance. *Accountancy International*, *68*, 69.

Collins, D. W., Maydew, E. L., & Weiss, I. S. (1997). Changes in the value-relevance of earnings and book values over the past forty years. *Journal of Accounting and Economics*, *24*(1), 39–67. doi:10.1016/S0165-4101(97)00015-3

Core, J. E., Guay, W. R., & Van Buskirk, A. (2003). Market valuations in the new economy: An investigation of what has changed. *Journal of Accounting and Economics*, *34*(1), 43–67. doi:10.1016/S0165-4101(02)00087-3

Dontoh, A., Radhakrishnan, S., & Ronen, J. (2004). The Declining Value-relevance of Accounting Information and Non-Information-based Trading: An Empirical Analysis. *Contemporary Accounting Research*, *21*(4), 795–812. doi:10.1506/J6P4-2UYP-HFXY-RBT1

Drake, M. S., Roulstone, D. T., & Thornock, J. R. (2012). Investor information demand: Evidence from Google searches around earnings announcements. *Journal of Accounting Research*, *50*(4), 1001–1040. doi:10.1111/j.1475-679X.2012.00443.x

Fama, E. F. (1970). Efficient capital markets: A review of theory and empirical work. *The Journal of Finance*, *25*(2), 383–417. doi:10.2307/2325486

Fama, E. F. (1991). Efficient capital markets: II. *The Journal of Finance*, *46*(5), 1575–1617. doi:10.1111/j.1540-6261.1991.tb04636.x

Francis, J., & Schipper, K. (1999). Have financial statements lost their relevance? *Journal of Accounting Research*, *37*(2), 319–352. doi:10.2307/2491412

Harris, L. (2002). *Trading and exchanges: Market microstructure for practitioners*. Oxford University Press.

Healy, P. M., & Palepu, K. G. (2003). The fall of Enron. *The Journal of Economic Perspectives*, *17*(2), 3–26. doi:10.1257/089533003765888403

Hellström, K. (2006). The value relevance of financial accounting information in a transition economy: The case of the Czech Republic. *European Accounting Review*, *15*(3), 325–349. doi:10.1080/09638180600916242

Holthausen, R. W., & Watts, R. L. (2001). The relevance of the value-relevance literature for financial accounting standard setting. *Journal of Accounting and Economics*, *31*(1), 3–75. doi:10.1016/S0165-4101(01)00029-5

Hung, M. (2000). Accounting standards and value relevance of financial statements: An international analysis. *Journal of Accounting and Economics*, *30*(3), 401–420. doi:10.1016/S0165-4101(01)00011-8

Kothari, S. (2001). Capital markets research in accounting. *Journal of Accounting and Economics*, *31*(1), 105–231. doi:10.1016/S0165-4101(01)00030-1

Land, J., & Lang, M. H. (2002). Empirical evidence on the evolution of international earnings. *Accounting Review*, *77*(Suppl. 1), 115–133. doi:10.2308/accr.2002.77.s-1.115

Lev, B., & Zarowin, P. (1999). The Boundaries of Financial Reporting and How to Extend Them (Digest Summary). *Journal of Accounting Research*, *37*(2), 353–385. doi:10.2307/2491413

Masters, B. (2011, December 1). Enron's fall raised the bar in regulation. *Financial Times*. Retrieved from http://www.ft.com/cms/s/0/9790ea78-1aa9-11e1-ae14-00144feabdc0.html-axzz4Hx8gXalq

Street, D. L., & Gray, S. J. (2001). *Observance of international accounting standards: Factors explaining non-compliance*. Certified Accountants Educational Trust.

Preface

In line with its predecessor volume, "Analyzing the Relationship between Corporate Social Responsibility and Foreign Direct Investment", this volume highlights and consolidates on the importance and significance of information asymmetries as a vital component and aspect of the rationale for financial regulation – with respect to the banking industry, as well as the insurance and securities sectors.

The following observations from a study also highlight the link and relationship between information asymmetries and systemic risks:

According to results from an investigation by Fernandes, Igan and Pinheiro (2015, p. 5),

Markets tend to react to stress test announcements, with the direction of the price reaction dependent on the nature of the news (e.g., whether the scenarios depict more or less stressful conditions than the markets foresee or whether a bank has failed or passed the quantitative thresholds). Higher moments of the distribution are also affected and trading activity picks up. Interestingly, the reaction is not limited to the tested banks only, affecting as well banks that are not subject to the tests. This suggests that stress tests reveal information about systemic risk (or the supervisor's perception thereof), which by definition is relevant for all banks.

As well as the above findings, they also conclude that public disclosure seems to help reduce informational asymmetries and that more importantly, public disclosure of stress test results (and methodology) does not seem to have reduced private incentives to generate information or to have led to distorted incentives.

Information uncertainty, as well as information asymmetries, generate far reaching and overwhelming consequences whose effects may prove difficult to reverse – as this volume and its individual chapters will seek to illustrate. The impact of information uncertainty, within the context of global and national financial markets could unleash domino effects whose impacts could be synonymous to those generated from the opening of "Pandora's box".

As illustrated by the recent EU Referendum in the United Kingdom, could the repercussions of the Brexit campaign results of 24th June 2016 be reversed – through the blocking of Brexit or a second referendum vote? Are the immediate domino effects merely temporary or would they sustain long term adverse repercussions? Is it justifiable to panic – given the volatility of financial markets?

A very vital lesson drawn from the build up to the Brexit poll results to its release, are problems associated with the disconnect between Westminster, many parts of England, as well as communities – particularly those communities who had lost mining industries – resulting in high unemployment levels, and the need to engage with changing communities. The EU Referendum also revealed wider repercussions of the failure of the executive to effectively engage with those who elected them – and this is clearly reflected in the surprising results inflicted by those voters whose actions have not only caused seismic repercussions, but also changed the course and path of the direction of the United Kingdom – being the first member state of the European Union to leave the Union after forty-three years.

The introductory chapter to the volume, "The Need for Global Adoption of International Financial Reporting Standards: Post Enron Consequences and the Restoration of Confidence to Capital Markets" considers the background culminating in the adoption of IFRS – as well as the need for the adoption of IFRS. It also highlights why the value relevance of accounting information is also of vital significance in certain emerging economies and why the successful implementation of IFRS in these jurisdictions may be crucial in restoring investor confidence – particularly in the aftermath of stock market crashes in these economies.

Chapter Two "Mitigating Information Asymmetries in Capital Markets: The Audit Expectations Gap" highlights the impact of the audit expectations gap (AEG) in assessing the extent to which accounting information can be relied upon based on given market values and its impact on assessing how a relationship or pattern could be established in certain jurisdictions. Further, the chapter is aimed at contributing to the literature on how accounting information could be interpreted or conveyed in such a way as to serve as a useful and vital indicator which will enable investors to interpret financial information in such a way which mitigates information asymmetries between management and investors.

Chapter Three "Value Relevance of Accounting Information in Capital Markets: The New York Stock Exchange", analyzes and investigates recent developments in vulnerabilities and volatility on the New York Stock Exchange. Further, the chapter investigates the topic of the value relevance of accounting information in global capital markets as a means of contributing to the topic of value relevance – and particularly highlighting the impact of monetary policies and growth rates of certain economies at a global level. It also highlights why fundamentals presently underlying present stock market volatilities differ from those of previous crises.

Chapter Four, Fundamental or Enhancing Roles?: The Dual Roles of External Auditors and Forensic Accountants, is aimed at highlighting why the roles of audits – and particularly accountants and auditors still serve as fundamental, vital and crucial means of verifying financial statements – such that these can be reasonably relied upon by investors in financial and capital markets. This chapter is also aimed at highlighting why such enhancing characteristics could be regarded as fundamental qualitative characteristics.

Chapter Five, Value Relevance of Accounting Information in the Emerging Chinese Stock Market (Re Visited), accentuates on why value relevance of accounting information is a very important issue – not just from the perspective of Foreign Direct Investment and the reliability and relevance of financial and accounting information for investors – whether institutional of individual, but also in respect of matters relating to Corporate Social Responsibility and financial reporting. This being of crucial importance given the need to enhance the quality and presentation of financial information, as well as the need for comparability and consistency as a means of enhancing the relevance and reliability of financial information. It is also highlights why the issue of reconciliation of discrepancies constitutes a matter in need of urgent redress in capital markets.

Chapter Six, Value Relevance of Accounting Information in Capital Markets: A Comparative Analysis between Jurisdictions from the Middle East, Africa and Asia, is specifically aimed at investigating the trends in value relevance of accounting information in these stock markets and exchanges. Further, amongst other goals and objectives, this chapter also seeks to illustrate why in light of recent developments which have resulted in decline of reliability - as a valued attribute, relevance and reliability still constitute fundamental characteristics which are required in the development of global stock markets and economies. It consolidates this aim in view of recent IASB and FASB's initiatives and the resulting framework which categorizes understandability, comparability, timeliness and verifiability as enhancing qualitative characteristics of accounting information.

Chapter Seven, Revisiting the Value Relevance of Accounting Information in the Italian and UK stock markets, investigates the results of the value relevance of accounting information with reference to the study: "The value relevance of accounting information in the Italian and UK stock markets". The chapter also seeks to contribute to the gap in the literature on the value relevance of accounting information in the UK and Italy. In so doing it investigates the relevance and reliability of results derived in this study, their applicability to current market developments – as well as recent fluctuations and volatility in the financial markets.

Chapter Eight, The Determinants of Stock Market Development in Emerging Economies: Examining the Impact of Corporate Governance and Regulatory Reforms (I), specifically focuses on investigating the validity of Efficient Markets Hypothesis and Efficient Capital Markets Hypothesis in emerging economies – as contrasted with advanced market economies. In so doing, it aims to contribute to the extant literature on stock market liquidity and liquidity in capital markets.

Chapter Nine, The Determinants of Stock Market Development in Emerging Economies: Examining the Impact of Corporate Governance and Regulatory Reforms (II), considers and addresses the impact of the sizes and development of capital markets on users of financial information – as well as other factors which could have a possible impact on the value relevance of accounting information. Recent financial regulatory reforms which embrace the Dodd Frank legislation – as well as Liikannen, Vickers, Volcker rules and reports, are also considered in the aim to provide a better understanding of financial regulatory reforms that have taken place in response to the recent global Financial Crisis.

The chapter, hence, also aims to highlight and enlighten on various factors which have contributed to difficulties in the implementation of such reforms, particularly in emerging market economies – further exacerbating the pace of the current global economic recovery – which has had considerable impact and bearing on recent stock market volatilities being experienced around the globe. Whilst it is evident that the decline in oil prices – largely attributed to excess supply by major oil exporting countries, has played a crucial part in the recent volatilities across global financial markets, other factors which, to a larger of lesser extent, have assumed a role in stock and capital market reactions, will be considered as illustrated through the chapters, and by way of specific reference to the value relevance of accounting information. Such factors, which include the level of transparency and public disclosure will also be analyzed and discussed comprehensively by way of reference to the Efficient Capital Markets Hypothesis and Efficient Markets Hypothesis.

Chapter Ten, The Determinants of Stock Market Development and Liquidity in Capital Markets, also investigates the validity of Efficient Markets Hypothesis and Efficient Capital Markets Hypothesis in emerging economies – as contrasted with advanced market economies. In so doing, it aims to contribute to the extant literature on stock market liquidity and liquidity in capital markets.

Under chapter Eleven, Estimating the Brand Image in the Process of Accounting Convergence. Perceptions and Practices Gap, the author attempts to highlight how "very important it is that those who investigate aspects of brand image (brand satisfaction, brand trust and brand loyalty) set realistic goals." Furthermore, it is accentuated that the auditor should consider also whether individual differences of brand image and reputation are accepted as reasonable or oriented in one direction as cumulated can have a significant effect on the financial statements. Are brands immune from financial markets' volatility? If so, to what extent? Diamond brands such as those of Nirav Modi, are considered to be "recession proof" – as revealed by its founder in a recent interview. Whilst gold is considered to be more volatile, diamonds are also considered to rise steadily in prices. However other brands such as Marks and Spencer have not fared so well with the pound's devaluation - particularly in the post Brexit world.

Under Chapter Twelve, Value Relevance of Accounting Information in Capital Markets of India, a study which focuses on the Indian situation, analyzing a sample of 114 companies listed on the Delhi Stock Exchange, constitutes the subject matter of consideration. A period of eight years (2008-2015) is analyzed - such length of analysis period, as stated by the author, constituting " a feature that distinguishes this study from previous studies on value relevance conducted in India." Furthermore, as highlighted in the chapter, insights about the usefulness of value relevance especially in periods of financial crisis are illustrated.

Chapter Thirteen, Impact of Declining Oil Prices on Global Markets and Economy, investigates recent global developments incorporating a consideration of countries which are likely to benefit from falling oil prices, as well as countries which are likely to bear the greatest impact of the oil price plunges. The chapter also considers developments which have resulted in the fall in global oil prices.

Chapter Fourteen, Information Uncertainty and Volatility in Global Financial Markets, further consolidates on chapter thirteen in comprehensively discussing the impact of commodity prices on global financial markets, as well as channels through which interest rate increases may be expected to impact prices. In so doing it considers the link between capital flows, commodity prices and common global factors in commodity exporters. It also attempts to highlight why much research is still needed in the field of empirical research, as contrasted with theoretical based research, in establishing a more conclusive link between interest rates and commodity prices.

Chapter Fifteen, The Value Relevance of Financial and Non-financial Information: Evidence from Recent Academic Literature, reviews and integrates recent findings, highlighting challenges and providing future directions for further research in this area through a consideration of a selected number of recently published studies that have documented the value relevance of different types of financial and non-financial information. Further, as highlighted by its authors, the chapter provides insight into the new types of information that have been proven to be value relevant and on incremental contributions made by researchers in other areas. The value relevance research findings have potential to be used by regulators and standard setters to increase the usefulness of financial and non-financial information.

Chapter Sixteen, Information Asymmetries in the Context of Restatement Announcements, provides an insight into whether sophisticated investors are able to predict certain events – in addition to a consideration of factors that influence their trading strategies. This chapter also clearly illustrates that sophisticated investors appear to trade at higher volumes when information asymmetries and risk associated events are higher – with disregard for the recent performance about the stock.

Further the chapter highlights that in contrast, unsophisticated investors are not influenced by a particular trading strategy – in relation to announcements – with less involvement in trading where there are indications of high risk levels and with greater involvement in relation to data based on positive past performance.

The results provided in the chapter also indicate and imply that sophisticated investors are able to "anticipate restatements and exploit information advantage to speculate around the event."

As highlighted by authors of the chapter, results and data provided in this chapter highlight the fact that unsophisticated investors mostly rely on accounting information in deciding their trading strategies while sophisticated investors integrate accounting information with other sources which allow them to better predict firm's future performance and detect the non-reliability of accounting information. Furthermore, in their opinion, the negative stock price reaction, which follows a restatement announcement, is partly due to the revision of accounting information and partly to lower trust in management capabilities and the accounting information they provide.

Chapter Seventeen, Volcker/Vickers Hybrid"?: Liikanen Report & Justifications For Ring Fencing, through a consideration of the merits of ring fencing and the establishment of separate legal activities and entities, aims to highlight why a suitable model aimed at mitigating risks of contagion can to a large extent, be justified on a cost-benefit analysis basis. Furthermore, the chapter ultimately concludes that even though a greater degree of separation of legal entities and activities persist with the model which is referred to as „total separation", a certain degree of independence between bank activities would also be necessary under ring fencing if its purposes and objectives are to be fulfilled.

Chapter Eighteen, Ring Fencing Volcker's Rule? Justifications for Ring Fencing and Separate Legal Entities Revisited, highlights why ring fencing not only presents a more feasible and cost effective option to other models, but also why its degree of flexibility provides the more appropriate balance in a financial environment whose trend is increasingly inclined towards conglomeration. Even though the Liikanen Report highlights why there is need for re-structuring of banks into separate legal entities – as a means of achieving ring fencing activities, the mandatory separation of banks' proprietary trading and other risky activities, such as that opted for under the Liikanen Report could be distinguished from the position under Volcker's Rule in the sense that it does not impose such stringent requirements as those applicable under Volcker's Rule – whilst not being as flexible as ring fencing recommendations proposed in the Vickers Report.

The EU Referendum which was held in the United Kingdom on the 23rd June 2016, as well as the build up to the process, has not only contributed immensely to the volatility triggered in global financial markets – but also to immense uncertainty in the coming months and years.

Table 1. The final results

Leave Voters	Remain Voters
17,410,742	16,141,241

The full and potential impact of the results of the Referendum were not evident till the morning of the 24th June 2016 – when the entire nation, as well as the global community, woke up to the shock which the Referendum results confirmed – as well further repercussions and ripples that were to be generated from the Brexit results.

The turnout amounted to 72.2%, the highest for 25 years (since 1992). Results of the Referendum confirmed a 51.9% victory margin for the Leave Campaign – as compared to the 48.1% of votes which were garnered by the Remain Voters.

Immediate broader and far reaching consequences of the results are as follows:

- The announcement of the Prime Minister's resignation at around 8.20am on the morning of the 24th June 2016 – as well as announcements that a new Prime Minister was to be elected by the end of October 2016.
- The depreciation of the pound to lowest levels (against the dollar) since 1985.
- Bank shares also amongst those hardest hit – with these plummeting by about 20%.
- With 62% of Scottish voters having chosen to remain in the EU, prospects of a second independence referendum (following that which was held in 2014), were also looming. The Scottish First Minister, Nicola Sturgeon, announced that options for these were open and were also on the table.

The global turmoil in financial markets following the release of the Referendum results, were also even more dramatic – given the announcements which had followed immediately the polls ended at 10pm on the 23rd June 2016 – namely, market indications that the pound was at its highest levels for months – owing to anticipations and optimism that the United Kingdom would remain in the European Union.

Such was the optimism that it was also rumored on the evening of the 23rd June 2016, that the UKIP leader, Nigel Farage, had also conceded.

Consequences of the results of the Referendum are namely, the triggering of Article 50 of the EU Treaty – process which could only be initiated by one party to the Agreement – the United Kingdom.

- The UK could unilaterally determine the date of its exit, but a decision to exit would most likely be irrevocable. Once triggered, Article 50 of the EU Treaty provides for a two-year process for negotiating the terms of the departing

> state's withdrawal and its future relations with the EU, but there is no requirement for remaining EU countries to reach agreement with an exiting party. An extension to negotiations could be granted, but would require unanimous consent from other EU governments (IMF, IMF Country Report No 16/168, June 2016).

It was the UK's intention to trigger Article 50 of the EU Treaty within three months (during which a new Prime Minister was to be sought and elected by the end of October 2016). However, events of the following days and weeks confirmed that this would be more complicated and controversial than initially anticipated.

Given the shocks that were still reverberating round the global financial markets, as well as wider repercussions emanating from the EU Referendum results, the level of uncertainty and the need to mitigate such levels, were paramount.

As highlighted by the IMF (IMF, 2016:10,11), "A protracted period of uncertainty could weigh on confidence and investment and increase financial market volatility". It has also been reiterated by the IMF that a protracted period of uncertainty could weigh on confidence and investment and increase financial market volatility – with the further risk that markets may anticipate significant negative economic effects from an exit and bring them forward via an adverse market reaction in the immediate aftermath of an exit vote.

Such a risk scenario, it is further added by the IMF, could involve some combination of higher borrowing costs for households and individuals due to higher risk premia, downward pressure on equity and house prices, and even a sudden stop of investment inflows into key sectors such as commercial real estate and finance. The UK's record-high current account deficit and attendant reliance on external financing exacerbates these risks."

Closing results of the financial week, following the release of the EU Referendum results, are as shown in Table 2.

The financial market results above also highlight the impact and urgency reflected as investors seek to move their investments from more risky portfolios to safer havens – a shift from perceived risky investments.

Table 2.

Dow Jones	-610.32	
FTSE 100	-199.41	With the FTSE 100 having initially reached as low as -315.94 (-6025.68) in the immediate aftermath of the release of the results
Nikkei 225	-1,286.33	

Indeed, the EU Referendum results, generated seismic consequences – whose impact was to be felt and whose consequences were to be revealed in the days and weeks (and perhaps months) to come.

As well as the far reaching consequences generated from the EU Referendum results, the financial market's reaction to the EU Referendum on the eve of the release of the results, namely following the close of the voting process at 10pm on the 23rd June 2016, illustrates that even the markets cannot be relied upon in predicting eventual results.

As well as capping off, within positive regions (+73) on the FTSE 100, the value of the pound, it was announced, reached its highest levels in months, following the closing of the voting process at 10pm on the 23rd June 2016.

Consequences of the lower value of the pound (as revealed the following day are as follows):

- Higher import prices.
- Higher inflation levels.

However, lower export prices are also to be expected – which is good news for exports.

On the 25th of June 2016, two days after the Referendum had taken place, even greater and far reaching repercussions were to be revealed.

Having met and decided that greater uncertainty within the Eurozone should be avoided, six foreign ministers from founding nations of the European Union member states announced that Article 50 had to be triggered immediately by the United Kingdom – rather than accommodate a delay in the negotiating process.

Having highlighted the concerns relating to uncertainty, such a reaction is quite understandable – however it is probably also unexpected given the caution added in relation to the hasty election of a new Prime Minister – as well as the need to observe the markets for a while – given its susceptibility to volatilities and fluctuations.

Coupled with the now "more complicated" procedures involved in facilitating the triggering of Article 50, was also the decision of the Scottish First Minister to instigate negotiations aimed at securing Scottish interests in the European Union – a process which could eventually result in a second independent referendum. The Scottish National Party's move was also of such significance – not only because of the potential breakup of the United Kingdom (a possible consequence of a second independence referendum), but also the added uncertainty which this created and generated for the entire process.

In just about thirty-six hours (or less), following the announcement of the EU Referendum results, the UK's Economic Outlook had been altered from stable to negative by a leading credit agency (Moody's). Further, the UK's European Commissioner, Lord Hill announced his resignation.

Further wider repercussions are anticipated in the coming days and weeks to come. Whatever such repercussions may be, one thing is certain – elements or further actions and developments which could generate greater uncertainty and instability in the involved economies – as well as the global economy, need to be addressed or avoided, as swiftly as possible.

In echoing the French Foreign Minister (Jean Marc Ayrault):

It's in Britain's interest and in the interest of Europeans not to have a period of uncertainty.

Acknowledgment

To all those who have never stopped giving hope.

For all wonderful sources of inspiration.

For battles and sacrifices made in the name of love and peace.

For support, courage and unacknowledged sources of contribution and efforts.

For all noble causes whose selfless contributions continue to, and will continue to make enduring impact.

To all those dear and wonderful fountains of knowledge, past and present alma maters.

To the most memorable almas of "Queens" and Aberystwyth – my wonderful colleagues at Cwrt Mawr Hall, Pam Williams and Professor Holland, Kate Whittingham, Margaret, Cynthia, Mo, Sonia Mahoney, Maha Al Sayed, to name a few – and of course, one of the best friends ever – Maria Combarros Iglesias.

For all those whose memories continue to make positive impacts – and particularly those never knowing or having ever known just how powerful such impacts are.

To all the committed and dedicated editorial team members of IGI whose efforts have contributed towards generating high quality outputs.

To all staff at the American Accounting Association who have helped to solicit contributors for the volume.

Finally to all wonderful colleagues at various academic institutions of employment, past and present, who have supported and still continue to support over the years. And to the wonderful city of Frankfurt for providing the opportunity to work in, and experience such an amazing period in such an amazing city. Vielen Dank!

Brexit and the US Presidential elections have surely constituted the focal points of information uncertainty in 2016 - as well as their impacts on the global financial markets - particularly stock exchanges in London and New York.

Chapter 1
The Need for Global Adoption of International Financial Reporting Standards:
Post-Enron Consequences and the Restoration of Confidence to Capital Markets Following the 2008 Financial and Stock Market Crises

Marianne Ojo
George Mason University, USA

ABSTRACT

Many questions have been raised as to whether financial accounting has become more conservative. The value relevance and qualitative characteristics of accounting information have become topics of particular relevance given the role they have assumed in influencing the value judgment of investors in deciding whether or not to invest in a certain market. Given the quality of accounting information – which has resulted in misleading and inaccurate information, it became evident, particularly following Enron's collapse, to adopt improved, enhanced, better quality standards: namely, International Financial Reporting Standards. This chapter considers the background culminating in the adoption of IFRS – as well as the need for the adop-

DOI: 10.4018/978-1-5225-1900-3.ch001

Copyright ©2017, IGI Global. Copying or distributing in print or electronic forms without written permission of IGI Global is prohibited.

tion of IFRS. It also highlights why the value relevance of accounting information is also of vital significance in certain emerging economies and why the successful implementation of IFRS in these jurisdictions may be crucial in restoring investor confidence – particularly in the aftermath of stock market crashes in these economies.

INTRODUCTION

Post Enron consequences such as the introduction of various legislation – most notable of which is the Sarbanes Oxley Act, as well as the need for embracing International Financial Reporting Standards (IFRS), have certainly had immense impact, not only within the United States, but also globally.

Part of the problems attributed to Enron's collapse is considered to have originated from the use of off balance sheet instruments. One consequence of the global adoption and implementation of IFRS will be the operation of larger balance sheets since a lot of financial instruments which had not previously been accounted for on the face of the balance sheet, will now be brought under the scope of the balance sheet.

IAS 32 and IAS 39 address off-balance sheet instruments. Off balance sheet instruments created problems in the Parmalat and Enron cases as they were not reflected in the balance sheet – even though sizes could have been as large as two to three times global GDP. The standards bring the financial instruments under the balance sheet. One of the biggest challenges facing the IASB constitutes reconciling IAS 32 and 39 globally – with the US in particular. Other debates relating to IAS 32 and 39 include the distinction between debt and equity as this distinction does not exist in the markets. Bond converts to equity under certain circumstances and vice versa. Under IAS 32 what you could call equity may not be permitted under banking regulation.

There are currently four standards in issue by the International Accounting Standards Board (IASB),which relate to financial instruments. These are: IAS 32[1] financial instruments: presentation; IAS 39 financial instruments: recognition and measurement; IFRS 7 financial instruments: disclosures, and IFRS 9 financial instruments.

As well as being a replacement for IAS 39, IFRS 9 will not be mandatory until 2015 (although early application is permitted)."[2]

IAS 32 deals with all types of financial instruments, both recognized and unrecognized and should be applied to contracts to buy or sell a non-financial item that can be settled net

- In cash,
- By another financial instrument, or

- By exchanging financial instruments, as if the contracts were financial instruments (with the exception of contracts for the purpose of the receipt or delivery of a non-financial item, in accordance with the entity's expected purchase, sale, or usage requirements).

The presentation requirements for IAS 32 apply to the classification of financial instruments into:

- Financial assets;
- Financial liabilities; or
- Equity instruments.

and income should be classified into:

- Related interest;
- Dividends; and
- Losses and gains.[3]

The International Financial Reporting Standards (IFRS) refers to a series of accounting pronouncements published by the IASB to help preparers of financial statements, throughout the world to produce and present high quality, transparent, and comparable financial information. (Impey, n. d.).

Globalization is an inevitable process and high quality standards are crucial to securing and restoring the trust reposed by investors in financial and non-financial information (also playing a crucial role in contributing to a country's economic growth and development.

IFRS 1 deals with the First Time Adoption of IFRS

The objective of this International Financial Reporting Standard (IFRS) is to ensure that an entity's first IFRS financial statements and its interim financial reports for part of the period covered by those financial statements contain high-quality information that is

- *Transparent for users and comparable over all periods presented.*
- *Provides a suitable starting point for accounting under IFRS.*
- *Can be generated at a cost that does not exceed the benefits to users.*

The value relevance and qualitative characteristics of accounting information have become topics of particular relevance given the role they have assumed in influencing the value judgment of investors (local or international) in deciding whether or not to invest in a certain market.

Improved transparency and comparability of accounting and financial information, as well as other benefits of high quality standards which should be derived from the adoption of IFRS: benefits such as improved attributes of information (such as relevance, reliability, understandability), will certainly ensure that users of financial information benefit from better decision making as well as restoring the confidence of investors in the aftermath of economic, capital market and financial crises, which have damaged the credibility of audits, and financial reporting.

As already highlighted, IFRS 9 (Financial Instruments), replaces IAS 39, one of the Standards inherited by the IASB when it began its work in 2001 (IFRS, 2014a, p. 4). Based on the IFRS project summary (IFRS, 2014a, p. 4), the IASB previously published versions of IFRS 9 that introduced new classification and measurement requirements (in 2009 and 2010) and a new hedge accounting model (in 2013). Further it confirms that the July 2014 publication represents the final version of the Standard, replaces earlier versions of IFRS 9 and completes the IASB's project to replace IAS 39.

The above represents one of the many initiatives currently being undertaken by the IASB and FASB to facilitate coherence, consistency and the convergence of financial reporting standards.

Ongoing Efforts by the FASB to Facilitate the Consistency of Standards: Codification

Based on the FASB Codification Guide (FAF, 2014, p. 35), before the Codification, authoritative US GAAP was not just a proliferation of thousands of standards established by a variety of standard setters over the last 50-plus years the standards lacked a consistent and logical structure. Furthermore, the Guide states that in the 20 years leading up to the Codification, there had been an explosive increase in financial reporting guidance compounding the difficulties in using US GAAP.

Table 1. Brief comparison between IFRS 9 and IAS 39

IAS 39	IFRS 9
Rule based	Principles based
Difficult to apply	Classification based on business model and nature of cash flows
Multiple impairment models	One impairment model
Own credit gains and losses recognized in profit or loss for fair value option (FVO) liabilities	Own credit gains and losses presented in OCI for FVO liabilities
Complicated reclassification rules	Business model-driven reclassification

Source of Table: IFRS. (2014, July). 9 Financial Instruments (p. 6).

According to the Codification Guide, there were three major reasons to pursue a Codification:

- First, the vast majority of constituents believed that the then-current structure of US GAAP was unwieldy, difficult to understand, and difficult to use. In addition, due to the dispersed nature of US GAAP, constituents believed that they may have missed relevant literature when they performed research. They believed that it took excessive levels of research to gain comfort that they had adequately researched an issue. The volume, complexity, and lack of integration made it difficult for professionals to stay up-to-date and to train staff. These issues increase financial reporting risks and create inefficiencies that lead to increased costs.

Hence the mission of the FASB, according to the Guide, was directed at improving the standards of financial accounting and reporting for issuers, auditors, and users of financial information.

- Second, the Codification would simplify several aspects of the FASB's standard-setting process.

Integrating all related literature into one location, as highlighted in the Guide, would allow the FASB to more easily (p. 35 & 36):

1. Integrate the new conceptual framework when completed.
2. Adopt a more principles-based or objectives-based model.
3. Identify differences and converge FASB and IASB standards.
4. Identify all relevant guidance for new projects e. Identify outdated literature for removal.
5. Identify internal inconsistencies between different pieces of literature that may address related matters.

The third major reason for pursuing a codification, as indicated in the Codification Guide related to "the disorganized state of authoritative US GAAP literature before the Codification - a result of 50+ years of effort by multiple standard-setting entities." It was also stated that each of the multiple standard-setting entities issued numbered standards with different sequencing and in different documents – and that with more than 2,000 such standards, the sequential numbering did not facilitate easy research or retrieval. The importance of designing a database with ease of retrieval in mind would, accordingly, it was reiterated, "significantly simplify and improve the efficiency of electronic research by constituents."

Among other things, the Codification is expected to (see FAF, 2014, p. 5 & 45):

1. Reduce the amount of time and effort required to solve an accounting research issue
2. Mitigate the risk of noncompliance through improved usability of the literature
3. Provide accurate information with realtime updates as Accounting Standards Updates are released
4. Assist the FASB with the research and convergence efforts.

As regards Basel III regulatory convergence, the United States is definitely better accustomed to the current Basel III framework – hence making the process of convergence less challenging than is the current situation with IFRS. Having operated at similar levels to current Basel III leverage ratio requirements for decades, greater challenges are currently and evidently being encountered (by) and demonstrated with many emerging economies who had not operated within the same requirements.

Capital Conservation Buffers

Whilst no capital conservation buffer existed under Basel II, regulatory requirements under Basel III will require banks to retain a capital conservation buffer of 2.5% as a means of "withstanding future periods of stress." As well as bringing the total common equity requirements to 7%, such a move "reinforces the stronger definition of capital agreed by Governors and Heads of Supervision in July and the higher capital requirements for trading, derivative and securitization activities to be introduced at the end of 2011.

Counter Cyclical Buffers

As is the case with the capital conservation buffer, counter cyclical buffers did not exist under Basel II. Basel III imposes a requirement of a counter cyclical buffer within a range of 0% and 2.5% of common equity or "other fully loss absorbing capital will be implemented according to national circumstances."

Additional Capital Requirements for Systemically Relevant Financial Institutions

Another vital distinction between Basel II and Basel III is evident from the fact that under Basel III, "systemically important banks will be required to have loss absorbing capacity beyond the standards approved and announced on the 12th September 2010 and work in relation to this is expected to continue between the Financial Stability

Table 2. Capital requirements: Expressed as a percentage of risk-weighted assets Basel III

	Min	Conservation Buffer	Countercyclical Buffer	SIFI Surcharge	Total
Common equity (core Tier 1) Predominant form: common shares, retained earnings and other comprehensive income	4.5	2.5	0-2.5	1-2.5	7-12
Tier 1	6				8.5-13.5
Total (Tier 1 + Tier 2)	8				10.5-15.5

(Notes: common equity + additional going concern capital = Tier One Capital)
Sources: see BIS (2015) and Ojo (2010).

Table 3. Capital requirements: Expressed as a percentage of risk-weighted assets Basel II

	Min
Common equity	2
Tier 1	4
Total (Tier 1 + Tier 2)	8

Board (FSB) and relevant Basel departments." Furthermore, the Basel Committee and the FSB are "developing a well-integrated approach to systemically important financial institutions which could include a combination of capital surcharges, contingent capital and bail-in debt."

Total Regulatory Capital for systemically important banks is therefore considered to be: [Tier One Capital Ratio] + [Capital Conservation Buffer] + [Counter Cyclical Capital Buffer] + [capital for systemically important banks

Basel III Leverage Ratios and Increased Volatility.

According to the Committee on the Global Financial System Markets Committee (BIS, 2015, p. 8):

- The leverage ratio may also lead to increased rate volatility, for two reasons. First, given that activity levels are expected to fall, liquidity is also likely to be lower, which will tend to push up bid-ask spreads (and reduce the size of the contracts to be traded – "clip size") and lead to an increase in volatility.

> Second, if banks seek to economize on the amount of central bank reserves that they are willing to hold at given levels of interest rates, then smaller reserve buffers may leave them needing to bid up for cash in short-term money markets in response to unexpected shocks, increasing market volatility. This may be particularly relevant for banks within a floor-based operating framework.

As will be demonstrated under chapters eight, nine and ten, several emerging economies face challenging tasks of adjusting to recent Basel III regulatory reforms – as well as IFRS global convergence particularly with respect to IFRS 9 (Financial Instruments). This very important standard has already been introduced in this chapter.

In the face of all the challenges currently being encountered, one theme resonates prominently – efforts and initiatives aimed at facilitating global convergence, consistency and disclosure. Further, it is evident that progress is continually being achieved by the IASB and FASB.

Figure 1. Process for determining the classification and measurement of financial assets
Source: IFRS. (2014, July). 9 Financial Instruments (p. 7).

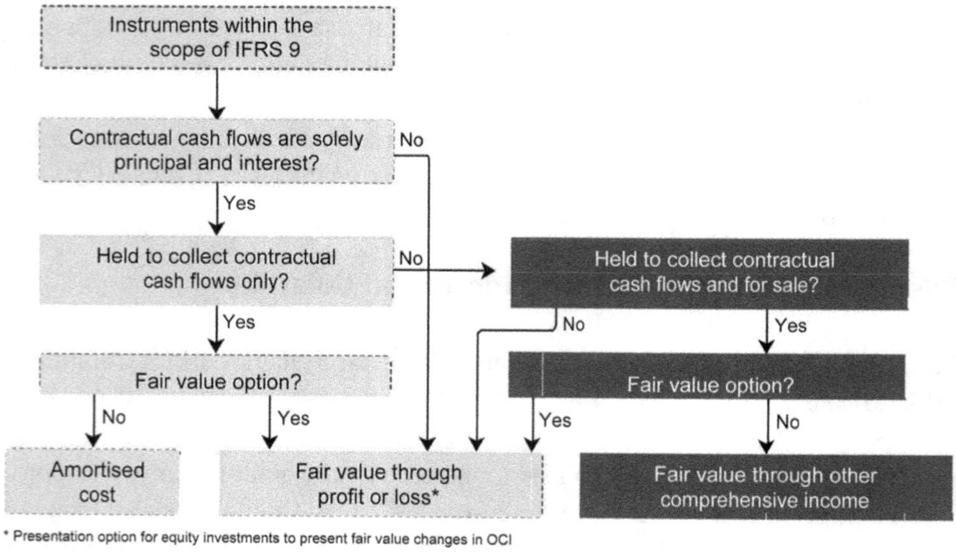

Figure 2. Fundamental review of hedge accounting aspects reconsidered
Source: IFRS. (2014, July). 9 Financial Instruments (p. 26).

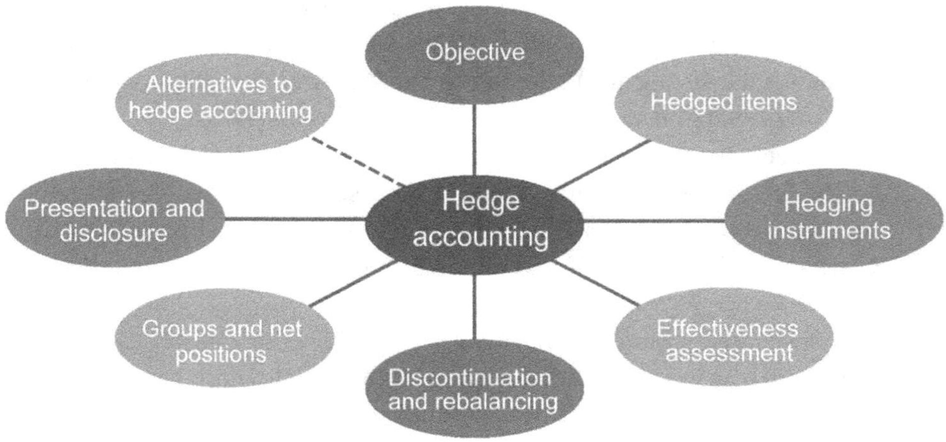

REFERENCES

Bank for International Settlements. (2015). CGFS Papers No 54 Regulatory change and monetary policy. Committee on the Global Financial System and the Markets Committee.

Ernst & Young. (2014). *Applying IFRS IFRS 15 Revenue from Contracts with Customers: A closer look at the new revenue recognition standard June 2014.* Retrieved from http://www.ey.com/Publication/vwLUAssets/Applying_IFRS:_A_closer_look_at_the_new_revenue_recognition_standard_(June_2014)/%24FILE/Applying-Rev-June2014.pdf

Financial Accounting Foundation. (2014). *FASB Accounting Standards Codification about the Codification (v 4.9).*

IFRS. (2014). *IFRS 9 Financial Instruments.*

IFRS. (2016). *IFRS 16 Leases, Project Summary and Feedback Statement.*

Impey, A. (n. d.). *Understanding IFRS.* PwC. Retrieved from: http://www.pwc.com/ng/en/publications/understanding-ifrs.html

ENDNOTES

1 IAS 32 and IAS 39 were issued as separate standards but are applied in practice as a unit because they deal with the same accounting phenomenon. IAS 39 (Financial Instruments: Recognition and Measurement) also contains some disclosures supplementary to those required by IAS 32. IAS 32 prescribes requirements for the presentation of on- balance sheet financial instruments and identifies information that should be disclosed about both on-balance sheet (recognized) and off balance sheet (unrecognized) financial instruments.

2 Raggay, D. (2012, May 10). Accounting for Financial Instruments. *Business Day*.

3 Further, IAS 32 requires disclosure by means of: Future cash flows relating to financial instruments, accounting policies applied to those instruments, the entity's use of financial instruments, the business purposes they serve, the risks associated with them, and management's policies for controlling those risks.

Chapter 2
Mitigating Information Asymmetries in Capital Markets:
The Audit Expectations Gap

Marianne Ojo
George Mason University, USA

ABSTRACT

As well as highlighting the impact of the audit expectations gap (AEG) in assessing the extent to which accounting information can be relied upon based on given market values and its impact on assessing how a relationship or pattern could be established in certain jurisdictions, this chapter is aimed at contributing to the literature on how accounting information could be interpreted or conveyed in such a way as to serve as a useful and vital indicator which will enable investors to interpret financial information in such a way which mitigates information asymmetries between management and investors. It also elaborates on factors which could affect the quality of accounting information – by way of reference to contributing elements of the audit expectations gap. As a result, it recommends measures aimed at addressing issues being faced by jurisdictions which have implemented accounting and legislative reforms as a means of improving the quality of accounting information.

DOI: 10.4018/978-1-5225-1900-3.ch002

Copyright ©2017, IGI Global. Copying or distributing in print or electronic forms without written permission of IGI Global is prohibited.

INTRODUCTION

If a survey were carried out within the general public and members of the public were asked to give a "true" or "false" answer to the statement: "The role of the auditor is to detect fraud and error in financial statements", most people would say true. In Re Kingston Cotton Mills (No 2) (1896), LJ Lopes of the Appeal Court stated that the auditor was a watchdog but not a bloodhound. This remark underlines the fact that the auditor's *primary role* is not the detection of fraud. The probable lack of clarity between users of financial statements, the general public and auditors as relating to the proper definition of the role and definition of an audit is what contributes to the "expectations gap."

The "expectations gap" is the difference between what users of financial statements, the general public perceive an audit to be and what the audit profession claim is expected of them in conducting an audit. In this respect, it is important to distinguish between the audit profession's expectations of an audit on one hand, and the auditor's perception of the audit on the other hand. Apart from users of financial statements and the general public, an auditor may also perceive a somewhat different interpretation or worse still, fail to comply with the standards set by the audit profession. The debate surrounding the "expectations gap" often revolves around whether such a gap can be eliminated. Sikka, Puxty, Cooper and Wilmott argue that within a social context, the expectations gap will be difficult to eliminate due to social conflict and the fact that the meaning of social practices is always subject to challenges (Sikka et al., 2003).It will however be argued that even though the *whole* component definition of an audit cannot be objective, elements within the definition of an audit and in particular, the fraud and error detection role of an audit is relatively objective. A return to the primary role of detection and prevention would also be welcomed since there are at present, not sufficient measures to hold the auditor liable for negative consequences of his actions.

Some sources of academic literature assume that the meaning of an audit is not objective/fixed whilst other sources such as contents of audit reports assume that the meaning of an audit is fixed (Sikka et al., 2003). In relation to the latter assumption, there is the belief that the expectations gap could be significantly reduced – if not possible to eliminate (Sikka et al, 2003). The remaining sections of this column are organized as follows: The first section deals with different meanings attributed to the expectations gap. It also considers why a stable meaning should be adopted. Section two then considers components of the expectations gap and possibilities of eliminating these components. Section three discusses the historical background of the expectations gap – including two very important cases which have been foundations of certain auditing standards. Section four, through an analysis and assessment of various standards, considers how clear, unambiguous standards could help reduce the expectations gap. The fifth section of this article then examines the social framework of the audit before arriving at a conclusion.

BACKGROUND AND LITERATURE REVIEW

Definitions of the Expectations Gap

The issue revolving around the expectations gap debate relates to the different and inconsistent meanings attributed to the definition of an audit by users of financial statements, the public and the audit profession. The "expectations gap" is the difference between what the public and users of financial statements perceive the role of an audit to be and what the audit profession claim is expected of them during the conduct of an audit. As mentioned in the introduction, this definition is preferred as it is important to distinguish between the audit profession's expectations of an audit on the one hand, and the auditor's perception of an audit on the other hand. Apart from users of financial statements and the general public, an auditor may also perceive a somewhat different interpretation or worse still, fail to comply with the standards set by the audit profession.

According to Pierce and Kilcommins (1995), the audit expectations gap is when external auditors' understanding of their role and duties is compared against the expectations of user groups and the general public. Liggio (1974) defined the audit expectations gap as the difference between the levels of expected performance as interpreted by the independent accountant and the user of financial statements. These definitions use external auditors as their bench mark rather than the audit profession. The use of the audit profession as bench mark would provide a less subjective element and help narrow the expectations gap. In this sense it would be a preferred definition and would also provide a more stable element of the expectations gap – as the audit profession's expectations are more well-defined than individual auditors' expectations. Reference by Liggio (1974) to "users of financial statements," as opposed to members of the general public, however, provides opportunity to narrow the expectations gap as it is obviously more feasible to educate users of financial information (via general meetings, etc.) than it is to educate members of the general public. This will be discussed in detail later.

The Cohen Commission in 1978 considered whether a gap might exist between what the public expected and what auditors could reasonably expect to accomplish. As rightly stated by Porter (1993), many definitions have failed to mention the possibility of sub-standard performance by auditors. Even though Porter highlights the importance of considering the *full extent* of the audit expectations gap which can be done by comparing society's expectations of auditors against the perceived performance of auditors, an *easier* comparison can be achieved through an analysis of the more objective components of the expectations gap.

The subjective components of the expectations gap could be made "more objective" by considering and analyzing each component and measures which could be taken to reduce the expectations gap created by each of these components. Unreasonable expectations from the public could be transformed to reasonable expectations of users of financial statements (since it is more feasible to educate users of financial information and since not all members of the public use financial information). After measures have been taken to eliminate the expectations gap relating to the components, a comparison of the reasonable expectations of users of financial statements against what the audit profession expect can then be made. This would provide for a more objective and stable analysis of the expectations gap.

Components of the Expectations Gap

Some commentators have attributed the expectations gap to users' confusion, widespread misunderstanding, ignorance and/or lack of education (Sikka et al., 2003). Porter analyses the total expectations gap into three separate components (Porter, 1993); namely, sub-standard performance (16%), deficient standards (50%) and unreasonable expectations (34%). As seen from these components, deficient standards component is the most objective component whilst unreasonable expectations and sub-standard performance are the subjective components. Even though unreasonable expectations are subjective, it still constitutes a significant proportion of the expectations gap and cannot be ignored.

Sub-standard performance should also not be ignored even though it constitutes just 16% of the expectations gap. After all possible measures have been taken to reduce this component it could be ignored. The sub-standard performance element is a problem arising from individual auditors, deficient standards stemming from the audit profession whilst unreasonable expectations emanate from the public. An analysis of the individual components of the expectations gap this way helps to know and understand better how to deal with and reduce these problems creating the expectations gap. In particular, it provides knowledge as to where more efforts should be concentrated namely, the reforms of auditing standards (since this constitutes half the problem).

The expectations gap is an issue for auditors as a greater "expectations gap" would lead to lower credibility, earning potential and prestige associated with their work (Sikka et al., 2003). It is also an issue for the public and investors in particular since wealth creation and political stability in a capitalist economy depends significantly on confidence and accountability and external audit is supposed to provide such confidence and accountability (Sikka et al., 2003).

MAIN FOCUS OF THE CHAPTER

Issues, Controversies, Problems

Is It Possible to Eliminate the Expectations Gap?

The nature of the components of the expectations gap make it difficult to eliminate.[1] Perceived performance of auditors is an element which is difficult to measure and changes constantly. It is possible to substantially reduce but not totally eliminate.

A number of suggestions have been put forward as a means of narrowing the expectations gap. These include an expanded audit report which offers scope to inform users of what auditors actually do; broadening the role and responsibility of auditors in the areas of fraud, illegal acts and strengthening the perceived independence of auditors (Pierce & Kilcommins, 1995). The implementation of auditing education has been suggested as a means of reducing the expectation gap (Pierce & Kilcommins, 1995). Audit education would surely help reduce the expectations gap but would not on its own be sufficient to solve the problem of expectations gap as other components of the expectations gap exist. Audit education would partly solve the problem of unreasonable expectations but not address deficient standards and sub-standard performance. Porter adds that in order for audit education to be effective, society should be educated on duties which may reasonably be expected of auditors (Pierce & Kilcommins, 1995).

The MacDonald Commission expressed their opinion that audit education was unlikely to be effective in reducing the gap since it concluded that for the most part, public expectations were reasonable and achievable (Pierce & Kilcommins, 1995). Sikka et al (2003) also argue that he expectations gap can be addressed by the audit profession widening the responsibilities of auditors. Even if new standards were implemented, the issue of enforcement is another matter which needs to be addressed.. As a result, enforcement and audit liability measures are also required.

Elements of the user misunderstanding gap investigated in the study by Pierce and Kilcommins (1995) include:

1. Duties;
2. Ethical and legislative framework;
3. Liability;
4. Audit report.

The duties' component consists of fraud and error and many commentators have found the expectations gap to be widest in relation to detection and reporting of fraud (Pierce & Kilcommins, 1995). The second element, the ethical and legislative framework included issues such as auditor independence, auditor appointment and audit regulation (Pierce & Kilcommins, 1995). In relation to auditor liability, Gloeck and de Jager argue that the *Caparo* case added a liability gap to the expectations gap since the public does not know to whom the auditor is liable.

However, it could also be said that the substandard performance component of the expectations gap already embraces the liability gap as auditors are encouraged to underperform – especially where no economic incentives exist for them to owe a duty of care to third party stakeholders.

HISTORICAL BACKGROUND OF THE EXPECTATIONS GAP

The origins of auditing date back to Greek, Egyptian and earlier civilisations and whilst there was the emergence of large manufacturing organisations in the eighteenth century, the usual association between audits and fraud detection remained (Sikka et al, 2003). Towards the end of the nineteenth century, a more prominent accountancy profession associated audits with fraud detection even though there was opposition by those who argued that it was unreasonable to expect the auditor to expose fraudulent acts (Sikka et al., 2003). Lawrence Dicksee's textbook is often considered to be the first major auditing textbook and his original book which was published in 1892 (Dicksee, 1892) stated clearly that the scope of an audit included namely, the detection of fraud, technical errors, and errors of principle (Dicksee, 1892). He also stated that the detection of fraud was a most important portion of the auditor's duties and that the whole duty of the auditor was to ascertain the exact state of the client's affairs on a certain date (Dicksee, 1892). However, other authors such as Robertson and Montgomery argued on the contrary and considered the detection of fraud to be a secondary audit objective (Sikka et al., 2003).

Humphrey et al noted that the position adopted by the profession in Britain during the twentieth century played down any suggestion that auditors had responsibility linked to fraud apart from that which arose from the need to confirm the truth and fairness of financial statements (Humphrey, Moizer, & Turley, 1993). Chandler et al (1993) reviewed the development of audit objectives between 1840 and 1940 and concluded that the primary objective in relation to public companies between 1830 and 1860 was the verification of financial statements and that more emphasis was put on fraud detection in the late nineteenth century (Chandler, Edwards, & Anderson, 1993). They also added that the primary audit objective reverted back to financial statements verification in the early part of the twentieth century. However, according to some, in the early part of the twentieth century, fraud detection continued to be regarded as a major audit objective (Chandler, Edwards, & Anderson, 1992; Sikka et al., 1993).

According to Brown (1962), the confusion over audit objectives was finally resolved after 1940 and fraud detection was generally accepted to be a secondary objective. However, the objectives of auditing have not been adjusted to conform with operational processes of auditing (Power, 1997). For example, selective sampling would have corresponded to a primary objective of financial statements verification whilst 100% testing would correspond with the detection of fraud (Power, 1997).

One important difference between mid-to-late Victorian England and more recent times is the presence or lack of presence of audit expectations (Eu-Jin & Cobbin, 2005). Victorian England is seen as a time of evolution and formulation of expectations and whilst gaps existed in the nineteenth century, they were mainly to do with inconsistencies and not expectations (Eu-Jin & Cobbin, 2005). The differing inconsistent expectations between the judiciary and the auditing profession is illustrated in the landmark cases of *London and General Bank (No 2)* [1895] and *Kingston Cotton Mill (No 2)* [1896] in which the UK Court of Appeal delivered two significant judgements.

London and General Bank (No2) [1895]

This case concerned the adequacy of security on bank loans, whether shareholders had been deceived as to the condition of the company, whether dividends had been paid out of capital and not available profits. The first instance decision had been against the defendants (the auditor). However in the Appeal Court, LJ Lindley overturned the previous court's decision. His opinion on the auditor's duty is as follows:

...the duty of an auditor is to convey information not to arouse inquiry and although an auditor might infer from an unusual statement that something was seriously wrong, it by no means followed that ordinary people would have their suspicions aroused. (Eu-Jin & Cobbin, 2005)

Lindley also stated that it was not the auditor's duty to guarantee the books showing the true position of the company's affairs or to guarantee that the balance sheet was accurate.

Kingston Cotton Mill (No 2) [1895]

The first instance decision involved the auditor relying on managers' certificates without the auditor conducting a physical observation of the inventory or taking steps to confirm valuation. In that decision, Vaughan Williams found that the auditors and directors were liable for dividends paid from non-existent profits. However damages sought against them in respect of consequent insolvency on the basis of tort was denied. There was a lot of concern by the audit profession following this decision and the validity of managers' certificates was also called into question. However Lopes in the Appeal Court over-turned the decision in his famous judgement:

It is the duty of an auditor to bring to bear on the work he has to perform that skill, care and caution which a reasonably competent, careful and cautious auditor would use. What is reasonable skill, care and caution must depend on the particular circumstances of each case. An auditor is not bound to be a detective or as was said to approach his work with suspicion or with a foregone conclusion that there is something wrong. He is a watchdog but not a bloodhound. He is justified in believing tried servants of the company in whom confidence is placed by the company. (Eu-Jin & Cobbins, 2005)

These two cases were the foundations of certain auditing standards which focused on the accepted fraud and error objectives and placed the nature of the audit on center stage (Eu-Jin & Cobbins, 2005). Apart from establishing that the auditor was not expected to fish out every fraud it established the use reasonable care and skill in his handling of relevant books and records (Eu-Jin & Cobbins, 2005). However, the fact that *London and General Bank (No 2)* [1895] and *Kingston Cotton Mill (No 2)* [1896] confirmed the "reasonableness" test did not completely remove any concern created due to the subjective nature of the reasonableness test (Eu-Jin & Cobbins, 2005).

During the early years of the twentieth century, fraud detection as an audit objective came to be replaced by the objective of checking that the appropriate accounting standards had been adopted and correctly used in constructing financial statements (Sikka et al., 2003). Between 1940 and 1970, fraud detection seemed to be regarded as a secondary audit objective even though this move had not been approved by the Companies Acts of 1948 and 1967.

The re-emergence of fraud detection as an audit objective occurred during the Thatcher administration and was also strongly highlighted during the mid-1970s property and secondary banking crisis (Powers, 1997). In 1985, a working party of the Institute of Chartered Accountants in England and Wales (ICAEW) was established to consider the matter relating to auditors' responsibilities in relation to fraud (Powers, 1997). This was prompted as a result of criticisms about the audit function following the collapse of Johnson Matthey Bankers (Sikka et al., 2003). The collapse of Johnson Matthey Bankers in 1984 also brought about questions on regulation of financial markets and the government being unhappy with the role of auditors, wanted to impose upon auditors a duty to report fraud to the Bank of England even without the knowledge of the client organization (Powers, 1997). In response to this, the Institute of Chartered Accountants in England and Wales argued against Lord Justice Bingham's recommendations for an imposition of statutory duty. The working party of the Institute of Chartered Accountants in England and Wales suggested instead that companies should be required by statute to maintain adequate systems of internal control (Powers, 1997). Problems which could threaten the auditor client relationship, duty of confidentiality were mentioned and these issues though apparent seemed more important than the protection of the public's interests.

It took another three years for the Institute of Chartered Accountants in England and Wales to issue draft guidance on the auditor's responsibility for detecting fraud and other irregularities (Powers, 1997). This document was amended further and published as a full operational guideline in February 1990. Management responsibility for setting up adequate systems of internal controls is highlighted but auditors are reminded to plan the audit to provide a "reasonable expectation" of detecting material misstatement (Powers, 1997). "Materiality" has been interpreted in professional guidance as the degree of tolerable or acceptable error in financial statements but like the term "reasonable expectation" it is not specified beyond this (Powers, 1997). It is important that further clarification in relation to these terms are provided as the question to whether auditors have a responsibility to detect fraud depends on the interpretation of these terms (Powers, 1997). The guidance document does not deny the auditor's duty to detect fraud – however, it qualifies this duty by the "reasonable expectation" term (ASB, n.d.).

Materiality

The International Standard on Auditing (ISA UK and Ireland) 320 establishes standards and provides guidance on the concept of materiality and how this relates to audit risk (Eu-Jin & Cobbin, 2005). The concept of "materiality" is defined in the International Accounting Standards Board's "Framework for the Preparation and Presentation of Financial Statements" as follows:

Information is material if its omission or misstatement could influence the economic decisions of users taken on the basis of the financial statements. Materiality depends on the size of the item or error judged in the particular circumstances of its omission or misstatement. Thus, materiality provides a threshold or cut off point rather than being a primary qualitative characteristic which information must have if it is to be useful.

The problem with this definition revolves round the word "judged". The assessment of materiality is based on professional judgement (ISA (UK and Ireland) 320. 5).

In planning the audit, the auditor establishes an acceptable level of materiality in order to detect quantitatively material misstatements (ISA). In addition, both the amount (quantity) and nature (quality) of misstatements need to be considered (ISA).

The auditor also needs to consider the possibility of misstatements of relatively small amounts which could cumulatively have a material effect on the financial statements 59 (ISA (UK and Ireland) 320. 6). An error could be potentially material if it is repeated each month for a particular month end procedure 59 (ISA (UK and Ireland) 320. 6). Materiality at both the entire financial statement level and in relation to classes of transactions, account balances and disclosures also need to be considered 59 (ISA (UK and Ireland) 320. 6). Legal and regulatory requirements may also affect materiality (ASB, n.d.).

From the above definition and standard, it can be seen that a lot of subjective issues affect the concept of materiality. Legal and regulatory issues which may affect materiality need to be more clearly defined and an error estimate given by the Auditing Practices Board. A lot of matters left to be judged by the individual auditor should be also be determined and clearly set out in the standards.

"Material significance" is defined by ISA (UK and Ireland) 250 Section B:

A matter or group of matters is normally of material significance to a regulator's function when, due either to its nature or its potential financial impact, it is likely of itself to require investigation by the regulator. (ISA (UK and Ireland) 250. 62)

Whilst judgement is also required by the auditor in determining whether a matter is or likely to be of material significance, material significance does not have the same meaning as materiality in the context of financial audit (ISA (UK and Ireland) 250.62). A particular event which may have little impact on the financial statements of an entity may be of a nature or type that is likely to change the perception of the regulator (ISA (UK and Ireland) 250.24).

ISA (UK and Ireland) 240: The Auditor's Responsibility to Consider Fraud in an Audit of Financial Statements

In carrying out the above function, the auditor is expected to maintain a sceptic attitude throughout the audit despite the fact that his past experience with the entity about the honesty and integrity of management.[67] The auditor also considers reports from the deposit taker's compliance department, legal department and money laundering reporting officer with reviews undertaken by third parties such as reports prepared under section 166 of the Financial Services and Markets Act 2000 (Sikka et al, 2003).

Examining the Social Framework of the Audit

Sikka et al have argued that meanings of the audit are determined by particular social arrangements which are always subject to change and as a result it is difficult for the audit to have a fixed meaning.[2] However it will be argued that even though social and global changes have shaped the role of the auditor and hence the role of an audit, some components within the definition of an audit can still be considered as fixed. The advancement of technology, internal control systems have definitely transformed the environment within which an audit operates. Periodical surveys should be carried out in the general public to ascertain what many perceive to be the role of an auditor. These surveys should be carried out only after the public has been sufficiently educated about the role of the audit. After this draft proposals should be made whereby public is still involved is invited to submit their ideas or challenge any proposals. The draft proposals on the definition of an audit should be a more acceptable definition by popular consensus – as realized through the opinions received from surveys carried out on the public. There should be an objective component within the definition of an audit which would be the public's reasonable expectations. These expectations could be deemed reasonable as public would already have been educated about the role of auditors, nature of audits before a survey is carried out to find out what the public want from an audit.

SOLUTIONS AND RECOMMENDATIONS

The subjective component definition of an audit would be revised from time to time – depending on social, environmental changes. The objective component would also be revised from time to time based on periodical surveys. In the absence of an imposition of statutory duty on auditors, the fraud and error detection role of an auditor seems to be a role which should become a primary audit objective – as this would help bring about some form of accountability. Of course, the auditor cannot be expected to sniff out every form of fraud – only material ones. The cases of Enron and Parmalat certainly involved huge amounts of money which are deemed significant and material from a subjective or an objective point of view. Why were the auditors involved not able to detect such material amounts?

In the absence of appropriate audit liability measures, there are no incentives to deter the external auditor from such gross misconduct. The re-instatement of fraud detection (and also error detection) as a primary audit objective which constitutes a fixed component definition of an audit (as the public has every right to expect this duty from the auditor – provided issues relate to material fraud) would certainly help bring some form of accountability within the audit profession.

Fraud and Error Detection Role of an Audit

The meaning attributed by users of financial statements as regarding the definition of an audit cannot be fixed but elements within the definition of what constitutes an audit can. Such components within the definition of an audit include the fraud and error role.

The role of fraud and error detection is one which is encouraged. If the public (and more specifically, users of financial statements) were educated about this role, it would be deemed to be a reasonable expectation. Surveys should be conducted frequently to determine if this role is one which is perceived by the greater part of users of financial information as that which is the role of the auditor.

Users of financial information should also be made aware that the fraud and error role is applicable to *material* misstatements. The role of the auditor in verifying financial statements and providing an opinion in relation to those statements is one which relies greatly on the subjective professional judgment as to materiality.

Before concluding, let us consider various ways through which the individual components of the expectations gap might be directly addressed, thus narrowing the expectations gap.

The Sub-Standard Performance Component

Bringing back the fraud and detection role should help reduce this component. Prem Sikka adds that the threat of a punitive action by the DTI could create *economic* incentives for accounting firms to reflect on the consequences of their actions – as a reduction in their revenue, due to fines incurred, would make them think twice before indulging in acts with negative consequences. In contrast, Huepkes (2006) argues that the threat of litigation could lead to further concentration in the auditing industry and also increase the trend towards defensive auditing – whereby audit partners tend to interpret rules prescriptively rather than exercising subjective judgment.

Deficient Standards Component

Unambiguous wordings within Statements of Auditing Standards should be avoided and clearer definitions provided to give the auditor a better understanding about his duties. The Dearing Committee, which had been established by the Consultative Committee of Accounting Bodies (CCAB) comprising the six professional accounting bodies, published its report, *The Making of Accounting Standards* in 1988. In addition to the setting up of the Accounting Standards Board (ASB), the Dearing Report (1997) recommended the redress of the issue of how accounting standards were to be applied to the public sector. It stated:

...there should be an underlying unity of approach to accounting standards across the public and private sectors, with accounting standards normally applicable in the public sector so that unnecessary differences in accounting and financial reporting between the two sectors are reduced and so that standards apply evenhandedly to both sectors, except where clearly appropriate. (Dearing Report, 1997)

The ASB also stated in the Dearing Report that:

Strong unambiguous accounting standards covering the main issues that arise in preparing financial statements are needed for the good working of a market economy.[3]

Post-Enron reforms which led to the Audit Practices Board being responsible for setting standards on objectivity, integrity and independence should improve the standard setting process and provide more consistency to the way standards are interpreted.

The year 2005 was a year of major change for many companies with the introduction of international accounting standards and new auditing standards (FRC Annual Report, 2005/2006). Public concerns about the continuing relevance of the "true and fair view" have been highlighted especially with the advent of the introduction of international standards on accounting and auditing in the UK (FRC Annual Report, 2005/2006). Responding to this, the FRC published a report in August 2005 in which it concluded that the "true and fair view" continues to remain a cornerstone in the UK system of financial reporting (FRC Annual Report, 2005/2006).

Reducing Unreasonable Public Expectations

Unreasonable public expectations might be reduced, and more reasonable public expectations obtained, with proper education of the public about the role of the auditor and the auditing standards relating to his role. Public education about the auditor's role could be facilitated through annual shareholders' meetings and other events which are organized for the purposes of educating users of financial information. As mentioned numerous times already, it would be more feasible to educate users of financial information as opposed to members of the general public – especially since not all members of the public use financial information.[4]

CONCLUSION

Humphrey (1997) describes the issue of auditor independence as "going to the heart of the audit expectations debate" (Dewing & Russell, 2005). The reality and notion of auditor independence is vital to public confidence in financial reporting (Singh, 2005; Porter, Simon & Hatherly, 2005). Public confidence in financial markets and the conduct of public interest entities relies partly on the credibility of the opinions and reports given by auditors in relation with financial audits (ASB, n.d.; Cooper, 1984).

It could be inferred that this issue of auditor independence relates to the role of the auditor and that factors which could prevent the auditor from performing his expected role – hence compromising his independence, would definitely increase the expectations gap. This is not surprising as any misconception of (by the public or users of financial information) or diversion from the auditor's expected role (by the auditor) contributes to increasing the expectations gap. As a result of the additional role of auditors and reporting accountants/skilled persons of financial services firms in reporting to supervisors under the Financial Services and Markets Act 2000 and under prior legislation, there is greater possibility for further misunderstandings – thus increasing the expectations gap further (Dewing & Russell, 2005).

However, arguments have been made in favor of the dual nature of the auditor. Interviewees from firms have seen little conflict between the dual role of auditors and reporting accountants/ skilled persons viewing the issue from a cost benefit analysis (Dewing & Russell, 2005).

Measures have been adopted by the FSA to safeguard against possibilities of a conflict of interest. Chapter 5 of the FSA Supervision Manual provides examples of circumstances where the FSA may use skilled persons. The FSA may nominate or approve the appointment of the auditor of a bank as a skilled person if it is cost effective to do so but also takes into account any conflicts the auditor may have in relation to the matter to be reported on. There are also defined and limited circumstances in which a firm can use skilled persons.[5]

The audit expectations gap is of serious concern to the UK accounting profession with the Department of Trade and Industry proposing a new framework for independent regulation of the accounting profession.[6] However the new Accounting Foundation had its role placed under review following the Enron collapse and introduction of the Sarbanes-Oxley Act 2002 (Dewing & Russell, 2005; Humphrey, Mozier & Turley, 1992; Lehman & Tinker; Sikka et al., 2003). This resulted in responsibility for independent regulation of the accounting profession being transferred to the reconstituted Financial Reporting Council.

Whilst sufficient measures are in place to protect the auditor's independence – hence no threat of widening the expectations gap – more work is needed to ensure that the role of the auditor is better defined.

REFERENCES

Brown, R. E. (1962). Changing Audit Objectives and Techniques. *Accounting Review*, *37*(4), 696.

Chandler, R. A., Edwards, J. R., & Anderson, M. (1993). Changing Perceptions of the Role of the Company Auditor: 1840 – 1940. In Accounting and Business Research, 23.

Dewing, P., & Russell, P. O. (2005). *The Role of Auditors, Reporting Accountants and Skilled Persons in UK Financial Services Supervision Institute of Chartered Accountants of Scotland*. The Institute of Chartered Accountants of Scotland. Retrieved from https://www.icas.com/__data/assets/pdf_file/0016/10582/63-The-Role-of-Auditors-Reporting-Accountants-And-Skilled-Persons-In-UK-FInancial-Services-Supervision-ICAS.pdf

Dicksee, L. (1892). Auditing: A Practical Manual for Auditors. Retrieved from https://archive.org/details/auditingpractica00dickuoft

FRC. (2004). Ethical Statement: Integrity, Objectivity and Independence. Retrieved from https://www.frc.org.uk/Our-Work/Publications/APB/ES-1-Integrity,-objectivity-and-independence-2004.pdf

Eu Jin, T., & Cobbin, P. (2005, July). A Re Visitation of the Audit Expectations Gap: Judicial and Practitioner Views on the Role of the Auditor in late- Victorian England. *Sage. Accounting History*, *10*(2), 35–66. doi:10.1177/103237320501000203

Financial Services and Markets Act 2000 (2000). Retrieved from: http://www.legislation.gov.uk/ukpga/2000/8/contents

FRC. (2006). Financial Reporting Council Annual Report 2005/2006. Retrieved from https://www.frc.org.uk/FRC-Documents/FRC/Annual-Report-2005-06.pdf

Huepkes, E. H. G. (2005). The External Auditor and the Bank Supervisor: Sherlock Holmes and Doctor Watson? *Journal of Banking Regulation*, *7*(1-2), 145–159. doi:10.1057/palgrave.jbr.2340010

Humphrey, C. (1997). Debating Audit Expectations. In M. Sherer & S. Turley (Eds.), Current Issues in Auditing (3rd ed.). London: Paul Chapman.

Humphrey, C. P., Turley, S., Moizer, P. (1993). Protection Against Detection: The Case of Auditors and Fraud. *Accounting, Auditing & Accountability Journal*, *6*(1).

IASplus. (n.d.). IAS 8 Accounting Policies, Changes in Accounting Estimates and Errors. Retrieved from http://www.iasplus.com/en/standards/ias/ias8

ISA (UK and Ireland). (n. d.). 250 Section B: Material significance. Retrieved from https://www.frc.org.uk/Our-Work/Publications/APB/ISA-250B-The-auditor-s-right-and-duty-to-report-to.pdf

ISA (UK and Ireland). (n. d.). 320 Retrieved from https://www.frc.org.uk/Our-Work/Publications/APB/ISA-320-Materiality-in-planning-and-performing-an.aspx

ISA (UK and Ireland). (n. d.). The Auditor's Responsibility to Consider Fraud in an Audit of Financial Statements. Retrieved from https://www.frc.org.uk/Our-Work/Publications/APB/240-The-auditor-s-responsibility-to-consider-fraud.pdf

Liggio, C.D. (1974). The Expectation Gap. *The Accountant's Waterloo Journal of Contemporary Business*, 3(3)

Ojo, M. (2006, June 2). Auditor Independence - Its Importance to the External Auditor's Role in Banking Regulation and Supervision. *Paper presented at the 2006 Global Conference on Business and Finance*, San Jose, Costa Rica.

Pierce, B. & Kilcommins, M. (1996). The Audit Expectations Gap: The Role of Auditing Education. University Business School Research Papers, Dublin City.

Porter, B. (1993). An Empirical Study of the Audit Expectation. Performance Gap Accounting and Business Research, 24(93).

Power, M. (1999). The Audit Society: Rituals of Verification. Oxford University Press.

Sikka, P., Puxty, A., Willmott, H., & Cooper, C. (2003). The Impossibility of Eliminating the Expectations Gap: Some Theory and Evidence. *Critical Explorations on Accounting*, *9*(3), 299–330. doi:10.1006/cpac.1997.0159

Singh, D. (2006). The Role of Third Parties in Banking Regulation and Supervision. *Journal of International Banking Regulation*, 4(3).

ENDNOTES

1 P. Sikka et al argue that due to social conflict the meaning of social practices continually face challenges and the gap between competing meanings of audit cannot be eliminated.

2 The auditor's role in relation to fraud detection has been concluded to be the critical component of the Audit Expectations Gap, according to most studies researching the nature of the gap. See Ali, A. (n. d.). Practical Training and the Audit Expectations Gap: The Case of Accounting. Universiti Utara Malaysia.; Humphrey et al., 1993, pp. 395- 411.

3 See Report of the Review Committee under Sir Ronald Dearing "The Making of Accounting Standards" (Dearing Report 1988); also see "Resource Accounting: Framework of Accounting Standard Setting in the UK Central Government Sector." International Federation of Accountants, June 2002 http://www.ifac.org (last visited September 28 2007). Subsequent to the publication of the Dearing Report in 1988, the ASB became successor to the ASC on 1 August 1990 with Sir David Tweedie being its first chairman. In contrast to the ASC, the ASB does not reflect solely the opinions of the accountancy profession. Its members include representatives of the government and the business and financial communities, as well as members of the accountancy profession. The ASB is also presently funded through the FRC, jointly by the Government, the financial community (City of London – through the London Stock Exchange) and the accountancy profession. See 'Development of the ASB' www.horwathcw.com/press/article_details.asp?article_id=39 (last visited September 28 2007); Willmott, H.C. (1985). Setting Accounting Standards in the UK: The Emergence of Private Accounting Bodies and their Role in the Regulation of Public Accounting Practice. London.
Ever since the 1844 Companies Act came into force and assumed formal control over accounting, the UK regulatory framework has changed significantly. Prior to 1970, no mandatory requirements in the UK outside company law existed to govern the presentation of financial statements of companies. See R.G. Day 'UK Accounting Regulation: An Historical Perspective.' *Bournemouth University School of Finance and Law Working Paper Series* No 20 (2000) p. 26. During the 1960s, following a period in which the accounting profession felt under threat from government intervention, the English Institute of Chartered Accountants published 'A Statement of Intent on Accounting Standards' which resulted in the formation of the Accounting Standards Steering Committee (ASSC) in January 1970. The first accounting standard was issued in 1971 and between then and 1976, membership of the ASSC embraced the six major accountancy bodies in the UK. At the same time, the ASSC was re-named the Accounting Standards Committee (ASC). Standards were approved by the Consultative Committee of Accounting Bodies (CCAB) issued by each professional body to its members. The CCAB is comprised of the six professional accounting bodies. The ASC however, had no legal or disciplinary authority, gave no interpretation of standards and provided no appeal measures against standards. In 1978, a review took place and its conclusions and recommendations were published in 1979 as 'Setting Accounting Standards'. Further review of the standard setting process in 1983 resulted in little change and it was only in 1987 when a major review was commissioned under Sir Ron Dearing, that significant changes took place.

Although accounting standards retained more force than the older recommendations, a number of major problems remained. Apart from there being no direct legal responsibility to comply, and the fact that it was the individual professional body's responsibility to discipline non-compliant members, there were two other problems. Firstly, the lack of a conceptual framework of accounting resulted in contradiction between individual standards, and secondly, there was lack of funding. The ASC was dependent on the accountancy profession for its funding and for voluntary participation. There were criticisms of undue influence being exerted by those who contributed. See Day, R.G. (n. d.). UK Accounting Regulation: An Historical Perspective (pp. 21-24). Also see Bromwich, M. (1992). Financial Reporting, Information and Capital Markets. London: Pitman.; Macve, R.H. (1981). A Conceptual Framework for Financial Accounting and Reporting: Possibilities for an Agreed Structure. London: ICAEW.; Edwards, J.R. (1989). A History of Financial Accounting. London: Routledge.; Accounting Standards Steering Committee A Statement of Intent on Accounting Standards (1970); Accounting Standards Steering Committee The Corporate Report (1975); Accounting Standards Committee Consultative Document: Setting Accounting Standards (1979)

4 Though audit education is considered to be a way of reducing the audit expectations gap, results from an internship programme, carried out to educate groups of accounting students in Malaysia, showed that even though there were significant changes in perceptions amongst students after the internship programme, mis-perceptions were still found among students on audit related issues after completion of the internship programme. The internship programme was found to have failed to correct some of the misperceptions as to audit objectives and as a result it was implied that an internship programme was unlikely to be used as a method of eliminating the audit expectations gap. It was, however, also concluded that an internship programme could still be used to complement audit education in a university as it was ideal for exposing students to professional issues and enabling them to have a better insight into the actual performance and duties of auditors. See A. Ali 'Practical Training and the Audit Expectations Gap: The Case of Accounting Undergraduates of Universiti Utara Malaysia' forthcoming. Also see Frank, E.K., Lowe, D.J., & Smith, J.K. (2001). The Expectation Gap: Perceptual Differences between Auditors, Jurors and Students. *Managerial Auditing Journal,* 16(3), 146-149.; Guy, D.M., & Sullivan. J.D. (1988). The Expectation Gap Auditing Standards. *Journal of Accountancy, April,* 36-44.; Lowe, D.J. (1994). The Expectation Gap in the Legal System: Perception Differences between Auditors and Judges. *Journal of Applied Business Research,* 1994, 39-44.; Monroe, G.S.,

& Woodliff, D.R. (1993). The Effect of Education on the Audit Expectation Gap. *Accounting and Finance,* 1993, 61-78.

5 According to chapter 5 of the Supervision Manual, the FSA states that firms are to appoint skilled persons only for specific purposes; not to use them as a matter of routine; to use skilled persons only after having considered alternatives; to use skilled persons because of the added value to be gained due to their expertise or knowledge and not because of resource restraints; to take into account cost implications, and to use the tool in a focused and proportionate way.

6 In contrast to the UK where interests of the public (as users of financial statements) are of great concern, the audit process in Malaysia appears highly politicized and has been criticized for serving special interests. See A. Ali 'Politics and Audit in Malaysia.'

Chapter 3
Value Relevance of Accounting Information in Capital Markets:
The New York Stock Exchange

Marianne Ojo
George Mason University, USA

James A DiGabriele
Montclair State University, USA

ABSTRACT

"The sell-off in US Treasury bonds in 2013 had global repercussions, impacting broad ranges of asset classes in both advanced and emerging market economies. The sell-off in 1994 is distinguished from 2003 and 2013 episodes in that, in 1994, not only did long-term rates surge, short-term rates also picked up significantly. By contrast, in both 2003 and 2013, bond market stress was confined mostly to longer maturities, although drivers of the 2003 event were different from those in 2013." As well as analyzing and investigating recent developments in vulnerabilities and volatility on the New York Stock Exchange, this chapter investigates the topic of the value relevance of accounting information in global capital markets as a means of contributing to the topic of value relevance – and particularly highlighting the impact of monetary policies and growth rates of certain economies at a global level. It also highlights why fundamentals presently underlying present stock market volatilities differ from those of previous crises.

DOI: 10.4018/978-1-5225-1900-3.ch003

Copyright ©2017, IGI Global. Copying or distributing in print or electronic forms without written permission of IGI Global is prohibited.

INTRODUCTION

The U.S. stock market principally operates on the two largest exchanges: the NASDAQ and the New York Stock Exchange (NYSE) and in response to the Crash which affected the NASDAQ in August 2013, a third exchange, the BATS Global Marketplace, was formed "to create a more efficient technology." (U.S Economy About, 2014).

The recent volatilities and vulnerabilities to which major leading stock markets and exchanges – notably the New York Stock Exchange have been attributed to stock market corrections, which hopefully, is intended to be a temporary matter.

Towards the end of August 2015 and amidst very high volume trading on the New York Stock Exchange, explanations of a possible market correction, and the consolation that trading markets worldwide had also been affected by the recent Crash in China's stock markets, it was concluded and predicted that a rebound in the stock markets would take place – based on stock crashes which had taken place in the previous decades.

The closing bell at the end of August 24th 2015 saw the NYSE closing with -585 points and explanations of the 10% stock market correction were considered to be something of an occurrence which stock market analysts had been anticipating for a while. However, even though these had been anticipated, the extent and degree of the plunge still took traders by surprise - resulting in a stock market sell off. In addition to the release of China's stock market figures – which revealed that expected prognosis about growth – particularly in China's manufacturing sector may not be as robust as forecasted, and questions relating to the reliability of accounting data, other issues resulting in a loss of investor confidence included how to adequately price stocks. Further, commodities such as gold and silver, and not just oil lost their value on that day. These factors, as well as uncertainty surrounding the Federal Reserve's decision to raise or decrease interest rates contributed to the Dow's plunge.

The 31st August 2015 witnessed the Dow capping its worst month in five years – with a loss of 6+% of its value for the month of August – ending August with the worst monthly percentage since 2010. The following day continued with a similar trend – partly attributed to further release of China's worst manufacturing data in three years, which sent the Dow plunging to -467 points amidst revelation of reports.

The immense impact of a slowdown in China's economy, on global stock markets, and particularly the NYSE was made evident again on the 7th January 2016 where a continuation of incidents attributed to a slowdown, coupled with plunging oil prices (which reached lowest level in twelve years, resulted in shares plunging. The Dow not only witnessed a 2.4% drop, but also impact of the global slowdown were experienced in other major financial markets around the globe.

The events were further accentuated the following week when all three major indices: the Dow (Dow Industrial), S & P (S&P 500) and NASDAQ composite went into correction zones - with the S & P 500 reaching its lowest level since September 2015.

Plunges were also triggered by falling oil prices which reached their lowest levels in twelve years.

This chapter is aimed at exploring the following objectives:

1. To investigate the extent to which accounting information can be relied upon based on given market values and whether a relationship or pattern can be established in certain jurisdictions based on given operating variables which function in such economies.
2. To demonstrate and highlight the validity of the Efficient Markets Hypothesis (as well as the Efficient Capital Markets Hypothesis)
3. To demonstrate how accounting information can serve as a useful and vital indicator which will enable investors to interpret financial information in such a way which mitigates information asymmetries between management and investors
4. To highlight those areas and factors which influence the quality of accounting information - and which must be addressed by markets if the audit is to achieve its intended aims and functions.
5. To illustrate why the semi-strong and strong forms of the Efficient Markets Hypothesis (EMH) appear to accord, to a greater degree, with the random walk theory whilst the weak form of the EMH increasingly appears to be contradictory to the random walk hypothesis – in terms of predictability – and based on past information.

Background and Literature Review

A stock market correction, is considered to be when the stock market declines 10% from its 52-week high and it is distinguished from a stock market crash, which is regarded as occurring where stock prices plummet more than 10%, in just one day (U.S Economy About, 2016).

As highlighted under the introductory section, financial markets are sensitive and vulnerable to various factors which include monetary policies, slowdown in growth from certain economies, as well as plunges in commodity prices – to name a few. Whilst stock markets are supposed to serve as good economic indicators, it is also evident that certain developments which have built up over the years may affect the value relevance of accounting information in major stock markets.

Value relevance approach "measures both relevance and reliability because accounting information is reflected in the price." (Khanagha, 2011; Barth, Beaver & Landsman, 2001). Further, "value relevance approach is an instrument used to estimate quality of accounting information – this being of vital importance to the economy." This view is in line with the Efficiency Market Hypothesis (EMH).

As constitutes the theme of the volume and in line with its objectives, even though various studies have been carried out on value relevance accounting (these including those undertaken by Graham, King and Bailes (1998), Filip & Raffournier (2010), Qystein, Kjell & Saettem (2007) and Khanagha (2011), recent developments which have resulted in the replacement of relevance and reliability with characteristics of relevance and faithful representation as fundamental qualitative accounting characteristics and verifiability, understandability, timeliness and comparability as enhancing qualitative accounting characteristics call for a redress in the secondary importance currently being accorded to such enhancing qualitative characteristics and also justification for such a redress in the light of the recent volatilities across global stock markets.

This section is also aimed at providing a background of developments which may have contributed to current events which are occurring on the New York Stock Exchange – which relate to the value relevance of accounting information – as well as whether the quality of accounting information, as reflected in stock prices, can be confidently relied upon by investors.

The ensuing section is dedicated to highlighting the importance of two vital characteristics of accounting information – namely, verifiability – which is embodied in the role of audits; as well as comparability.

Comparability being intricately linked to understandability – another very important quality whose focus is not only vital from the perspective that its results in the mitigation of informational asymmetries between management and users of financial information, but also from the perspective of mitigating the Audit Expectations Gap.

As highlighted under the introductory chapter, the issue of investor confidence and the restoration thereof, constitutes an important issue in light of recent volatilities, vulnerabilities and stock market corrections within the financial markets.

The Current IASB and FASB Framework

The links between comparability and understandability are evident since comparability facilitates and enhances understandability. Comparability is also an essential tool towards global regulatory convergence and harmonization.

Figure 1. Fundamental and enhancing qualitative characteristics
Source of Figure 1: KPMG Briefing Sheet Conceptual Framework for Financial Reporting October 2010 Issue 213 at page 3

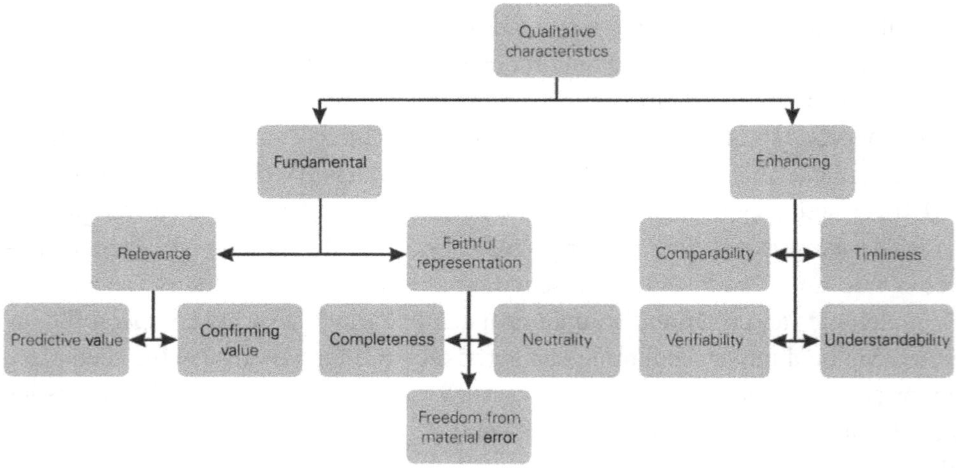

The importance accorded to comparability by the Basel Committee on Banking Supervision is highlighted in its BIS (84th) Annual Report (BIS, 2014: 138):

- Having substantially strengthened the banking system's regulatory framework, the Committee has now turned to the matter of its complexity and the comparability of capital adequacy ratios across banks and jurisdictions.
- The Committee considers it essential to the ongoing effectiveness of the Basel capital standards to simplify them where possible and to improve the comparability of their outcomes (eg regulatory capital, risk-weighted assets and capital ratios). In 2012, the Committee commissioned a small group of its members to review the Basel capital framework, aware that, over time, the framework has steadily grown and that more sophisticated risk measurement methodologies have been introduced.
- The goal of the task force was to point to areas of undue complexity within the framework and opportunities to improve the comparability of its outcomes. In July 2013, the Committee released a discussion paper on the trade-offs between the risk sensitivity of the Basel capital standards and their simplicity and comparability.
- Related developments in the analysis of comparability were the Committee's release of two studies on the risk-weighting of assets, the first regarding credit risk in the banking book, and the second regarding market risk in the trading book

Some Flaws Revealed in Accounting Measurements and Policies

Based on the BIS 84th Annual Report (BIS, 2014:105):

- The definition of the denominator of the Basel III leverage ratio, a simple ratio of capital to total bank exposure that complements the risk-based capital requirements, was finalized in January 2014. The exposure measure represents progress in two respects. First, it is universal, as it overcomes discrepancies in the way different accounting standards capture off-balance sheet exposures, including derivatives. Its definition adopts an established regulatory practice that is highly comparable across jurisdictions.
- Second, the measure is comprehensive, as it ensures adequate capture of both on- and off-balance sheet sources of leverage.

Stock Market Developments: Distinguishing between Business and Financial Cycles

In view of recent plunges on the Wall Street, should there be concern that an impending recession or Financial Crisis is about to occur? Stock market corrections are known to occur even where accounting information is accurate and whilst there may be apparent similarities between recent developments and previous financial turbulences, the fundamentals underlying these are different.

In distinguishing business and financial cycles the BIS highlights the following (BIS, 2014:66):

- Financial cycles are much longer than business cycles. As traditionally measured, business cycles tend to last from one to eight years, and financial cycles around 15 to 20 years. The difference in length means that a financial cycle can span several business cycles.
- Peaks in the financial cycle tend to coincide with banking crises or periods of considerable financial stress.
- Financial cycles are often synchronized across economies.
- Financial cycles change with the macroeconomic environment and policy frameworks.

Following the labor data announcement, US stocks weakened, and a series of speeches by Fed officials which markets viewed as preparing the ground for a December rate hike followed (see BIS, 2015:7). Even though the Paris terrorist attack

Figure 2. Financial cycle peaks to coincide with crises

[1] *The financial cycle as measured by frequency-based (bandpass) filters capturing medium-term cycles in real credit, the credit-to-GDP ratio and real house prices (Box IV.A). Vertical lines indicate financial crises emerging from domestic vulnerabilities.*

[2] *Belgium, Finland, France, Ireland, Italy, the Netherlands, Portugal and Spain.*

[3] *Australia, Canada, New Zealand, Norway and Sweden.*

[4] *Indonesia, Hong Kong SAR and Singapore.*

Sources: National data; BIS; BIS calculations.

Source of Figure 2: BIS 84th Annual Report page 67 June 2014

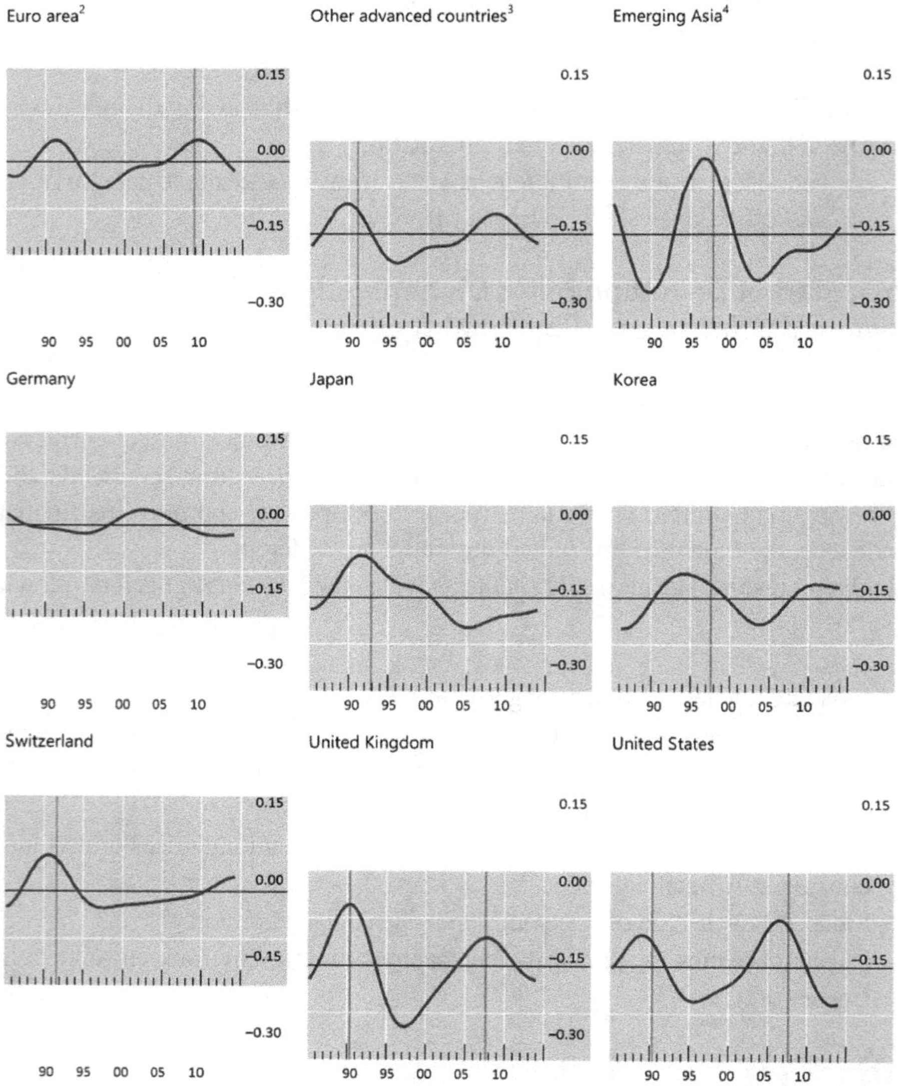

in November 2015 and heightened tensions in Syria resulted to increased concerns over geopolitical risks, these had little impact on the market (BIS, 2015:7).

The Fed had decided in October to put on hold interest rate hikes – to which the markets appeared to respond very favorably.

Markets' Recovery Following Corrections in August and September 2015

See Figure 3 and Figure 4.

Distinguishing the Efficient Markets Hypothesis from the Random Walk Theory: Historical Based Information as Reliable Information Predictors

Even though the Efficient Markets Hypothesis (EMH) is also commonly referred to as the random walk theory (Clarke et al, 2001:1), there are several reasons why

Figure 3. Markets' recovery
[1] MSCI World Index. [2] MSCI Emerging Markets Index.
[3] Implied volatility of at-the-money options on long-term bond futures of Germany, Japan, the United Kingdom and the United States; weighted average based on GDP and PPP exchange rates.
[4] JPMorgan VXY Global index.
[5] US dollars per unit of local currency. A decline indicates a depreciation (appreciation) of the local currency (US dollar).
Sources: Bloomberg; Datastream; national data.
[1] See "EME vulnerabilities take centre stage", BIS Quarterly Review, September 2015.

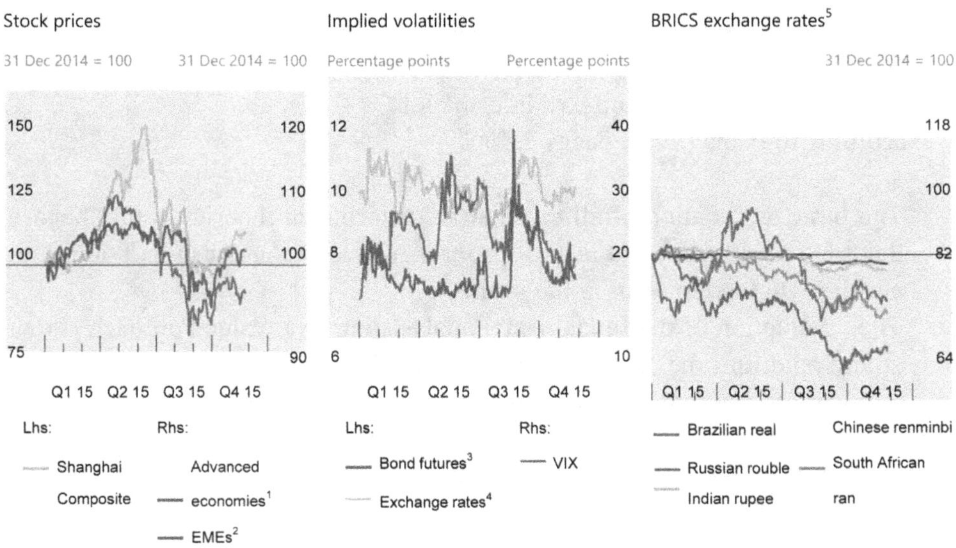

Figure 4. Impact of policy announcements on markets[1]
In per cent
[1] *Vertical lines represent the US Federal Reserve Federal Open Market Committee meetings on 17 September and 28 October 2015, the European Central Bank Governing Council meeting on 22 October 2015 and the release of US nonfarm payrolls report on 6 November 2015.*
[2] *Based on Bloomberg implied probabilities from fed funds futures.*
Source of Figure 3: BIS Quarterly Review December 2015 at page 2
[3] *Three-month government bond yields.*
[4] *Ten-year government bond yields.*
Source: Bloomberg.
Source: BIS Quarterly Review December 2015 at page 3

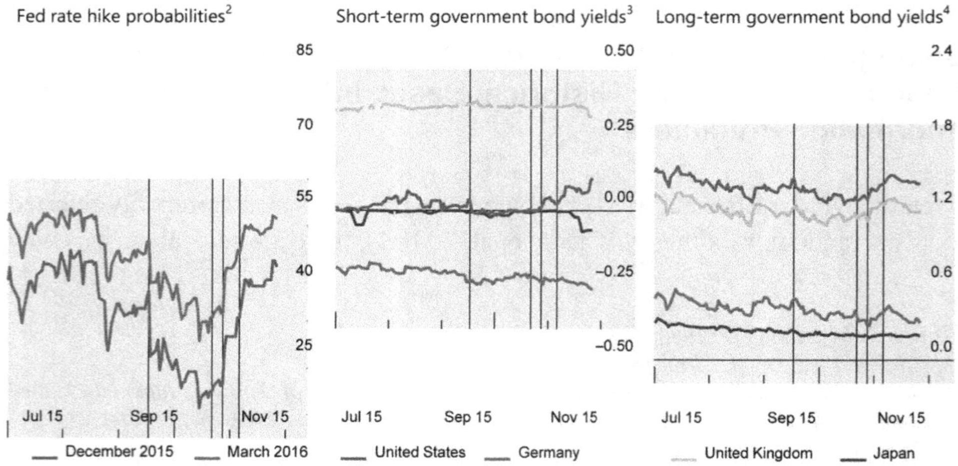

both can be distinguished. This chapter will also aim to illustrate why the semi-strong and strong forms of the Efficient Markets Hypothesis appear to accord, to a greater degree, with the random walk theory whilst the weak form of the EMH increasingly appears to be contradictory to the random walk hypothesis – in terms of predictability – and based on past information.

According to Fama (1965, pages 2, 3):

- The basic assumption of all the chartist or technical theories is that history tends to repeat itself, that is, past patterns of price behavior in individual securities will tend to recur in the future.
- The assumption of the fundamental analysis/intrinsic value approach is that at any point in time an individual security has an intrinsic value (or, in the terms of the economist, an equilibrium price) which depends on the earning potential of the security. The earning potential of the security depends in turn on such fundamental factors as quality of management, outlook for the industry and the economy, etc.

Is "important current information almost freely" available to all participants? (as assumed under the EMH?, Fama:1965, page 4).

This requires a consideration of what constitutes:

1. Important current information
2. Availability to all participants (users of such financial information)

Fama (page 4) argues that "If the discrepancies between actual prices and intrinsic values are systematic rather than random in nature, then knowledge of this should help intelligent market participants to better predict the path by which actual prices will move toward intrinsic values".

Further, random walk, according to Fama (page 6) is implied to be the past history of the series of stock price changes which cannot be used to predict the future in any meaningful way – basically independent on past results.

"If the random-walk theory is valid and if security exchanges are "efficient" markets, then stock prices at any point in time will represent good estimates of intrinsic or fundamental values. Thus, additional fundamental analysis is of value only when the analyst has new information which was not fully considered in forming current market prices, or has new insights concerning the effects of generally available information which are not already implicit in current prices." (Fama, 1965:16)

Even though empirical studies which support the independence assumption of the random walk model have been referred to in the literature, Kohlsheen et al (2016) provide "extensive evidence" that supports the claim that "distinct commodity-related driver of exchange rate movements", exist - even at relatively high frequencies.

The three forms of the Efficient Market Hypothesis (EMH)

1. **Strong Form of the Efficient Market Hypothesis:** In its strongest form, the Efficient Markets Hypothesis postulates that you cannot beat the market – either through insider information or insider privileges as all relevant information is reflected fully and instantaneously impounded in stock market prices.
2. **Semi Strong Form of the Efficient Market Hypothesis (EMH):** The semi strong form, which is defined from the perspective of publicly available information, holds that where access to such information is gained, then stock prices fully reflect and transmit relevant and fundamental information.
3. **Weak Form of the Efficient Market Hypothesis (EMH):** The weak form reflects the Efficient Markets Hypothesis from the point of view that the market transmits relevant information based on past prices and historical data.

What Constitutes Current Important Information?

Backward looking information – This particularly, is excluded from the IASB and FASB's current framework and definition of what constitutes fundamental qualitative accounting characteristics. Whilst relevance and faithful representation now constitute fundamental qualitative accounting characteristics, enhanced qualitative accounting characteristics are said to comprise comparability, timeliness, verifiability and understandability.

This is underlined by further qualifications attributed to predictive and confirmability attributes of accounting information – which are assigned under the heading of fundamental qualitative accounting characteristics (categorized under relevance).

In respect of forward looking information, a distinction needs to be drawn between information that cannot be directly verified – as well as that which can be directly verified, in designating the categorization of verifiability as a fundamental and required characteristic or merely an enhancing characteristic.

Forward looking information that can be directly verified: Given the importance attributed to forward looking information, verifiability in respect of such information should be designated under the category of fundamental qualitative characteristic.

Forward looking information that cannot be directly verified: This is still considered very important by IASB and FASB – hence the reason for relegating verifiability to a "desirable but not required enhancing qualitative characteristic."

Forward Looking Information That Cannot Be Directly Verified

According to Petersen (2012: page 8),

- Bonds have three variables in their pricing, coupon yield, time to maturity and the relevant interest rate with which to discount the returns as per the maturity. When the interest rate used in discounting future income streams increases, the price of the bond goes down so that the coupon yield adjusts to the market interest rate – in the basic model, which to a large extent still reflects market behavior.

Based on Keynes model (2000) and the basic relationship between the market for foreign exchange and the interest rate, which in her opinion, has been "translated to modern equilibrium models – as well as reduced to equating the premium for foreign exchange to the relevant interest-rate differential between the countries of origin" she makes the following observations (pages 8, 9):

- Given that both the interest rates and the exchange rates depend on more variables, one equation cannot solve this.
- Even if interest rates in two countries are relatively stable, still the forward exchange rate may move because other currency-rate determinants are at play than one interest-rate differential.
- Whilst it is true that interest-rate differentials deliver the basis for foreign-exchange hedging through the forward market, there is a difference between benchmarks used to hedge exposure in foreign-trade business dealings and a theoretical model for financial trades which, despite the theories stating that excessive gains cannot be had, tend to be motivated by such gain.
- Further, when looking at actual pricing, there is always a residual that is nowadays attributed to volatility rather than preference.

On the other hand, Kohlscheen, Avalos & Schrimpf (2016: pages 2,3) argue that changes in the prices of key exports may well bear a close link with exchange rate movements. In reconciling their views with those of Petersen, they add that whilst it is possible that commodity price movements also affect the exchange rates of commodity importers, the link in such cases is likely to be less clear-cut, as there may be greater symmetry in the effects of import price fluctuations on different countries.

The use of daily Constructing Country-Specific Commodity Export Price Indices (CXPIs), in their opinion allows them to analyze the relationship between commodity prices and exchange rates with greater precision at different frequencies. Further, they illustrate how the information that is provided in the indices explicitly improves the predictive performance of exchange rate models for all 11 of the commodity exporters being studied.

Further important observations and derivations from their studies are as follows (see pages 3 and 4):

- That commodity prices predict exchange rate movements of commodity exporters up to two months ahead when the analysis is based on in-sample panel regressions.
- That out-of-sample estimations also show that simple linear predictive models based on their commodity price indices tend to have superior predictive performance for exchange rates when compared to random walk benchmarks (these being illustrated through investigations carried out on the three advanced economies and the eight emerging economies used in their sample).
- Their key finding that commodity price models dominate random walk models is based on the usual approach of utilizing realized variables as predictors (Meese and Rogoff: 1983).

As well as testing for the reverse link, namely, whether exchange rates predict CXPIs, they conclude (page 26) that the relationship between commodity prices and exchange rates is "economically and statistically significant" - even at high-frequency. Furthermore, they deduce that the commodity price-exchange rate nexus is largely unaffected – even when changes in uncertainty and global risk appetite are taken into consideration.

Given the classification of verifiability as a desirable but not required enhancing qualitative characteristic, could the definition of fundamental, as embodied within the scope of the Efficient Market Hypothesis be considered to provide and fully reflect relevant information?

Forward looking information, which could relate to the strong form of EMH – as well as to historical data, is distinguished from the weak form of the EMH in matters relating to the degree of time. With timeliness also being categorized as an enhancing qualitative characteristic, the definition attributed to what constitutes fundamental information appears to exclude timeliness.

Where the random walk theory applies, then there could be justification that capital markets are efficient at any point in time – regardless and independent of past data – which are not being used or cannot be used to predict future prices. However, where the theory does not hold, then time – which also determines accessibility to (current) information, could play a pivotal role in determining how efficient the markets really are.

Petersen (page 11) adds that "The EMH excludes two notions: using the past to predict the future and consistent disagreement about how to incorporate 'information'. With the tendency to ensure the efficient outcome, EMH is in line with Bachelier's statement that no extraordinary profits can be had. However, she continues, EMH does not openly say that the outcome is that markets allocate capital efficiently to enterprises, but this is often implied when ordinary people opine "markets are efficient".

Fama and Miller (1971) argue that the theory of finance is an attempt to account for how solutions to the problems faced in the allocation of resources over time are facilitated by the existence of capital markets (which in their opinion provides a means for economic agents to exchange resources for availability at different points in time), as well as firms.

Given the credibility of information in financial reporting and the extent to which certain information can be directly or indirectly verified – and particularly in view of the relegated status of verifiability – as a qualitative characteristic, the Efficient Markets Hypothesis appears to have greater relevance than ever. How predictive are stock market prices and changes in price movements? The weak form of the Efficient Markets Hypothesis is supposed to constitute the most opposing form (of EMH) to the random walk hypothesis – and it appears that the Efficient Markets

Hypothesis is growing more in line with the random walk hypothesis in the sense that even more forward looking information and the predictability of such information have increasingly less bearing on the predictability of information – and that markets are more efficient in providing investors with information than publicly accessible or inside based information.

ISSUES, CONTROVERSIES, PROBLEMS

However, just as the weak form of the EMH is supposed to strongly contradict the random walk hypothesis, the potential for historical based data to provide predictable information to investors is evidenced by the results of empirical based studies which will be highlighted in this chapter – as well as results from the tables and figures. Thus whilst confirming the fact that the Efficient Markets Hypothesis is growing more in line with the random walk hypothesis in the sense that even more forward looking information and the predictability of such information increasingly, appear to have less bearing on the predictability of information, the weak form of the EMH appears to also be increasingly contradictory to the random walk hypothesis – in terms of the level of predictability which it is able to provide - based on past and historical information.

Where greater recognition is not accorded to the status and attribute of verifiability of information – regardless of whether such information is backward or forward looking, there is also the tendency for greater incidences of manipulation of data to occur – and particularly inside information – and this would lend greater credibility and support to the Efficient Markets Hypothesis. No matter how many cover ups or degree of transparency, it would only be a matter of time when the full impact and scale of such inaccuracies are revealed through the markets.

Reliability of Accounting Data and Loss of Investor Confidence

Discrepancies in the way various accounting standards are applied across several jurisdictions are evident – not just in relation to off-balance sheet exposures, and particularly derivatives, but also in relation to the rise of nonbanking financial intermediation.

Addressing such discrepancies and the potential to manipulate accounting data, can best be facilitated through clear accounting concepts, policies and standards which are not only understandable to users of such financial information, but are applied in a consistent and comparable manner. Comparability from this perspective, is not only a vital characteristic which needs to be incorporated by standard setters but also from the perspective of users.

Verifiability gives credibility to the value of accounting information – as well as the work of auditors. Where such a fundamental quality is undermined, there is every possibility that users of such information will be encouraged to give less attention to the credibility of financial statements which are generated by the management of an enterprise – further undermining investor confidence.

Even though backward looking information cannot be directly verified, investors rely to a huge extent on stock markets as reliable economic indicators – particularly with respect to forward looking information. If stock prices are regarded as being not directly verifiable, then the value relevance of such information reflected through stock prices can be questioned. In matters relating to whether stock prices fully reflect information, whilst stock market corrections occur from time to time, the extent and frequency to which they occur, does not provide conclusive and concrete evidence to justify the accuracy of such information. In certain cases, the nature and rationale of surrounding events is needed to judge the accuracy of information being transmitted through stock markets prices.

Further stock market corrections should not be misinterpreted as the failure of markets to accord with the Efficient Markets Hypothesis – since stock market corrections should be distinguished from such developments heralding and signaling the beginning of a recession.

Which is why recent developments categorizing timeliness into an enhancing qualitative characteristic could also mean the difference between delineating a stock market correction from a major Crash - with recession inducing consequences.

FUTURE RESEARCH DIRECTIONS

As highlighted by the Bank for International Settlements in its BIS 84th Annual Report (BIS, 2014:151):

- The G20 and FSB support the development of a single set of high-quality global accounting standards. The FSB continues to encourage the IASB and the Financial Accounting Standards Board to complete their convergence project, and it is monitoring their progress in implementing specific G20 and FSB accounting recommendations.

Regulatory and global convergence initiatives and related research are thereby encouraged as a means of fostering the realization of comparability, consistency, verifiability and understandability of accounting information as fore and core objectives and characteristics.

Further in January 2014, in view of ongoing initiatives aimed at fostering consistency, the Committee published information to assist supervisors in their evaluation of the liquidity profile of assets held by banks (BIS, 2014:140). Even though the document, Guidance for supervisors on market-based indicators of liquidity, is aimed at promoting greater consistency in the classification of so-called high-quality liquid assets (HQLA) across jurisdictions in the context of the Basel III LCR, the definition of HQLA within the LCR is not changed; rather, the document assists supervisors assess whether assets are suitably liquid for LCR purposes (BIS, 2014:140).

CONCLUSION

Three big influences on stock market volatilities during 2016 have been oil prices, the EU Referendum in the United Kingdom, and the November 2016 United States Presidential elections – with oil prices having impacted global stock markets since the end of 2014. Volatility can arise across stock markets for many reasons – some of which include political risks and currency devaluations. Whatever the reasons attributable to such volatilities, these turbulences across financial markets boil down generally and frequently to one common denominator and underlying issue and cause – namely, information uncertainty - which this presents, in many cases to investors.

More recently and of greater relevance, political risks and currency devaluations have been typically and best illustrated through the results of the 2016 U.S Presidential elections which were released on the 8th November, and the UK Brexit Referendum results. All in all, financial markets, it has been demonstrated, hate uncertainty.

Further repercussions of information uncertainty on global stock markets in the immediate aftermath of the 2016 United States Presidential elections are attributed to inflationary policies of the incoming Trump administration which triggered bond sell offs across markets. Indications that bond stocks will be weaker with a surge in yields of ten year bonds and long term interest rates also up – in anticipation of higher interest rates – which should be good for equities. Uncertainties have also been generated in relation to US domestic and foreign policies, as well as the unexpected strength of the dollar – following the Presidential elections, with crude oil prices at a 3 month low.

Does value relevance accord with the definition attributed to an alignment of accounting information and capital market values (market values)? This chapter has sought to underline the importance of certain characteristics, namely, verifiability, understandability, timeliness, and comparability, as crucial in determining the extent to which accounting information may be considered as relevant in stock and capital markets.

In so doing it not only contributes to existing and previous literature and investigations which have regarded value relevance as being "the evaluation of the relationship between accounting information and capital market values (market values)", but also highlights the need for the incorporation of such vital characteristics in the definition of value relevance – if accounting information is to be considered value relevant – and particularly from within the scope of capital and stock markets.

As revealed from the results of empirical studies discussed in this chapter, and based on sample periods used, some market data may prove to be more reliable and relevant sources of information for investors than merely relying on financial information and statements which are generated by management of an enterprise.

Three big influences on stock market volatilities during 2016 have been oil prices, the EU Referendum in the United Kingdom, and the November 2016 United States Presidential elections – with oil prices having impacted global stock markets since the end of 2014. Volatility can arise across stock markets for many reasons – some of which include political risks and currency devaluations. Whatever the reasons attributable to such volatilities, these turbulences across financial markets boil down generally and frequently to one common denominator and underlying issue and cause – namely, information uncertainty - which this presents, in many cases to investors.

More recently and of greater relevance, political risks and currency devaluations have been typically and best illustrated through the results of the 2016 U.S Presidential elections which were released on the 8th November, and the UK Brexit Referendum results. All in all, financial markets, it has been demonstrated, hate uncertainty.

Further repercussions of information uncertainty on global stock markets in the immediate aftermath of the 2016 United States Presidential elections are attributed to inflationary policies of the incoming Trump administration which triggered bond sell offs across markets. Indications that bond stocks will be weaker with a surge in yields of ten year bonds and long term interest rates also up – in anticipation of higher interest rates – which should be good for equities. Uncertainties have also been generated in relation to US domestic and foreign policies, as well as the unexpected strength of the dollar – following the Presidential elections, with crude oil prices at a 3 month low.

In terms of financial markets' reaction, such was the certainty in the United Kingdom that the "Remain" voters would be triumphant in the aftermath of the EU Referendum that it was rumored on the night before the release of the results, that the UKIP leader, Nigel Farage had conceded. Further, the financial markets soared to very high levels – with the value of the pound also reaching all-time highs on the night before the 24th June.

Having predicted the results of the EU Referendum wrongly, the 24th June, a day after (during which it had been revealed that the Remain voters had lost by a margin of about 4%), witnessed the value of the pound dropping to historically low levels. The impact of the Referendum on the pound has not only resulted in lower export prices, higher import prices, but also higher inflation levels. Further, the FTSE 100 closed the day – as well as the week ending, the 24th June at about -200. Other major indices such as the Nikkei 225 and the Dow Industrial closed in extremely negative regions of -1286.33 and – 610.32 respectively. Even though volatilities are still being experienced across the markets, a huge degree of stability has occurred Post Brexit.

Higher inflation levels attributed to the value of the pound and initial panics and volatilities across the market were responded to swiftly by the Governor of the Bank of England through a cut in interest rates to 0.25% – during the first week of August 2016. Quantitative easing measures were also introduced in a bid to add some monetary stimulus to the levels of economic activity. Interestingly it was not the reaction of the Bank that was later criticized but the emphasis of "Project Fear" whereby many claimed that undue fears and uncertainty had been instilled into the general public in the build up to the EU Referendum – as regards possible detrimental consequences for the UK economy - should it leave the European Union. This particularly being the case Post Brexit – when markets appear to have recovered and the country weathering all the storms of Brexit reasonably well.

Just as the Brexit results were wrongly predicted and it was demonstrated that markets cannot be relied upon, the same scenario was echoed during the days culminating to the November 8th 2016 US Presidential elections. In response to announcements that the FBI had cleared Hilary Clinton of any alleged mishandling and criminal investigations relating to her Emails, markets soared in the anticipation that a Clinton victory, one which was seen to favor certainty, was inevitable. The financial markets were also considered to be anti-Trump – not only given the levels of uncertainty which a President-elect Trump was viewed as generating, but also in respect of his alleged approaches of protectionism in trade matters.

Even before the election results had been confirmed on the morning of the 9th November 2016, with 137 electoral college votes being declared for Trump, and just 104 for Clinton, and more significantly with the 270 magic target having not even been confirmed, the Dow Futures had already dropped by 500 points. Further, the Mexican Peso dropped to record lows against the dollar – and most stocks in Asia down 1-2%. In view of risk aversion, transfers were witnessed with movements to safer haven stocks. The Mexican Peso which had been performing well the day before – based on anticipations of a Clinton victory, was now reacting to possible consequences of a Trump victory – namely, higher trade tariffs, taxes on cars and the building of "the Wall".

At this stage, the markets were already clearly reacting to a shock and historically low and volatile levels were understandable following confirmation of the Presidential results. The value of the dollar also dropped to low levels. However, in contrast to

Table 1. Exchange rate predictability by commodity prices (out-of-sample analysis) forecasting performance vs RW benchmark

		RW without drift			RW with (time-varying) drift		
Currency	**Observations**	**RMSE ratio**	**DM stat**	**p-value**	**RMSE ratio**	**DM stat**	**p-value**
AUD							
	1607	0.858	-5.30***	0.000	0.858	-5.29***	0.000
CAD							
	1607	0.850	-4.16***	0.000	0.850	-4.16***	0.000
NOK							
	1607	0.908	-3.79***	0.000	0.908	-3.78***	0.000
BRL							
	1607	0.936	-3.51***	0.001	0.937	-3.45***	0.001
CLP							
	1607	0.918	-4.64***	0.000	0.918	-4.63***	0.000
COP							
	1607	0.953	-3.83***	0.000	0.953	-3.82***	0.000
MXN							
	1607	0.910	-4.29***	0.000	0.910	-4.32***	0.000
PEN							
	1607	0.965	-4.12***	0.000	0.966	-4.09***	0.000
ZAR							
	1607	0.905	-5.36***	0.000	0.905	-5.34***	0.000
RUB							
	802	0.958	-2.04**	0.041	0.960	-1.99**	0.046
MYR							
	1195	0.972	-1.95*	0.052	0.972	-1.95*	0.051

Notes: The null hypothesis of the Diebold Mariano test is that forecast accuracy is equal. Negative DM statistics indicate that the tested model has superior predictive performance when compared to benchmark. The coefficients were estimated with a 5 year rolling window, following the Meese-Rogoff approach. RMSE ratios refer to the RMSE of the model based on commodities divided by the RMSE of the RW benchmark in question. *, **, *** denote statistical significance at 10%, 5% and 1%, respectively.

Source: BIS Publications, Kohlscheen., E., Avalos., F. H. and Schrimpf., A. (2016). When the Walk is not Random: Commodity Prices and Exchange Rates (page 41)

Table 2. Exchange rate predictability (in-sample) in a panel setting

	k=1	k=5	k=22	k=44	k=66
CXPI	-0.020***	-0.016*	-0.044***	-0.047***	-0.018
t-stat	3.51	1.89	5.19	2.65	0.88
R2 overall	0.0032	0.0113	0.0540	0.0934	0.1228
R2 within	0.0032	0.0111	0.0530	0.0917	0.1206
R2 between	0.5714	0.5608	0.6062	0.6143	0.6055
Observations	30,294	30,283	30,096	29,854	29,612
Groups	11	11	11	11	11
Fixed effects	yes	yes	yes	yes	Yes

Notes: Dependent variable: log change of bilateral exchange rate

Prediction horizon in days

This table shows the results of the panel regression $\Delta s_{i,t+k} = \alpha + \Delta CXPI_{i,t} + \gamma_i + \theta_{t+k} + \varepsilon_{i,t+k}$, where k stands for the length of the prediction horizon. t-statistics are based on clustered standard errors. *, **, *** denote statistical significance at 10%, 5% and 1%, respectively. The estimation is based on information from Jan 2004 to

Source: Kohlscheen., E., Avalos., F. H. and Schrimpf., A. (2016). When the Walk is not Random: Commodity Prices and Exchange Rates (page 40)

Table 3. The reverse link: commodity price predictability by exchange rates

			Prediction horizon in days		
	k=1	k=5	k=22	k=44	k=66
bilateral exchange rate	-0.017	-0.005	-0.030	-0.037	-0.077
t-stat	1.41	0.46	0.71	0.94	0.75
R2 overall	0.0066	0.0228	0.0912	0.1700	0.1802
R2 within	0.0065	0.0226	0.0907	0.1690	0.1794
R2 between	0.5762	0.5413	0.5957	0.6280	0.5290
Observations	28,941	28,897	28,710	28,468	28,226
Groups	11	11	11	11	11
Fixed effects	yes	yes	yes	yes	yes

Notes: Dependent variable: log change of commodity prices

This table shows the results of the fixed effects regression $\Delta CXPI_{i,t+k} = \alpha + \Delta s_{i,t} + \gamma_i + \theta_{t+k} + \varepsilon_{i,t+k}$, where k stands for the length of the prediction horizon. t-statistics are based on clustered standard errors. *, **, *** denote statistical significance at 10%, 5% and 1%, respectively. The estimation is based on information from Jan 2004 to Feb 2015, except for observations of the six months after the collapse of Lehman Brothers.

Source: BIS Publications, Kohlscheen., E., Avalos., F. H. and Schrimpf., A. (2016) (page 44)

Table 4. Exchange rate predictability by commodities by country

		k=0	k=1	k=5	k=22	k=44	k=66
AUD							
	CXPI	-0.579***	-0.044	-0.091**	-0.074***	-0.026	0.002
	t-stat	12.12	1.30	2.20	3.07	1.43	0.18
	R2	0.2286	0.0013	0.0068	0.0083	0.0012	0.0000
CAD							
	CXPI	-0.287***	-0.019	-0.014	-0.057***	-0.089***	-0.071***
	t-stat	18.96	1.33	0.83	4.22	7.51	8.53
	R2	0.2248	0.0010	0.0006	0.0136	0.0399	0.0275
NOK							
	CXPI	-0.180***	-0.018*	0.001	-0.074***	-0.060***	-0.025**
	t-stat	15.31	1.78	0.14	8.89	5.40	2.51
	R2	0.1446	0.0015	0.0000	0.0326	0.0196	0.0034
BRL							
	CXPI	-0.545***	-0.060	-0.074	-0.244***	-0.261***	-0.154***
	t-stat	11.86	1.25	1.55	8.54	11.69	9.17
	R2	0.1073	0.0013	0.0027	0.0503	0.0718	0.0267
CLP							
	CXPI	-0.190***	-0.027**	-0.058***	-0.027**	0.027**	0.074***
	t-stat	14.66	2.23	3.93	2.23	2.56	9.21
	R2	0.1405	0.0029	0.0105	0.0026	0.0034	0.0263
COP							
	CXPI	-0.152***	-0.025*	0.000	-0.046***	-0.099***	-0.094***
	t-stat	10.43	1.74	0.02	3.71	7.45	9.76
	R2	0.0657	0.0017	0.0000	0.0071	0.0329	0.0310
MXN							
	CXPI	-0.195***	0.002	-0.032**	-0.076***	-0.143***	-0.121***
	t-stat	13.70	0.15	2.04	6.90	13.00	13.97
	R2	0.1336	0.0000	0.0039	0.0274	0.1054	0.0807
PEN							
	CXPI	-0.050***	-0.004	-0.016**	-0.058***	-0.076***	-0.065***
	t-stat	6.64	0.55	2.05	9.89	16.44	16.08
	R2	0.0319	0.0002	0.0029	0.0445	0.0796	0.0610
ZAR							
	CXPI	-0.558***	0.036	-0.015	-0.033	-0.034	0.014

continued on following page

Table 4. Continued

		k=0	k=1	k=5	k=22	k=44	k=66
	t-stat	13.75	1.08	0.38	1.22	1.50	1.16
	R2	0.1592	0.0007	0.0001	0.0012	0.0016	0.0004
RUB							
	CXPI	-0.277***	-0.075***	-0.050*	-0.170***	-0.315***	-0.348***
	t-stat	14.44	3.52	1.87	7.23	10.28	9.55
	R2	0.1293	0.0097	0.0044	0.0569	0.1202	0.1165
MYR							
	CXPI	-0.067***	-0.0280***	-0.005	-0.041***	-0.041***	-0.039***
	t-stat	10.88	5.15	0.89	7.89	7.62	9.66
	R2	0.0549	0.0096	0.0003	0.0240	0.0245	0.0257

Notes: Prediction horizon in days

This table shows the results of the OLS regression $\Delta s_{t+k} = \alpha + \Delta CXPI_t + \varepsilon_{t+k}$, where k stands for the length of the prediction horizon. Constants are not tabulated. t-statistics, which are reported below the coefficients, are based on Newey-West standard errors. *, **, *** denote statistical significance at 10%, 5% and 1%, respectively. The estimation is based on information of the full sample period (ie Jan 2004 - Feb 2015), except for Russia and Malaysia were the sample period starts in February 2009 and August 2005, respectively.

Source BIS Kohlsheen et al (2016)

Table 5. Exchange rate predictability with lagged commodity prices (out-of-sample analysis)

		Prediction of exchange rate vs. USD				Prediction of exchange rate vs. JPY			
		RW without drift		RW with drift		RW without drift		RW with drift	
Currency	obs	DM stat	p-value	DM stat	p-value	DM stat	p-value	DM stat	p-value
AUD									
	1607	-0.01	0.994	-0.07	0.944	1.24	0.212	0.69	0.486
CAD									
	1607	-0.10	0.922	-0.07	0.937	1.31	0.190	1.22	0.221
NOK									
	1607	2.35**	0.019	2.58***	0.010	2.58***	0.010	2.27**	0.023
BRL									
	1607	-1.66*	0.095	-1.12	0.248	0.08	0.938	-0.12	0.902
CLP									
	1607	-2.13**	0.034	-2.37**	0.018	-2.78***	0.005	-2.70***	0.007
COP									
	1607	-1.62	0.105	-1.62	0.104	-1.58	0.113	-1.68*	0.092

continued on following page

Table 5. Continued

		Prediction of exchange rate vs. USD				Prediction of exchange rate vs. JPY			
		RW without drift		RW with drift		RW without drift		RW with drift	
Currency	**obs**	**DM stat**	**p-value**	**DM stat**	**p-value**	**DM stat**	**p-value**	**DM stat**	**p-value**
MXN									
	1607	1.62	0.105	1.20	0.231	1.23	0.218	0.66	0.505
PEN									
	1607	-1.01	0.311	-0.46	0.643	0.14	0.893	-0.51	0.608
ZAR									
	1607	0.36	0.722	-0.23	0.818	-0.87	0.384	-0.91	0.359
RUB									
	802	0.21	0.836	0.08	0.933	-1.69*	0.091	-1.80*	0.071
MYR									
	1195	-1.71*	0.087	-1.84*	0.065	-2.05**	0.040	-2.20**	0.028

Notes: forecasting performance vs RW benchmark

The null hypothesis of the Diebold Mariano test is that forecast accuracy is equal. Negative DM statistics indicate that the tested model has superior predictive performance when compared to benchmark. The coefficients were estimated with a 5 year rolling window. RMSE ratios refer to the RMSE of the model based on commodities divided by the RMSE of the RW benchmark in question. *, **, *** denote statistical significance at 10%, 5% and 1%, respectively

Source: BIS, Kohlscheen., E., Avalos., F. H. and Schrimpf., A. (2016) (page 50)

Table 6. Exchange rate predictability: carry vs. commodities

		Carry model			Carry + CXPI model		
Currency	**Observations**	**RMSE ratio**	**DM stat**	**p-value**	**RMSE ratio**	**DM stat**	**p-value**
AUD							
	1607	0.951	-4.66***	0.000	0.819	-6.15***	0.000
CAD							
	1607	0.992	-2.85***	0.004	0.841	-4.42***	0.000
NOK							
	1607	1.000	0.23	0.817	0.908	-3.80***	0.000
BRL							
	1607	1.036	2.62	0.009	0.958	-2.66***	0.008
CLP							
	1607	1.000	0.74	0.460	0.918	-4.69***	0.000
COP							
	1607	1.009	1.64	0.100	0.961	-3.31***	0.001

continued on following page

Table 6. Continued

		Carry model			Carry + CXPI model		
Currency	**Observations**	**RMSE ratio**	**DM stat**	**p-value**	**RMSE ratio**	**DM stat**	**p-value**
MXN							
	1607	0.998	-0.72	0.474	0.909	-4.29***	0.000
PEN							
	1607	1.003	0.90	0.368	0.961	-3.42***	0.001
ZAR							
	1607	1.023	0.61	0.544	0.919	-2.20**	0.028
RUB							
	802	0.808	-1.125	0.261	0.776	-1.25	0.210
MYR							
	1195	1.000	1.702	0.089	0.972	-1.90*	0.057

Notes: The null hypothesis of the Diebold Mariano test is that forecast accuracy is equal. The benchmark that is used as a reference is the random walk model with a time-varying drift. Negative DM statistics indicate that the tested model has superior predictive performance when compared to benchmark, while positive values indicate that the random walk benchmark is superior. The coefficients were estimated with a 5 year rolling window, following the Meese-Rogoff approach. RMSE ratios refer to the RMSE of the model based on commodities divided by the RMSE of the RW benchmark in question. *, **, *** denote statistical significance at 10%, 5% and 1%, respectively.

Source: BIS, Kohlscheen., E., Avalos., F. H. and Schrimpf., A. (2016) (page 45)

Table 7. Exchange rate predictability by commodities by country

		k=0	**k=1**	**k=5**	**k=22**	**k=44**	**k=66**
AUD							
	CXPI	-0.579***	-0.044	-0.091**	-0.074***	-0.026	0.002
	t-stat	12.12	1.30	2.20	3.07	1.43	0.18
	R2	0.2286	0.0013	0.0068	0.0083	0.0012	0.0000
CAD							
	CXPI	-0.287***	-0.019	-0.014	-0.057***	-0.089***	-0.071***
	t-stat	18.96	1.33	0.83	4.22	7.51	8.53
	R2	0.2248	0.0010	0.0006	0.0136	0.0399	0.0275
NOK							
	CXPI	-0.180***	-0.018*	0.001	-0.074***	-0.060***	-0.025**
	t-stat	15.31	1.78	0.14	8.89	5.40	2.51
	R2	0.1446	0.0015	0.0000	0.0326	0.0196	0.0034
BRL							
	CXPI	-0.545***	-0.060	-0.074	-0.244***	-0.261***	-0.154***

continued on following page

Table 7. Continued

		k=0	k=1	k=5	k=22	k=44	k=66
	t-stat	11.86	1.25	1.55	8.54	11.69	9.17
	R2	0.1073	0.0013	0.0027	0.0503	0.0718	0.0267
CLP							
	CXPI	-0.190***	-0.027**	-0.058***	-0.027**	0.027**	0.074***
	t-stat	14.66	2.23	3.93	2.23	2.56	9.21
	R2	0.1405	0.0029	0.0105	0.0026	0.0034	0.0263
COP							
	CXPI	-0.152***	-0.025*	0.000	-0.046***	-0.099***	-0.094***
	t-stat	10.43	1.74	0.02	3.71	7.45	9.76
	R2	0.0657	0.0017	0.0000	0.0071	0.0329	0.0310
MXN							
	CXPI	-0.195***	0.002	-0.032**	-0.076***	-0.143***	-0.121***
	t-stat	13.70	0.15	2.04	6.90	13.00	13.97
	R2	0.1336	0.0000	0.0039	0.0274	0.1054	0.0807
PEN							
	CXPI	-0.050***	-0.004	-0.016**	-0.058***	-0.076***	-0.065***
	t-stat	6.64	0.55	2.05	9.89	16.44	16.08
	R2	0.0319	0.0002	0.0029	0.0445	0.0796	0.0610
ZAR							
	CXPI	-0.558***	0.036	-0.015	-0.033	-0.034	0.014
	t-stat	13.75	1.08	0.38	1.22	1.50	1.16
	R2	0.1592	0.0007	0.0001	0.0012	0.0016	0.0004
RUB							
	CXPI	-0.277***	-0.075***	-0.050*	-0.170***	-0.315***	-0.348***
	t-stat	14.44	3.52	1.87	7.23	10.28	9.55
	R2	0.1293	0.0097	0.0044	0.0569	0.1202	0.1165
MYR							
	CXPI	-0.067***	-0.0280***	-0.005	-0.041***	-0.041***	-0.039***
	t-stat	10.88	5.15	0.89	7.89	7.62	9.66
	R2	0.0549	0.0096	0.0003	0.0240	0.0245	0.0257

Notes: Prediction horizon in days

This table shows the results of the OLS regression $\Delta s_{t+k} = \alpha + \Delta CXPI_t + \varepsilon_{t+k}$, where k stands for the length of the prediction horizon. Constants are not tabulated. t-statistics, which are reported below the coefficients, are based on Newey-West standard errors. *, **, *** denote statistical significance at 10%, 5% and 1%, respectively. The estimation is based on information of the full sample period (ie Jan 2004 - Feb 2015), except for Russia and Malaysia were the sample period starts in February 2009 and August 2005, respectively

Source: BIS Publications, Kohlscheen., E., Avalos., F. H. and Schrimpf., A. (2016) (page 49)

Brexit – during which stock markets remained volatile for a longer period, the shock appeared to be temporary and shares rallied throughout the day. The Brexit effect, it appears, has greater consequences – not just in respect of initial inflation levels – which prompted the central bank governor to take inflationary targeting measures, but also other possible repercussions which have necessitated the Government to take those fiscal initiatives of taxation of high earners and a focus on long term investment - all aimed reducing the current Government deficit. Such initiatives and post Brexit developments, it appears, will impact UK and global trade relations.

Whilst stock market reactions across the globe, in response to the US Presidential election results, were clearly attributable to uncertainty, it appears that markets are now reacting and adjusting well to news of a Trump Presidency – following initial shocks. And whilst it is clear that financial markets dislike uncertainty, it is also evident from Brexit and the US Presidential result experiences, that markets can and do over react to certain announcements.

REFERENCES

Alexander, S. S. (1964). Price Movements in Speculative Markets: Trends or Random Walks Bank for International Settlements.

Bank for International Settlements. (2008). Transmission mechanisms for monetary policy in emerging market economies. BIS Papers.

Bank for International Settlements. (2014). The transmission of unconventional monetary policy to the emerging markets. BIS Papers.

Bank for International Settlements. (2015, December). Uneasy calm awaiting lift-off. BIS Quarterly Review.

Bank for International Settlements. (2015). What do new forms of finance mean for EM central banks? BIS Papers.

Borio, C, McCauley, R., & McGuire, P. (2011, September). Global credit and domestic credit booms. BIS Quarterly Review.

Cashin, P., Cespedes, L. F., & Sahay, R. (2004). Commodity Currencies and the Real Exchange Rate. *Journal of Development Economics*, *75*(1), 239–268. doi:10.1016/j.jdeveco.2003.08.005

Chen, Y., & Rogoff, K. (2003). Commodity Currencies and Empirical Exchange Rate Puzzles. *Journal of International Economics*, *60*(1), 133–160. doi:10.1016/S0022-1996(02)00072-7

Chui, M., Kuruc, E., & Turner, P. (2016). *Emerging market companies: currency mismatches, leverage and profitability*. Mimeo.

Clarke, J., Jandik, T., & Mandelker, G. (2001). The Efficient Markets Hypothesis. Retrieved from http://m.e-m-h.org/ClJM.pdf

Cooper, G. (2008). *The Origin of Financial Crises: Central Banks, Credit Bubbles and the Efficient Market Fallacy*. New York: Vintage Books.

Eichengreen, B. (2002). Can emerging markets float? Should they inflation target? *Banco Central do Brasil Working Papers*.

Engel, C., & West, K. D. (2005). Exchange rates and fundamentals. *Journal of Political Economy*, *113*(3), 485–517. doi:10.1086/429137

Executive Office of the President of the United States. (2015, July). Long-term interest rates: a survey.

Fama, E. (1970). Efficient Capital Markets: A Review of Theory and Empirical Work. *The Journal of Finance*, *25*(2), 383. doi:10.2307/2325486

Fama, E. F., & Miller, M. H. (1971). *Theory of Finance Dryden Press*. Hinsdale, Illinois.

Ferraro, D., Rogoff, K., & Rossi, B. (2015). Can Oil prices Forecast Exchange Rates? *Journal of International Money and Finance*, *54*, 116–141. doi:10.1016/j.jimonfin.2015.03.001

Gali, J., & Monacelli, T. (2005). Monetary policy and exchange rate volatility in a small open economy. *The Review of Economic Studies*, *72*(3), 707–734. doi:10.1111/j.1467-937X.2005.00349.x

Genberg, H. (2008). The changing nature of financial intermediation and its implications for monetary policy. BIS Working Papers.

Grossman, S. J., & Stiglitz, J. E. (1980, June). On the Impossibility of Informationally Efficient Markets. *The American Economic Review*, *70*(3), 393–408.

Keynes, J.M. (2000). A Tract on Monetary Reform, New York: Great Minds Series, Prometheus Books. (First published in 1924)

Kohlscheen, E. (2014). Long-run Determinants of the Brazilian Real: A Closer Look at Commodities. *International Journal of Finance & Economics*, *19*(4), 239–250. doi:10.1002/ijfe.1493

Kohlscheen, E., Avalos, F. H., & Schrimpf, A. (2016, March). When the Walk is not Random: Commodity Prices and Exchange Rates. Bank for International Settlements Working Papers.

Kohlscheen, E., & Miyajima, K. (2015). The transmission of monetary policy in EMEs in a changing financial environment: A longitudinal analysis. BIS Working Papers.

Kohlscheen, E., & Rungcharoenkitkul, P. (2015). Changing financial intermediation: implications for monetary policy transmission. BIS Papers.

KPMG. (2010, October). Briefing Sheet Conceptual Framework for Financial Reporting.

Laffont, J., & Maskin, E. S. (1990, February). The Efficient Market Hypothesis and Insider Trading on the Stock Market. *Journal of Political Economy*, *98*(1), 70–93. doi:10.1086/261669

MacDonald, R., & Ricci, L. (2004). Estimation of the Equilibrium Real Exchange Rate for South Africa. *The South African Journal of Economics*, *72*(2), 282–304. doi:10.1111/j.1813-6982.2004.tb00113.x

Mohanty, M (2014). Market volatility and foreign exchange intervention in EMEs: what has changed? BIS Papers.

Mohanty, M., & Turner, P. (2008). *Monetary policy transmission in emerging market economies: what has changed?* BIS Papers.

Mohanty, M. S., & Rishabh, K. (2016). Financial intermediation and monetary policy transmission in EMEs: What has changed post-2008 crisis? BIS Working Papers.

Murcia, A., & Kohlscheen, E. (2016, March). Moving in tandem: bank provisioning in emerging market economies BIS Working Papers.

Pesando, J. E. (1979, November). On the Random Walk Characteristics of Short- and Long-Term Interest Rates In an Efficient Market. *Journal of Money, Credit and Banking*, *11*(4), 457–466. doi:10.2307/1992047

Petersen, K. H. (2012). Risk and Modern Finance Theory: A Non-mathematical Analysis of Mathematical Models.

Peterson, K.H. (n.d.). Risk and modern finance theory: a non-mathematical analysis of mathematical models. Retrieved from http://ntu.ac.uk/nbs/document_uploads/108661.pdf

Poterba, J. M., & Summers, L. H. (1988). Mean Reversion in Stock Prices: Evidence and Implications. *Journal of Financial Economics*, *22*(1), 27–59. doi:10.1016/0304-405X(88)90021-9

Seiler, M. J., & Rom, W. (1997). A Historical Analysis of Market Efficiency: Do Historical Returns Follow a Random Walk? *Journal Of Financial And Strategic Decisions*, 10(2).

Shin, H. S. (2012, November 7). The second phase of global liquidity and its impact on emerging economies (Keynote address). *Proceedings of the Asia Economic Policy Conference*, Federal Reserve Bank of San Francisco.

Shin, H. S., & Turner, P. (2015). What does the new face of international financial intermediation mean for emerging market economies?" *Bank of France Financial Stability Review*, 19.

Singh, K., & Kalirajan, K. (2007). Monetary transmission in post-reform India: An evaluation. *Journal of the Asia Pacific Economy*, *12*(2), 158–187. doi:10.1080/13547860701252371

Sobrun, J., & Turner, P. (2015a). Bond markets and monetary policy dilemmas for emerging market economies. BIS Working Papers.

Turner, P. (2014). The long-term interest rate, financial risks and policy choices in EMEs. BIS Working Papers.

Fama, E.F. (1965). Random Walks in Stock Market Prices Selected Papers. University of Chicago. Retrieved from https://www.chicagobooth.edu/~/media/34F68FFD9CC04EF1A76901F6C61C0A76.PDF

Upson, R. B. (1972). Random Walk and Forward Exchange Rates: A Spectral Analysis. *Journal of Financial and Quantitative Analysis*, *7*(4), 1897. doi:10.2307/2329624

U.S Economy About. (2016). Stock Market Correction. Retrieved from http://useconomy.about.com/od/glossary/g/Market_Correcti.htm

U.S Economy About. (2016). How does the stock market work? Retrieved from http://useconomy.about.com/od/themarkets/f/Stock_Market_Co.htm

Chapter 4
Fundamental or Enhancing Roles?
The Dual Roles of External Auditors and Forensic Accountants

Marianne Ojo
George Mason University, USA

James A. DiGabriele
Montclair State University, USA

ABSTRACT

In view recent developments which have resulted in the replacement of attributes of relevance and reliability with a new categorization of fundamental qualitative characteristics of accounting information and enhancing qualitative characteristics of accounting information, this chapter is aimed at highlighting why the roles of audits – and particularly accountants and auditors still serve as fundamental, vital and crucial means of verifying financial statements – such that these can be reasonably relied upon by investors in financial and capital markets. Fundamental qualitative characteristics of accounting information are categorized into relevance and faithful representation – a change from the IASB's 1989 framework. The enhancing qualitative characteristics of accounting information now comprise verifiability, understandability, comparability and timeliness. This chapter is aimed at highlighting why such enhancing characteristics could be regarded as fundamental qualitative characteristics.

DOI: 10.4018/978-1-5225-1900-3.ch004

Copyright ©2017, IGI Global. Copying or distributing in print or electronic forms without written permission of IGI Global is prohibited.

INTRODUCTION

In view recent developments which have resulted in the replacement of attributes of relevance and reliability with a new categorization of fundamental qualitative characteristics of accounting information and enhancing qualitative characteristics of accounting information, this chapter is aimed at highlighting why the roles of audits – and particularly accountants and auditors still serve as fundamental, vital and crucial means of verifying financial statements – such that these can be reasonably relied upon by investors in financial and capital markets. Fundamental qualitative characteristics of accounting information are categorized into relevance and faithful representation – a change from the IASB's 1989 framework. The enhancing qualitative characteristics of accounting information now comprise verifiability, understandability, comparability and timeliness. This chapter is aimed at highlighting why such enhancing characteristics could be regarded as fundamental qualitative characteristics which not only facilitate the mitigation of information asymmetries between management and investors – but also assume crucial roles in the present volatile environment which prevails in major economies in respect of their financial and capital markets.

This chapter also considers the dual roles of both external auditors and forensic accountants: whether acting in the dual capacity of external auditor and internal auditor (with respect to internal and external audits), as well as whether the overlapping roles of testifying and consulting experts [3] (with respect to forensic accountants) do (significantly or not significantly), affect the objectivity and independence attributes required in exercising their functions.

It is also important to highlight that a consideration of the dual roles of the external auditor and internal auditor will involve examining whether it is appropriate for the external auditor to incorporate internal audit responsibilities in certain circumstances (as provided for by *ISA 610, Using the Work of Internal Auditors*, as well as provisions of the Sarbanes Oxley Act which imposes limitations on external auditors' abilities to perform in a dual capacity—particularly with respect to internal audit outsourcing services). It will consider the impact of the performance in such a dual capacity on the ability of the external and internal audit work to be carried out with the required attributes of objectivity and independence.

According to Stewart and Subramaniam (2010), the motivation for increased interest in the objectivity and independence of internal audit is associated with "the evolving and expanding role of internal audit as key corporate governance mechanism, as well as an internal consultancy service. In this respect, internal auditors occupy the unique position as providers of both assurance services within the organization, and consultancy services to managers." The controversial debates which such dual role has generated, as well as the dual role's impact in placing internal auditors in a situation where conflicts of interest, and a compromise of "true objectivity" may arise, was also highlighted (Subramanian, 2010; Paape, 2007).

BACKGROUND AND LITERATURE REVIEW

Integrity, Independence, and Objectivity: Key Attributes in External and Internal Audits

The APB (Auditing Practices Board) Ethical Standards are concerned with the integrity, objectivity and independence of auditors (paragraph 5).

- Integrity is a prerequisite for all those who act in the public interest. It is essential that auditors act, and are seen to act, with integrity, which requires not only honesty but a broad range of related qualities such as fairness, candor, courage, intellectual honesty and confidentiality (paragraph 7) (Auditing Practicing Board, n.d.).
- Objectivity, according to the definition provided by the APB, is considered to be "a state of mind that excludes bias, prejudice and compromise and that gives fair and impartial consideration to all matters that are relevant to the task in hand, disregarding those that are not" (Auditing Practicing Board, n.d.).

Paragraph 13 distinguishes between objectivity and independence:

Independence is freedom from situations and relationships which make it probable that a reasonable and informed third party would conclude that objectivity either is impaired or could be impaired. Independence is related to and underpins objectivity. However, whereas objectivity is a personal behavioral characteristic concerning the auditor's state of mind, independence relates to the circumstances surrounding the audit, including the financial, employment, business and personal relationships between the auditor and the audited entity and its connected parties. (Auditing Practicing Board, n.d.)

Other definitions of independence have been provided as follows (Beattie, Fearnley & Brandt; 2001):

the conditional probability of reporting a discovered breach" by DeAngelo; the ability to resist client pressure (Knapp): a function of character - with characteristics of integrity and trustworthiness being essential (Magill and Previts); and an absence of interests that create an unacceptable risk of bias - this definition being provided by the AICPA White Paper definition (AICPA, 1997) which defines independence as an absence of interests that create an unacceptable risk of bias.

Independence and objectivity are also considered to be key and crucial features of the internal audit function. According to the Basel Committee on Banking Supervision, "continuously performing similar tasks or routine jobs may negatively affect an individual internal auditor's capacity for critical judgment because of possible loss of objectivity. It is therefore a sound practice, whenever practicable and without jeopardising competence and expertise, to periodically rotate internal audit staff within the internal audit function."[1] Furthermore, the Committee recommends that remuneration of top officials of the internal audit function should be determined correspondingly with the remuneration policies and practices of the organisation or bank (since independence and objectivity are thought to be undermined where internal audit staff's remuneration is linked to the financial performance of sector for which internal audit responsibilities are carried out).

Further, integrity, objectivity and independence constitute vital principles - in respect of ethical principles which are considered to be essential to the exercise and conduct of the internal audit function. These principles are mentioned under the first four principles relating to the supervisory expectations which are considered relevant to the internal audit function. The principles (Basel Committee on Banking Supervision; 2012) are as follows:

Principles Relating to the Supervisory Expectations Relevant to the Internal Audit Function

Principle 1: An effective internal audit function provides independent assurance to the board of directors and senior management on the quality and effectiveness of a bank's internal control, risk management and governance systems and processes, thereby helping the board and senior management protect their organisation and its reputation.

Principle 2: The bank's internal audit function must be independent of the audited activities, which requires the internal audit function to have sufficient standing and authority within the bank, thereby enabling internal auditors to carry out their assignments with objectivity.

Principle 3: Professional competence, including the knowledge and experience of each internal auditor and of internal auditors collectively, is essential to the effectiveness of the bank's internal audit function.

Principle 4: Internal auditors must act with integrity.

Fundamental or Enhancing Roles?

From what has been highlighted so far, great focus is attached to the importance of objectivity and independence as pre requisites in exercising internal and external audit functions. Threats which are common and are likely to compromise objectivity and independence, during the exercise of internal and external audit functions, will now be analysed.

The Institute of Internal Auditors (IIA)'s published framework of independence lists seven threats to audit independence (which are similar to those threats faced by external auditors) and these threats include (Stewart & Subramanian, 2010):

- Self review threat
- Social pressures
- Economic interests
- Personal relationships
- Familiarity threat
- Cultural, racial and gender biases
- Cognitive biases

The Auditing Practices Board (n. d.) identifies the following principal types of threats to the auditor's objectivity and independence:

- Self-interest threat[2]
- Self-review threat [3]
- *Management threat*
- Advocacy threat[4]
- *Familiarity (or trust) threat*
- *Intimidation threat*

MAIN FOCUS OF THE CHAPTER

Changing Roles of Internal and External Auditors

As well as evidence which suggests that the internal auditor's role has changed in recent years to one of a consultant nature, in contrast to that of a policing role (Stewart & Subramanian, 2010), evidence has also been provided to support the fact that the external auditor's role changed during the nineties from that synonymous to a watch dog to a less vigilant and scrutinising role (Cunningham; 2006). Such evidence which include:

- Firstly, the widening scope of audit firm services beyond the audit function - which has resulted in relationships which have affected audit firms' independence, (Cunningham, 2006) secondly, increase in accounting irregularities during the 1990s which have arisen in the form of widespread premature revenue recognition and other forms of creative accounting, and thirdly, evidence of auditor ability to influence audit quality and liability risk (Cunningham, 2006).

Traditional auditing techniques focus on internal controls and demonstrate the auditor's thorough reputation as compared to the lax and complacent attitude which has been evidenced through recent increases in creative accounting practices and the widespread use of off balance sheet instruments as illustrated in the case of Enron. For this reason, a return to and focus on traditional auditing techniques, as well as auditing techniques which focus on internal controls is a much needed move - whilst also supporting audits which also take into consideration, strategic and operational controls. Such a stance would be greatly facilitated in cases where an external auditor is able to undertake certain permitted internal audit responsibilities.

Limitations on the Use of Internal Audit Work and the Assumption of Internal Audit Roles: As Performed by External Auditors

To prevent or avoid situations where over reliance on internal audit work could result in a compromise of the external auditor's objectivity, certain safeguards serve to assist in "clarifying the circumstances where the work of the internal audit function cannot be used and therefore is prohibited." Such instances, as provided for by the ISA 610 (Revised), paragraphs 14] are as follows (IFAC, n. d.): [20]

- Where the function's organizational status and relevant policies and procedures do not adequately support the objectivity of internal auditors;
- Where the function lacks sufficient competence; or
- Where the function does not apply a systematic and disciplined approach, including quality control.

According to Paragraph 9 of the INTERNATIONAL STANDARD ON AUDITING 610 (REVISED) (2013), the external auditor's sole responsibility for the audit opinion expressed, is not reduced by the external auditor's use of the work of the internal audit function on the engagement.

Paragraph 24 also expressly states that the following information should be included in the audit documentation - where the external auditor incorporates the work of the internal audit function:

- Evaluation of whether the function's organizational status and relevant policies and procedures adequately support the objectivity of the internal auditors; the level of competence of the function; and whether the function applies a systematic and disciplined approach, including quality control.
- The nature and extent of the work used and the basis for that decision; and
- The audit procedures performed by the external auditor to evaluate the adequacy of the work used.

Outsourcing and Co-Sourcing of Internal Audit Services

As highlighted in the previous sections, there are certain duties and responsibilities which the external auditor is capable of undertaking and permitted to undertake by law. Under the Sarbanes Oxley Act, the prohibition of the external auditor's capacity to perform dual roles in respect of performing certain non audit services which include internal audit outsourcing services, is highlighted.

Section 201 of the Sarbanes Oxley Act of 2002 lists certain prohibited services which do not lie within the scope of practice of external auditors of U.S public companies. The prohibited services[5] are based on three primary criteria, namely:

1. An auditor cannot function in the role of management;
2. An auditor cannot audit his or her work; and
3. An auditor cannot serve in an external advocacy role for the client.

Internal audit outsourcing services constitute one of the services listed as prohibited and even though the provision of such services by external auditors to their clients is no longer permissible, it is reported by Ernst and Young (2006; Stewart & Subramanian, 2010) that public accounting and specialist firms provide these services to non audit clients. Section 201 of Sarbanes-Oxley, with regard to internal audit outsourcing, may have been over-reactionary and may continue to hinder both companies and their auditors. The following sections relating to knowledge spillover gains, cost management and financial reporting quality illustrate why.

Knowledge Spillover Gains

Knowledge spillover is the result of accounting firms benefiting from the relationship between the audit and non-audit services offered to their clients. In the case of internal audit outsourcing, the efficiency of financial audits is bolstered because the auditor is able to benefit from knowledge gained during the performance of internal audit functions. The auditor is able to gain a better understanding of the client's internal controls because the auditor has had close experience with the internal control environment as part of the client's internal audit function. As stated earlier, the auditor is better equipped during the financial audit and the amount of work needed to document internal controls, assess control risk, and design tests of control is reduced. (Aldhizer, 2003) The cost of performing the audit to the audit firm may also be lowered because of knowledge spillover gains, as Al-Harshani (2003) states in his dissertation:

Knowledge spillover may generate a quasi-economic rent to the audit firm, where the marginal cost of the joint provision of the two types of services to the same client is less than the marginal cost of separately providing the same amount of audit and NAS to two different clients. The joint provision, therefore, is expected to lead to lowering the cost of performing the external audit work. Accordingly, we would expect the audit firm that provides both audit and NAS to the same audit client to rely less on the client's internal auditors' work as a cost-reduction technique due to potential cost savings from knowledge spillover.

Cost Management

Audit firms are not the only party to monetarily benefit from the outsourcing of internal audit. Companies that outsource their internal audit function may reap potential cost benefits as well. In the article "Internal Audit Outsourcing" Aldhizer and Cashell (2003) explain:

For companies, outsourcing the internal audit function offers potential cost benefits. Internal audit outsourcing may reduce overlapping positions and audit effort by creating more flexibility in increasing and decreasing workloads. Additionally, outsourcing allows a company to replace "fixed" cost employees with "variable" fees for services. Finally, a wide range of expertise is available from large firms that would be too expensive for a company to maintain internally.

Accounting Risk Management and Financial Reporting Quality

An investigation by Prawitt et., al. (2011) found evidence that suggested that high quality internal audit functions (regardless of outsourcing) are associated with lower accounting risk. Furthermore, Prawitt et. Al. (2003) found that companies that outsourced their internal audit function to their external auditor prior to the passage of Sarbanes-Oxley had lower accounting risk than companies that outsourced their internal audit function to another third-party service provider and companies that maintained their own in-house internal audit function.

Based on an empirical analysis of the relationship between restatements and non-audit fees paid by a client to its external auditor, it was found that companies that were not required to restate their financial statements paid more in internal audit outsourcing fees to their external auditors than companies that did, in fact, have to record material restatements (Prawitt et. Al. 2003). This evidence suggests a negatively correlating relationship between the outsourcing of internal audit functions and the occurrence of material financial restatements.

Arguments have also been put forward to bolster the stance that "an outsourced provider may be more independent than an in-house internal audit function since it is difficult for an employee to be truly independent of management, and that on the other hand, there also factors which could affect the objectivity of outsourced providers in the same manner that external auditor independence can be compromised."[6] It is also argued that "regardless of whether external assurance is obtained for sustainability reports (which contain a combination of quantitative[7] and qualitative data), that internal audit can play a role in verifying this data for management purposes."

The Institute of Internal Auditors (IIA) also recommends a list of factors to be considered when assessing potential outsourcing engagements (IIA, 2009): available resources, size of the organization, types of outsourcing alternatives, Law, Statute, or regulation (since some companies may be prohibited by statute or regulation from outsourcing internal audit services to their external auditors), taking into consideration an analysis of the advantages and disadvantages of outsourcing, as well as the following[8]:

- Independence of the external service providers,
- Allegiance of in-house resources versus that of external service provider,
- Professional standards followed by the external service provider,
- Qualifications of the service provider,
- Staffing – training, turnover, rotation of staff, management,
- Flexibility in staffing resources to meet engagement needs or special requests,
- Availability of resources,
- Retention of institutional knowledge for future assignments.

External Auditors Also Undertaking the Role of Skilled Persons

Section 166 of the Financial Services and Markets Act (FSMA) 2000 deals with the powers of the UK's financial services regulator, the Financial Services Authority (FSA), to obtain a report by a skilled person (also referred to as a reporting accountant) to assist the FSA in performing its functions under the FSMA 2000.

In addition to its powers to appoint skilled persons to carry out certain functions under section 166, sections 167 and 168 of the Act also empower the FSA to appoint competent persons to carry out investigative tasks.

The differences between the roles of skilled persons (also known as reporting accountants) and competent persons, are demonstrated by the bearer of the costs for work carried out by these persons. For work undertaken by skilled persons, the regulated firm (who employs them) bears the cost directly whilst for work undertaken by competent persons, the FSA bears the cost (Hitchens, Hogg & Mallet, 2001).

According to Singh (2003), even though skilled persons are usually approved by the FSA, the role is usually performed by auditors of the regulated firm (Singh, 2003). This "raises the question of independence since both roles of auditors of the regulated firm and skilled persons (or reporting accountants) employed by the regulator (the FSA) are distinct roles which still overlap occasionally (Singh, 2003). The use of skilled persons' reports has been controversial and concerns have been expressed in relation to the FSA using a skilled person's report instead of devoting its own resources to investigating a matter" (Singh, 2003).

Certain measures have been adopted to safeguard against possibilities of a conflict of interest arising between the auditors of the regulated firm who are commissioned by the FSA as skilled persons but paid by the regulated firm. Chapter Five of the FSA Supervision Manual provides examples of circumstances where the FSA may use skilled persons. According to chapter five of the Supervision Manual, the FSA states that firms are to appoint skilled persons only for specific purposes, not to use them as a matter of routine, to use skilled persons only after having considered alternatives, to use skilled persons because of the added value to be gained due to their expertise or knowledge and not because of resource restraints, and to take into account cost implications as well as using the tool in a focused and proportionate way.

The Impact of Internal Auditor Compensation on External Auditor's Objectivity and Independence

It is widely agreed in many academic and social spheres that compensation related performances have the potential and tendency to affect the objectivity and independence attributes required by an auditor to effectively perform his duties and responsibilities. Where an audit firm places great reliance on the income generated from a particular client (and particularly with respect to non-audit services), there are greater possibilities for situations involving threats to the auditor's objectivity and independence, to occur–since such an audit firm will be unwilling to lose such a lucrative client. DeZoort et al (2001) argue that Institute of Internal Auditors' (IIA's) are vague in respect of factors which threaten internal auditor's objectivity (DeZoort et al, 2001). Their prior research is based on the attribution theory which indicates "that external auditors should recognize this incentive bias". Their hypotheses also include the basic statement that "the effect of internal auditor compensation on external auditors' reliance judgments will be greater when internal auditors perform subjective tasks than when they perform objective tasks."

This can also be linked to the argument by Stewart and Subramaniam (2010) that objectivity issues and threats (arising from social pressure and familiarity) are more likely to arise when information being verified by internal audits for management is not quantifiable. The more objective and quantifiable the information being dealt with, the less likelihood for the impact of internal audit compensation to significantly affect internal audit work as well as external auditors' reliance judgments.

Other Means of Safeguarding Audit Independence: Audit Committees

According to a publication by Grant Thornton (2010), "being on an audit committee is a part-time job with full-time responsibilities. Audit committees rely heavily on the hands-on analysis provided by internal and external auditors…" As well as being considered a "specialised committee within the board of directors—which prepares the work of, and reports to the board of directors in specific areas for which it has designated responsibility, other responsibilities of an audit committee are as follows (Basel Committee on Banking Supervision; 2012):

- Monitoring of the financial reporting process, its output and integrity of the entity's financial statements;
- Oversight of the establishment of accounting policies and practices by the entity;
- Reviewing the significant qualitative aspects of the entity's accounting practices (including accounting estimates and financial statement disclosures), significant financial reporting judgments contained in the statements, and arrangements through which staff of the entity may privately and confidentially raise concerns about.

The audit committee is also responsible for "reviewing and monitoring the independence of the statutory auditor or external audit firm; reviewing and monitoring the statutory auditor's objectivity, as well as the effectiveness of the audit process" (Basel Committee, 2012).

Other generally acknowledged responsibilities of audit committees include the appointment and assessment of remuneration for external auditors, ensuring that adequate resources exist for the internal audit function, reviewing and reporting on the effectiveness of the firm or entity's internal controls and ensuring that coordination[9] is retained between the internal audit function and external auditors.

Empirical Evidence on Whether Audit Independence Is Compromised Where External Auditors Serve in the Dual Capacities (Exercising Both External and Internal Audit Functions): Results of a Study

According to a study by Geiger et al (2002), whose purpose partly consists in providing some empirical evidence on whether audit independence is compromised when external auditors serve in the dual capacities in exercising both external and internal audit functions, " Little evidence exists as to whether financial statement users believe that auditor independence or financial statement reliability is jeopardized where the external auditors are engaged to perform internal audit activities."[10]

The study also made reference to some important observations:

- That financial statement users may have perceived some positive synergy in performing internal audit work for the external audit client. This dual role might improve audit quality by providing external auditors with greater insight into the client, making it more likely that business transactions will be understood and key audit risks identified. In addition, being engaged to perform internal audit work for the audit client may be perceived as a signal of high quality work.
- Regardless of whether performing the internal audit work leads to a better external audit, or performing the external audit well leads to an internal audit engagement, the loan officers in their study perceived this relationship favorably.
- While the AICPA has requested (and the SEC originally proposed) that CPA firms should be strictly prohibited from performing outsourced internal audits for public attest clients, the study suggests that external auditors performing outsourced internal audit work for clients was not, by itself, perceived negatively.

SOLUTIONS AND RECOMMENDATIONS

Objectivity and the Overlapping Roles of Testifying and Consulting Experts in Forensic Accounting

Forensic accounting experts are usually classified among the following three groups; expert witness (testifying expert), consulting expert, and fact witness. An expert witness generally appears before a Trier of fact (Judge and/or Jury) and provides an opinion by deposition or testimony before the court. A consulting expert can advise on an attorney's work product by providing additional support in resolving a case. When an accounting expert is called to testify as a fact finding witness, he or she is expected to offer only factual analysis regarding the case without rendering an opinion (Michaelson, 2005). The main differences lie between the testifying expert and consulting expert.

The testifying expert must be mindful of the Daubert standard, which is codified in the Federal Rules of Evidence 702 and states; a witness may only testify if, the testimony is based upon sufficient facts or data, the testimony is the product of reliable principles and methods, and the witness has applied the principles and methods reliably to the facts of the case. This standard creates an environment where an expert's opinion should maintain a character of transparent objectivity. Conversely, a consulting expert owes objectivity to the client rather than the Trier of fact. A consulting expert advocates their position on a client's behalf (Michaelson, 2005).

The perception of objectivity is an important element for a forensic accountant engaging in expert testimony. The transparency of an experts' impartiality is vital from a critical position because this ultimately establishes the credibility of the expert's findings. As exemplified in Monsanto v. Tidball (2009) (Monsanto), the defendant retained an accountant and tax professor to consult on economic damages claimed. The expert eventually testified in the case. According to the Court, there were reservations regarding the expert's objectivity and ultimately deemed the report "unreliable and unable to assist the jury." The expert was referred as a consultant and expert throughout the case literature. These dual roles likely occur as the litigation process develops and the mounting costs conceivably prohibit the addition of a second expert exclusively for testimony. This quandary compels litigation attorneys to put forward an expert initially retained in a consulting role hoping for the best result (Pedneault 2009). Ethical risks persist with the revised rules as regards Amended Rule 26 Communications (DiGabriele, 2012) and particularly with reference to the fact that full disclosure of draft expert reports (as well as the expansive disclosure of communications between experts and attorneys) will no longer be required. As argued, (DiGabriele, 2012) attorney influence on the objectivity and independence of testifying experts is likely to increase, not only as a result of the dual roles assumed by the testifying and consulting expert, but also because of the consequences of the Amended Rule 26 Communications (as regards disclosures).

Even though cost considerations are partly attributed to the revised rules (Amended Rule 26 Communications), cost savings could still be achieved through a focus on cost reductions during the discovery phase – and particularly also owing to the fact that:

- The majority of the cost of litigation is incurred during the discovery phase; and
- A focus on the final opinion of the testifying expert – rather than the thought process, will help mitigate and minimise overall cost expenditure. (DiGabriele, 2012)

Unnecessarily protracted discovery costs should be avoided. Given the nature of the process involving the final opinions of the testifying expert and the tendency for attorneys to do everything possible to waive or shift opinions in favour of their clients, greater measures should be in place to avoid potential manipulations of opinions (of the testifying expert) or potentials for the objectivity and independence of the testifying expert to be influenced. The increased protection afforded to attorney and expert communications via the waiver of the need for full disclosures of such communications would only increase the likelihood that attorney influence (over objectivity and independence of testifying expert opinions) will increase.

CONCLUSION

This chapter has highlighted how objectivity and independence serve as vital tools – not only in ensuring that the external auditor and forensic accountants' roles are effectively executed, but also in securing the essence of audits – in ensuring that the main objective of the audit in verifying the financial statements of an enterprise, is realized. Where verifiability cannot be achieved, there is less likelihood that comparability, consistency and reliability in the financial reporting process can ultimately, be derived.

It has been demonstrated that certain capacities exist in which the dual role of the external auditor (in undertaking internal audit roles as well as skilled persons roles) could be immensely beneficial to an entity or organisation. This arises as a result of the invaluable skills and expertise which such a role provides and incorporates into the audit process. Even where such an exercise of a dual role is prohibited by law or as a result of organisational policies, opportunities exist whereby close cooperation between external and internal auditors could provide for increased scope in implementing and benefiting from each other's work. The opportunities and benefits of drawing on the skills and expertise gained by an external auditor who has acquired so much knowledge by virtue of the exercise of both roles and the experience acquired from having exercised such roles, should not be under estimated.

As recommended in chapter five of the Supervision Manual of the FSA, there are certain situations whereby such a dual role may not be warranted, where such dual roles should not be exercised routinely, where such dual role should only be implemented after having considered other alternatives, and more importantly, why such dual role could contribute and generate added value by virtue of the increased expertise or knowledge which such a dual role brings. Where concerns relating to a compromise of independence and objectivity arise, then prohibitions and restrictions imposed by section 201 of the Sarbanes Oxley Act are, to a great extent, justified.

As stated previously in this chapter, under the heading which highlights a return to and focus on traditional auditing techniques, as well as auditing techniques which focus on internal controls is a much needed move—whilst also supporting (internal) audits which to a greater extent, take into consideration, strategic and operational controls. Such a stance would be greatly facilitated in cases where an external auditor is able to undertake certain permitted internal audit responsibilities. There is support for the opinion that a certain degree of compromise of objectivity and independence does occur where the forensic accounting expert assumes a dual role (acts in both capacities of testifying expert and consulting expert). However, the degree to which such a compromise occurs is another issue. Where reliable, well tested techniques have been incorporated into the process, then the disadvantages of having a forensic accountant acting in both capacities/roles may be mitigated or nullified by the potential advantages in having a forensic accountant in both positions.

As is particularly the case with external auditors, the reliability of internal controls also plays a huge and crucial role in the audit process—as well as those in charge of those internal controls. Where safeguards such as the segregation of duties and other measures are incorporated into the process to reduce instances or situations whereby such controls could be manipulated, then benefits of having an external auditor serve in a dual role capacity may well extend beyond its stated disadvantages.

Benefits accruing from having a dual role include namely the acquisition of knowledge and expertise gained during the latter stages of the process—which could assist in providing more accurate judgments during latter stages of the process. This is also similar to the position which exists with external auditors: whereby the mandatory rotation of audit firms, whilst serving to ensure that independence and objectivity is not compromised, could also be detrimental where the external auditor leaves the firm shortly/prematurely after having been employed by the firm. In the case of internal audit outsourcing, the efficiency of financial audits is bolstered because the auditor is able to benefit from knowledge gained during the performance of internal audit functions. The auditor is able to gain a better understanding of the client's internal controls because the auditor has had close experience with the internal control environment as part of the client's internal audit function.

The firm incurs greater costs in employing a new auditor in re acquiring the knowledge which the previous auditor had acquired - having left the firm prematurely. Further, the knowledge which could have been employed by the leaving auditor is not fully maximized in the process.

Whilst a segregation of duties and the incorporation of court appointed experts may serve to introduce some degree of greater objectivity into the process, greater focus should also be given to nonhuman information gathering techniques which could also generate greater savings—if not initially, but subsequently after the purchase of these techniques. Furthermore, unnecessary protracted discovery costs should be avoided whilst according greater focus to the process involving the final opinions of the testifying expert—particularly given the tendency for attorneys to do everything possible to waive or shift opinions in favor of their clients.

REFERENCES

Ahlawat, S.S., & Lowe. (2004). An Examination of Internal Auditor Objectivity: In-House versus Outsourcing. *Auditing: A Journal of Practice & Theory, 23*(2), 147-58.

Aldhizer, G. R. III, Cashell, J. D., & Martin, D. R. (2003). Internal Audit Outsourcing. *The CPA Journal, 8*(3), 30–25.

Al-Harshani, M. (2003). *The Effect of Inherent Risk, Knowledge Spillover, and Litigation Risk on External Auditors' Reliance on Client's Internal Audit Functions* [Dissertation]. University of Arkansas. Retrieved from http://www.frc.org.uk/Our-Work/Publications/APB/ES-1-(Revised)-Integrity,-objectivity-and-inde-(1).aspx

Basel Committee on Banking Supervision. (2012). *The Internal Audit Function in Banks*. Retrieved from www.bis.org/publ/bcbs223.pdf

Beattie, V., Fearnley, S., & Brandt, R. (2001). *Behind Closed Doors: What Company Audit Is Really About*. Institute of Chartered Accountants in England and Wales. doi:10.1057/9780230599413

Cunningham, L. (2006). *Too Big to Fail: Moral Hazard in Auditing and the Need to Restructure the Industry Before it Unravels*. Boston College Law School Faculty Papers.

DeZoort, , Houston, R. W., & Peters, M. F. (2001, Summer). The Impact of Internal Auditor Compensation and Role on External Auditors Planning Judgments and Decisions. *Contemporary Accounting Research*, *18*(2), 257–281. doi:10.1506/7ERQ-LD54-BTQV-TUVE

DiGabriele, J. A. (2011). An Observation of Differences in the Transparent Objectivity of Forensic Accounting Expert Witnesses. *Journal of Forensic & Investigative Accounting, 3*(2).

DiGabriele J. A. (2012). Narrative Inquiry of the Inchoate Ethical Risks of Forensic Accounting Experts under Amended Rule 26 Communications. *Ethics & Critical Thinking Journal*, (1).

Ernst & Young. (2006). *Trends in Australian and New Zealand Internal Auditing, Third Annual Benchmarking Survey 2006*. Australia: Ernst & Young.

Garrett, A. (2012). The Role of Internal Audits in External Audits. *CAE Conference*, Abu Dhabi, UAE.

Geiger, M., Jordan Lowe, D., & Pany, K. (2002). Outsourced Internal Audit Services and The Perception of Auditor Independence. *The CPA Journal*. Retrieved from http://www.nysscpa.org/cpajournal/2002/0402/features/f042002.htm

Thornton. (2010). Evaluating the Internal and External Audit Function. Wiley and Sons.

Hitchins, J., Hogg, M., & Mallet, D. (2001). *Banking: A Regulatory Accounting and Auditing Guide.* Institute of Chartered Accountants England and Wales HM Treasury "Cooperation Between Internal and External Auditors", A Good Practice Guide. Retrieved from http://www.hm-treasury.gov.uk/d/auditors_190105.pdf

IFAC. (n. d.). *Basis for Conclusions on ISA 610 and ISA 315.* Prepared by the Staff of the IAASB.

Institute of Internal Auditors (IIA). (2009). *The Role of Internal Auditing in Resourcing the Internal Audit Activity*. IIA Position Paper. Retrieved from https://na.theiia.org/standards- guidance/Public %20Documents/IPPF_PP_Role_of_IA_in_Resourcing_the_IAA_01- 09.pdf

KPMG. (2010). *Briefing Sheet Conceptual Framework for Financial Reporting*. KPMG.

Michaelson, W. M. (2005). Advocacy and the Expert Witness. *Expert Witnessing in Forensic Accounting.*, *1*(1), 63–70.

Monsanto v. Tidball 2009 WL 2757047 (E.D. Mo.)

Ojo, M. (2006). General Literature on the Audit Expectations Gap. *Journal of Forensic Accounting, 8*(1-2).

Paape, L. (2007). *Corporate Governance: The Impact on the Role, Position, and Scope of Services of the Internal Audit Function* (Unpublished PhD Dissertation). Erasmus Research Institute of Management, Erasmus University.

Pedneault, S. (2009). *Fraud 101 Techniques and Strategies for Understanding Fraud*. Hoboken, NJ: John Wiley & Sons Inc.

Prawitt, D.F., Sharp, & Wood. (2011). Internal Audit Outsourcing and the Risk of Misleading or Fraudulent Financial Reporting: Did Sarbanes-Oxley Get It Wrong? *Contemporary Accounting Research, 19*(11), 38-46.

Singh, D. (2003). The Role of Third Parties in Banking Regulation and Supervision. *Journal of International Banking Regulation, 4*(3).

Stewart, J., & Subramaniam, N. (2010). *Internal Audit Independence and Objectivity: Emerging Research Opportunities*. Academic Press.

ENDNOTES

1 It is also added that "The independence and objectivity of the internal audit function may be undermined if the internal audit staff's remuneration is linked to the financial performance of the business lines for which they exercise internal audit responsibilities." Basel Committee on Banking Supervision, "The Internal Audit Function in Banks" June 2012, pages 5 (particularly paragraphs 15 and 16) www.bis.org/publ/bcbs223.pdf

2 "A self-interest threat arises when the auditor has financial or other interests which might cause the auditor to be reluctant to take actions that would be adverse to the interests of the audit firm or any individual in a position to influence the conduct or outcome of the audit (for example, where the auditor has an investment in the audited entity, is seeking to provide additional services to the audited entity or needs to recover long-outstanding fees from the audited entity)", see ibid.

3 "A self-review threat arises when the results of a non-audit service performed by the auditor or by others within the audit firm are reflected in the amounts included or disclosed in the financial statements (for example, where the audit firm has been involved in maintaining the accounting records, or undertaking

valuations that are incorporated in the financial statements). In the course of the audit, the auditor may need to re-evaluate the work performed in the non-audit service. As, by virtue of providing the non-audit service, the audit firm is associated with aspects of the preparation of the financial statements, the auditor may be (or may be perceived to be) unable to take an impartial view of relevant aspects of those financial statements", ibid.

4 This arises when "the audit firm undertakes work that involves acting as an advocate for an audited entity and supporting a position taken by management in an adversarial context (for example, by acting as a legal advocate for the audited entity in litigation or a regulatory investigation). In order to act in an advocacy role, the audit firm has to adopt a position closely aligned to that of management. This creates both actual and perceived threats to the auditor's objectivity and independence", ibid.

5 Prohibited services include: Book keeping or other services related to the accounting records or financial statements of the client whose statements are being audited; Financial reporting systems design and implementation; Internal audit outsourcing services.

6 For instance, where the audit firm is dependent on a client for a major source of income and would not wish to lose such a client, self review threats etc; see ibid at pages 17 and 18.

7 Furthermore, "where information being verified is not quantifiable, internal auditors could face objectivity threats arising from social pressure and familiarity." see ibid at page 21.

8 Other factors to be considered include "access to best practice or insight to alternative approaches; culture of the organization – receptiveness to external service providers; insight into the organization by the external service provider; coverage of remote locations; coordination with in-house internal auditing; coordination with external auditor; use of internal auditing as a training ground for internal promotions; retention, access to and ownership of work papers; acquisition and availability of specialty skills; cost considerations; and good standing membership in an appropriate professional organization." see ibid.

9 Section two of the Guide published by HM Treasury "Cooperation Between Internal and External Auditors", A Good Practice Guide, highlights the conditions necessary for effective cooperation and the benefits which can be gained. Such benefits include: "More effective audits based on a clearer understanding of respective audit roles and requirements; a reduced audit burden resulting in less disruption; a better informed dialogue on the risks facing the organisation or entity; better coordinated internal and external audit activity based on joint planning and communication of needs; increased scope for use by both internal and external auditors of each other's work; and the opportunity for each party

to draw on a wider and more flexible skills base." HM Treasury "Cooperation Between Internal and External Auditors", A Good Practice Guide http://www.hm-treasury.gov.uk/d/auditors_190105.pdf

10 Furthermore, results of their study "provide important insights into the effects of various internal audit outsourcing arrangements. The findings support the former AICPA position that having outsourced internal audit activities performed by the company's external audit firm does not, by itself, appear to negatively affect financial statement users' perceptions of auditor independence and other related decisions. This type of outsourcing arrangement would be expected to increase in the future if audit firms are allowed to provide these services to their clients. While the SEC and AICPA have implemented certain constraints regarding these arrangements, in certain cases audit firms are still allowed to provide these services."

Chapter 5
Value Relevance of Accounting Information in the Emerging Chinese Stock Market (Re Visited)

James A Rossi
University of Greenwich, UK

ABSTRACT

Value relevance of accounting information is a very important issue – not just from the perspective of Foreign Direct Investment and the reliability and relevance of financial and accounting information for investors – whether institutional of individual, but also in matters of Corporate Social Responsibility and financial reporting. This being of crucial importance given the need to enhance the quality and presentation of financial information, the need for comparability and consistency as a means of enhancing the relevance and reliability of financial information. This issue of reconciliation of discrepancies hence constitutes a matter in need of urgent redress in capital markets.

INTRODUCTION

Value relevance of accounting information is a very important issue – not just from the perspective of Foreign Direct Investment and the reliability and relevance of financial and accounting information for investors – whether institutional of indi-

DOI: 10.4018/978-1-5225-1900-3.ch005

Copyright ©2017, IGI Global. Copying or distributing in print or electronic forms without written permission of IGI Global is prohibited.

vidual, but also in matters of Corporate Social Responsibility and financial reporting. This being of crucial importance given the need to enhance the quality and presentation of financial information, the need for comparability and consistency as a means of enhancing the relevance and reliability of financial information. This issue of reconciliation of discrepancies hence constitutes a matter in need of urgent redress in capital markets.

As highlighted in Enron (IFRS:2014):

Enron's accounting was misleading to users and that specifically, the accounting risks for Enron were too high to be considered acceptable or presented fairly. To make them acceptable, adjustments would have been necessary to the reported estimates. Accounting risks should have been reduced to an acceptable level (as suggested by ISA 540) so that the reported numbers were more reliable.

This chapter seeks to contribute to the gap in the literature on the value relevance of accounting information in China. In so doing it investigates the relevance and reliability of results derived in this study, their applicability to current market developments – as well as recent fluctuations and volatility in the financial markets.

Conclusions derived from previous study undertaken by Chen et al, (2001). Is Accounting Information Value-Relevant in the Emerging Chinese Stock Market? Journal of International Accounting, Auditing & Taxation 10 (2001) 1–22 are as follows:

Conclusions of the Study

1. Using a sample of all available observations in the Shanghai and Shenzhen Stock Exchanges from 1991 to 1998, the authors obtain evidence of value-relevance of accounting information in China based on a return and a price model. The results provide evidence that accounting information is value-relevant in the Chinese market according to both the pooled cross-section and time-series regressions or the year-by-year regressions. The evidence is consistent between the return model and the price model.
2. Authors examine whether value-relevance changes in a predictable manner with respect to four factors including positive versus negative earnings, firm size, earnings persistence, and percentage of public share holdings. Overall, the results support the conclusion that value-relevance in China changes in a predictable manner. Chen et al find that while accounting earnings are value-relevant for companies reporting positive earnings, there is no value-relevance evidence for companies reporting losses.

3. Finally, the study conducted by Chen et al examines two competing predictions about the value-relevance of accounting information between A-share and AB-share companies. While accounting information is value-relevant for both types of companies, they find that value-relevance is higher for companies issuing only A-shares.

In their paper, "Is accounting information value-relevant in the emerging Chinese stock market?", Chen et al (2001) make reference to the following set of factors which, in their opinion, constitute "discernible factors suggesting that accounting information may not be as value-relevant in the Chinese market as in a mature market":

1. First, Chinese accounting systems and regulations were traditionally not market-oriented. Most listed companies were state-owned before going public and the purpose of their accounting was not to provide useful information to investors but to facilitate centralized state planning and control. Although the Chinese government issued a separate accounting standard for listed companies as early as in 1992, there have been numerous unresolved issues in implementing a shareholder-oriented accounting system. Consequently, the value of accounting information in the Chinese market has been questioned in the literature.
2. Second, the reliability of accounting information in China has been a source of concern.
3. Independent auditing is relatively a new phenomenon in China. While it is true that financial statements of listed companies must be audited by CPAs, the quality of audits in China has been generally perceived low (Aharony et al., 2000). A relatively weak monitoring role by outside auditors may contribute to a lack of confidence in and less use of financial statements.
4. Finally, in their view, compared to a mature market such as the U.S. market, the Chinese market lacks a sufficient level of corporate governance such as independent outside directors, audit committee, and competition in the managerial labor market, which weakens investors' confidence in their use of accounting information.

Further, they add that:

Whilst individual investors are active in the market, the investment profession in China is not well established and comprises only a small number of financial analysts and institutional investors such as mutual funds. Most transactions are executed by individual investors with limited access to information other than publicly available accounting numbers. As a result, price may be less informative and accounting information may contain more surprises in the Chinese market, both of which lead to an increased reliance upon accounting numbers by investors.

The following research questions, in line with the theme and volume of the Call for Chapters, will also be addressed:

1. What is the extent to which accounting information can be relied upon based on given market values and can a relationship or pattern be established in certain jurisdictions based on certain operating variables which function in such economies?
2. How valid and applicable is the Efficient Markets Hypothesis (as well as the Efficient Capital Markets Hypothesis)?
3. How can accounting information be harnessed in such a way as to serve as a useful and vital indicator which will enable investors to interpret financial information in such a way which mitigates information asymmetries between management and investors?
4. What factors influence the quality of accounting information - and how can these be addressed by markets if the audit is to achieve its intended aims and functions?
5. Have accounting and legislative reforms undertaken in investigated jurisdictions actually achieved their desired goals of improving the quality of accounting information? If not, what measures could be proposed or recommended to address the current issues being faced by such jurisdictions?

BACKGROUND AND LITERATURE REVIEW

This chapter is aimed at consolidating on, as well as contributing to gaps in the literature on the topic.

Chen et al focused on two models: The return model and the price model.

The return model used in their study is as follows (Chen et al, 2001:9,10):

RETjt 5 a0 1 a1Ejt/Pjt21 1 a2(Ejt 2 Ejt21)/Pjt21 1 ejt (1)

where:

RETjt: A-share annual return (including cash dividends) of firm j between the current and last year's annual report announcement months;

Ejt: annual earnings per share;

Ejt-Ejt-1: change of annual earnings per share;

Pjt-1: stock price at the beginning of the last year's annual report announcement month.

Their study also employed a price model. They argue that while return models are heavily relied upon in market based accounting research, price models persist in the literature. Further they employ a modified Ohlson model (1995) as follows:

MVjt 5 a0 1 a1BVjt 1 a2Ejt 1 ejt (2)

In consolidating on the investigations undertaken by Chen et al, the essential and vital qualitative characteristics of accounting information are now considered in analyzing and evaluating the relevance of these attributes in the Chinese stock market.

International Financial Reporting Standards (IFRSs) as adopted by the International Accounting Standards Board (IASB), comprise the following elements:

- International Financial Reporting Standards;
- International Accounting Standards; and
- Interpretations developed by the International Financial Reporting Interpretations Committee (IFRIC) or the former Standing Interpretations Committee (SIC).

Figure 1. Qualitative characteristics of accounting information
Source: KPMG, Briefing Sheet Conceptual Framework for Financial Reporting, October 2010 Issue 213 at page 3

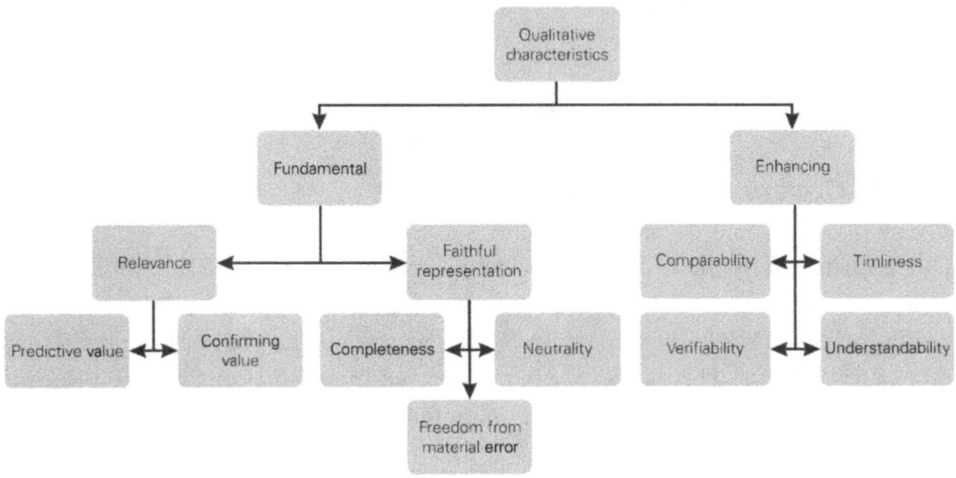

Pursuant to the Standard (IAS 8), judgments and estimates are to be approached as follows:

- In the absence of a Standard or an Interpretation that specifically applies to a transaction, other event or condition, management shall use its judgement in developing and applying an accounting policy that results in information that is relevant and reliable. In making the judgement management shall refer to, and consider the applicability of, the following sources in descending order: (a) the requirements and guidance in IFRSs dealing with similar and related issues; and (b) the definitions, recognition criteria and measurement concepts for assets, liabilities, income and expenses in the Conceptual Framework.

Material omissions or misstatements of items are material if they could, individually or collectively, influence the economic decisions that users make on the basis of the financial statements. Materiality depends on the size and nature of the omission or misstatement judged in the surrounding circumstances. The size or nature of the item, or a combination of both, could be the determining factor (IAS 8 Accounting Policies, Changes in Accounting Estimates and Errors: 2012).

Table 1 as presented by the IFRS (2015:5) provides a list of the 140 jurisdictions whose profiles were posted as of June 2015.

As highlighted by the IFRS, the 116 jurisdictions that require IFRS for all or most publicly accountable entities are bolded.

With respect to jurisdictions where IFRS are required – contrasted to those where IFRS are permitted, the determination of the value relevance of accounting information in capital markets in jurisdictions where IFRS are permitted would have to be considered by way of reference to the national standards currently being applied.

MAIN FOCUS OF THE CHAPTER

Issues, Controversies, Problems

As demonstrated by the results and evidence gathered from the 2015 IFRS report, the main challenges for the global economy as it currently appears, will be the reconciliation of national standards with IFRS – as well as the goal of harmonization across jurisdictions. This is also further evidenced in jurisdictions where IFRS are permitted – and who do not only apply national standards, but also other jurisdictions' standards.

Table 1. 140 jurisdiction profiles as of June 2015

Afghanistan	**Bulgaria**	**Ghana**	**Liechtenstein**	**Palestine**	**Sweden**
Albania	**Cambodia**	**Greece**	**Lithuania**	Panama	Switzerland
Angola	**Canada**	**Grenada**	**Luxembourg**	Paraguay	**Syria**
Anguilla	Cayman Islands	Guatemala	Macao	**Peru**	**Taiwan**
Antigua and Barbuda	**Chile**	Guinea-Bissau	**Macedonia**	**Philippines**	**Tanzania**
Argentina	China	**Guyana**	Madagascar	**Poland**	Thailand
Armenia	**Colombia**	Honduras	**Malaysia**	**Portugal**	**Trinidad and Tobago**
Australia	**Costa Rica**	**Hong Kong**	**Maldives**	**Romania**	**Turkey**
Austria	**Croatia**	**Hungary**	**Malta**	**Russia**	**Uganda**
Azerbaijan	**Cyprus**	**Iceland**	**Mauritius**	**Rwanda**	**Ukraine**
Bahamas	**Czech Republic**	India	**Mexico**	**Saint Lucia**	**United Arab Emirates**
Bahrain	**Denmark**	Indonesia	**Moldova**	Saudi Arabia	**United Kingdom**
Bangladesh	**Dominica**	**Iraq**	**Mongolia**	**Serbia**	United States
Barbados	**Dominican Republic**	**Ireland**	**Montserrat**	**Sierra Leone**	**Uruguay**
Belgium	**Ecuador**	**Israel**	**Myanmar**	**Singapore**	Uzbekistan
Belarus	Egypt	**Italy**	**Nepal**	**Slovakia**	**Venezuela**
Belize	**El Salvador**	**Jamaica**	**Netherlands**	**Slovenia**	Vietnam
Bermuda	**Estonia**	Japan	**New Zealand**	**South Africa**	**Yemen**
Bhutan	**European Union**	**Jordan**	Nicaragua	**Spain**	**Zambia**
Bolivia	**Fiji**	**Kenya**	Niger	**Sri Lanka**	**Zimbabwe**
Bosnia and Herzegovina	**Finland**	**Korea (South)**	**Nigeria**	**St Kitts and Nevis**	
Botswana	**France**	**Kosovo**	**Norway**	**St Vincent and the Grenadines**	
Brazil	**Georgia**	**Latvia**	**Oman**	Suriname	

The IFRS Report (2015:10,11) also highlights the following:

- While Chinese companies that trade on Mainland China stock exchanges use national standards, it should be noted that Chinese companies whose securities trade on the Stock Exchange of Hong Kong may choose either IFRS,

Hong Kong Financial Reporting Standards (HKFRS) or Chinese Accounting Standards (ASBEs) for purposes of financial reporting to Hong Kong investors. Those financial reports are in addition to the ASBE financial reports that the Chinese companies issue within mainland China.

- India has recently adopted a new set of accounting standards for listed and large companies that is generally converged with IFRS, but with some mandatory and some optional modifications.
- In Japan, listed companies may use Japanese Accounting Standards, IFRS or US GAAP.
- In Saudi Arabia, IFRS is required for banks and insurance companies. There is a plan to adopt IFRS for all listed companies and financial institutions, which is most likely to be effective in 2017.
- IFRS is permitted for non-US companies without reconciliation to US GAAP. Around 500 cross-border SEC registrants now use IFRS.

Hence the above demonstrate challenges relating to comparability, consistency and harmonization across jurisdictions and markets. Reverting back to Figure 1, it is quite understandable to have comparability – which is synonymous with consistency and harmonization, as categorized under the enhancing qualities – rather than fundamental qualities. Whilst some would argue that comparability, timeliness, understandability and verifiability should be regarded as fundamental qualitative characteristics, faithful representation, with components – neutrality and completeness – in addition to freedom from material error, could also arguably be relegated to enhancing attributes.

How realistic is it to obtain complete, neutral accounting information? Factors governing the derivation of such information are, to a large extent, very judgmental and subjective. In the same manner, whilst it may be possible to mitigate material errors, the subjective nature and judgmental elements to which it is governed, makes possibilities of its elimination highly unlikely.

Whilst reliability is a credible and necessary quality and characteristic of accounting information – the very essence of generating and auditing financial statements – such that investors are able to judge and rely on the results and performance of a firm, faithful representation presents a more watered down and less stringent criteria which permits greater flexibility by the virtue of subjective and judgmental elements.

Chen et al also highlight four factors affecting value relevance in China (2001:12), namely, positive versus negative earnings, firm size, earnings persistence, and liquidity of stocks.

FUTURE RESEARCH DIRECTIONS

As rightly highlighted by Chen et al (2001:19), other important factors – particularly those related to supporting infrastructure, such as auditing quality, and corporate governance merit careful examination. Further, in their opinion, there may be better measures for some of the variables studied such as earnings persistence in China – all of which could be improved through a focus on further research.

The mandatory and permissible adoption of IFRS is still a work in progress. Greater research and initiatives should be directed in respect of accounting and legislative reforms currently being undertaken in jurisdictions – as a means of achieving their desired goals of improving the quality of accounting information. Greater collaboration between the G20 Finance Ministers and Central Bank Governors, IASB, FASB, Financial Stability Board, IOSCO and the Basel Committee on Banking Supervision – as well as how such collaboration can be fostered could constitute future research work.

CONCLUSION

Chen et al (2001: 3,4) make reference to investigations undertaken by Haw et al. (1998a) which not only confirm that information based on Chinese GAAP is value-relevant and that reconciliation to IAS has limited value to foreign investors in the B-share market, but also findings of "significant incremental information content of IAS reconciliation for H shares traded on the Hong Kong Stock Exchange". In their opinion, such results infer that the same accounting information may have varying degrees of value-relevance in different markets. In consolidating their view, they cite Bao and Chow (1999) as providing "conflicting evidence" in their conclusion that accounting information based on IAS has greater information content than that based on Chinese GAAP to B-share investors in China.

"IFRS provides the financial information for capital markets covering more than half of the world's GDP." (IFRS, 2015:18). Hence, initiatives and efforts aimed at fostering, achieving and realizing harmonization, comparability and consistency should be encouraged.

REFERENCES

G20 Finance Ministers and Central Bank Governors. (2012). Retrieved from http://g20watch.edu.au/g20-leaders-declaration-loscabos-2012

Aharony, J., Lee, C. J., & Wang, T. J. (2000). Financial packaging of IPO firms in China. *Journal of Accounting Research, 38*(1), 103–126. doi:10.2307/2672924

Amir, E., Harris, T., & Lev, B. (1996). Value-relevance of nonfinancial information: The wireless communications industry. *Journal of Accounting and Economics, 22*(1-3), 3–30. doi:10.1016/S0165-4101(96)00430-2

Amir, E., Harris, T., & Venuti, E. (1993). A comparison of the value-relevance of US versus non-US gap accounting measures using form 20-f reconciliations. *Journal of Accounting Research, 31*(Suppl.), 230–264. doi:10.2307/2491172

Bao, B. H., & L. Chow. (1999). The usefulness of earnings and book value for equity valuation in emerging capital markets: evidence from listed companies in the People's Republic of China. *Journal of International Financial Management and Accounting*, 10(2), 85–104.

Basel Committee on Banking Supervision. (2013, October). The Regulatory Framework: Balancing Risk Sensitivity, Simplicity and Comparability.

Chen, C. J. P., Chen, S., & Su, X. (2001). S, Chen & S, Su (2001). Is accounting information value-relevant in the emerging Chinese stock market? *Journal of International Accounting, Auditing & Taxation, 10*(1), 1–22. doi:10.1016/S1061-9518(01)00033-7

Curran, J. (1994). China's investment boom. *Fortune*, (March 7), 116–122.

European Commission. (2009). Paragraph 10 International Accounting Standard 8 Accounting Policies, Changes in Accounting Estimates and Errors Financial Stability Board. Retrieved from http://www.financialstabilityboard.org/2014/09/pr_140918

Haw, I. M., Qi, D., & Wu, W. (1998a). Value-relevance of financial reporting disclosures in an emerging capital market: the case of B-shares and H-shares in China (Working paper). The Chinese University of Hong Kong.

Haw, I. M., Qi, D., & Zhang, W. G. 1998b earnings management of listed firms in response to security regulations in China's emerging capital market (Working paper). The Chinese University of Hong Kong.

IAS. (n. d.). 8 Accounting Policies, Changes in Accounting Estimates and Errors.

IFRS. (2014). Fairness of Reporting, Acceptable Accounting Risk and the IASB's Conceptual Framework Review: Insights from the Enron Trial.

IFRS. (2015, June). Financial Reporting Standards for the World Economy 2015 IOSCO. Retrieved from http://www.iosco.org/library/pubdocs/pdf/IOSCOPD282.pdf

Kothari, S., & Zimmerman, J. (1995, September). Price and return models. *Journal of Accounting and Economics*, *20*(2), 155–1. doi:10.1016/0165-4101(95)00399-4

Ohlson, J. (1995). Earnings, book values, and dividends in equity valuation. *Contemporary Accounting Research*, *11*(Spring), 661–687. doi:10.1111/j.1911-3846.1995.tb00461.x

Ojo, M. (2014, October). The Basel Capital Adequacy and Regulatory Framework: Balancing Risk Sensitivity, Simplicity and Comparability. *Centre of Excellence for Scientific & Research Journalism*, *3*(4), 516–522.

Xiang, B. (1998). Institutional factors influencing China's accounting reforms and standards. *Accounting Horizons*, (June), 105–119.

Chapter 6
Value Relevance of Accounting Information in Capital Markets:
A Comparative Analysis between Jurisdictions from the Middle East, Africa and Asia

James A Rossi
University of Greenwich, UK

ABSTRACT

By way of reference to a comparative analysis between three selected jurisdictions from the Middle East, Africa and Asia, this chapter aims to investigate the trends in value relevance of accounting information in these stock markets and exchanges. Further, amongst other goals and objectives, this chapter also seeks to illustrate why in light of recent developments which have resulted in decline of reliability - as a valued attribute, relevance and reliability still constitute fundamental characteristics which are required in the development of global stock markets and economies. It consolidates this aim in view of recent IASB and FASB's initiatives and the resulting framework which categorizes understandability, comparability, timeliness and verifiability as enhancing qualitative characteristics of accounting information.

DOI: 10.4018/978-1-5225-1900-3.ch006

Copyright ©2017, IGI Global. Copying or distributing in print or electronic forms without written permission of IGI Global is prohibited.

INTRODUCTION

By way of reference to a comparative analysis between three selected jurisdictions from the Middle East, Africa and Asia, this chapter aims to investigate the trends in value relevance of accounting information in these stock markets and exchanges.

As highlighted in the theme to the volume:

Value relevance approach "measures both relevance and reliability because accounting information is reflected in the price. (Khanagha, 2011; Barth, Beaver & Landsman, 2001). Further, "value relevance approach is an instrument used to estimate quality of accounting information – this being of vital importance to the economy."

An efficient market is one in which security prices adjust rapidly to the infusion of new information, and current stock prices fully reflect all available information including the risks involved. (Reilly, 1989).

To what extent can accounting information be expected to provide or convey complete information to investors? Further to what extent can capital markets of advanced market economies and emerging market economies be considered to be efficient?

Amongst other goals and objectives, this chapter also seeks to illustrate why in light of recent developments which have resulted in decline of reliability - as a valued attribute, relevance and reliability still constitute fundamental characteristics which are immensely required in the development of global stock markets and economies.

As well as contributing to the literature on the topic, the following constitute the aims and objectives of the chapter:

1. To investigate the extent to which accounting information can be relied upon based on given market values and whether a relationship or pattern can be established in certain jurisdictions based on given operating variables which function in such economies.
2. To demonstrate and highlight the validity of the Efficient Markets Hypothesis (as well as the Efficient Capital Markets Hypothesis)
3. To demonstrate how accounting information can serve as a useful and vital indicator which will enable investors to interpret financial information in such a way which mitigates information asymmetries between management and investors
4. To highlight those areas and factors which influence the quality of accounting information - and which must be addressed by markets if the audit is to achieve its intended aims and functions

5. To highlight whether accounting reforms undertaken in investigated jurisdictions actually achieved their desired goals of improving the quality of accounting information and if such reforms were not successful, to propose measures which could address the current issues being faced by such jurisdictions.

BACKGROUND AND LITERATURE REVIEW

Analyzing the Results Derived from the Value Relevance of Accounting Information in the United Arab Emirates

Conclusions derived from the study and investigation carried out between 2001 and 2008 by Khanagha (2011, p. 43) indicate the following:

1. The result of the study revealed accrual based information were more value relevant than cash based information. And also the coefficient of EPS was more than BVP.
2. Investors tend to be more tolerant towards overvaluation when the economy and financial markets are doing well and less lenient during market bears and economic slowdowns (Al-Hogail, 2004).

The first of these results could be related with recent developments which have witnessed a change in fundamental qualitative characteristics from the IASB's existing framework published in 1989 (the 1989 framework). Such fundamental qualitative characteristics comprise relevance and faithful representation and whilst relevance has been retained in both frameworks, faithful representation has taken the position previously occupied by reliability.

As highlighted in KPMG's Briefing Sheet (2010, p. 3), this was prompted by the IASB's goals to clarify the meaning of reliability – further, the Financial Accounting Stability Board (FASB) and the International Accounting Stability Board (IASB) decided it was better to use a new term rather than to try to clarify the use of "reliability".

Also of significance is the following statement by the Board:

- Verifiability embodies the concept of the ability to use information with confidence. The Boards (FASB and ISAB) noted that this is a desirable but not required enhancing qualitative characteristic in acknowledging the importance of forward-looking information in financial reporting that cannot be directly verified.

Methodology and Further Findings of the Study

According to Khanagha (2011, p. 35), the regression-variations and the portfolio-returns approaches was used to investigate and to operationalize the value relevance of accounting information because they provide different perspective on the issue of value relevance of accounting information. Further he adds that by using the regression-variations approach, the value relevance was estimated as the percentage of variations in the returns or market value explained by the accounting figures and that portfolio-returns approach reflected a proportion of total returns that could be earned from financial statement information which control for changes in the volatility of market returns over time.

Findings are as follows (2011, p. 42):

- Accounting information is value relevant in Abu Dhabi Securities Market.
- Value relevance of accounting information is not the same between small and large companies.
- Value relevancy of accounting information in small companies is more than large companies in Abu Dhabi Securities Market and that in Abu Dhabi Securities Markets, small companies are more likely to include start-up companies and investors may focus more on accounting numbers of these companies than large companies.
- Findings of both methods based on the portfolio returns approach showed that selected accounting numbers are value relevant for Abu Dhabi Securities Market investors. A comparison of the results of the two methods periods before and after reform showed value relevancy of ΔEARN and ΔROE decreased during the period after reform. The results also indicated that value relevancy of ΔCASH increased in the period after reform based on both portfolio methods.
- Confirmation that value relevance of accounting information in UAE decreased after reform in accounting standards.

Based on the 2015 IFRS Report (page 5) the UAE comprises one of those 116 jurisdictions, from a total of 140 jurisdictions that require IFRS for all or most publicly accountable entities – with most of the remaining 24 jurisdictions permitting the use of IFRS.

Some observations included in the report are as follows:

- That modifications to IFRS are rare.
- That, as regards auditor's report wording, in the majority of jurisdictions, the auditor's report refers to compliance with IFRS.

The above observations not only highlight the degree to which consistency can be retained and preserved within IFRS, but also the binding force which the auditor's report confer in respect of matters of compliance with IFRS. Whilst a move to principles based accounting is evidenced through recent developments which have witnessed the replacement of reliability with faithful representation, characteristics which compel users of financial information to comply with regulations – as well as facilitate a degree of consistency, particularly with large enterprises, should be regarded as fundamental in their application and importance.

Benefits of IFRS (IFRS, 2015, p. 21)

- IFRS brings transparency by enhancing the international comparability and quality of financial information, enabling investors and other market participants to make informed economic decisions.
- IFRS increases accountability by reducing the information gap between the providers of capital and the people to whom they have entrusted their money. Our standards provide information that is needed to hold management to account. As a source of globally comparable information, IFRS is also of vital importance to regulators around the world.
- IFRS contributes to economic efficiency by helping investors to identify opportunities and risks across the world, thus improving capital allocation.

Analyzing the Results Derived from the Value Relevance of Accounting Information in the Bombay Stock Exchange

The following conclusions are based on results derived by Mulenga (2015) "Value Relevance of Accounting Information of Listed Public Sector Banks in Bombay Stock Exchange":

- The fixed effect model, random effect model and correlation analysis were used to examine value relevance of accounting information and ascertaining if there was significant relationship between share prices and accounting information.
- The study also provided empirical evidence that earnings per share constituted the most relevant accounting information for equity valuation in public sector banks.
- On the other hand accounting information such as earnings per share, book value per share were reported to have positive correlation with share prices at 5% level of significance

- Further, return on equity was reported to have positive correlation with share prices at 1% level of significance but positive correlation existing between return on equity and share price was found to be very low. Only asset turnover ratio was reported to have weak negative correlation with market share price at 5% level of significance.

Based on the Financial Reporting Standards for the World Economy (2015, p. 10), in India:

- IFRS is currently permitted on a limited voluntary basis. A few listed companies (approximately 11 companies) use IFRS.
- India has recently adopted a new set of accounting standards for listed and large companies that is generally converged with IFRS, but with some mandatory and some optional modifications. Those standards are known as Indian Accounting Standards (Ind AS).

The initiatives and future focus would then appear to be the facilitation of mandatory adoption IFRS – as a means of enhancing transparency, disclosure of financial information within capital markets. This is not only very significant given the current role assumed by India as an emerging market economy, but also in relation to the previously mentioned benefits conferred by the mandatory adoption of IFRS, namely and including, reducing the information gaps and asymmetries between management and investors, as well as enhancing comparability and consistency between accounting information.

Analyzing the Results Derived from the Value Relevance of Accounting Information in the Nigerian Stock Exchange

The following conclusions were derived by Olugbenga and Atanda (2014):

- The study revealed that accounting information on quoted companies in Nigeria is value relevant. However, as highlighted by the author, the study also revealed that the value relevance of accounting information does not follow a particular trend within the period under study.
- While the value relevance was weak in the periods of political crisis caused by military dictatorship (1992-1998) and global economic crisis (2005-2009), it was high in the other periods.

- Based on the finding that accounting information directly influences the value of securities in the capital market, it was therefore recommended by Olugbenga and Atanda that Accounting Standards should be complied with by Nigerian companies and that more standards that could curtail information overload should be introduced.

By way of reference to Bouvatier & Lepetit (2012) and Bushman & Williams (2012), Murcia & Kohlscheen (BIS, 2016, p. 6) have highlighted how backward-looking provisioning systems tend to amplify the procyclicality of loan market fluctuations - even if, in their opinion, no concrete evidence exists to explain differences in the health measures of banking sectors based on a representative panel of EMEs (see Murcia & Kohlscheen (BIS, 2016, p. 6,7).

Hence forward looking provisioning may be encouraged – and verifiability as an enhancing fundamental accounting characteristics (as categorized by the IASB and FASB) be restricted particularly to practices such as backward looking provisioning. The IASB and FASB, whilst making the observations that verifiability embodies the concept of the ability to use information with confidence, also added that verifiability was a desirable but not required enhancing qualitative characteristic of accounting information (KPMG, 2010, p. 3). In so doing, it made reference to the importance of forward looking information in financial reporting – information which could not be directly verified.

Figure 1. A bar graph showing the trend analysis of the value relevance
Source: Olugbenga and Atanda (2014)

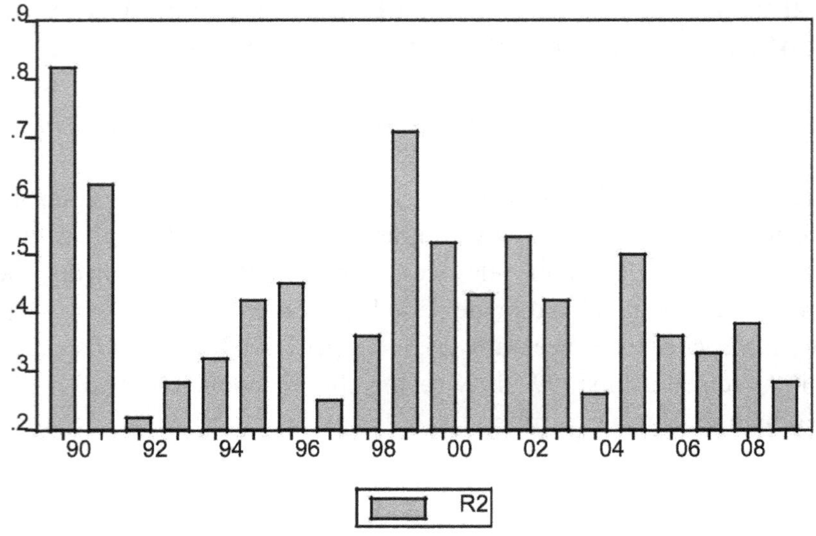

Figure 2.
Source: KPMG Briefing Sheet Conceptual Framework for Financial Reporting Oct 2010 Issue 213 at page 3

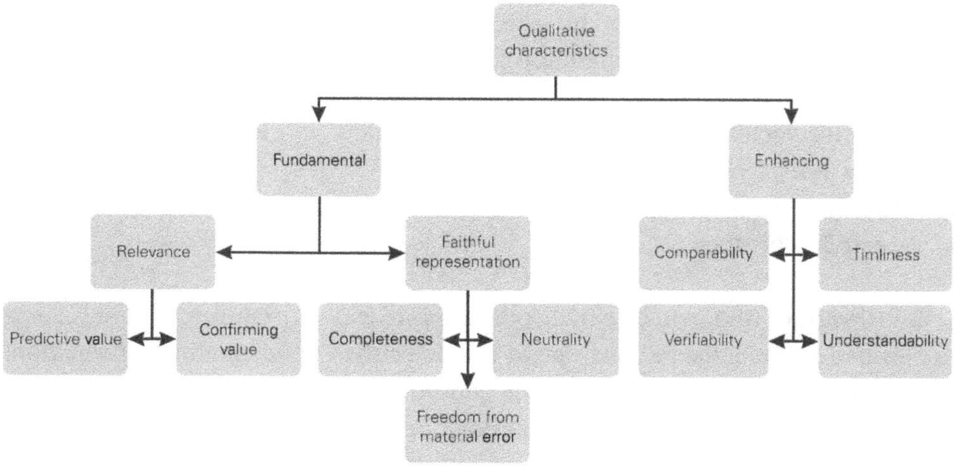

Issues, Controversies, Problems

How can accounting information be harnessed in such a way as to serve as a useful and vital indicator which will enable investors to interpret financial information in such a way which mitigates information asymmetries between management and investors?

Comparability, consistency and reliability of financial and accounting information appear to have greater relevance than ever – as highlighted by the goals and objectives of IFRS. However such objectives appear to have been undermined by the categorization of understandability, verifiability, timeliness and comparability as enhanced qualitative accounting characteristics- pursuant to Figure 2.

- In Abu Dhabi, as well as confirmation that value relevance of accounting information in UAE decreased after reform in accounting standards, it was also highlighted that value relevancy of accounting information in small companies is more than large companies in Abu Dhabi Securities Market and that in Abu Dhabi Securities Markets, small companies are more likely to include start-up companies and investors may focus more on accounting numbers of these companies than large companies.
- In India, IFRS is currently permitted on a limited voluntary basis.
- In Nigeria, value relevance was weak during periods of political crisis.

The above factors, as highlighted, which affect value relevance of accounting information indicate that value relevance as impacted and influenced, is jurisdiction specific.

The following are identified by Chen at al (2001) as contributing to variations in value relevance of accounting information in the Chinese stock market:

1. Positive versus negative earnings,
2. Firm size,
3. Earnings persistence, and
4. Liquidity of stocks.

It is therefore very evidence that comparability and verifiability, at least, should be elevated to fundamental qualitative characteristics of accounting information. Herein lies a role for the IASB, FASB and other strategic international standard setters such as the Basel Committee on Banking Supervision, the Financial Stability Board and IOSCO to strengthen coordination initiatives aimed at aligning their goals and initiatives – such that harmonization can be facilitated and the goals on consistency and comparability realized.

As highlighted in the previous section, forward looking provisioning may be encouraged – and verifiability as an enhancing fundamental accounting characteristics (as categorized by the IASB and FASB) be restricted particularly to practices such as backward looking provisioning. The IASB and FASB, whilst making the observations that verifiability embodies the concept of the ability to use information with confidence, also added that verifiability was a desirable but not required enhancing qualitative characteristic of accounting information (KPMG, 2010, p. 3). In so doing, it made reference to the importance of forward looking information in financial reporting – information which could not be directly verified.

This would appear to infer that the Boards did not regard verifiability as being of little importance – but rather were trying to highlight the importance of information which whilst not being directly verifiable, were still important – namely information such as forward looking information. However the categorization of verifiability as an enhancing qualitative characteristic – and not a required enhancing qualitative characteristic – and even more so, its mere characterization as an enhancing qualitative characteristic – rather than a fundamental qualitative characteristic would appear to send misleading signals that verifiability, generally, was not as important and required characteristic as those characteristics which were either classified as required enhancing qualitative characteristics or fundamental qualitative characteristics.

SOLUTIONS AND RECOMMENDATIONS

Whilst the need for greater collaboration between international regulatory standard setters has been highlighted, this is not to undermine the current initiatives of such international bodies in their efforts to realize a global set of consistent harmonized standards – particularly with respect to IFRS. As highlighted in the 2015 IFRS Report, immense progress has been achieved and efforts are constantly being made to mandatorily adopt IFRS across all jurisdictions.

To the extent that variations in value relevance of accounting information is jurisdiction specific, the need for comparability and a degree of consistency in financial reporting cannot be over emphasized.

CONCLUSION

As highlighted in the theme to this volume, The important role which auditors serve in facilitating good corporate governance practices, the monitoring of directors and management of an enterprise, ensuring accountability through the provision of a „true and fair view" on the financial statements of an enterprise, all constitute means whereby the auditor provides important vital, reliable and relevant information and indicators to current and potential stakeholders of an enterprise.

If investors cannot rely on the auditor's report – in respect of the financial statements generated by the management of an enterprise, and management of an enterprise are not compelled to comply with vital financial reporting standards, how are such users of financial information expected to use reasonable judgement which is vital for purposes of forecasting and sound decision making? What is the role of the audit then reduced or relegated to?

It is needs to be added that mandatory compliance with fundamental concepts, elements, codes, ethics, standards and rules underlie the basis for successful principle based application and sound judgment.

In the present volatile financial environment where information asymmetries have increased considerably as a result of lack of information certainty, there is vital and unprecedented need to accord a greater recognition for the need for verifiability, understandability, comparability – and even timeliness as irreplaceable and fundamental characteristics of accounting information. Whilst forward looking provisioning may be encouraged, verifiability as an enhancing fundamental accounting characteristics (as categorized by the IASB and FASB) should primarily be restricted to practices such as backward looking provisioning.

REFERENCES

Aljifri, K., & Hussainey, K. (2007). The determinants of forward-looking information in annual reports of UAE companies. *Managerial Auditing Journal, 22*(9), 881–894. doi:10.1108/02686900710829390

Aljifri, K., & Khasharmeh, H. (2006). An investigation into the suitability of the international accounting standards to the United Arab Emirates environment. *International Business Review, 15*(5), 505–526. doi:10.1016/j.ibusrev.2006.05.009

Amir, E., Harris, T. S., & Venuti, E. K. (1993). A comparison of the value-relevance of US versus non-U.S. GAAP accounting measures using Form 20-F reconciliations. *Journal of Accounting Research, 31*, 230–264. doi:10.2307/2491172

Barth, M. E., Beaver, W. H., & Landsman, W. R. (2001). The relevance of the Value Relevance Literature for Financial Accounting Standard Setting: Another View. *Journal of Accounting and Economics, 31*(1-3), 77–104. doi:10.1016/S0165-4101(01)00019-2

Bikker, J., & Metzemakers, P. (2005). Bank provisioning behavior and procyclicality. *Journal of International Financial Markets, Institutions and Money, 15*(2), 141–157. doi:10.1016/j.intfin.2004.03.004

Bouvatier, V., & Lepetit, L. (2008). Banks pro cyclical behavior: Does provisioning matter? *Journal of International Financial Markets, Institutions and Money, 18*(5), 513–526. doi:10.1016/j.intfin.2007.07.004

Bouvatier, V., & Lepetit, L. (2012). Provisioning rules and bank lending: A theoretical model. *Journal of Financial Stability, 8*(1), 25–31. doi:10.1016/j.jfs.2011.04.001

Chen, C. J. P., Chen, S., & Su, X. (2001). Is accounting information value-relevant in the emerging Chinese stock market? *Journal of International Accounting, Auditing & Taxation, 10*(1), 1–22. doi:10.1016/S1061-9518(01)00033-7

Francis, J., & Schipper, K. (1999). Have Financial Statements Lost Their Relevance? *Journal of Accounting Research, 37*(Suppl. 2), 319–352. doi:10.2307/2491412

Francis, J., Schipper, K., & Vincent, L. (2002). Expanded disclosures and increased usefulness of earnings announcements. *Accounting Review, 77*(3), 515–546. doi:10.2308/accr.2002.77.3.515

Holthausen, R. W., & Watts, R. L. (2001). The Relevance of Value Relevance Literature for Financial Accounting Standard Setting. *Journal of Accounting and Economics, 31*(1-3), 3–75. doi:10.1016/S0165-4101(01)00029-5

IFRS, (2015). Financial Reporting Standards for the World Economy June 2015.

Khanagha, J. B. (2011). Value Relevance of Accounting Information in the United Arab Emirates. *International Journal of Economics and Financial Issues*, 1(2), 33-45.

KPMG. (2010, October). Briefing Sheet Conceptual Framework for Financial Reporting.

Modigliani, F., & Miller, M. (1959). The Cost of Capital Corporate Finance and the theory of Investment. *The American Economic Review*, *48*, 261–297.

Mulenga, M. J. (2015). Value Relevance of Accounting Information of Listed Public Sector Banks in Bombay Stock Exchange. *Research Journal of Finance and Accounting*, 6(8).

Murcia, A., & Kohlscheen, E. (2016, March). Moving in tandem: bank provisioning in emerging market economies. BIS Working Papers.

Ohlson, J. A. (1995). Earnings, book values, and dividends in equity valuation. *Contemporary Accounting Research, 11*(2), 661–687. doi:10.1111/j.1911-3846.1995.tb00461.x

Olugbenga, A. A., & Oyerinde, A. A. (2014). Value Relevance of Financial Accounting Information of Quoted Companies in Nigeria: A Trend Analysis. *Research Journal of Finance and Accounting*, 5(8).

Oshodin and Chijoke. (2014). The comparative study of value relevance of financial information in the Nigeria banking and petroleum sectors. *Journal of Business Studies Quarterly*, *6*(1).

Pathirawasam, C. (2010). Value relevance of accounting information: Evidence from Sri Lanka. *International Journal of research in commerce & management.*

Sharma, A., Kumar, S., & Singh, R. (2012). Value Relevance of Financial Reporting and Its Impact on Stock Prices: Evidence from India. *South Asian Journal of Management*, *19*(2), 60–77.

Sharma, M. (2014). Value relevance of accounting information: A comparative study of public and private sector companies in India. *Asia Pacific Journal of Research, 1*(12).

Chapter 7
Revisiting the Value Relevance of Accounting Information in the Italian and UK Stock Markets

James A Rossi
University of Greenwich, UK

ABSTRACT

This chapter aims to investigate the results of the value relevance of accounting information with reference to the study: "The value relevance of accounting information in the Italian and UK stock markets". Results revealed from this study are as follows: - First, evidence shows the greater value relevance of accounting information in Italy than in the UK, even if this result must be explained according to the sample's characteristics. Second, the study underlines that in Italy the most value relevant accounting data refer to earnings while in the UK the focus is mainly on cash flows. The chapter also seeks to contribute to the gap in the literature on the value relevance of accounting information in the UK and Italy. In so doing it investigates the relevance and reliability of results derived in this study, their applicability to current market developments – as well as recent fluctuations and volatility in the financial markets.

DOI: 10.4018/978-1-5225-1900-3.ch007

Copyright ©2017, IGI Global. Copying or distributing in print or electronic forms without written permission of IGI Global is prohibited.

INTRODUCTION

This chapter aims to investigate the results of the value relevance of accounting information with reference to the study: "The value relevance of accounting information in the Italian and UK stock markets." Results revealed from this study are as follows:

- First, evidence shows the greater value relevance of accounting information in Italy than in the UK, even if this result must be explained according to the sample's characteristics. Second, the study underlines that in Italy the most value relevant accounting data refer to earnings while in the UK the focus is mainly on cash flows.

The chapter also seeks to contribute to the gap in the literature on the value relevance of accounting information in the UK and Italy. In so doing it investigates the relevance and reliability of results derived in this study, their applicability to current market developments – as well as recent fluctuations and volatility in the financial markets.

The following research questions, in line with the theme and volume of the Call for Chapters, will also be addressed:

1. What is the extent to which accounting information can be relied upon based on given market values and can a relationship or pattern be established in certain jurisdictions based on certain operating variables which function in such economies?
2. How valid and applicable is the Efficient Markets Hypothesis (as well as the Efficient Capital Markets Hypothesis)?
3. How can accounting information be harnessed in such a way as to serve as a useful and vital indicator which will enable investors to interpret financial information in such a way which mitigates information asymmetries between management and investors?
4. What factors influence the quality of accounting information - and how can these be addressed by markets if the audit is to achieve its intended aims and functions?
5. Have accounting and legislative reforms undertaken in investigated jurisdictions achieved their desired goals of improving the quality of accounting information? If not, what measures could be proposed or recommended to address the current issues being faced by such jurisdictions?

Based on IAS 8 Accounting Policies, Changes in Accounting Estimates and Errors:

- An entity shall change an accounting policy only if the change: (a) is required by an IFRS; or (b) results in the financial statements providing reliable and more relevant information about the effects of transactions, other events or conditions on the entity's financial position, financial performance or cash flows.

"Accounting policies are the specific principles, bases, conventions, rules and practices applied by an entity in preparing and presenting financial statements. When an IFRS specifically applies to a transaction, other event or condition, the accounting policy or policies applied to that item shall be determined by applying the IFRS and considering any relevant Implementation Guidance issued by the IASB for the IFRS."

Pursuant to the Standard (IAS 8), judgments and estimates are to be approached as follows:

- In the absence of a Standard or an Interpretation that specifically applies to a transaction, other event or condition, management shall use its judgement in developing and applying an accounting policy that results in information that is relevant and reliable. In making the judgement management shall refer to, and consider the applicability of, the following sources in descending order:
    - The requirements and guidance in IFRSs dealing with similar and related issues; and
    - The definitions, recognition criteria and measurement concepts for assets, liabilities, income and expenses in the Conceptual Framework.

Whilst the investigation undertaken by Camodeca et al focus on statistical associations and models, this chapter incorporates vital concepts and developments that have shaped the definition of what really constitutes value relevance – a discussion which was not considered in their paper.

BACKGROUND AND LITERATURE REVIEW

Based on paragraph 10 International Accounting Standard 8 Accounting Policies, Changes in Accounting Estimates and Errors (2009):

In the absence of an IFRS that specifically applies to a transaction, other event or condition, management shall use its judgement in developing and applying an accounting policy that results in information that is:

1. Relevant to the economic decision-making needs of users; and
2. Reliable, in the financial statements:
    a. Represent faithfully the financial position, financial performance and cash flows of the entity
    b. Reflect the economic substance of transactions, other events and conditions, and not merely the legal form
    c. Are neutral, i.e. free from bias
    d. Are prudent
    e. Are complete in all material respects (IAS, 2009)

Figure 1 highlights the developments that have taken place since 1989.

As accentuated in the Briefing Sheet (KPMG, 2010), the fundamental qualitative characteristics have changed from the IASB's framework which was published in 1989. Whilst relevance is reflected in both frameworks, reliability has been replaced with faithful representation. Further, it is highlighted that faithful representation does not embrace substance over form and prudence – which were included as part of the 1989 framework and definition of reliability. The IASB and FASB, in citing their reasons for the removal of characteristics related to substance over form and prudence, highlighted the following justifications:

- That substance over form was redundant as a separate characteristic – and that presenting the form – which differed from the substance, could not pro-

Figure 1. Qualitative characteristics of accounting information
Source: KPMG, Briefing Sheet Conceptual Framework for Financial Reporting, October 2010 Issue 213 at page 3

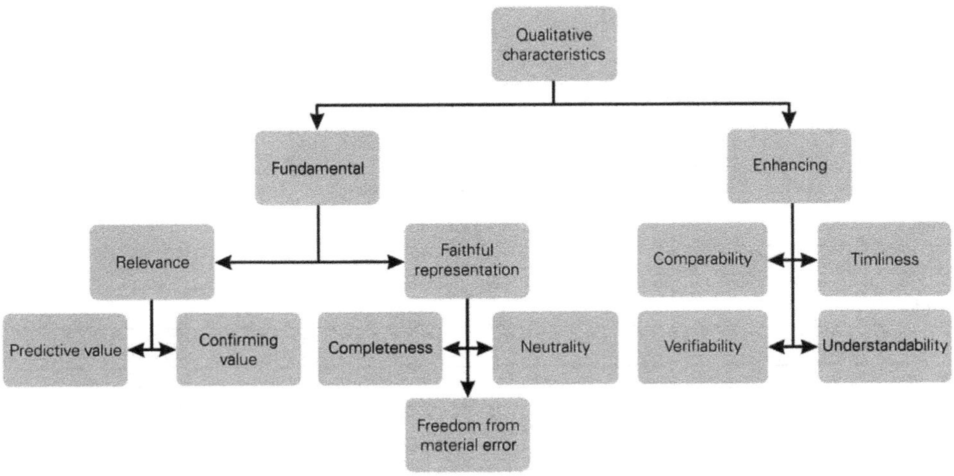

vide faithful representation of the facts. It was also accentuated that faithful representation reflected merely the substance.

- That prudence conflicted with neutrality.

Table 2 , as presented by the IFRS (2015, p. 5) provides a list of the 140 jurisdictions whose profiles were posted as of June 2015.

As highlighted by the IFRS, the 116 jurisdictions that require IFRS for all or most publicly accountable entities are bolded.

Addressing the extent to which accounting information can be relied upon - based on given market values and whether a relationship or pattern be established in certain jurisdictions based on certain operating variables which function in such economies.

In order to assess the relevance of International Financial Reporting Standards and the extent to which judgments and estimates are exercised in jurisdictions, in the absence of such standards, the following observations, based on the 140 jurisdictional profiles in the IFRS report, in addition to the qualitative characteristics of accounting information, as highlighted under Table 1, must also be taken into consideration (IFRS, 2015):

Observation 1: Support for global accounting standards. Nearly all jurisdictions have publicly stated a commitment in support of global accounting standards.

Observation 2: IFRS as the global accounting standard. The relevant authority in nearly all jurisdictions has publicly stated that IFRS should be the global accounting standards.

Observation 3: IFRS requirement for domestic listed companies and financial institutions. IFRS is required for all or most domestic publicly accountable entities (listed companies and financial institutions) in 116 jurisdictions of the 140 jurisdictions profiled.

Table 1.

Region	Number of jurisdictions	Percent of total
Europe	43	31%
Africa	19	14%
Middle East	9	6%
Asia and Oceania	32	23%
Americas	37	26%
Total	140	100%

Source: (IFRS, 2015, p. 3)

Table 2. 140 jurisdictions

Afghanistan	**Bulgaria**	**Ghana**	**Liechtenstein**	**Palestine**	**Sweden**
Albania	**Cambodia**	**Greece**	**Lithuania**	Panama	Switzerland
Angola	**Canada**	**Grenada**	**Luxembourg**	Paraguay	**Syria**
Anguilla	Cayman Islands	Guatemala	Macao	**Peru**	**Taiwan**
Antigua and Barbuda	**Chile**	Guinea-Bissau	**Macedonia**	**Philippines**	**Tanzania**
Argentina	China	**Guyana**	Madagascar	**Poland**	Thailand
Armenia	**Colombia**	Honduras	**Malaysia**	**Portugal**	**Trinidad and Tobago**
Australia	**Costa Rica**	**Hong Kong**	**Maldives**	**Romania**	**Turkey**
Austria	**Croatia**	**Hungary**	**Malta**	**Russia**	**Uganda**
Azerbaijan	**Cyprus**	**Iceland**	**Mauritius**	**Rwanda**	**Ukraine**
Bahamas	**Czech Republic**	India	**Mexico**	**Saint Lucia**	**United Arab Emirates**
Bahrain	**Denmark**	Indonesia	**Moldova**	Saudi Arabia	**United Kingdom**
Bangladesh	**Dominica**	**Iraq**	**Mongolia**	**Serbia**	United States
Barbados	**Dominican Republic**	**Ireland**	**Montserrat**	**Sierra Leone**	**Uruguay**
Belgium	**Ecuador**	**Israel**	**Myanmar**	**Singapore**	Uzbekistan
Belarus	Egypt	**Italy**	**Nepal**	**Slovakia**	**Venezuela**
Belize	**El Salvador**	**Jamaica**	**Netherlands**	**Slovenia**	Vietnam
Bermuda	**Estonia**	Japan	**New Zealand**	**South Africa**	**Yemen**
Bhutan	**European Union**	**Jordan**	Nicaragua	**Spain**	**Zambia**
Bolivia	**Fiji**	**Kenya**	Niger	**Sri Lanka**	**Zimbabwe**
Bosnia and Herzegovina	**Finland**	**Korea (South)**	**Nigeria**	**St Kitts and Nevis**	
Botswana	**France**	**Kosovo**	**Norway**	**St Vincent and the Grenadines**	
Brazil	**Georgia**	**Latvia**	**Oman**	Suriname	

Observation 4: IFRS required for more than just listed companies. Around 60 per cent of the 116 jurisdictions that require IFRS for domestic listed companies also require IFRS for unlisted financial institutions and/or large unlisted companies.

Observation 5: IFRS permitted for unlisted companies. Around 90 per cent of the 116 jurisdictions that require IFRS for domestic listed companies also require or permit IFRS for many unlisted companies.

Observation 6: IFRS permitted for listed companies.

- Most of the remaining 24 jurisdictions that do not yet require IFRS for all or most domestic listed companies already permit IFRS for at least some domestic listed companies:
    - Twelve jurisdictions permit, instead of require, IFRS: Bermuda, Cayman Islands, Guatemala, Honduras, India, Japan, Madagascar, Nicaragua, Panama, Paraguay, Suriname and Switzerland
    - Two require IFRS for financial institutions but not for other listed companies: Saudi Arabia and Uzbekistan
    - One is in the process of adopting IFRS in full: Thailand
    - One is in the process of converging its national standards substantially (but not entirely) with IFRS: Indonesia
    - Eight use national standards: Bolivia, China, Egypt, Guinea-Bissau, Macao, Niger, United States and Vietnam. Note that China's standards, while not IFRS, are substantially converged with IFRS

With respect to jurisdictions where IFRS are required – contrasted to those where IFRS are permitted, the determination of the value relevance of accounting information in capital markets in jurisdictions where IFRS are permitted would also have to be considered by way of reference to the national standards currently being applied.

In their paper, "The Value Relevance of Accounting Information in the Italian and UK Stock Markets", Camodeca, Almici and Brivio make the following observations (2014):

- Firstly, that evidence shows the greater value relevance of accounting information in Italy than in the UK, even if this result must be explained according to the sample's characteristics.
- Second, that the study underlines that in Italy the most value relevant accounting data refer to earnings while in the UK the focus is mainly on cash flows.

Focusing on factors such as the legal system, capital markets' features and role of accountancy profession – and with reference to the legal system, they identify two main systems: the Civil law and the Common law.

The four different interpretations of value relevance of accounting information, as postulated by Francis and Schipper (1999) also make interesting points for reference:

Interpretation 1: "Financial statement information leads stock prices by capturing intrinsic share values towards which stock prices drift."

Interpretation 2: Defines a financial information value relevant if "it contains the variables used in a valuation model or assists in predicting those variables". Consequently, "the value relevance of earnings (…) might be measured by the ability of earnings to predict future dividends, future cash flows, future earnings, or future book values.

Interpretations 3 and 4: Assume the value relevance as a statistical association between financial information and stock returns.

A distinction is also made between value relevance and market value relevance. Value relevance is highlighted as being:

- The explanatory power of accounting variables, such as earnings and book value of equity (Ali and Hwang, 1999), cash flows (Bartov, Goldberg and Kim, 2001), or other relevant variables selected by other authors (Göttsche and Schauer, 2011); whilst

Market value relevance is distinguished as:

- A statistical association between financial information and market prices or stock returns. Consequently, under the efficient market hypothesis that share-prices reflect available information, the accounting-based measures could explain market price in an effective way (Francis and Schipper, 1999).

Reference is also made to findings whereby numerous authors have concluded their investigations on the Felham and Ohlson model that, over the past 40 years, the value relevance of earnings had decreased while the value relevance of book value has increased.

Six different regression models were implemented by Camodeca et al, they conclude, based on their findings, that cash flows in the United Kingdom have a greater explanatory power than earnings, with contrasting results being derived for Italy.

They add that this could be explained by some of the differences which exist between Italy and the UK, namely, that:

- In Anglo Saxon countries financial markets are larger, more efficient and more active than Italian ones, such that investors look to financial statements as a tool that should help them to assess prospective company's net cash inflows. On the other hand, in Italy - where financial markets are not so well-developed and they are bank-based, investors probably still pay more attention to income statements and statements related to financial position than to cash flow statements.

What is clear and certain from Table 2, however, is that Italy and the United Kingdom fall under the category of those jurisdictions where IFRS are required. From the investigations undertaken by Camodeca et al, it can also be concluded that investors rely on financial statements – even if the degree of attention accorded to income statements – as opposed to cash flow statements, varies between both countries. The importance of reliability and the influence of sizes of capital markets – as well as their development, on users of financial information, is also emphasized.

ISSUES, CONTROVERSIES, PROBLEMS

The re definition of what constitutes qualitative characteristics of accounting information, as highlighted under Figure 1, would also appear to highlight greater pre-eminence in relation to principles based accounting – even though the element of "substance" is accorded attention.

Faithful representation would be better placed as an enhancing qualitative characteristic – whilst comparability, timeliness, verifiability and understandability be elevated to fundamental qualitative characteristics.

Verifiability by its very nature, serves as the primary purpose of an audit. To classify it as enhancing qualitative characteristics not only appears to undermine the role of the audit, but responsibilities of auditors. As regarding timeliness, and understandability, the importance of such attributes cannot be over emphasized. Whilst stock market corrections in respect of insignificant misstatements or accounting errors may generate consequences which are capable of being overlooked or rectified, the same cannot be said of material misstatements or errors.

In addressing how accounting information can be harnessed in such a way as to serve as a useful and vital indicator which will enable investors to interpret financial information in such a way which mitigates information asymmetries between management and investors, greater focus should hence be given to characteristics such as consistency, understandability, timeliness, comparability and verifiability.

Whether the qualitative characteristics of accounting information, as highlighted under Figure 1, should be classified at all, presents another matter of controversy. However, if they should, then certainly those characteristics considered to be enhancing, or rather complementary attributes – namely, comparability, timeliness, verifiability and understandability, should assume greater priority than those which are more susceptible to judgment and subjectivity. Others may also argue that those attributes which are more susceptible to material misstatements, judgment and error, should be accorded greater attention.

In any case, it is worth aligning the work of the International Accounting Standards Board, and that of the Financial Accounting Standards Board, with the initiatives of the Basel Committee on Banking Supervision – whose focus in recent documents has accentuated the need for comparability and consistency. It also worth noting that leading economies such as the United States, China and the United Kingdom have been very progressive with Basel initiatives.

SOLUTIONS AND RECOMMENDATIONS

Perhaps the Basel framework present the best chances of achieving and realizing harmonization, comparability and consistency. These goals have been instrumental in the evolvement of the original 1988 Basel Capital Accord to its present form – in addition to the realization to address practices relating to capital arbitrage.

The Boards (the International Accounting Standards Board, and that of the Financial Accounting Standards Board) highlighted (KPMG, 2010, p. 3) that verifiability "embodies the concept of the ability to use information with confidence". Further, it is acknowledged that this is a desirable – but not required enhancing qualitative characteristic – by way of reference to forward looking information in financial reporting which cannot be "directly verified."

If this is the case, then there should be a distinction between forward looking information in financial reporting which cannot be "directly verified" and directly verifiable current-relevant information whose value is of such importance that inaccuracy or lack of timeliness in its generation or release, would trigger financial shocks or cause vulnerability and volatility within financial markets – such of immense magnitude and proportion.

If investors or users of financial information cannot use information with confidence anymore, then the purpose of the audit, namely the verifiability of financial statements, is certainly defeated.

CONCLUSION

How valid and applicable is the Efficient Markets Hypothesis (as well as the Efficient Capital Markets Hypothesis)? "IFRS provides the financial information for capital markets covering more than half of the world's GDP." (IFRS, 2015, p. 18). As highlighted in the IFRS report (2015, p. 22), "The long-term benefits likely to result from the use of a harmonized set of international accounting standards are considerable, in particular from a market transparency and cost perspective." Further initiatives such as the "development and use of robust, internationally accepted, and consistently applied financial reporting standards" (IOSCO), as well as "the objective of achieving a single set of high-quality global accounting standards" (Financial Stability Board) are accentuated.

REFERENCES

G20 Finance Ministers and Central Bank Governors. (2012). Leaders declaration. Retrieved from http://g20watch.edu.au/g20-leaders-declaration-loscabos-2012

Alexander, D., & Nobes, C. (2013). Financial Accounting: An International Introduction (5th ed.).

Ali, A., & Hwang, L.-S. (1999). Country-Specific Factors Related to Financial Reporting and the Value Relevance of Accounting Data. *Journal of Accounting Research*, *38*(1), 1–21. doi:10.2307/2672920

Barth, M. E., Beaver, W. H., Hand, J. R. M., & Landsman, W. R. (1999). Accruals, Cash Flows and Equity Values. *Review of Accounting Studies*, *3*(3/4), 205–229. doi:10.1023/A:1009630100586

Barth, M. E., Beaver, W. H., & Landsman, W. R. (2001). The Relevance of the Value Relevance Literature for Financial Accounting Standard Setting: Another View. *Journal of Accounting and Economics*, 31.

Barth, M. E., & Clinch, G. (2009). Scale Effects in Capital Market-Based Accounting Research. *Journal of Business Finance & Accounting*, *36*(3-4), 253–288. doi:10.1111/j.1468-5957.2009.02133.x

Bartov, E., Goldberg, S. R., & Kim, M. S. (2001). The Valuation-Relevance of Earnings and Cash Flows: An International Perspective. *Journal of International Financial Management and Accounting*, *12*(2), 103–176. doi:10.1111/1467-646X.00068

Basel Committee on Banking Supervision. (2013, October). The Regulatory Framework: Balancing Risk Sensitivity, Simplicity and Comparability.

Camodeca, R., Almici, A. & Brivio, A.R. (2014). The value relevance of accounting information in the Italian and UK stock markets. *Problems and Perspectives in Management*, 12(4).

European Commission. (2009). *Paragraph 10 International Accounting Standard 8 Accounting Policies*. Changes in Accounting Estimates and Errors.

Feltham, G. A., & Ohlson, J. A. (1995). Valuation and Clean Surplus Accounting for Operating and Financial Activities. *Contemporary Accounting Research, 11*(2), 689–732. doi:10.1111/j.1911-3846.1995.tb00462.x

Financial Stability Board. (2014). FSB Plenary meets in Cairns, Australia. Retrieved from http://www.financialstabilityboard.org/2014/09/pr_140918

Francis, J., & Schipper, K. (1999). Have financial statements lost their relevance? *Journal of Accounting Research, 37*(2), 319–352. doi:10.2307/2491412

Göttsche, M., & Schauer, M. (2011). The value relevance of accounting figures in the European market reconsidered, European Accounting Association (EAA). *Proceedings of the34th Annual Congress*, Roma.

IAS 8 Accounting Policies, Changes in Accounting Estimates and Errors. (2009).

IFRS. (2015, June). Financial Reporting Standards for the World Economy.

IOSCO. (2008). Letter to Chairman, Financial Stability Forum. Retrieved from http://www.iosco.org/library/pubdocs/pdf/IOSCOPD282.pdf

Chapter 8
The Determinants of Stock Market Development in Emerging Economies:
Examining the Impact of Corporate Governance and Regulatory Reforms (I)

Sarah Newton
University of Kent, UK

ABSTRACT

"The chief concerns of EMEs (emerging market economies) in relation to their financial systems remain developmental rather than regulatory: increasing financial savings to accelerate growth and development, and deepening their financial system to develop long term funding instruments for infrastructure financing, absorb large inflows of capital to counter the uphill backwash from EMEs to AMEs, reduce the cost of capital and reduce the leads and lags in monetary policy transmission. Advanced market economies (AMEs), on the other hand, need major regulatory changes that inoculate them more effectively against the new risks their financial systems face." As well as investigating these observations, this chapter is aimed at investigating the validity of Efficient Markets Hypothesis and Efficient Capital Markets Hypothesis in emerging economies – as contrasted with advanced market economies. In so doing, it aims to contribute to the extant literature on stock market liquidity and liquidity in capital markets.

DOI: 10.4018/978-1-5225-1900-3.ch008

Copyright ©2017, IGI Global. Copying or distributing in print or electronic forms without written permission of IGI Global is prohibited.

INTRODUCTION

The chief concerns of EMEs (emerging market economies) in relation to their financial systems remain developmental rather than regulatory: increasing financial savings to accelerate growth and development, and deepening their financial system to develop long term funding instruments for infrastructure financing, absorb large inflows of capital to counter the uphill backwash from EMEs to AMEs, reduce the cost of capital and reduce the leads and lags in monetary policy transmission. advanced market economies (AMEs), on the other hand, need major regulatory changes that inoculate them more effectively against the new risks their financial systems face. (Sheel & Ganguly, 2016: 197).

As well as investigating these observations, this chapter is aimed at investigating the validity of Efficient Markets Hypothesis and Efficient Capital Markets Hypothesis in emerging economies – as contrasted with advanced market economies. In so doing, it aims to contribute to the extant literature on stock market liquidity and liquidity in capital markets. Results appear to confirm the theory that stock market liquidity impacts and influences the ability of the market to fully reflect information.

Recent financial regulatory reforms which embrace Basel III regulations and Volcker rules – along with their impact and the issues presented for EMDEs (emerging market and developing economies), will be also considered in this chapter.

Sheel and Ganguly (2016:197) also argue that the immediate impact of recently introduced financial regulatory reforms are most likely to take effect in the "relatively lightly regulated AMEs", rather than, in their opinion, the more tightly regulated EMEs.

The literature review section however, highlights concerns which have been expressed by EMDEs (emerging market and developing economies) as a result of recent regulatory reforms. This also raises concerns as to whether such reforms may have had greater far–reaching unintended consequences which are currently impacting the growth of these economies than originally expected or anticipated.

In line with the theme of the volume, the chapter will amongst other objectives, aim to contribute to the extant literature on whether capital markets in emerging markets economies, in particular, fully reflect information - hence demonstrating and highlighting the validity of the Efficient Markets Hypothesis (as well as the Efficient Capital Markets Hypothesis.

It will attempt to realize this aim by way of reference to an evaluation and analyses of determinants of stock market developments – as well as stock market liquidity.

BACKGROUND AND LITERATURE REVIEW

In their findings (1999), Garcia and Liu conclude that:

1. Real income, saving rate, financial intermediary development, and stock market liquidity are important determinants of stock market capitalization;
2. Macroeconomic volatility does not prove significant; and
3. Stock market development and financial intermediary development are complements instead of substitutes.

Further, stock market development is considered by Garcia and Liu (1999:30) to be a multi-dimensional concept which is usually measured by stock market size, liquidity, volatility, concentration, integration with world capital markets, and the legal rule (regulation and supervision) in the market. Market capitalization is employed by them as a measure for stock market development in their study since, in their opinion, "it is a good proxy for such general development because it is less arbitrary than other individual measures and indexes of stock market development."

In explaining the differences in stock market development in the major stock markets in Latin America as compared with those in East Asia and selected industrial countries, pooled data for fifteen countries from a period ranging 1980 to 1995, are also used in their study (see 1999: 31) and the countries involved include seven countries in Latin America, six countries in East Asia, and two industrial countries: the United States and Japan.

As well as examining, common determinants of stock and bond liquidity over the period 1991 through 1998, Chordia, Sarkar and Subrahmanyam (2001:21) also examine the impact of financial crises, monetary policy, and mutual fund flows on financial market liquidity. The results of their findings are as follows (2001:21,22):

- That liquidities in stock and bond markets are codetermined: returns, bid-ask spreads, and volume in one market affect the bid-ask spread and volume in the other market – with the results being consistent with asset allocation strategies being conducted simultaneously in both stock and bond markets.
- Stock and bond market bid-ask spreads can be forecasted to a remarkable degree using publicly available variables and lagged market returns, lagged interest rates, the lagged bid-ask spread and lagged volume are strong predictors of the bid-ask spread and volume changes in both markets- with the notable result being that bond spreads lead stock spreads and the result being consistent with order imbalances due to portfolio reallocations reflected first in the institution-dominated bond markets, followed by stock markets.

- That time-series properties of bond and stock liquidity are different during crises as compared to normal circumstances. Levels of stock and bond volume, spread volatility, and the correlation between stock and bond liquidity are all significantly higher during crises - such results being consistent with increased investor uncertainty leading to frequent and correlated portfolio reallocations during financial crises.
- That monetary policy affects financial market liquidity during crises – with the effect being particularly pronounced for stock market liquidity. Further the results support the notion that increases in money supply loosen credit constraints faced by investors and dealers, which has a beneficial effect on financial market liquidity.
- Lagged money flows into stock mutual funds have a positive effect on stock market liquidity changes, as measured by changes in stock bid-ask spreads, during normal periods. During crises, this effect is not significant. However, there is an inverse relation between lagged bond fund flows and bond spread changes during crises, and the results indicate a net inflow into government bond funds (a flight to quality) in turbulent periods that eventually has a beneficial effect on liquidity in the bond markets.

As well as indicating that asset allocation strategies in periods of enhanced liquidity should be executed first in the bond market their analysis and findings, in their opinion, helps provide an understanding of how practitioners can use public information to forecast periods of enhanced liquidity and thereby design strategies to reduce trading costs.

Based on their empirical results which reveal that that the main determinants of stock market development in emerging markets are banking sector development, private capital flows, income level, and political risk, Yartey (2008:25) investigates if such factors could explain the development of the stock market in South Africa. Further, the impact of banking sector development, private capital flows, and political risk in determining the development of the stock market in South Africa are evaluated.

Using a model and econometric method considered to be "basic", a dummy variable for South Africa (referred to as SAdummy) is introduced in the regression and then interacted with the variables of interest (political risk, banking sector development, the square of banking sector development, and private capital flows). Through such interactions, four new variables (SAcredit, SAcredit2, SAPolitical and SAflows) are derived (see Yartey, 2008:25). The four new models used in their analyses are then sequentially estimated with each regression having an interaction of the SA dummy and one of the four variables under consideration and then a T-test conducted on the coefficient of the new variables (page 25).

A description of the five models used in their study is as follows (Yartey, 2008:27):

Model 1: The baseline model with lagged dependent, bank credit, valued traded, the square of bank credit, investment, inflation, and the South African dummy as the explaining variables. Their result reveals that the South African dummy is positive and statistically insignificant – with further inference that the main factors identified in the previous section as determining the development of the stock market in emerging market countries also apply to the specific case of South Africa.

Model 2: Incorporates the examination of the impact of banking sector credit on stock market development in South Africa – with positive and significant results being reflected – and with income level, value traded, bank credit, the square of bank credit, and the lagged dependent variable, proving again to be significant.

Model 3: Incorporating the examination of the impact of the square of bank credit on stock market development in South Africa revealed that very high levels of banking sector development tends to have a negative impact on stock market development as banks and stock markets substitute each other as vehicles for financing investments.

Model 4: Results implied that the resolution of political risk could broaden appeal in equity investment in South Africa and lead to the development of the stock market.

Model 5: Results revealed that private capital flows is positive and statistically significant in explaining the development of the stock market in South Africa.

As well as confirming that "income level, domestic investment, banking sector development, private capital flows, and stock market liquidity are important determinants of stock market development in emerging markets" (see pages 27 and 28), the relationship between banking sector development and stock market development in emerging market countries were found to be "non-monotonic". Further, institutional factors such as political risk, law and order, democratic accountability and bureaucratic quality were found to be important determinants of stock market development in emerging markets – with a final conclusion based on the premises that the main factors explaining the development of the stock market in emerging market countries could also help us to understand the determinants of stock market development in South Africa (see page 28).

Wuyts considers four "beneficiaries" of liquidity to be (2007: 309): traders, stock exchanges (or alternative trading systems), listed firms and the stability of the financial system. In accentuating the fact that liquidity is vital to traders, he adds that liquidity not only directly impacts their cost of trading, but also, that it is a determinant of the return traders require to invest in a stock. He also adds that whilst certain traders prefer transparent systems, other might favor less transparent structured markets.

The above results do not only demonstrate the impact of stock market liquidity on capital markets, but also their significance in the growth and development of financial and capital markets.

ISSUES, CONTROVERSIES, PROBLEMS

In their executive summary (Financial Stability Board, 2012:3), the following potential unintended consequences and issues for EMDEs (emerging market and developing economies), were highlighted by the IMF, World Bank and Financial Stability Board – as a result of recent regulatory reforms:

- **Basel III Capital Framework:** That the risk weighting of assets in the trading book and for securitised products under Basel 2.5, the convertibility of certain capital instruments, differences in the measurement of risk between a parent bank and its subsidiary, capital requirements for certain business activities (such as trade finance) as well as higher overall capital requirements may exacerbate deleveraging and increase the costs of global banks operating in EMDEs, thereby reducing credit and financial market liquidity;
- **Basel III Liquidity Framework:** That the definition of high quality liquid assets and the calibrations used in the calculation of the liquidity ratios do not accurately reflect EMDEs' financial market structures, which may adversely affect the functioning of the domestic financial markets and the lending capacity of banks in EMDEs;
- Policy measures for global systemically important financial institutions (G-SIFIs);
- Over-the-counter (OTC) derivatives reforms.

As regards Basel regulatory reforms (2012: 12):

- Respondents from some EMDEs with a large foreign bank presence identified unintended consequences associated with Basel 2.5's introduction of an incremental risk capital charge to capture default and migration risk, as well as a stressed value-at-risk requirement.
- Since the level and composition of capital in many EMDEs already exceed Basel III requirements, some respondents stated that their concern is not necessarily with the overall level of capital, but with the complexity of the Basel

Table 1. Size of debt markets in EMDEs (2010)

		EMDE Debt 1/		
	Government		Corporate	
	% GDP	**% Total**	**% GDP**	**% Total**
		banking		banking
		system		system
Advanced Economies		assets		assets
Germany	49.8	19.3	10.6	4.1
Japan	195.0	114.4	15.4	9.0
United Kingdom	55.9	14.4	1.0	0.2
United States	75.8	77.7	21.2	21.8
Emerging Market and Developing Economies				
Argentina	12.9	41.3	1.9	6.0
Brazil	41.9	44.7	0.5	0.5
Chile	15.4	14.3	14.1	13.0
China	26.2	16.8	7.4	4.8
Colombia	22.6	37.3	0.5	0.8
Hungary	51.6	47.0	0.3	0.2
India	34.9	37.8	1.4	1.5
Indonesia	12.6	37.3	0.8	2.4
Korea	44.4	30.9	34.0	23.7
Lebanon	78.2	-	-	-
Malaysia	44.8	19.6	30.6	13.4
Mexico	22.1	56.9	3.1	8.0
Pakistan	29.4	70.7	-	-
Peru	12.6	28.8	2.6	5.8
Philippines	28.8	41.9	1.0	1.5
Portugal	46.6	16.3	20.1	7.0
Russia	3.9	7.2	-	-
Slovak Republic	26.8	31.0	-	-
Slovenia	11.1	-	1.4	-
South Africa	29.7	23.7	7.0	5.6
Thailand	45.7	41.3	17.2	15.5
Turkey	30.6	36.4	0.2	0.2
Venezuela	28.7	75.2	1.8	4.6

Source: BIS Quarterly Review, IMF World Economic Outlook, and Economic Intelligence Unit
Note: 1/ Period average.

Source: Financial Stability Board, (2012). Identifying the Effects of Regulatory Reforms on Emerging Market and Developing Economies page 28

Table 2. Covered banks and activities under the Volcker Rule

Nature of Prohibition or Requirement	Type of Financial Institution	Covered Activities	Exempt Activities
Proprietary Trading 1/	U.S. licensed depositories affiliates, parents, holding companies, wherever located; U.S. branches/subsidiaries of non-US banks	Short-term buy-to-resell or arbitrage Transactions subject to market-risk capital charge Broker-dealer desks transactions	Market making; Underwriting; Risk hedging, including liquidity management; Repo, reverse repo, and securities lending; Client facing transactions; Trading of U.S. government, state, municipal, federal agency, and GSE debt

Non-U.S. banking units any of the above, if of non-U.S. banks. Transacted with U.S. residents, using U.S. personnel, or on U.S. execution facilities.

All of the above, plus all proprietary trading if not transacted with U.S residents, not using U.S. personnel nor U.S. execution facilities.

Source: Financial Stability Board, (2012). Identifying the Effects of Regulatory Reforms on Emerging Market and Developing Economies page 32

Source: U.S. Treasury (2011). Notes: 1/ All transactions of covered banks' broker-dealer desks are prohibited, except for direct trading of loans and spot market transactions in commodities and foreign exchange.

III rules, the negative effect that it may have on certain types of banking activities (e.g. trade finance) and on the development and functioning of capital markets in their jurisdiction.

- Some EMDEs expressed concern about aspects of the leverage ratio and measures to reduce procyclicality that may impact domestic credit and output growth.
- Respondents were particularly concerned that challenging macroeconomic conditions and fragile financial markets may exacerbate pressure on some banks to deleverage and thereby adversely affect their economies.

Identified actual or potential negative effects "from other regional and national regulatory measures, adopted mainly in Europe and in the US - which go beyond the financial reforms agreed to by the G20" as highlighted in the FSB Report, relate to the EBA requirements and the Volcker Rule (see FSB, 2012:20).

With EBA requirements, the measures involved the building up a temporary capital buffer such that the Core Tier 1 capital ratio of those banks reaches 9% by the end of June 2012 (FSB, 2012:20,21).

With the Volcker Rule – an Act which seeks to promote financial stability by improving accountability and transparency in the domestic financial system, including policies to address the risks arising from SIFIs and; which particularly prohibits regulated and insured depositories from undertaking proprietary trading, and also

Table 3. Potential effects of the Volcker Rule on EMDEs

What is affected	Who is affected	Where is the direct impact
Proprietary trading of EMDE sovereign and corporate debt	Covered U.S. banks	Liquidity in EMDE sovereign and corporate debt markets
Curtailing of activities arising from restrictions on their dealings with U.S. counterparties	Covered non-U.S. banks	Liquidity in EMDE sovereign and corporate debt markets
Proprietary trading of EMDE government securities	EMDE affiliates of covered U.S. and non-U.S. banks	Liquidity in local EMDE government securities markets
Restriction on the ability to execute or clear proprietary trading on US infrastructure	Covered non-U.S. banks	Execution of international trades moving away from the United States
Market making inadvertedly affected	Covered U.S. and non-U.S. banks	Liquidity in EMDE capital markets
Stringent requirements on payments and settlements	Covered U.S. and non-U.S. banks as counterparties	Limited access to covered banks by EMDE banks
Failure to prove trading activities as market making activities	Covered affiliates of U.S. and non-U.S. banks	Principal dealer status in EMDEs
Differentiation between market making and proprietary trading	Covered U.S. and non-U.S. banks	Reporting requirements for EMDE affiliates
Reporting compliance	Covered U.S. and non-U.S. banks	Establishment of a wide array of programs, policies, procedures, and information structures for compliance purposes Exemptions for market-making and hedging activities leading to misreporting

Source Financial Stability Board, (2012). Identifying the Effects of Regulatory Reforms on Emerging Market and Developing Economies page 33

For comprehensive information on the indirect effects of the Volcker Rule on EMDEs, see Financial Stability Board, (2012). Identifying the Effects of Regulatory Reforms on Emerging Market and Developing Economies page 33

seeks to reduce systemic risk by prohibiting these firms from investing in private equity and hedge funds (FSB, 2012:21), concerns were expressed about its cross border effects.

FUTURE RESEARCH DIRECTIONS

As added by Wuyts (2007: 311), while the extant literature confirms the fact that liquidity and liquidity risk are priced in the market, little is known about which elements of market design affect this pricing of liquidity (risk). Hence this area constitutes a suitable candidate for future research focus and direction.

CONCLUSION

Whilst Garcia and Liu (1999) conclude that stock market development and financial intermediary development serve as complements rather than substitutes, Yartey (1998), on the on hand, concludes that at early stages of its development, the banking sector is a compliment to the stock market in financing investment. However, as they both develop, banks and the stock market begin to compete with each other as vehicles for financing investment.

However he reconciles some results of his investigations with those derived by Garcia and Liu by highlighting the fact that Garcia and Liu (1999) found that income level and financial intermediary development have positive impacts on stock market development in a sample of Latin American and Asian countries – a result which correlates with his findings that the development of the stock market in emerging market countries could also help to understand the determinants of stock market development in South Africa.

Whilst the concerns of emerging markets economies may appear to be developmental, it has also been demonstrated that many issues and concerns have arisen in respect of recently introduced and implemented regulatory concerns. This is also evidenced by the impact of such reforms on the current growth levels – as well as forecasted growth for emerging market economies.

REFERENCES

Amihud, Y.; Mendelson, H. & Pedersen, L. (2005). Liquidity and Asset Prices. *Foundations and Trends in Finance*, 1(4), 269-364.

Bacidore, J. (1997). The Impact of Decimalization on Market Quality: An Empirical Investigation of the Toronto Stock Exchange. *Journal of Financial Intermediation*, *6*(2), 92–120. doi:10.1006/jfin.1997.0213

Barclay, M., Christie, W., Harris, J., Kandel, E., & Schultz, P. (1999). Effects of Market Reform on the Trading Costs and Depths of NASDAQ Stocks. *The Journal of Finance*, *54*(1), 1–34. doi:10.1111/0022-1082.00097

Barclay, M., Hendershott, T., & McCormick, T. (2003). Competition Among Trading Venues: Information and Trading on Electronic Communications Networks. *The Journal of Finance*, *58*(6), 2637–2666. doi:10.1046/j.1540-6261.2003.00618.x

Baumol, J.W. (1960). The Stock Market and Economic Efficiency. New York: Furham University Press.

Bhattacharya, U., & Spiegel, M. (1998). Anatomy of a Market Failure: NYSE Trading Suspensions (1974-1988). *Journal of Business & Economic Statistics*, *16*, 216–222.

Chordia, T., & Ball, C. (2001). True Spreads and Equilibrium Prices. *The Journal of Finance*, *56*(5), 1801–1836. doi:10.1111/0022-1082.00390

Chordia, T., Roll, R., & Subrahmanyam, A. (2000). Commonality in Liquidity. *Journal of Financial Economics*, *56*(1), 3–28. doi:10.1016/S0304-405X(99)00057-4

Chordia, T., Sarkar, A., & Subrahmanyam, A. (2001, December 11). Common Determinants of Bond and Stock Market Liquidity: The Impact of Financial Crises. Monetary Policy, and Mutual Fund Flows.

Demirguc-Kunt, A., & Levine, R. (1996). Stock Markets, Corporate Finance and Economic Growth: An Overview. *The World Bank Economic Review*, *10*(2), 223–239. doi:10.1093/wber/10.2.223

El-Erian, M., & Kumar, M. S. (1995, February 16–17). Emerging Stock Markets in Middle Eastern Countries. *Paper presented at theWorld Bank Conference on Stock Markets, Corporate Finance and Economic Growth*, Washington DC.

Financial Stability Board. (2012). Identifying the Effects of Regulatory Reforms on Emerging Market and Developing Economies: A Review of Potential Unintended Consequences. Report to the G20 Finance Ministers and Central Bank Governors. *Financial Stability Board in coordination with Staff of the International Monetary Fund and the World Bank.*

Garcia, F. V., & Liu, L. (1999). Macroeconomic Determinants of Stock Market Development. *Journal of Applied Econometrics*, *2*(1), 29–59.

La Porta, R., Lopez-de-Silanes, F., Shleifer, A. & Vishny, R. (1996). Law and Finance. *NBER*.

Pagano, M. (1993). Financial Markets and Growth: An Overview. *European Economic Review*, *37*(2-3), 613–622. doi:10.1016/0014-2921(93)90051-B

Sheel, A., & Ganguly, M. (2016). *Financial Regulatory Reforms – A Mid Term Assessment from an Emerging Market Perspective. In*R. Kathuria & N. K. Nagpa, (Eds.), *Global Economic Cooperation.* Springer Verlag.

Wuyts, G. (2007). Stock Market Liquidity. *Determinants and Implications Tijdschrift voor Economie en Management, LII*(2).

Yartey, C. A. (2007). Macroeconomic and Institutional Determinants of Stock Market Development in Africa. In J. Okpara (Ed.), *Management and Economic Development in Sub-Saharan Africa: Theoretical and Applied Perspectives.* London: Adonis and Abbey Publishers.

Yartey, C.A. (2008). The Determinants of Stock Market Development in Emerging Economies: Is South Africa Different? *IMF.*

Chapter 9
The Determinants of Stock Market Development in Emerging Economies:
Examining the Impact of Corporate Governance and Regulatory Reforms (II)

Sarah Newton
University of Kent, UK

ABSTRACT

Results appear to confirm the theory that stock market liquidity impacts and influences the ability of the market to fully reflect information. The impact of the sizes and development of capital markets on users of financial information will also be considered in this chapter – as well as other factors which could have a possible impact on the value relevance of accounting information. So will the issue of Shadow Banking and recent financial regulatory reforms which embrace the Dodd Frank legislation – as well as Liikannen, Vickers, Volcker rules and reports.

DOI: 10.4018/978-1-5225-1900-3.ch009

Copyright ©2017, IGI Global. Copying or distributing in print or electronic forms without written permission of IGI Global is prohibited.

INTRODUCTION

Results appear to confirm the theory that stock market liquidity impacts and influences the ability of the market to fully reflect information. The impact of the sizes and development of capital markets on users of financial information will also be considered in this chapter – as well as other factors which could have a possible impact on the value relevance of accounting information. So will the issue of shadow banking and recent financial regulatory reforms.

As well as investigating these observations, this chapter is aimed at investigating the validity of Efficient Markets Hypothesis and Efficient Capital Markets Hypothesis in emerging economies – as contrasted with advanced market economies. In so doing, it aims to contribute to the extant literature on stock market liquidity and liquidity in capital markets. Results appear to confirm the theory that stock market liquidity impacts and influences the ability of the market to fully reflect information.

In line with the theme of the volume, the chapter will amongst other objectives, aim to contribute to the extant literature on whether capital markets in emerging markets economies, in particular, fully reflect information - hence demonstrating and highlighting the validity of the Efficient Markets Hypothesis (as well as the Efficient Capital Markets Hypothesis.

Other objectives of the chapter are as follows:

1. To investigate the extent to which accounting information can be relied upon based on given market values and whether a relationship or pattern can be established in certain jurisdictions based on given operating variables which function in such economies.
2. To demonstrate and highlight the validity of the Efficient Markets Hypothesis (as well as the Efficient Capital Markets Hypothesis)
3. To demonstrate how accounting information can serve as a useful and vital indicator which will enable investors to interpret financial information in such a way which mitigates information asymmetries between management and investors
4. To highlight those areas and factors which influence the quality of accounting information - and which must be addressed by markets if the audit is to achieve its intended aims and functions
5. To highlight whether accounting reforms undertaken in investigated jurisdictions achieved their desired goals of improving the quality of accounting information and if such reforms were not successful, to propose measures which could address the current issues being faced by such jurisdictions.

BACKGROUND AND LITERATURE REVIEW

The term global liquidity is used by the Bank for International Settlements to mean the ease of financing in global financial markets (BIS 2016). Credit is among the key indicators of global liquidity and the focus of the global liquidity indicators estimated by the BIS and these indicators constitute part of the BIS's support for the G20's activities (see BIS Global Liquidity Indicators, 2016).

- Deep and liquid financial markets are considered important to financial stability. Market participants require liquid markets in order to effectively manage risks and their own funding needs. There is a significant body of literature that suggests that financial derivatives reduce risk. A resilient and effective financial system enables corporates to manage business risks, such as currency, interest rates or commodity price risks. Market liquidity is also critical in maintaining the resiliency of financial markets during times of stress. Benos and Zikes (2014) find that frictions in inter-dealer markets inhibited dealers' ability to share risk and manage their inventories, which translated into a higher cost of trading above and beyond what can be explained by funding costs and aggregate uncertainty (PWC, Global Markets Liquidity Study, 2015, p. 19).

It is argued that in order for important economic activities such as the capital allocation process, monetary policy implementation and government borrowing to take place efficiently, economies must continue their efforts to develop financial markets (Sundaresan, 2009, p. 85). Further, according to Sundaresan, these efforts must be expended along multiple dimensions - such as the development of deep and liquid financial markets depends on a number of factors, including, regulatory policies, fiscal and exchange rate policies, bankruptcy code/laws, trade-patterns, infrastructure for trading and intermediation (financial and informational), access to markets for global investors and issuers, and incentives for financial innovation.

According to PWC, Global Markets Liquidity Study (2015, p. 19):

- Financial markets are a key source for financing business growth and government spending. They also provide important access for investors to invest and earn returns.
- In most regions, such as in Europe, Latin America and Asia where businesses have been historically reliant on bank financing, capital markets are less developed compared to markets such as the US. However, policymakers are increasingly recognising the importance of developing capital markets as

an alternative to bank finance: the recent proposal for the EU Capital Markets Union seeks to develop deep and liquid capital markets across borders that complement banks as a source of financing. Policy developments which have encouraged further financial integration are also underway in Asia and in, other regions to promote growth in capital markets.

Further, the sources of liquidity are identified (see p. 20):

- Financial markets liquidity facilitates the efficient allocation of economic resources through a number of channels:
- Efficient capital markets facilitate the global flow of capital between investors, or savers, and borrowers. Well-functioning capital markets also provide diversified sources of funding, in addition to traditional bank lending.
- Liquid capital markets also facilitate the distribution of financial risks to market participants most able and willing to bear them, and enable investors to manage and hedge against risks, as well as adjust their portfolios effectively.
- Liquidity is necessary for the effective generation and dissemination of issuer specific information. In the context of equity markets, movements in the share price are likely to reveal important information about changes in the firm's value in liquid markets, and can also reflect liquidity risks. Chordia et al. (2001) and Acharya and Pedersen (2005) show that there is a positive and statistically significant relationship between liquidity in equity markets and asset returns. Friction in the system, as characterised by high transaction costs, can therefore hinder the price discovery process.
- The effectiveness of monetary policy also depends on liquidity conditions in financial markets. Abbassi and Linzert (2012) analyse the effectiveness of monetary policy in steering money market rates in the euro area, and find that money market rates after the crisis became less responsive to the expected path of the European Central Bank's (ECB) policy rate, compared to before August 2007. The loss of monetary policy effectiveness is partly attributed to money market rates being driven by higher liquidity premia. Therefore, financial markets liquidity is a key factor in ensuring the effectiveness of monetary policy.

The impact of central bank policies on financial markets was clearly highlighted in the Bank for International Settlements 2014 Annual Report which highlighted the volatility – as well as sensitivity of financial markets to central bank policies by way of illustration to responses of asset prices to monetary policy changes (BIS, 2014, p. 23). The Report also underlines the fact that expectations regarding US monetary policy were central – resulting in a bond market sell-off in May–June 2013 that reverberated around the globe – a measure which was instigated as a means of addressing and stabilizing monetary policy effects.

The Report also draws attention to the fact that whilst advanced economies fared well – in matters relating to shifting monetary policies, emerging market economies were more vulnerable and suffered heavier losses than was the case with advanced economies in the wake of the 2013 sell-off "with persistent declines in bond, equity and currency markets".

The Bank for International Settlements also observes that "the transformation of the banking industry and, in particular, the shift to a more market determined process of intermediation has also had implications for central banks to the extent that it has affected the effectiveness of monetary policy instruments, the relative importance of the different transmission channels and/or their ability to react to non-policy shocks" (BIS, 2007, p. 1).

Mohanty and Kumar Rishabh (BIS, 2016) argue that there has been growing evidence in recent years that the size and the structure of financial intermediation play a critical role in the transmission of monetary policy. Further they add that, the globalization of debt markets means that monetary policy can no longer be conducted through the short-term interest rate alone.

In their report (BIS, 2016, p. 2), they highlight the fact that the introduction of inflation targeting by many EMEs in the 1990s, together with reforms to abolish interest rate controls, to strengthen central bank credibility and to develop local bond markets, had marked a major turning point for monetary policy in many countries. Further, they add that these reforms had helped not only to reduce earlier constraints on monetary policy stemming from a high degree of fiscal dominance and liability dollarization but also to increase the role of interest and exchange rates in monetary policy transmission, leading to an environment of low and stable inflation.

Whilst Kohlscheen and Miyajima (2015) argue that financial systems in EMEs tend to be more bank-oriented, Mohanty and Kumar Rishabh (BIS, 2016) add that historically, banks have been at the centre of financial intermediation in EMEs – however, the environment in which monetary policy is conducted in EMEs has undergone a major transformation over the past decade (see page 4).

However see Kohlscheen and Rungcharoenkitkul (2015): "Changing financial intermediation: implications for monetary policy transmission", BIS Papers, no 83

The importance of transparency has also been brought to the fore by various sources in the literature. Its contribution to the Asian Financial Crisis is also highlighted thus:

- The importance of transparency in financial markets in helping to dampen crisis in financial markets has been noted in the context of Asian financial crisis by an IMF staff report (1998), which cites lack of transparency as a possible contributor to the crisis. "Problems resulting from the limited availability of data and a lack of transparency, both of which hindered market participants from taking a realistic view of economic fundamentals" (Sundaresan, 2009, p. 88).

Mohanty and Kumar Rishabh (BIS, 2016, p. 6) highlight how financial intermediation through debt markets has increased sharply and a large part of that intermediation has moved offshore. Further, they add: "what is striking is that EME non-financial corporations have sharply increased their international debt issuance which registered a more than three-fold expansion between 2008 and 2013. Again, Asia seems to be leading the EMEs".

In view of the above mentioned recent developments – as well as changes in financial intermediation, the rise of shadow banking – and offshore activities, the importance of enhanced transparency cannot be over emphasized.

The above results do not only demonstrate the impact of stock market liquidity on capital markets, but also their significance in the growth and development of financial and capital markets.

ISSUES, CONTROVERSIES, PROBLEMS

Impact of current financial regulations on financial markets liquidity as highlighted by PWC, Global Markets Liquidity Study (2015, p. 35):

- Since the financial crisis, policymakers have introduced new regulations designed to: improve banks' capital and liquidity positions, improve market infrastructure and capital market transparency, restrict certain activities that may be undertaken by financial institutions, and ensure the resolvability of financial institutions.
- The suite of regulatory reforms across banking and capital markets has undoubtedly led to a more resilient banking industry. However, these reforms do not necessarily improve financial markets liquidity. For certain financial market activities, this may have been intended, but broader, presumably unanticipated, reductions in financial markets liquidity may have been deeper than intended.
- Financial markets liquidity has been affected by a combination of bank deleveraging and shrinkage in capital-intensive businesses, reduction in market making activity and complete exits of other market activities, shifts in trading patterns, liquidity contraction in repo markets, and the demand for and hoarding of liquid assets.

Table 1. Factors influencing financial markets development

Factors	Manner in which factors influence financial markets development
1. Regulatory framework	Corporate governance
	Investor protection
	Disclosure requirements
	Insider trading
	Market surveillance
	Underwriting standards/bank supervision
2. Fiscal and exchange rate policies	Captive (nationalised) banks to hold debt
	Auctions to sell sovereign debt – government benchmarks – active
	Primary and secondary government bond markets
	Controlled exchange rates
3. Legal framework and bankruptcy code	Integrity of contract enforcement
	Transparent ownership of assets such as residential and commercial properties
	Bankruptcy code that leads to efficient outcome in financial distress and provides correct incentives ex-ante. This can have huge consequences for the development of corporate bond markets
4. Trade patterns	An export-oriented economy has greater incentives to access and develop foreign currency debt instruments
	An economy driven by domestic consumption may have innovative and informal credit markets to tap pools of local currency capital
5. Infrastructure for trading and intermediation	Developing settlement and clearing systems
	National and international standards for accounting/auditing statements
	Developing and enforcing standards for investment advisors and other intermediaries
6. Access to global issuers and investors	Access to global issuers allows foreign currency markets to develop within the country
	Access to global investors generates global portfolio flows that move in and out of the country
7. Incentives for financial innovation	Light touch regulation tends to promote innovation as well as excessive risk-taking
	Tough regulation can lead to stagnant financial markets

- The impact on financial markets liquidity is compounded across regulatory reforms. In addition, the lack of regulatory equivalence across jurisdictions is increasing the complexity and the costs of complying with regulations. So, while reform assessments are usually undertaken at the individual reform level, market participants are making commercial responses across all reforms. This means the aggregate impact can be far greater than apparent from individual reforms.

It is also highlighted that regulation is a key driver of financial market liquidity (see p. 35 & 152); see also Table 1. Further it is accentuated that although the impact of structural reforms on capital markets liquidity will not be immediate, it is likely to be considerable (PWC, Global Markets Liquidity Study 2015, p. 47): The removal of proprietary trading removes one portion of market trading activity. Further, the regulatory risk of some inventories being requalified, together with strong governance requirements, will also drive down trading inventories. The separation of retail and trading activities will put commercial pressure on the funding and capital costs for the separated trading entities, further constraining market making activities (PWC, Global Markets Liquidity Study 2015, page 47 of 152).

Table 2. Global liquidity: credit aggregates

	Amount Outstanding (USD trn)			Annual Percentage Change		
	Q1 15	**Q2 15**	**Q3 15**	**Q1 15**	**Q2 15**	**Q3 15**
International bank credit						
Claims on banks	18.2	17.9	17.5	1.7	–1.0	–2.5
Claims on non-banks	14.4	14.3	14.3	3.8	2.2	1.7
Total bank credit						
All countries						
Local claims	88.3	89.0	90.3	7.7	6.8	6.9
Cross-border claims	8.9	8.6	8.6	9.9	4.4	3.0
Advanced economies						
United States						
Local claims	19.0	19.0	19.0	6.0	4.6	2.9
Cross-border claims	2.6	2.5	2.5	3.7	1.0	2.5
Euro area						
Local claims	17.2	16.7	16.9	1.5	0.0	–0.1
Cross -border claims	2.9	2.7	2.7	14.0	5.0	3.2
Emerging market economies (EMEs)						
Asia-Pacific						
Local claims	24.4	25.1	25.6	10.6	10.4	10.2
Cross-border claims	0.6	0.6	0.6	12.8	6.5	1.1
Latin America						

continued on following page

Table 2. Continued

	Amount Outstanding (USD trn)			Annual Percentage Change		
	Q1 15	Q2 15	Q3 15	Q1 15	Q2 15	Q3 15
Local claims	2.6	2.5	2.5	11.2	10.3	10.7
Cross-border claims	0.3	0.3	0.3	7.0	6.7	3.6
Emerging Europe						
Local claims	0.8	0.8	0.8	–0.2	3.4	3.2
Cross-border claims	0.1	0.1	0.1	–9.2	–8.5	–6.7
Global credit						
US dollar credit						
To US residents (non-financial sector)	43.1	43.5	43.8	4.0	4.0	3.4
Of which: government	17.4	17.5	17.5	3.2	3.0	1.9
To non-residents (non-bank sector)	9.7	9.8	9.8	6.6	6.7	4.7
Bank lending	5.3	5.3	5.3	4.5	4.6	2.2
Debt securities	4.4	4.5	4.5	9.2	9.3	7.7
Of which: non-financial sector	2.5	2.5	2.5	8.9	8.0	6.4
Memo: To EMEs (non-bank sector)	3.3	3.4	3.3	5.4	5.3	3.9
Euro credit						
To euro area residents (non-financial sector)	30.0	29.5	29.8	4.1	1.2	2.1
Of which: government	12.8	12.4	12.5	8.5	1.8	2.0
To non-residents (non-bank sector)	2.7	2.7	2.7	11.3	9.0	7.4
Bank lending	1.3	1.2	1.2	10.3	3.6	1.0
Debt securities	1.4	1.5	1.5	12.2	13.9	13.1
Of which: non-financial sector	1.0	1.0	1.0	13.7	15.1	15.0
Japanese yen credit						
To Japanese residents (non-financial sector)	16.2	16.2	16.2	2.7	1.7	1.7
Of which: government	9.7	9.8	9.7	4.1	2.7	2.6
To non-residents (non-bank sector)	0.5	0.5	0.5	0.6	–0.5	–4.7
Bank lending	0.3	0.3	0.3	3.7	2.9	–2.7
Debt securities	0.2	0.2	0.2	–5.4	–7.2	–8.4
Of which: non-financial sector	0.1	0.1	0.1	–9.3	–12.9	–13.5

Sources: IMF, *International Financial Statistics*; Datastream; BIS debt securities statistics; BIS locational banking statistics; BIS calculations.

Source: Bank for International Settlements *6 March 2016*

Table 3. Covered banks and activities under the Volcker Rule

Nature of prohibition or requirement	Type of financial institution	Covered activities	Exempt activities
Proprietary Trading 1/	U.S. licensed depositories, affiliates, parents, holding, companies, wherever located; U.S. branches/subsidiaries of non-U.S. banks	Short-term buy-to-resell or arbitrage Transactions subject to market-risk capital charge Broker-dealer desks transactions	Market making; Underwriting; Risk hedging, including liquidity management; Repo, reverse repo, and securities lending; Client facing transactions; Trading of U.S. government, state, municipal, federal agency, and GSE debt

Non-U.S. banking units Any of the above, if of non-U.S. banks transacted with U.S. residents, using U.S. personnel, or on U.S. execution facilities.

All of the above, plus all proprietary trading if not transacted with U.S residents, not using U.S. personnel nor U.S. execution facilities.

Source: U.S. Treasury (2011). Notes: 1/ All transactions of covered banks' broker-dealer desks are prohibited, except for direct trading of loans and spot market transactions in commodities and foreign exchange.

Pro Cyclical Effects Which Usually Result from Credit Booms: Preceding Financial Crises

Financial crises are generally considered to be often preceded by periods of booms or bust cycles. However, as argued by Murcia & Kohlscheen (2016, p. 2), credit expansions do not always imply future loan portfolio deterioration.

According to Murcia, and Kohlscheen (2016, p. 5), bank behavior is said to be procyclical if the relationship between provisions and credit growth or GDP growth is negative. Further they add that, during good times, when credit and incomes are increasing, provisions tend to fall – and in contrast, during bad times, provisions tend to increase as losses materialize.

Whilst the principal issue with Basel II related to procyclicality, Basel III generates further concerns in matters relating to the shifting of supply and demand. As highlighted by the Committee on the Global Financial System Markets Committee (BIS, 2015, p. 7), absent a binding leverage ratio requirement, a bank would generally be indifferent to the choice between keeping cash at the central bank or lending it out via repo (using government securities) at the same rate as these two transactions are both free of a capital charge. Yet, the bank would charge a higher rate to lend the cash in the unsecured money market, not only because of the greater credit risk, but also because unsecured transactions would require more capital (see p. 7).

As concluded by the Committee on the Global Financial System Markets Committee, a consequence of this would be other things being equal, a reduced demand

Table 4. Potential effects of the Volcker Rule on EMDEs

What is affected	Who is affected	Where is the direct impact
Proprietary trading of EMDE sovereign and corporate debt	Covered U.S. banks	Liquidity in EMDE sovereign and corporate debt markets
Curtailing of activities arising from restrictions on their dealings with U.S. counterparties	Covered non-U.S. banks	Liquidity in EMDE sovereign and corporate debt markets
Proprietary trading of EMDE government securities	EMDE affiliates of covered U.S. and non-U.S. banks	Liquidity in local EMDE government securities markets
Restriction on the ability to execute or clear proprietary trading on U.S. infrastructure	Covered non-U.S. banks	Execution of international trades moving away from the United States
Market making inadvertedly affected	Covered U.S. and non-U.S. banks	Liquidity in EMDE capital markets
Stringent requirements on payments and settlements	Covered U.S. and non-U.S. banks as counterparties	Limited access to covered banks by EMDE banks
Failure to prove trading activities as market making activities	Covered affiliates of U.S. and non-U.S. banks	Principal dealer status in EMDEs
Differentiation between market making and proprietary trading	Covered U.S. and non-U.S. banks	Reporting requirements for EMDE affiliates
Reporting compliance	Covered U.S. and non-U.S. banks	Establishment of a wide array of programs, policies, procedures, and information structures for compliance purposes Exemptions for market-making and hedging activities leading to misreporting

Source Financial Stability Board, (2012). Identifying the Effects of Regulatory Reforms on Emerging Market and Developing Economies page 33

For comprehensive information on the indirect effects of the Volcker Rule on EMDEs, see Financial Stability Board, (2012). Identifying the Effects of Regulatory Reforms on Emerging Market and Developing Economies page 33

for cash in the money market (and for secured transactions relative to unsecured ones), pushing down on rates.

SOLUTIONS AND RECOMMENDATIONS

As highlighted by Murcia, and Kohlscheen (2016, p. 6), and in response to addressing pro cyclical effects which usually result from credit booms – preceding financial crises, banks can smooth their earnings by drawing from loan loss reserves if actual losses exceed expected losses and by increasing loan loss provisions in the opposite case – the advantage of this behavior being that it can reduce the volatility of reported bank profits, reducing the need to draw on capital in adverse times.

Focus on how to address and prevent further cyclical generating crises – as well as addressing root causes of the volatility to which EMEs are more susceptible – in the face of monetary policy changes, as well as regulatory reforms, are recommended as areas in need of greater attention.

FUTURE RESEARCH DIRECTIONS

According to Jeanneau (2007, p. 9):

The banking sector in EMEs has traditionally been a highly protected industry. However, global competitive forces and banking crises in the 1990s forced market participants and the authorities to deregulate the industry and open it to domestic non-banks and foreign intermediaries. The removal of restrictions, such as ceilings on deposit rates, has led to a progressive switch to market-based monetary policy techniques that have made it easier for central banks to signal their intentions, guide the economy and better respond to shocks (Archer (2006)). It has also been a catalyst for stronger market competition and efficiency (Hawkins and Mihaljek (2001)). However, the process of deregulation has been followed in many countries by major banking crises. Poor bank management and supervision encouraged a rapid expansion of credit which was ultimately followed by mounting loan losses, an erosion of bank capital and an eventual collapse of financial institutions (Kaminsky and Reinhart (1999) and Demirgüç-Kunt and Detragiache (2005)).

In view of their role as drivers of economic growth, the current slowdown in the pace of growth of emerging market economies, has also impacted the global economy. As a result, it is worth directing future research which would facilitate a redress of the present challenges encountered by emerging market economies in response to regulatory reforms – issues which include poor bank management and supervision.

CONCLUSION

This chapter – as well as its predecessor have highlighted the challenges currently faced by emerging market economies in coping with regulatory reforms – as well as central bank policies – in contrast to their more advanced counterparts. Do stock markets and the banking sector serve as complements rather than substitutes – even at various stages of the evolution? History has revealed that even though the banking sector – as well as capital markets are essential components and vehicles for economic development in any economy, financial crises – resulting from debt or triggered by a failure of operating policies, or otherwise, have always served to obstruct the progress and potential that could ultimately be derived where the banking sector and capital markets complement and enhance each component's activities. Whilst it is argued that the banking sector competes with the investment sector, it cannot be denied that a failure in one system ultimately affects optimal operation of the other.

How does commercial banking impact investment activities in capital markets – and particularly developed capital markets? Is it true then that in certain economies, the banking sector serves as a complementary component of the financial system – up till a stage where it begins to compete with the securities sector?

These are questions which the final chapter of the volume - which deals exclusively with stock market development, hopes to consolidate on. In particular, it illustrates how and why growth in the nonbanking sectors, have accelerated over the years – with the result that detrimental consequences within capital markets also strongly impact the banking sector.

REFERENCES

Amihud, Y.; Mendelson, H. & Pedersen, L., (2005). *Liquidity and Asset Prices*. Foundations and Trends in Finance.

Bacidore, J. (1997). The Impact of Decimalization on Market Quality: An Empirical Investigation of the Toronto Stock Exchange. *Journal of Financial Intermediation*, *6*(2), 92–120. doi:10.1006/jfin.1997.0213

Bank for International Settlements. (2007). Evolving banking systems in Latin America and the Caribbean: challenges and implications for monetary policy and financial stability.

Bank for International Settlements. (2014). 84th Annual Report.

Bank for International Settlements. (2015). CGFS Papers No 54 Regulatory change and monetary policy.

Barclay, M., Christie, W., Harris, J., Kandel, E., & Schultz, P. (1999). Effects of Market Reform on the Trading Costs and Depths of NASDAQ Stocks. *The Journal of Finance*, *54*(1), 1–34. doi:10.1111/0022-1082.00097

Barclay, M., Hendershott, T., & McCormick, T. (2003). Competition Among Trading Venues: Information and Trading on Electronic Communications Networks. *The Journal of Finance*, *58*(6), 2637–2666. doi:10.1046/j.1540-6261.2003.00618.x

Baumol, J.W. (1960). The Stock Market and Economic Efficiency. New York: Furham University Press.

Bhattacharya, U., & Spiegel, M. (1998). Anatomy of a Market Failure: NYSE Trading Suspensions (1974-1988). *Journal of Business & Economic Statistics*, *16*, 216–222.

Bikker, J., & Metzemakers, P. (2005). Bank provisioning behaviour and procyclicality. *Journal of International Financial Markets, Institutions and Money*, *15*(2), 141–157. doi:10.1016/j.intfin.2004.03.004

Cavallo, M., & Majnoni, G. (2002). Do banks provision for bad loans in good times? Empirical evidence and policy implications. In R. Levich, G. Majnoni, & C. Reinhart (Eds.), *Ratings, rating agencies and the global financial system*. Kluwer Academic Publishers. doi:10.1007/978-1-4615-0999-8_19

Chordia, T., & Ball, C. (2001). True Spreads and Equilibrium Prices. *The Journal of Finance*, *56*(5), 1801–1836. doi:10.1111/0022-1082.00390

Chordia, T., Roll, R., & Subrahmanyam, A. (2000). Commonality in Liquidity. *Journal of Financial Economics*, *56*(1), 3–28. doi:10.1016/S0304-405X(99)00057-4

Chordia, T., Sarkar, A., & Subrahmanyam, A. (2001). Common Determinants of Bond and Stock Market Liquidity: The Impact of Financial Crises.

Demirguc-Kunt, A., & Levine, R. (1996). Stock Markets, Corporate Finance and Economic Growth: An Overview. *The World Bank Economic Review*, *10*(2), 223–239. doi:10.1093/wber/10.2.223

El-Erian, M., & Kumar, M. S. (1995, February 16–17). Emerging Stock Markets in Middle Eastern Countries. *Paper presented at the World Bank Conference on Stock Markets, Corporate Finance and Economic Growth*, Washington DC.

Financial Stability Board. (2012). Identifying the Effects of Regulatory Reforms on Emerging Market and Developing Economies: A Review of Potential Unintended Consequences. Report to the G20 Finance Ministers and Central Bank Governors.

Garcia, F. V., & Liu, L. (1999). Macroeconomic Determinants of Stock Market Development. *Journal of Applied Econometrics*, *2*(1), 29–59.

Kohlscheen, E., & Miyajima, K. (2015). The transmission of monetary policy in EMEs in a changing financial environment: A longitudinal analysis. BIS Working Papers.

Kohlscheen, E., & Rungcharoenkitkul, P. (2015). Changing financial intermediation: implications for monetary policy transmission. BIS Papers.

La Porta, R., Lopez-de-Silanes, F., Shleifer, A., & Vishny, R. (1996). Law and Finance. NBER.

Mihaljek, D., Scatigna, M. & Villar, A. (2002). Recent Trends in Bond Markets BIS Papers.

Mohanty, M.S., & Rishabh, K. (2016). Financial intermediation and monetary policy transmission in EMEs: What has changed post-2008 crisis? BIS Working Papers.

Nakaso, h. (2016, March 3). Japan's Economy and Monetary policy (Speech). Bank of Japan business leaders meeting, Okinawa.

Pagano, M. (1993). Financial Markets and Growth: An Overview. *European Economic Review*, *37*(2-3), 613–622. doi:10.1016/0014-2921(93)90051-B

PWC. (2015, August). Global Markets Liquidity Study.

Rossi, S. (2016). The launch of Solvency II – the implementation of the new regime: open issues, implications for business models, and effects on institutional and financial communication/ Keynote address by Mr Salvatore Rossi, Senior Deputy Governor of the Bank of Italy and President of IVASS (Istituto per la Vigilanza sulle Assicurazioni), at the IVASS Conference 2016, Rome, 3 March 2016.

Sheel, A., & Ganguly, M. (2016). Financial Regulatory Reforms – A Mid Term Assessment from an Emerging Market Perspective. In R. Kathuria, N.K. Nagpal, (Eds.), Global Economic Cooperation. Springer Verlag.

Sundaresan, S. (2009). *Development of financial markets in Asia and the Pacific: the international financial crisis and policy challenges*. BIS Papers.

Wuyts, G. (2007). Stock Market Liquidity. *Determinants and Implications Tijdschrift voor Economie en Management*, *LII*(2), 2007.

Yartey, C. A. (2007). Macroeconomic and Institutional Determinants of Stock Market Development in Africa. In J. Okpara (Ed.), *Management and Economic Development in Sub-Saharan Africa: Theoretical and Applied Perspectives*. London: Adonis and Abbey Publishers.

Yartey, C. A., (2008). The Determinants of Stock Market Development in Emerging Economies: Is South Africa Different? IMF.

Chapter 10
The Determinants of Stock Market Development and Liquidity in Capital Markets

Sarah Newton
University of Kent, UK

Ingrid O'Connor
University of Cardiff, UK

ABSTRACT

"At the early stages of its establishment the stock market is a complement rather than substitute for the banking sector. Developing the banking sector can promote stock market development as demonstrated by the experiences of many East Asian countries. However, when stock markets are sufficiently developed they tend to compete with the banking sector as shown by findings." How does commercial banking impact investment activities in capital markets – and particularly developed capital markets? Is it true then that in certain economies, the banking sector serves as a complementary component of the financial system – up till a stage where it begins to compete with the securities sector? As well as investigating these observations, this chapter is aimed at investigating the validity of Efficient Markets Hypothesis and Efficient Capital Markets Hypothesis in emerging economies – as contrasted with advanced market economies. In so doing, it aims to contribute to the extant literature on stock market liquidity and liquidity in capital markets.

DOI: 10.4018/978-1-5225-1900-3.ch010

Copyright ©2017, IGI Global. Copying or distributing in print or electronic forms without written permission of IGI Global is prohibited.

INTRODUCTION

How does commercial banking impact investment activities in capital markets – and particularly developed capital markets? Is it true then that in certain economies, the banking sector serves as a complementary component of the financial system – up till a stage where it begins to compete with the securities sector?

At the early stages of its establishment the stock market is a complement rather than substitute for the banking sector. Developing the banking sector can promote stock market development as demonstrated by the experiences of many East Asian countries. Support services from the banking system contribute significantly to the development of the stock market. However, when stock markets are sufficiently developed they tend to compete with the banking sector as shown by our findings. (Yartey, 2008)

As well as investigating these observations, the chapter will amongst other objectives, aim to contribute to the extant literature on whether capital markets in emerging markets economies, in particular, fully reflect information - hence demonstrating and highlighting the validity of the Efficient Markets Hypothesis (as well as the Efficient Capital Markets Hypothesis.

Other objectives of the chapter are as follows:

1. To investigate the extent to which accounting information can be relied upon based on given market values and whether a relationship or pattern can be established in certain jurisdictions based on given operating variables which function in such economies.
2. To demonstrate and highlight the validity of the Efficient Markets Hypothesis (as well as the Efficient Capital Markets Hypothesis)
3. To demonstrate how accounting information can serve as a useful and vital indicator which will enable investors to interpret financial information in such a way which mitigates information asymmetries between management and investors
4. To highlight those areas and factors which influence the quality of accounting information - and which must be addressed by markets if the audit is to achieve its intended aims and functions
5. To highlight whether accounting reforms undertaken in investigated jurisdictions actually achieved their desired goals of improving the quality of accounting information and if such reforms were not successful, to propose measures which could address the current issues being faced by such jurisdictions.

BACKGROUND AND LITERATURE REVIEW

According to PWC, Global Markets Liquidity Study (2015, page 105 of 152):

- Regulations yet to be implemented, such as FRTB, MiFID II, the US G-SIB surcharge, EU bank structural reform and FTT, if inappropriately calibrated, will have a significant impact on the viability of dealers' market-making activities and increase transaction costs for capital markets participants.
- These reforms are likely to have extra-territorial impacts beyond Europe and the US. Although the majority of recently-proposed or implemented reforms originate in Europe and the US, regulators in other parts of the world may follow suit with similar reforms, which will directly affect market participants based in other regions.

Three developments which in PWC's view "could improve financial markets liquidity in a sub-set of asset classes" are as follows: Firstly, the growth of exchange-traded funds (ETFs) – which they conclude, provides investors with a more tradeable instrument for investment, in the absence of directly investing in the underlying asset, which may not be as liquid.

Second,

- More widespread uptake of electronic trading which could further reduce transaction costs for market participants by providing additional platforms to match buyers and sellers.

Such platforms, they add, will, in some cases, help reduce the time required to locate buyers and sellers and improve the process of price discovery and they also argue that although electronic trading platforms have seen growth in recent years, they do not replace liquidity provision by dealers - in particular the ability to bear proprietary risk and thereby provide immediacy.

Lastly, they state that the retreat of banks from financial markets has also been accompanied by the entrance or growth of other market participants taking on some principal risk-taking activities.

Size of Financial Intermediaries

Mohanty and Kumar Rishabh (BIS, 2016) argue that there has been growing evidence in recent years that the size and the structure of financial intermediation play a critical role in the transmission of monetary policy. Further they add that, the globalization of debt markets means that monetary policy can no longer be conducted through the short-term interest rate alone.

In their report (BIS, 2016:2), they highlight the fact that the introduction of inflation targeting by many EMEs in the 1990s, together with reforms to abolish interest rate controls, to strengthen central bank credibility and to develop local bond markets, had marked a major turning point for monetary policy in many countries. Further, they add that these reforms had helped not only to reduce earlier constraints on monetary policy stemming from a high degree of fiscal dominance and liability dollarization but also to increase the role of interest and exchange rates in monetary policy transmission, leading to an environment of low and stable inflation.

Based on reports by Murcia and Kohlscheen (BIS, 2016: 15,16) evidence is found that bank-specific earnings and the size of the intermediaries have an effect on provisions:

- The level of provisions and actual losses are negatively related to lagged economic growth and positively related to lagged aggregate credit growth. At least at the country level, EME banks seem to move in tandem.
- The strong negative relationship between GDP growth and provisioning clearly points to pro cyclical behavior on the part of EME banks.
- There is greater uncertainty about business cycle patterns in EMEs, as well as greater exposure to terms of trade shocks, which are often hard to anticipate. In other words, banks in EMEs may face a more challenging signal extraction problem than their advanced economy counterparts, which is then reflected in their provisioning behavior.
- The results of their BIS report suggest that the design of macro prudential policies based on simple aggregate indicators could be instrumental in smoothing credit cycles. Further, they add that early indications from EMEs that have enacted regulation for dynamic provisioning suggests this may have reduced the procyclicality of banking provisions and increased the effectiveness of provisions as buffers for future losses.

Whilst Kohlscheen and Miyajima (2015) argue that financial systems in EMEs tend to be more bank-oriented, Mohanty and Kumar Rishabh (BIS, 2016) add that even though, historically, banks have been at the centre of financial intermediation in EMEs – the environment in which monetary policy is conducted in EMEs has undergone a major transformation over the past decade (see page 4).

However Kohlscheen, and Rungcharoenkitkul (2015): "Changing financial intermediation: implications for monetary policy transmission", BIS Papers, no 83 also add that:

- Changes in financial intermediation may, first of all, affect monetary policy via the equilibrium or neutral interest rate in the economy;
- Changes in financial intermediation may also have cyclical implications for monetary policy.

They also re iterate the continued importance and prominent role assumed by banks (see page 67).

In order to review potential effects of recent changes in financial intermediation on the transmission mechanism, three channels are taken into account by Mohanty & Kumar Rishabh (BIS, 2016:10), namely the interest rate, exchange rate and credit channels.

As regards post crisis financial changes, Mohanty and Kumar Rishabh (BIS, 2016:17), by reference to companies (Chui et al (2016), add that since 2010, currency mismatches in many emerging markets have increased – notably because of a substantial increase in foreign currency borrowing by emerging market non-financial companies.

They conclude (see page 30) that the globalisation of debt markets, together with a sharp decline in the global long-term interest rate and the accumulation of large dollar debts by EME non-financial corporations, have complicated the transmission mechanism of monetary policy in many countries.

Issues, Controversies, Problems

Threats to Banking Development and New Forms of Risks

According to the BIS Report for Evolving banking systems in Latin America and the Caribbean: challenges and implications for monetary policy and financial stability (BIS, 2007:17)

- Macroeconomic imbalances and external shocks appear to be main sources of banking sector fragility. However, in smaller economies important macroeconomic risks may result from a lack of economic diversification, making the banking systems of these countries highly dependent on the fortunes of the main sectors of the economy and, therefore, even more vulnerable to external shocks than in larger economies.

Such risks and contagion affecting the banking system, and possibly the financial system as a whole include credit risks, liquidity risks, market risks and currency risk. The evolving nature of risks – as well as the rise of the shadow banking system all contribute to the likelihood that the detection and prevention of more sophisticated and complex forms of risks – particularly those associated with derivatives, will be identified or easily controlled.

As highlighted in the previous section, and according to Kohlscheen & Miyajima (2015:6), financial systems in EMEs tend to be much more bank-oriented so in their view, developments within this sector typically have larger macroeconomic effects when compared with advanced economies. Further, they add that the pro cyclicality of the financial sector may deserve particular attention in emerging market economies, which often exhibit larger macroeconomic volatility due to less diversified economic structures and greater exposure to capital flow reversals. Moreover, they argue, in the recent past, credit growth in EMEs has been much higher than in advanced economies.

Between 2009 and 2014, annual credit growth in the EMEs considered in their study (see Murcia, A. & Kohlscheen, E. (2016:8) and according to their reports: averaged 8.1% in real terms, compared with only 0.5% in the G7 economies. In their view, these factors, taken together, suggest that a systematic evaluation of the long-term effects of credit growth on the financial health indicators of EME banks is currently of special interest.

Figure 1. Price hikes by firms the share of price-increasing items minus the share of price-decreasing items in the CPI in the Japanese economy
Sources of Charts: BIS Central Bank Speeches. Nakaso, N. (2016). Japan's Economy and Monetary policy. Speech by Mr Hiroshi Nakaso, Deputy Governor of the Bank of Japan, at a meeting with business leaders, Okinawa, 3 March 2016.

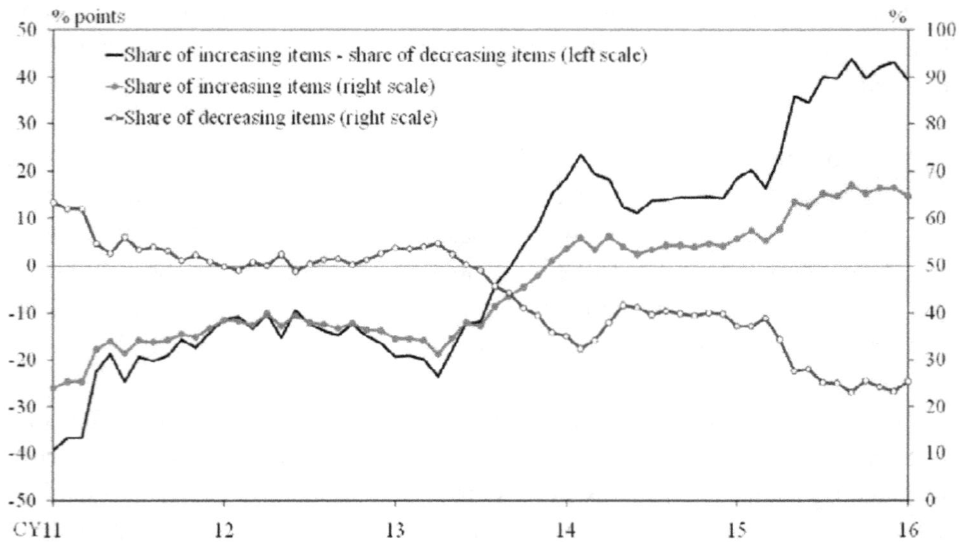

Figure 2. Reflecting outlook for major economies
Sources of Charts: BIS Central Bank Speeches. Nakaso, N. (2016). Japan's Economy and Monetary policy. Speech by Mr Hiroshi Nakaso, Deputy Governor of the Bank of Japan, at a meeting with business leaders, Okinawa, 3 March 2016.

Real GDP Growth Rate

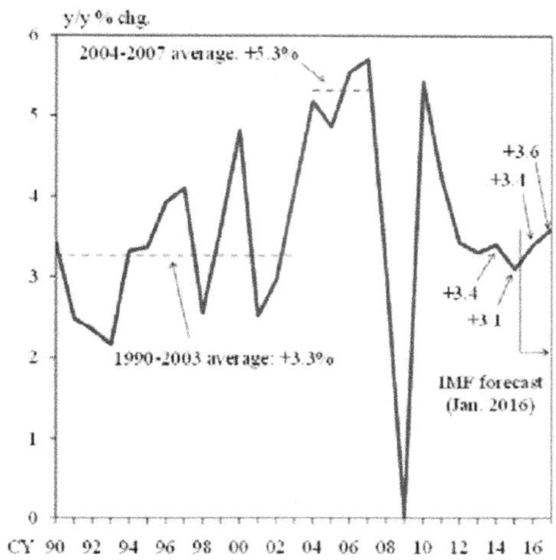

Projections for Major Economies

y/y % chg.

	2014	2015	Projections 2016	Projections 2017
World	3.4	3.1	3.4	3.6
Advanced Economies	1.8	1.9	2.1	2.1
United States	2.4	2.5	2.6	2.6
Euro Area	0.9	1.5	1.7	1.7
Japan	0.0	0.6	1.0	0.3
Emerging Market and Developing Economies	4.6	4.0	4.3	4.7
China	7.3	6.9	6.3	6.0
ASEAN5	4.6	4.7	4.8	5.1

Figure 3. Projections for the Chinese economy
Sources of Charts: BIS Central Bank Speeches. Nakaso, N. (2016). Japan's Economy and Monetary policy. Speech by Mr Hiroshi Nakaso, Deputy Governor of the Bank of Japan, at a meeting with business leaders, Okinawa, 3 March 2016.

(1) Manufacturing PMI *(2) Real GDP Growth Rate*

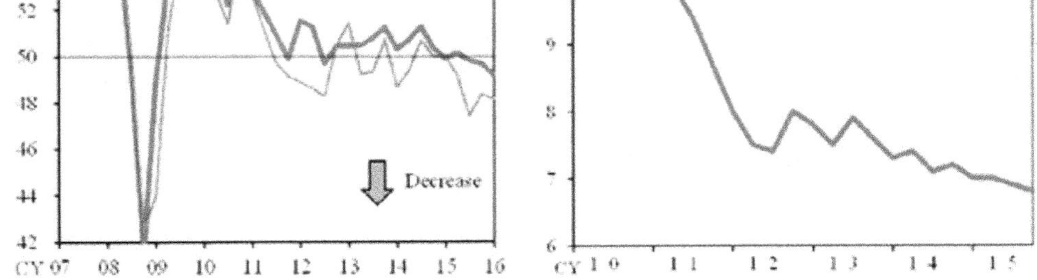

Figure 4. Qualitative and quantitative monetary easing
Sources of Charts: BIS Central Bank Speeches. Nakaso, N. (2016). Japan's Economy and Monetary policy. Speech by Mr Hiroshi Nakaso, Deputy Governor of the Bank of Japan, at a meeting with business leaders, Okinawa, 3 March 2016.

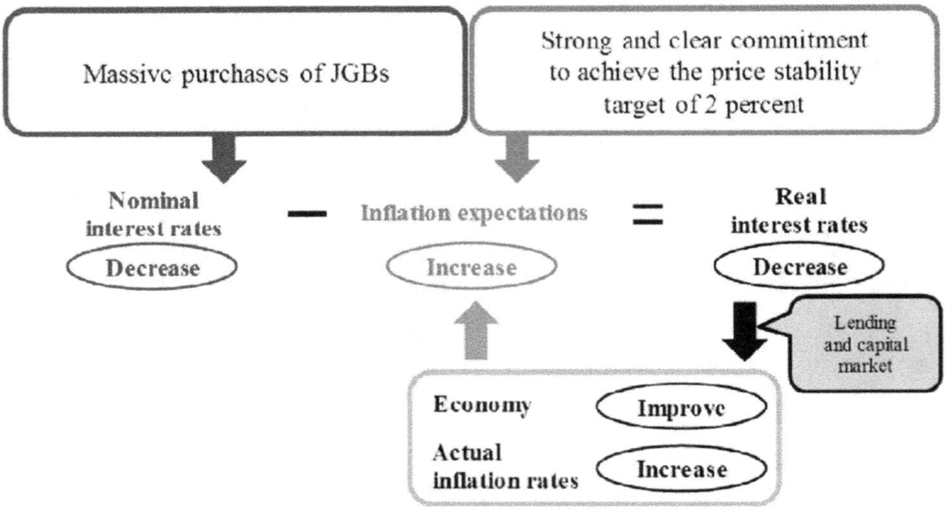

FUTURE RESEARCH DIRECTIONS

In view of changing financial intermediation in a changing financial environment, and the emergence of new forms of more sophisticated and complex risks which notably include liquidity risks, future research directions should embrace determinants of future financial markets liquidity as well as greater focus on the impact of the increase in the size of financial markets.

CONCLUSION

Having considered the impacts of banking on global financial developments – as well as the changing financial intermediation environment – with the nonbanking sector assuming prominence in recent years, and the rise of shadow banking activities, some reference needs to be made to the insurance sector.

As highlighted by Salvatore Rossi (2016),

Understanding the trends and the challenges behind the current state of affairs in the insurance market should be a common endeavor for regulators/supervisors

Figure 5. Yield curve

Sources of Charts: BIS Central Bank Speeches. Nakaso, N. (2016). Japan's Economy and Monetary policy. Speech by Mr Hiroshi Nakaso, Deputy Governor of the Bank of Japan, at a meeting with business leaders, Okinawa, 3 March 2016.

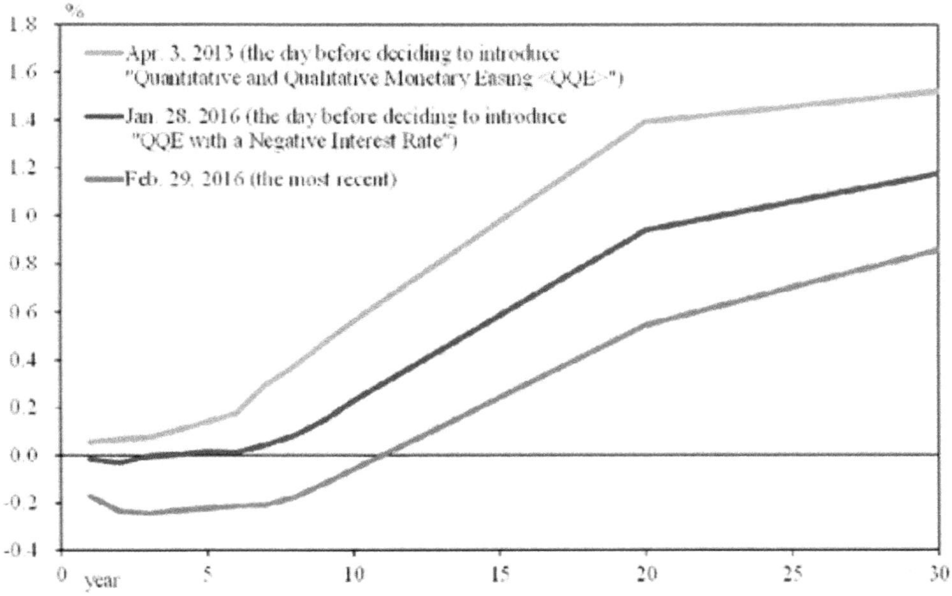

Figure 6. Inflation expectations

Sources of Charts: BIS Central Bank Speeches. Nakaso, N. (2016). Japan's Economy and Monetary policy. Speech by Mr Hiroshi Nakaso, Deputy Governor of the Bank of Japan, at a meeting with business leaders, Okinawa, 3 March 2016.

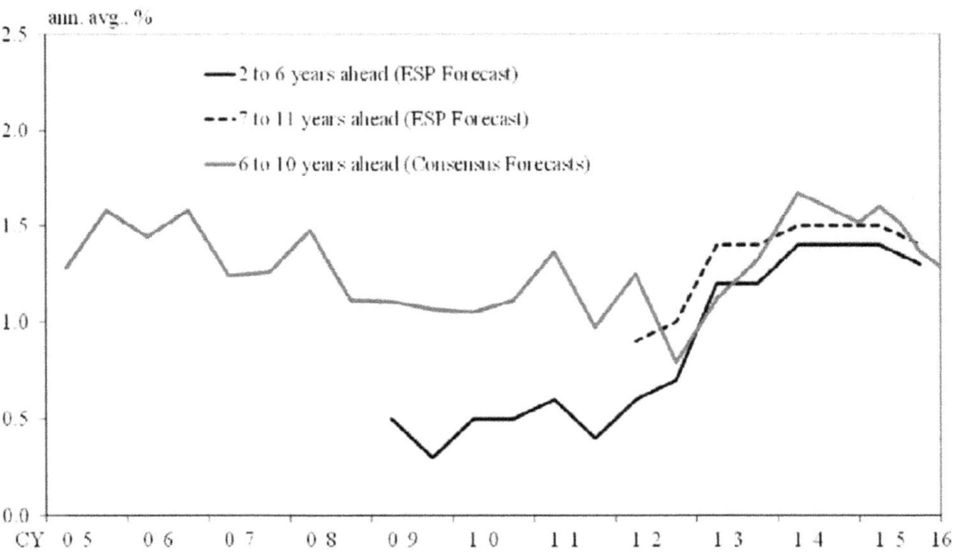

Figure 7. Three tier system
Sources of Charts: BIS Central Bank Speeches. Nakaso, N. (2016). Japan's Economy and Monetary policy. Speech by Mr Hiroshi Nakaso, Deputy Governor of the Bank of Japan, at a meeting with business leaders, Okinawa, 3 March 2016.

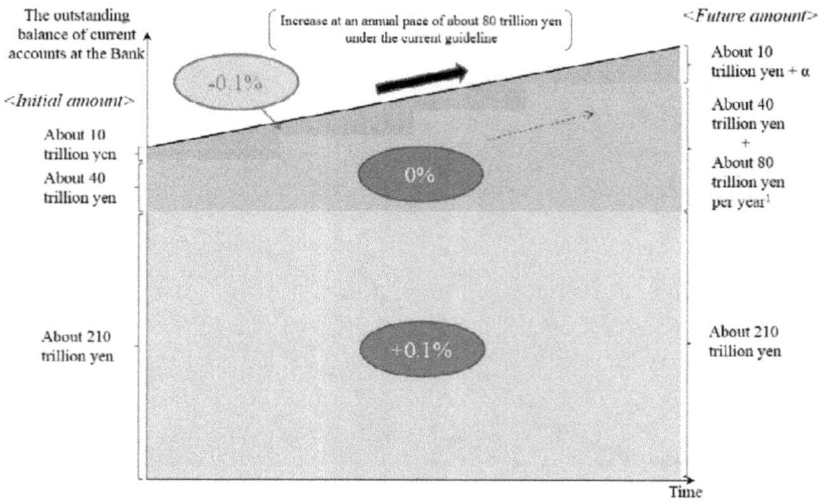

Figure 8. Negative interest rate policies in Europe
Sources of Charts: BIS Central Bank Speeches. Nakaso, N. (2016). Japan's Economy and Monetary policy. Speech by Mr Hiroshi Nakaso, Deputy Governor of the Bank of Japan, at a meeting with business leaders, Okinawa, 3 March 2016.

	Euro area	Denmark	Switzerland	Sweden
Policy rate	Rate on deposit facility, etc.	Certificates of deposit rate	Swiss franc Libor (3M)	Repo rate[1]
Timing when the decision was made	June 2014	July 2012 September 2014	December 2014	February 2015
Central bank's debt to which interest is applied, and its rate	Minimum reserve: 0.05% Deposit facility, etc.: -0.3%	Current account deposit Under or at the limit: 0% Over the limit[2]: -0.65%	Current account deposit Under or at the limit: 0% Over the limit: -0.75%	Main operation with the certificates: -0.5% Fine-tuning operation: -0.6% Deposit facility: -1.25%

Table 1. Classification of financial markets

Type of financial markets	Clearing house and settlement guarantees	Marking to market and collateral	Secondary market liquidity	Customisation vs. standardisation	Market transparency
Centralised markets	√	√	Typically high	Highly standardised	Typically very high
OTC markets	X With some exceptions	X With some exceptions	Typically low	Can be customised to the needs of investors	Typically moderate to low
Private and less-regulated markets	X	X	Typically poor	Highly customised	Typically very poor

Source: Sundaresan (2009). Development of financial markets in Asia and the Pacific: the international financial crisis and policy challenges. BIS Papers No 52 page 89

and the industry. What is important is to keep moving ahead – step by step but constantly – towards the main goal: a forward-looking approach in assessing risks and vulnerabilities.

Furthermore the theme of harmonization and regulatory convergence resonates in that speech.

Do capital markets, particularly in emerging market economies, fully reflect information? In view of recent developments and changes in the financial intermediation environment, the rise of shadow banking and offshore activities, as well as nonbanking intermediation, and having highlighted concerns related to transparency, stock market liquidity in previous chapters, the answer appears apparent. This should also be viewed against the backdrop of pressures faced by emerging market economies in response to recent regulatory reforms and monetary policies.

REFERENCES

Acharya, V., & Naqvi, H. (2012). The seeds of a crisis: A theory of bank liquidity and risk-taking over the business cycle. *Journal of Financial Economics*, *106*(2), 345–366. doi:10.1016/j.jfineco.2012.05.014

Adrian, T., & Shin, H.S. (2010). Prices and quantities in the monetary policy transmission mechanism. Federal Reserve Bank of New York Staff Report.

Amador, J., Gómez-Gonzalez, J., & Murcia, A. (2013). Loan growth and bank risk: New evidence. *Financial Markets and Portfolio Management*, *27*(4), 365–379. doi:10.1007/s11408-013-0217-6

Amihud, Y.; Mendelson, H. & Pedersen, L. (2005). *Liquidity and Asset Prices.*

Bacidore, J. (1997). The Impact of Decimalization on Market Quality: An Empirical Investigation of the Toronto Stock Exchange. *Journal of Financial Intermediation*, *6*(2), 92–120. doi:10.1006/jfin.1997.0213

Bank for International Settlements. (2008). Transmission mechanisms for monetary policy in emerging market economies. BIS Papers.

Bank for International Settlements. (2014). The transmission of unconventional monetary policy to the emerging markets. BIS Papers.

Bank for International Settlements. (2015). What do new forms of finance mean for EM central banks? BIS Papers.

Barclay, M., Christie, W., Harris, J., Kandel, E., & Schultz, P. (1999). Effects of Market Reform on the Trading Costs and Depths of NASDAQ Stocks. *The Journal of Finance*, *54*(1), 1–34. doi:10.1111/0022-1082.00097

Barclay, M., Hendershott, T., & McCormick, T. (2003). Competition Among Trading Venues: Information and Trading on Electronic Communications Networks. *The Journal of Finance*, *58*(6), 2637–2666. doi:10.1046/j.1540-6261.2003.00618.x

Baumol, J.W. (1960). The Stock Market and Economic Efficiency. New York: Furham University Press.

Bhattacharya, U., & Spiegel, M. (1998). Anatomy of a Market Failure: NYSE Trading Suspensions (1974-1988). *Journal of Business & Economic Statistics*, *16*, 216–222.

Bikker, J., & Metzemakers, P. (2005). Bank provisioning behaviour and procyclicality. *Journal of International Financial Markets, Institutions and Money*, *15*(2), 141–157. doi:10.1016/j.intfin.2004.03.004

Borio, C, McCauley, R., & McGuire, P. (2011, September). Global credit and domestic credit booms. BIS Quarterly Review.

Cavallo, M., & Majnoni, G. (2002). Do banks provision for bad loans in good times? Empirical evidence and policy implications. In R. Levich, G. Majnoni, & C. Reinhart (Eds.), *Ratings, rating agencies and the global financial system*. Kluwer Academic Publishers. doi:10.1007/978-1-4615-0999-8_19

Chordia, T., & Ball, C. (2001). True Spreads and Equilibrium Prices. *The Journal of Finance*, *56*(5), 1801–1836. doi:10.1111/0022-1082.00390

Chordia, T., Roll, R., & Subrahmanyam, A. (2000). Commonality in Liquidity. *Journal of Financial Economics*, *56*(1), 3–28. doi:10.1016/S0304-405X(99)00057-4

Chordia, T., Sarkar, A., & Subrahmanyam, A. (2001). Common Determinants of Bond and Stock Market Liquidity: The Impact of Financial Crises, Monetary Policy, and Mutual Fund Flows.

Chui, M., Kuruc, E., & Turner, P. (2016). *Emerging market companies: currency mismatches, leverage and profitability*. Mimeo.

Demirguc-Kunt, A., & Levine, R. (1996). Stock Markets, Corporate Finance and Economic Growth: An Overview. *The World Bank Economic Review*, *10*(2), 223–239. doi:10.1093/wber/10.2.223

Ehlers, T., & Villar, A. (2015). The role of banks. BIS Papers.

Eichengreen, B. (2002). Can emerging markets float? Should they inflation target? Banco Central do Brasil Working Papers Series.

El-Erian, M., & Kumar, M. S. (1995, February 16–17). Emerging Stock Markets in Middle Eastern Countries. *Paper presented at theWorld Bank Conference on Stock Markets, Corporate Finance and Economic Growth*, Washington DC.

Executive Office of the President of the United States. (2015, July). Long-term interest rates: a survey.

Financial Stability Board. (2012). Identifying the Effects of Regulatory Reforms on Emerging Market and Developing Economies: A Review of Potential Unintended Consequences.

Gali, J., & Monacelli, T. (2005). Monetary policy and exchange rate volatility in a small open economy. *The Review of Economic Studies*, *72*(3), 707–734. doi:10.1111/j.1467-937X.2005.00349.x

Garcia, F. V., & Liu, L. (1999). Macroeconomic Determinants of Stock Market Development. *Journal of Applied Econometrics*, *2*(1), 29–59.

Genberg, H. (2008). The changing nature of financial intermediation and its implications for monetary policy. BIS Working Papers.

Kohlscheen, E., & Miyajima, K. (2015). The transmission of monetary policy in EMEs in a changing financial environment: A longitudinal analysis. BIS Working Papers.

Kohlscheen, E., & Rungcharoenkitkul, P. (2015). Changing financial intermediation: implications for monetary policy transmission. BIS Papers.

La Porta, R., Lopez-de-Silanes, F., Shleifer, A. & Vishny, R. (1996). Law and Finance. NBER.

Mohanty, M. (2014). Market volatility and foreign exchange intervention in EMEs: what has changed? BIS Papers.

Mohanty, M., & Turner, P. (2008). *Monetary policy transmission in emerging market economies: what has changed?* BIS Papers.

Mohanty, M.S., & Rishabh, K. (2016). Financial intermediation and monetary policy transmission in EMEs: What has changed post-2008 crisis? BIS Working Papers.

Murcia, A., & Kohlscheen, E. (2016, March). Moving in tandem: bank provisioning in emerging market economies BIS Working Papers.

Pagano, M. (1993). Financial Markets and Growth: An Overview. *European Economic Review*, *37*(2-3), 613–622. doi:10.1016/0014-2921(93)90051-B

PWC. (2015). Global Markets Liquidity Study August 2015

Rossi, S. (2016, March 3). The launch of Solvency II – the implementation of the new regime: open issues, implications for business models, and effects on institutional and financial communication (Keynote address). *Proceedings of the IVASS Conference '16*, Rome.

Sheel, A., & Ganguly, M. (2016). *Financial Regulatory Reforms – A Mid Term Assessment from an Emerging Market Perspective. In*R. Kathuria & N.K. Nagpal (Eds.), *Global Economic Cooperation, Views From G20 Countries* (Springer Verlag.

Shin, H.S. (2012, November 7). The second phase of global liquidity and its impact on emerging economies (Keynote address). *Proceedings of the Asia Economic Policy Conference*, Federal Reserve Bank of San Francisco.

Shin, H.S., & Turner, P. (2015). What does the new face of international financial intermediation mean for emerging market economies? Bank of France Financial Stability Review.

Singh, K., & Kalirajan, K. (2007). Monetary transmission in post-reform India: An evaluation. *Journal of the Asia Pacific Economy*, *12*(2), 158–187. doi:10.1080/13547860701252371

Sobrun, J., & Turner, P. (2015a). Bond markets and monetary policy dilemmas for emerging market economies. BIS Working Papers.

Turner, P. (2014). The long-term interest rate, financial risks and policy choices in EMEs. BIS Working Papers.

Wuyts, G. (2007). Stock Market Liquidity. *Determinants and Implications Tijdschrift voor Economie en Management, LII*(2), 2007.

Yartey, C. A. (2007). Macroeconomic and Institutional Determinants of Stock Market Development in Africa. In J. Okpara (Ed.), *Management and Economic Development in Sub-Saharan Africa: Theoretical and Applied Perspectives*. London: Adonis and Abbey Publishers.

Yartey, C.A. (2008). The Determinants of Stock Market Development in Emerging Economies: Is South Africa Different? IMF.

Chapter 11
Estimating the Brand Image in the Process of Accounting Convergence:
Perceptions and Practices Gap

Ionica Oncioiu
Titu Maiorescu University, Romania

ABSTRACT

Globalization is an irreversible process accounting. The global economic crisis that cross, there is need for stronger global accounting standards, to ensure a common language for each type of transaction and for each business sector. The value of intangible assets has been the main focus in the debates between consumers' evaluations about brand name and business world for many decades. Today, this concept interferes with the international process of assessment, but also is influenced by the store name and the quality of merchandise it carries.

INTRODUCTION

The value of intangible assets has been the main focus in the debates between consumers' evaluations about brand name and business world for many decades. Today, this concept interferes with the international process of assessment, but also is influenced by the store name and the quality of merchandise it carries. The need to determine the value of these intangible assets lies in the more virulent criticism

DOI: 10.4018/978-1-5225-1900-3.ch011

Copyright ©2017, IGI Global. Copying or distributing in print or electronic forms without written permission of IGI Global is prohibited.

brought to the traditional accounting system, placed face to face with an increasing vision of financial assets of a company. In an uncertain world with imperfect and incomplete markets (financial crisis), no particular measurement objective should be regarded as having a monopoly, and different measurements should be regarded as complementing one another.

The problem is how to choose the best of them in the context of satisfying consumers' motivations in the purchasing process requirements, on the one hand and the brand image and reputation accounting estimates are often made in conditions of uncertainty because it involves the determination of their judgment, on the other hand. As a result, the risk of material misstatement is greater when these estimates are involved and in some cases the auditor may determine that the risk of material misstatement is greater that requires special audit.

According to Thomas et al., (2012) the most important asset of a company is the brand they own. For customers, a brand can simplify the choice process, promise quality, reduce risk (Keller & Lehmann, 2006) and also motivate repeated buying (Aaker, 1996; Keller, 2001).

A strong brand is a competitive advantage, a barrier for entry in some markets, easier acceptance among distributors and consumers etc. for the organization it owns (Farquhar, 1989).

The transition to IFRS represents the latest episode of brand image and reputation's often turbulent story. One striking feature of this framework for brand image and reputation measurement and reporting is its order magnitude increase in complexity compared to typical prior practice. Application of this system requires navigation through several layers of difficult and potentially contestable choices. It is for this reason in particular that much of the recent literature relating to this issue focuses on the incentive compatibility problems which may be associated with the implementation of impairment based approaches to brand image and reputation measurement and reporting (e.g; Beatty & Weber, 2006; Hayn & Hughes, 2006).

Producers and users of financial statements consider that in the measurement and presentation of accounting information regarding brand name, the most widely used is the historical cost, although it has some weaknesses. This is usually combined with other bases of evaluation. Moreover, the tendency is to use current cost accounting in response to failure based on historical cost model to solve problems connected with non-cash effect of changes in asset prices.

Accountants, in their turn, reflect accounting estimates only in registers and certainly not the value generated by the presentation of materials. It is a clear dichotomy between the historical cost accounting and fair value in accounting measurement, which creates a productive tension in discussions related to economy based on knowledge. However, it is more likely for a certain period of time to develop both paradigms in parallel and then become convergent, thus solving the paradox of intangible asset valuation.

Therefore, we can say that accounting estimates on brand image and reputation is one of the challenges of international accounting and auditing in the context of convergence.

BACKGROUND

In recent decades there was an idea almost unanimous on the growing importance of brand image. Also, many economists have stressed the importance of brand image as a production factor in comparison with traditional assets. There are two theories on economic growth: the theory of neo-classical growth theory exogenous and endogenous growth. Intangibles reflect different endogenous model.

According to endogenous growth model of production is defined as a function dependent accumulation of immaterial (intangible). Over time, permanent growth is possible only if the intangible capital stock changes virtually forever.

Over time, brand image has become one of the most controversial issues in accounting. Its value is generally determined by appraisal, which is based on evaluator's assumptions. As such, the value of brand image is determined subjectively. Subject recognition of brand image in financial statements found both supporters and opponents among professionals.

Supporters of recognized brand image say that brand image is „the present value of the surplus revenue that a company can get." This group claims to determine the fair value of these excess revenues is similar to determining the present value of cash flows associated with other activities and projects. Opponents of the recognition fund argue that the purchase price paid, many times proves to be based on unrealistic expectations, leading to further reductions default to zero of the brand image. Both arguments have merit. Many companies are able to achieve revenues in excess out of their investments. As such, the prices of ordinary shares of these companies must register first a book value of intangible assets. Consequently, investors who buy ordinary shares of such companies pay for intangible assets (reputation, brand names, etc.). Trademarks, copyrights, patents and even harder to classify intangible assets converge all the brands. There is no simple definition of what constitutes a trademark, but the basic idea is that it is an economic asset, not just a way to label a product. Brands are more than just names or trademarks. Tom Blackett at Interbrand (2003) writes about brands as assets: brands that fulfill their promise attract loyal customers who will return at regular intervals. The benefit obtained by the owner of the brand is that cash flow forecasting easier and it becomes possible to plan and coordinate development activities in terms of greater certainty.

The need to determine the value of these brand image lies in the more virulent criticism brought to the traditional accounting system, placed face to face with an increasing vision of financial assets of a company. In an uncertain world with imperfect and incomplete markets (financial crisis), no particular measurement objective should be regarded as having a monopoly, and different measurements should be regarded as complementing one another.

Brand image is the brand's current set of associations (in the consumer's mind), or how the brand is seen by consumers (Aaker & Joachimsthaler, 2000; Aaker, 1996; Park, Jaworski & MacInnis, 1986; Raggio & Leone, 2005).

Brand names are key indicators of the products that have become an imperative asset that influences consumer brand perceptions in today's highly competitive environment (Ailawadi & Keller, 2004).A brand can be basically delineated as a name, term, symbol, sign, design or any combination of them, intended to identify the goods and services of one seller or group sellers to differentiate them from those competitors (Kotler, 1994).Brand names simplify consumer choices by helping them to recognize products more easily (Friedman, 1985). Well-chosen brand names contribute to the strength of the product. Moreover, brand names that are associated with positive attributes score higher on overall liking (Kohli, Harich& Leuthesser, 2005).

IASB argues that brand image is the only item of intangible assets for which depreciation is very difficult to identify. It does not generate cash flows independently of other assets or groups of assets and, therefore, its recoverable amount cannot be measured individually. Accordingly, if there is any indication that brand image may be impaired, the recoverable amount is calculated for the cash-generating unit to which it belongs. So, the IASB and the FASB agree to work together and to pool their resources as both Boards considered that it was the most effective method to eliminate as many as possible of the differences between IFRS and US GAAP.

CHALLENGES ACCOUNTING FOR BRAND IMAGE: PERCEPTIONS AND PRACTICES GAP

The main issue in terms of measuring systems is that it is not possible to measure social phenomena with scientific precision. Thus it tends, in the absence of appropriate tools to use traditional methods based on the figures - financial indicators or remove the real cause of the phenomenon that caused the occurrence of these intangible assets.

The brand image concept one of the first articles that make a reference to the commercial fund was published in the year 1884, although this concept is much older. But he is also the one who claims the first references to the term brand image and reputation in a class about which Lord Eldon commented: "the goodwill that was the subject of the sale is nothing more than the probability of an old client to come back." Making a reference to one of the components of the brand image and reputation, clients' fidelity. Since then were written numerous articles and books about this subject, the same as generations of accountants were confronted with this problem.

In order to establish the arguments for and against the recognition of the brand image and reputation as an active, we will analyses the definition of the immaterial actives established by the International Organism of accountancy normalization and problems in identifying the immaterial actives which it faced. The accountancies of an element in the immaterial immobilizations category requires that an enterprise to demonstrate that the element fulfills the definition of an immaterial immobilization and the criteria to recognize the active (it is probably that the enterprise is to obtain future economic advantages due to the active and if its costs can be evaluated.).

Frustrations expressed by the studies mentioned on the measurement of brand image are interesting and suggest, on the one hand, the need for tangible measurement of intangible assets in general and particularly brand image, and on the other hand, that the attempt has been made now leaves room for improvement.

Considers that, before presenting in detail the different methods of reporting and measuring intangible are used so far, it is necessary to present a general classification will serve as a basis for analysis and will facility understanding of the specificity of each method. Sveiby proposed classification is presented in 2001 and is based primarily on the dichotomy that characterizes these methods and models: orientation atomistic/holistic orientation (e.g., models that measure and/or individual is intangible that models that measure and/or is intangibles overall available to organizations). Then, starting from this basic distinction is a distinction between methods of monetary and non-monetary:

- *Monetary methods are useful in mergers, acquisitions of new companies listing on stock exchanges*, comparisons made between companies in the same field of activity, moreover, the methods money have been developed based on accepted accounting rules so that they can be easily learned by accountants;
- *Non-monetary methods is the determination of innovation and performance management company* also may be noted that these methods have the advantage that it does not express the intangible assets in financial terms, so that they can be applied at any level of organization in non-profit, public companies, and/or organizations with social objectives.

According to these differences, results in a matrix with four categories of methods:

- **Cell A – Holistic and Monetary Methods:** A method includes using financial models and, on the one hand provides a general representation of the intellectual capital of organization supporting a determination of their money and, on the other hand, because of the nature their very general and brief no intangible enable administration for the purposes of creating value.
- **Cell B - Atomistic and Monetary Methods:** Using monetary methods include but are applied to individual intangible assets. However, although these methods focus on individual assets do not provide a clear vision of the organization in total intangible assets of total assets.
- **Cell C - Atomistic and Non-Monetary Methods:** Includes non-monetary atomistic methods, among them, being found most important innovations thousand and more in line with the "atmosphere" knowledge economy. But, and this presents some weaknesses, namely that it does not allow comparisons and that are not always able to accurately reflect the value of individual intangible assets and, therefore, often based on approximations.
- **Cell D - Holistic Methods, Non-Monetary:** It is observed that the literature does not provide such methods of measurement yet eloquent.

Another classification of the methods used so far was made all the Sveiby, based on ideas suggested by Luthy (1998) and Williams (2001), is as follows:

- **Direct Assessment of Intellectual Capital Methods (DIC):** Estimating the value in cash ($) of intangible assets by determining the various components. After these components are identified, they can be measured directly, either individually or with a compound coefficient.
- **Market Capitalization Methods (MCM):** Calculate the difference between a company's market capitalization and shareholder equity value as the value of its intellectual capital or intangible assets.
- **Method Returns on Assets (ROA):** Average pre-tax earnings of a company for a period of time are divided by average assets of the company's tangible. The result is ROA - return on assets of the company which then compares the average of its industry. The differences multiplied by the average of tangible assets of the company to calculate the average annual earnings from intangibles. Dividing the average earnings above the cost average capital company or the interest rate, you can estimate the value of intangible assets or intellectual capital thereof.
- **Method Scores (Scorecard - SC):** Establish various components of intangible assets or intellectual capital and generate indicators or indices that are reported as scores (scorecards) or graphics. These methods are similar meth-

ods in that DIC is based on identifying components of intangible assets, but unlike, they do not consider the need for a financial estimate of the value of intangible assets.

Methods offer different advantages. Thus the actual amount that provides evaluations ($), such as ROA and MCM, are useful in cases of merger and acquisition and stock assessments. May be used to compare companies within the same industry and are useful to illustrate the financial value of intangible assets, feature that tends to draw attention to managers. Because they are based on counting rules long established and recognized them in different national laws or regulations can be easily communicated to the accounting profession. The disadvantage is the fact that all the terms, making money, they can be superficial.

DIC and SC methods advantages are that it can create a more complex organization in terms of health than financial metrics and ROA and MCM can be applied easily to any level of organization. Measurement is made closer to the event and so reporting can be more accurate and faster than financial measurements. Their disadvantage is that the indicators are contextual and must be adapted to each organization and each objective, which makes comparison difficult. Also, the methods are new and are not easily accepted by the companies and managers who are accustomed to seeing it only in purely financial.

From the perspective of global experience in evaluating intangibles, we can remember the following methods:

- Skandia Navigator, is probably the most well-known and analyzed intellectual capital measurement model that literature offers to date. Thanks to its innovative qualities it is considered a kind of archetype for the class of models for non-monetary atomist measuring. Among the advantages of this model are: it initiated a series of efforts toward abandoning traditional ideas about the determinants of value in organizations and bringing to the fore the possibility of measuring intangible assets; it highlights the crucial role of customer relationships in business value creation and shows how the nature of the relationship between companies and their customers changed; for the first time a great importance is attached to the contribution that can bring renewal and development of the organization's value;
- The Intangible Assets Monitor is a model that can be applied to all companies and its indicators are chosen according to the characteristics of the company, industry, competitive variables, company's history, organizational culture and company management. According to the model, intangible income can be divided into: strengthening the company's image, strengthening the organization and enhancing its competence;

- The Balanced Scorecard model that Kaplan and Norton have designed does not present a general system of indicators to measure intellectual capital, the argument being that a general system of indicators could leave out certain aspects of each company related to its objectives, processes and the context in which it operates. Traditional indicators provide information about the past performance of the company, while non-financial indicators can measure, for example, customer satisfaction, corporate innovative activities and improvements to various processes of the company. Combining the two types of indicators allows managers to obtain a balanced image on company performance. Braam points out that diffusion of innovative practices of management or management accounting, such as the Balanced Scorecard, can bring a discrepancy between the "tag" of the implmented concept and its contents. Authors such as Bontis, Petty and Guthrie have shown that this model can be used for evaluating intellectual capital. Comparison made between Balance Scorecard and intellectual capital valuation methods reveal other similarities such as recognition strategy as an essential component of performance management need to find a concise and fully expressing the company's situation, attention to intangible assets and knowledge. In other words, it is possible that some organizations only claim that they use the Balanced Scorecard, while the implementation substance ignores the considered defining characteristics of Balanced Scorecard (connecting indicators to the strategy, causal relationships between indicators etc.). Therefore, to assess whether the Balanced Scorecard is used in practice is dependent on defining and clarifying the concept, ie the unequivocal identification of the characteristics that define a Balanced Scorecard;
- Lev's Knowledge Capital Formula Method for measuring knowledge capital is based on the traditional method for calculating goodwill. One difference is that, in Lev's model, additional revenues are replaced by residual income attributable to intangible assets. Based on these critical observations, in the scientific literature, the Value Chain Scoreboard has appeared, which is an atomistic method of measuring intangible assets which are pending completion;
- Criticism of the method Tobin's Q considered the volatility of the courses on the capital market, often beyond the control of management, which directly affect the market value of the intellectual capital of the company, and focused on the fact that this way of calculating the intellectual capital is not very robust. However, in his work, Stewart argues, by exemplifying, that both market value and book value may be diminished. Another weakness of the method is that the indicator "Q" may not be determined by the value of intangible assets;

- The Economic Value Added model was initially developed as an internal measure of performance used by managers to help them make decisions on investments. In practice, it has been demonstrated that an investment project which causes higher income than the net cost of its funding and thus generates profit, does not necessarily lead to an increased company value. A company should be interested only in those investment projects capable of generating a positive or even increasing Economic Value Added, because it will increase the shareholder value. Thus, it is clear that by applying the principles of this method, companies should change their priorities;
- Technology Broker stated that it is itself an intellectual asset for organizations. But the main weakness of the model is considered to be related to the possibility of transforming the qualitative results in monetary results. For example, using market-based approach is likely to not be identified on the market any information on prices of many of the elements that form the intellectual capital. Income-based approach suffers from the bias of the estimates and uncertainties inherent in the calculation of cash-flow;
- The Weighted Patents Citation model estimates a "technological factor" to identify the impact of research-development efforts leading to the creation of intellectual property and uses indicators such as research-development expenses / sales, number of patents, income / research-development expenses, etc. "The evaluation process of patents" is an effort that involves teamwork, in which specialists interact in marketing and research-development to decide the viability of abandoning or continuing the research-development process.

Based on this overview of the different methods of measuring intellectual capital of companies, we can say that the literature and practice offer several models, each with its strengths and weaknesses. Moreover, we can see that some of the intellectual capital valuation models are built on the same principles and using the same indicators, but they are named differently. For example, Skandia Navigator uses the term "human capital", Technology Broker uses the name "people-based activities" (human-centered assets) and Intangible Assets Monitor uses "staff competence" to denote the same concept. This demonstrates that the field is still at an early stage and no one wants to give up their own nomenclature borrowing aspects of the work of others, as long as it was shown that one method is generally valid. For this reason, an important aspect of research is to develop a common set of definitions and indicators that can be easily generalized.

FUTURE RESEARCH DIRECTIONS

Many companies are able to achieve revenues in excess out of their investments. As such, the prices of ordinary shares of these companies must register first a book value of intangible assets. Consequently, investors who buy ordinary shares of such companies pay for intangible assets (reputation, brand names, etc.).

Therefore, their representation in situations of brand image value as intangible asset, to a value as close as possible to the real one, is essential for users since they ground their decisions based on its level.

Moreover, the success of any company depends not least on whether the brand image has recognized the important role of an examination over several years of the development of intangible values both in the construction of the house of intangible values and the annual evaluation, and if it has implemented this knowledge consistently in everyday decisions.

The author believes that due to the high influence, both positively and negatively, of the brand image on its value is necessary for conducting more detailed studies of diagnostic analysis to identify and measure them, and also to determine a set of evaluation methods that leads to a correct result, close to the market.

Of course, the appeal to intangible resources in order to create value remains a significant challenge for specialists because the country's competitive advantage should be interpreted in relation to the skills, talent and brand image stock. Future research efforts of SMEs should turn those scales into operational parameters and promote the development of empirical methodological studies based on dialogue and the dissemination of knowledge and experience in interdisciplinary research teams.

CONCLUSION

Companies have recognized the importance of brand image as a key factor for success, looking for ways to measure and control this factor. Financial performance measurement is not sufficient that reflects how the profit is due to brand image. In the knowledge economy, wealth is created through a combination of services and products that generate value. Each company has its unique set of knowledge, skills, values and solutions, all intangible resources. Monitoring and management of these resources can be made with value creation efficiency analysis because it is a priority for managers to obtain and maintain productivity and efficiency in the enterprise.

Another aspect that can be observed is related to the fact that some researchers have developed theories based on reflection the results of case studies, others have developed some indicators that have applied in practice (as in the case of Skandia, for example) but without testing their validity in advance and others have developed sets of indicators were not tested. For this reason another challenge in the study of brand image is the need for researchers to base their conclusions on several empirical researches. And, to make conclusive statements about brand image, we need to consider that a coherent field theory has positive effects in multiple areas such as accounting, human resources, finance, strategic management, etc..

Very important is that those who investigate aspects of brand image (brand satisfaction, brand trust and brand loyalty) to set realistic goals. As with many challenges, such as efforts to conceptualization of the field, trying to measure brand image; setting causal relations - effect, demonstrating the accuracy of proxies, it happens that many companies have a brand image management system its use in some individual indicators whose relevance is not fully justified.

The auditor should consider also whether individual differences of brand image and reputation were accepted as reasonable or oriented in one direction as cumulated can have a significant effect on the financial statements. In such circumstances, the auditor must assess the brand image and reputation accounting estimates taken as a whole. Therefore, it can be said that accounting estimate on brand image and reputation is one of the challenges of international accounting and auditing in the context of convergence.

It is therefore important to determine and establish relevant indicators, the group of them in specific categories (quantitative or qualitative aspects related to individual company's business - e.g. employees - or macro issues) and not I just put together, and also to assign each category a specific weight in calculating the final result. Therefore, investigating the role of these factors can be considered possible avenues for further research.

REFERENCES

Aaker, D. A. (1996). Measuring brand equity across products and markets. *California Management Review*, *38*(3), 102–120. doi:10.2307/41165845

Aaker, D. A., & Joachimsthaler, E. (2000). *Brand Leadership*. New York: The Free Press.

Abernethy, M., Bianchi, P., Labory, S., Lev, S., Wyatt, A., & Zambon, S. (2003). *Study on the Measurement and Reporting of Intangible Assets and Associated Reporting Practices*. Commission of the European Communities.

Ailawadi, K., & Keller, K. L. (2004). Understanding retail branding: Conceptual insights and research priorities. *Journal of Retailing*, *80*(4), 331–342. doi:10.1016/j.jretai.2004.10.008

Anson, W. (2008). *The intangible assets handbook: maximizing value from intangible assets*. Washington, DC: American Bar Association, Section of Business Law.

Beatty, A., & Weber, J. (2006). Accounting Discretion in Fair Value Estimates: An Examination of SFAS 142 Brand image and reputation Impairments. *Journal of Accounting Research*, *44*(2), 257–288. doi:10.1111/j.1475-679X.2006.00200.x

Blackett, T. (2003). Brands and brand strategies (R. Clifton and J. Simmons Eds.). Princeton, NJ: Bloomberg Press.

Braam, G., & Nijssen, E.J. (2001). *Antecedents of the Adoption of the Balanced Scorecard* (Working Paper). University of Nijmegen.

Campisi, D. (2006). The measurement of intangible assets: a method to assess knowledge productivity. *Proceedings of the 2006 Business & Economics Society International Conference*, Florence.

Cravera, A., Maglione, M., & Ruggieri, R. (2001). *The Valuation of Intellectual Capital.*

Farquhar, P. H. (1989). Managing brand equity. *Marketing Research*, *1*(September), 24–33.

Hayn, C., & Hughes, P. (2006). Leading Indicators of Brand image and reputation Impairment. *Journal of Accounting, Auditing & Finance*, *21*(3), 223–265.

Kaplan, R.S., & Norton, D.P. (1992). The Balanced Scorecard – Measures that Drive Performances. *Harvard Business Review*, 1992, 71 – 79.

Keller, K. L. (2006). Building customer based brand equity: a blue print for creating strong brands. Marketing Science Institute Working Paper.

Kohli, C., Harich, K., & Leuthesser, L. (2005). Creating brand identity: A study of evaluation of new brand names. *Journal of Business Research*, *58*(11), 1506–1515. doi:10.1016/j.jbusres.2004.07.007

Kotler, P. (1994). *Principles of Marketing*. New Jersey: Prentice Hall.

Kwansa, F. A., Mayo, C., & Demirciftci, T. (2008). The importance of intangible assets: trends and patterns. In *M.D. Olsen (Ed.), Handbook of hospitality strategic management* (pp. 181–202). Amsterdam: Butterworth-Heinemann. doi:10.1016/B978-0-08-045079-7.00008-9

Lev, B. (2001). *Intangibles: Management, Measurement and Reporting*. Washington: Brookings Institute Press.

Lynn, L. E. (1999). *The Management of Intellectual Capital: The issues and the practice. In Management Accounting Issues Paper 16 Management Accounting Practices Handbook*. Hamilton, Ontario: Society of Management Accountants of Canada.

Martory, B., & Verdier, F. (2000). *Comment traiter le goodwill? Pratique d'une theorie, theorie d'une pratique. In Comptabilite, Controle* (Vol. 6). Audit.

Park, C. W., Jaworski, B. J., & Maclnnis, D. J. (1986). Strategic brand concept-image management. *Journal of Marketing*, *50*(October), 135–145. doi:10.2307/1251291

Petty, R., & Guthrie, J. (2000). *Journal of Intellectual Capital*, *3*.

Raggio, R., & Leone, P. R. (2005). Separating Equity and Value. *Proceedings of theZIBS Brand Valuation Workshop*, Atlanta, GA, USA.

Roos, J., Roos, G., Dragonetti, N.C. & Edvinsson, L. (1997). *Intellectual Capital: Navigating in the New Business Landscape*. Houndsmills, Basingtoke: Macmillan.

Sveiby, K.E. (n. d.). *Methods for Measuring Intangible Assets*. Retrieved from www.sveiby.com.au/Intangible Methods.htm

Chapter 12
Value Relevance of Accounting Information in Capital Markets of India:
Value Relevance

Manoj Kumar
International Engineering Services, India

ABSTRACT

This study belongs in the specific line of research into value relevance that aims to assess the consequences on companies' market values of the introduction of the International Accounting Standards. The specific research area concerns the role of the International Accounting Standards (IAS)/International Financial Reporting Standards (IFRS), investigating whether the adoption of the IAS/IFRS has led to a greater correlation between important financial statement values (earning, comprehensive income and equity) and stock market capitalization than in the pre-IAS/IFRS period. The study focuses on the Indian situation, analyzing a sample of 114 companies listed on the Delhi Stock Exchange. We analyze a period of eight years (2008-2015). In relation to the critique of value relevance studies by Holthausen and Watts (2001) and subsequent reactions of Barth et al. (2001), this chapter offers insights about the usefulness of value relevance especially in periods of financial crisis.

DOI: 10.4018/978-1-5225-1900-3.ch012

Copyright ©2017, IGI Global. Copying or distributing in print or electronic forms without written permission of IGI Global is prohibited.

INTRODUCTION

Accounting Standards are used as regulatory mechanisms for preparation of financial reports in almost all the countries of the world. Accounting Standard are written policy documents issued by expert accounting body or government or other regulatory body covering the aspects of recognition, measurement, treatment, presentation & disclosure of accounting transaction in the financial statement. Objective of accounting standard is to standardize the diverse accounting policies & practices with a view to eliminate to the extent the non-comparability of financial statements & add the reliability to the financial statements. The rapid growth of international trade & Internationalization of firms create need of global harmonization of accounting standards as a company having presence in different countries has to prepare financial reports as per GAAP of the country where it operates. Under this global business environment, companies are in need of common accounting language in the form of harmonized accounting standard across the world.

This chapter describes Value Relevance (VR) in India 2008-2015 before and after the mandatory adoption of international accountancy principles International Accounting Standards (IAS)/International Financial Reporting Standards (IFRS). There are three distinct phases in this time period: the period preceding mandatory adoption (2008-2009); the post-introduction period before the international financial crisis (2010-2012); and the period of the financial crisis (2013-2015). This article asks whether the adoption of the IAS/IFRS has produced more useful financial reporting for a wide range of users, particularly for investors in making financial decisions (IAS 1, par. 5). It extends previous Indian country-specific studies (i.e. Paglietti, 2009; Pavan & Paglietti, 2011) focusing on India in three ways:

1. It looks at the VR of two different aspects of income, income statement and comprehensive income (Goncharov & Hodgson, 2011);
2. The time period observed is longer;
3. It takes into account the financial crisis.

This third feature of assessing the validity of VR in periods of financial crisis (Laux & Leuz; 2009), has to date not been widely discussed in the literature (Barth & Landsman, 2010, p. 405).

The chapter focusing on the Indian market contributes to the debate on the relationship between market values and accounting in continental Countries. In fact VR has been widely studied in north America and northern Europe where the concept was first developed, but there is a dearth of studies of other areas. India in fact presents numerous marked differences with these areas. The first difference is that Indian companies tend to be credit-centred in finance, compared to the more market oriented approach overseas (Cesarini, 2003). And in India, management of companies is often in the hands of the ownership, whereas overseas public ownership is more common. A further characteristic of India is that stock ownership tends to be highly concentrated and investors tend to have low levels of management awareness and skills. Another reason because the chapter focus on the Indian market is the strong impact of the financial crisis in this Country, that makes especially urgent the need for empirical studies assessing the impact of the crisis on VR of accounting values.

There are various definitions of VR; Francis and Schipper in "Have financial statements lost their relevance?" (1999) propose four. The first is that financial reporting influences share prices capturing their intrinsic value. This means that VR is measured by the earnings determined by market value oriented accounting standards. The second interpretation is that financial statements are value relevant if they contain the variables used in an assessment model or can be used to predict these variables. This means that the VR of earnings (in a model based on present value of dividends, cash flow, or abnormal earnings) is measured by the capacity of earnings to supply indications on future dividends, future cash flows, future earnings or future market prices. The third and fourth interpretations present certain similarities; both see VR as a statistical association between financial information and market prices or returns. In the third interpretation, statistical association can be used to interpret whether investors use financial statements to fix market prices. This means that VR is measured by the capacity of financial information derived from financial reporting to alter the overall composition of information on the market. In this view, value relevant information affects share prices because it can persuade investors to rethink their forecasts. It is thus closely linked to the rapidity of information and how forecasts are formed. In the fourth and final interpretation, it is possible that a statistical association between financial information and market prices or returns could mean only that the information is the same or related to that used by investors. VR is measured by the capacity of financial reporting to capture information influencing share prices, regardless of its source. Clearly Francis and Schipper's work takes into account that financial reporting is not the only type of meaningful information available. But even so, it is undeniable that one of its declared aims is to supply investors with information useful for financial decisions (IAS 1, par. 5). And by their fourth interpretation, taking into consideration the link between share value and firm value, we can say that financial information can give an indication of firm value. In this view, in order to say that financial values reported are value relevant, they need to be linked to current firm value. This leads into a definition of VR useful for the aims of this article which derives from Francis and Schipper's fourth interpretation. If there is no link between accounting values and firm value, financial information cannot be considered value relevant. This definition thus includes the simpler definition by Barth *et. al.* (2001) of value relevance as "[. . .]

the ability of financial statement information to capture or summarise information that affects share values'' (Hellström, 2006, p. 325; Devalle et al., 2010, p. 93). Methodologically, VR indicates the association between prices or returns of shares quoted on regulated markets and accounting values (earning and equity). Market values are dependant variables and accounting values are independent variables. For an accounting value, the more significant the correlation with the dependant variable, the more value relevant it is.

LITERATURE REVIEW

The concept of VR is based on the Modigliani-Miller theorem (Modigliani & Miller, 1958) and the first pioneering contributions in the field were made in the next few years. VR studies can thus be placed in the wider of context of capital market-based accounting research, CMBAR, (Beaver, 2002) for example the work by Ball and Brown (1968) and Beaver (1968). These studies examine market reaction to period results, and focused on the reaction of prices to announcements of earnings, establishing an association between earnings of the financial statement and market prices. This association exists even though part of the financial reporting information is incorporated into market prices before the date the earnings are published. This link implies that earnings appearing on the financial statement are value relevant. The study by Ball and Brown is a short term event study, rather than a long term association study.

Watts and Zimmerman (1978) subsequently examined the link between accounting standards and firm market value. This work was methodologically similar to VR studies but in fact became the basis for positive accounting theory (Watt and Zimmerman, 1990). But the work of Ohlson (1995) and Feltham-Ohlson (1995) was decisive in relating firm market value to the availability of financial information. Their model linked firm market value with the main accounting values, earnings and equity. Feltham and Ohlson elaborated a coherent theory of firm value based on the concept of "clean surplus". Today VR studies are being enriched by more segmented focus on various sectors, markets, countries and groups of countries. Classifications and taxonomies of the numerous and widely differing works have been proposed by many authors (Barth *at al.,* 2001; Beaver, 2002; Courteau, 2008; Holthausen & Watts, 2001; Kothari, 2001; Paglietti, 2009; Devalle, 2010). Some taxonomies isolate VR as a field of research lying within CMBAR (Beaver, 2002), while others consider it as an independent field (Kothari, 2001). Critique has also been made; Holthausen and Watts (2001) for example have criticized the usefulness of VR for standard setters. They find that the association between book values and values usually used to measure firm capital such as market value are simply associations and have no use for standard setters. VR is not fully descriptive and has no capacity to explain or make accounting forecasts, evaluations or indications. These criticisms have however been met with rebuttals; Barth et al., (2001); Hellström, (2006) find that VR is indeed useful. Barth claims that VR studies are not a substitute for standard setting; they are not intended to be a complete descriptive theory. Standard setters already have complete reference frameworks. But VR is no less useful for not being a complete theory, according to Barth et al. (2001). Although it is not the only type of research useful for standard setting, it supplies relevant information.

Different econometric choices can be made in VR studies. These cannot be judged as positive or negative a priori; their usefulness depends on the aim of the research. The choice between specification of return levels or price levels underlines that these are different types of analysis rather than competing alternatives, and each has advantages and disadvantages, (Barth et al., 2001; Kothari & Zimmerman, 1995; Landsman & Magliolo, 1988). If the focus is on firm value, it may be more useful for the methodology to use price level specification, but if the focus is on term changes in value then return specification will prove more useful.

The research presented here lies in the specific area of VR. This study is to appreciate the consequences on the market values from the introduction of international accounting standards. Internationally, many important and detailed contributions have been made in this field on various aspects of the quality of financial reporting (Barth et al., 2008). Another important contribution on VR over time was made by Collins et al. (1997) who looked at the VR of earning and equity in the long term using the model developed by Ohlson (1995). In this study the R^2 is the main explanatory measurement of VR. In terms of R^2, explanatory power of the independent variables (earning and equity) can be broken down into three elements: explanatory power of earning; incremental explanatory power of equity; combined explanatory power of earning and equity. In this context, some of the main studies they reached different conclusions, due to different methodological choices made (equations and consideration of the effects of scale) and the different assumptions used (samples, number of observations, the chosen time period). For example Collins concludes that although the explanatory power of earning fell, the explanatory power of equity rose in the same period, as did the explanatory power of the two variables taken jointly. Francis and Schipper (1999) reached similar conclusions. Brown (Brown et al. 1999) observed that the increases in VR could be a result of scale effects, and that there would be a fall in VR if scale effects were eliminated. Lev and Zarowin (1999) showed how the VR of earning, cash flow and equity had deteriorated. They found that the accounting system of the intangible is what most seriously interferes with the representation of the value of corporate performance. Dontoh et al. (2004) confirmed the results of Francis and Schipper (1999) who found that market return volatility causes a fall in VR. In particular, "uninformed" trading, where there is no information about the product traded, decreases the R^2 between market and book values. Kim and Kross (2006) used the same methodology as Collins to study how the capacity of earnings to supply indications on future cash flows has evolved over time.

In VR studies examining the effect of the change in accounting standards, a further distinction is made between voluntary or mandatory adoption. Much research in fact focus on voluntary adoption (Paananen & Lin, 2008; Christensen et al., 2008; Jermakowicz et al., 2007; Bartov et al., 2005). But since the decisions taken by many governments for mandatory adoption of IAS/IFRS, numerous studies have addressed the impact of mandatory regulation on value relevance (Horton and Serafeim, 2007; Soderstrom and Sun, 2007: p. 695; Paglietti, 2009; Ghoncarov & Hodgson, 2011).

A further relevant aspect is the composition of the sample of firms, which may belong to one country or to different countries. It is undeniable that there are substantial differences between the economies, sizes, societies and environments in countries. So using firms from one country has clear advantages, for example in the uniform influence of institutional factors regulating the country itself (Schipper, 2005) and in decreasing the incidence of the scale effect on the R^2 (Brown et al., 1999, p. 107). Multi-country studies continue to appear (Barth and Landsman, 2010; Hung and Subramanyam, 2007) but other researchers have found country-specific studies advantageous (Hellström, 2006; Callao et al.; 2007). An increasing number of country-specific studies on VR in recent years have focused on Countries of continental accounting tradition (Schiebel, 2007; Callao et al.; 2007), and in particular among Italian studies there are many country-specific studies (Cordazzo, 2008; Paglietti, 2009; Pavan and Paglietti, 2011; Veltri and Silvestri, 2011). Most of these examine the effects on VR of the transition to IAS/IFRS. The present chapter thus contributes to a widely debated field.

RESEARCH QUESTIONS

The main aim of the research is to assess the evolution over time of the relationship or VR between market value and accounting value after two important events: the adoption of the IAS/IFRS and the financial crisis. Our survey of Indian firms quoted on the Delhi Stock Exchange covered an eight year period 2008-2015. To this study concerns the mandatory adoption of different accounting standards. Our main research questions are:

RQ1: Has the transition to international accounting standards produced an increase in VR of accounting values?

The evolution of accounting standards means that the effects on VR of the adoption of IAS/IFRS can be assessed by comparing figures from financial year 2008-2009, the last when financial statements were drawn up using Indian accounting standards, with figures from 2010-2012 and 2013-2015 when IAS/IFRS were used. And because comparative information is available on the first time adoption of IAS/IFRS in 2004, for which we have Indian accounting standards as well as IAS/IFRS figures, the effect of the transition can be identified. Our first research question (RQ1) is thus based on the evolution of VR of earning and equity 2008-2015. It has two parts. The first focuses on the transition to IAS/IFRS, year 2004. As figures derived by Indian accounting standards as well as figures derived by IAS/IFRS are available, the effect of the transition to International Accounting Standards on the correlation between book values and market values can be seen by comparing the figures. The second part of RQ1 develops the time period and compares the pre IAS period (2008-2009) with the post-IAS/IFRS adoption period IAS (2010-2012).

RQ2L Has the financial and economic crisis affected the usefulness of accounting data?

The second research question (RQ2) asks whether accounting values retain significance during periods of financial crisis. Comparison is made between 2010-2012, years when the crisis was not even forecast, and 2013-2015 when its effects were felt. There is in fact a view expressed in literature that fair accounting values lose their relevance and reliability when extreme financial turbulence affects the real world economy (Barth et al., 2008; Barth and Landsman, 2010). We therefore assess empirically whether and to what extent accounting information are still useful for investors.

RQ3: Has comprehensive income become over time a more relevant type of information than net income?

The third and last research question (RQ3) examines the role and informational importance of comprehensive income. For the period 2010-2015, the usefulness of accounting information can be analyzed in detail thanks to the different specifications of earning yielded by the application of IAS/IFRS. In particular, IAS 1 regulates the definition of comprehensive income and how it is represented. Comprehensive income differs from earning as it includes "Other Comprehensive Income" (OCI) and any reclassifications. RQ3 thus aims to assess the VR effects of reporting comprehensive income. The analysis covered 2010-2015, although IAS 1 made a statement of comprehensive income obligatory only from 01/01/2009. So for 2010-

2013, comprehensive income was indirectly derived as the sum of earning, other comprehensive income and any reclassifications.

The three research questions were investigated taking into account differences between sectors. Each sample was analyzed in its entirety and a sectoral analysis was also made. It was also possible to measure VR for groups of firms with similar core business, with similar management and financial structures and according to accounting standards used which were at least partially different. We focused on two different sectors; banking and insurance and a non-financial sector consisting of industrial, trading and service firms not operating in banking, insurance and financial intermediation.

METHODOLOGICAL ASPECTS

Method

Most existing VR studies (Barth et al. 2008; Collins et al., 1997; Devalle et al., 2010; Entwistle et al., 2010; Gu Z., 2007), both Indian and international, are based on Ohlson's (1995) model. Methodology is often based on Efficient Market Hypothesis proposed by Fama in the 1970s. Through the Efficient Market Hypothesis, it is possible to measure the degree of VR through the association between the accounting and market values. Ohlson's basic premise is the Discounted Dividend Model (DDM). For the DDM, firm value equals the present value of expected dividends. Ohlson added the Clean Surplus Relation (CSR) and the definition of the abnormal earning to demonstrate the equality between the DDM and the Residual Income Model (RIM). The Clean Surplus Relation formula is: $y_{t-1} = y_t + d_t - x_t$; when y_{t-1} is the equity in $t-1$, y_t is the equity in t, d_t is the dividend in t and x_t is the earning in t. The abnormal earning formula is: $x_t^a = x_t - (R_f - 1)y_{t-1}$; when x_t^a is the abnormal earning t, x_t is the earning t, R_f is $(1 + r_f)$ and y_{t-1} is the equity in $t-1$. CSR can specify the reasons that equity varies over time, which happens principally as a result of capital operations, dividends and earnings. So in absence of increase or reduction of capital, the equity in t is equal at the sum of the equity in $t-1$ including earning and subtracting dividend. Abnormal earning, on the other hand, is equal to the difference between the earning in t and the expected income from the use of equity.

On the basis of DDM and taking into account the CSR and the concept of abnormal earning, Ohlson proposes the following definition of the Residual Income Model, when the firm value is equal to the equity plus the present value of expected abnormal earnings. The equation is:

$$P_t = y_t + \sum_{\tau=1}^{\infty} R_f^{-\tau} E_t \left[x_{t-\tau}^a \right] \tag{1}$$

where P_t is the firm market value in t, y_t is the equity in t, $x^a_{t-\tau}$ is the abnormal earning in t-τ, $R_f^{-\tau}$ is $1/(1 + r_f)^\tau$ where r_f is the risk-free value and $E_t[...]$ is the expected value operator conditioned on the date t information.

Ohlson also introduces Linear Information Dynamics (LID) that describes how the accounting and extra-accounting information affect the determination of the earning. He shows that the abnormal earning in $t+1$ (x^a_{t+1}) depend on abnormal earnings in the previous period (x_t^a), on information present on the market at date t but not yet incorporated into accounting values (v_t) and on information which although not predicted at t appear at $t+1$ and influence the determination of the abnormal earning (ε_{1t+1}), in:

$$x^a_{t+1} = \omega x_t^a + v_t + \varepsilon_{1t+1} \tag{2}$$

In particular, ω is the coefficient of the x_t^a and measures its persistence in the determination of x^a_{t+1}. This coefficient can have values between zero and one (Courteau, 2008). If it is equal to zero, x_t^a has no effect on the expected earnings ($x^a_{t+1} = v_t + \varepsilon_{1t+1}$). If the coefficient is equal to one, there is persistence of the abnormal earnings in the determination of the expected earnings ($x^a_{t+1} = x_t^a + v_t + \varepsilon_{1t+1}$). The main result of (2) is that expected abnormal earnings depend on three different types of information. Ohlson shows that x^a_{t+1} is the result of:

1. Persistence over time (ω) of abnormal earning;
2. Information available at t which is not incorporated into the results of that financial year;
3. All information which becomes known at $t+1$ and which was not predicted at the end of the previous financial year; if it had been known it would have been reflected in x_t^a or in v_t. In formula: $v_{t+1} = \gamma v_t + \varepsilon_{2t+1}$; when γ is the persistence of the extra-accounting information in t and ε_{2t+1} is the unexpected events in t that influence the information in $t+1$.

In the final version of the model, which today underpins most VR studies, LID is substituted into the RIM as follows:

$$P_t = y_t + \alpha_1 x_t^a + \alpha_2 v_t \tag{3}$$

where:

$\alpha_1 = \omega/[(1 + r_f) - \omega]$;

$\alpha_2 = (1 + r_f)/\{[(1 + r_f) - \omega][(1 + r_f) - \gamma]\}$.

In (3) Ohlson shows that, at any time, the market value of a firm is the sum of the equity, the abnormal earnings and the extra-accounting information. The effect of x_t^a on market value is expressed by α_1 which rises as ω rises and falls as r_f falls. The incidence of v_t on P_t is measured instead by coefficient α_2 which rises as ω rises, and by γ which falls as r_f rises.

Equation (3) is the theoretical basis to measure the relation between firm market value and accounting information through regression analysis. It has however been slightly modified by previous researchers for the purposes of VR, as follows:

$$MV_{it} = \beta_0 + \beta_1 y_{it} + \beta_2 x_t^a + \beta_3 v_{it} + \varepsilon_{it} \quad (4)$$

where MV_{it} is the market value at t of the firm i, β_0 is the constant that describes market value when the other variables are equal to zero, y_{it} and x_{it} are the equity and the earning at t of the firm i, v_{it} are the extra-accounting information, ε_{it} is the standard error and β_1, β_2 and β_3 are the coefficients of the independent variables. For the purposes of VR, (4) uses earning instead of abnormal earnings in order to keep to a minimum the errors of measurement that may be caused from estimating x_t^a. Variable v_{it} is often omitted for the same reason.

Assessing the VR of accounting values involves taking scale effects (Barth and Clinch, 2009) into account. Scale effects appear every time the firms in the sample present different sizes, as these are used as values for regression. It has been shown (Barth and Kallapur 1996; Easton and Sommers, 2003) that scale effects can in fact alter the value of R^2 as well as the value of coefficients. The most widely used technique to eliminate the problem is to divide all the terms in the regression model by a scale factor selected from the following:

- The total number of shares issued at 31/12/t;
- Equity at 01/01/t;
- Equity at 31/12/t;
- Firm market value at 01/01/t;
- Firm market value at 31/12/t.

Heteroscedasticity is another big problem (Verbeek, 2006), and needs to be identified through the White test. In the literature (Barth & Clinch, 2009), it is linked to the scale effect, as the techniques used to eliminate the scale effect also contribute to lowering heteroscedasticity, although they may not remove it completely.

These two equations, which take account of the problems outlined above, are used to test our research questions:

$$P_{it} = \beta_0 + \beta_1 BVS_{it} + \beta_2 EPS_{it} + \varepsilon_{it} \quad (5)$$

$$P_{it} = \beta_0 + \beta_1 BVS_{it} + \beta_2 CIPS_{it} + \varepsilon_{it} \quad (6)$$

where:

P_{it} is the share price four months after the end of the year;
β_0 is the constant;
BVS_{it} is the book value per share at 31/12/t;
EPS_{it} is the earning per share at 31/12/t;
$CIPS_{it}$ is the comprehensive income per share at 31/12/t;
β_1 and β_2 are the coefficients respectively of the equity and earning.

Starting from (4), the scale effect was tackled by dividing all variables in the model by the number of shares issued at the end of the financial year. The two equations differ in the composition of income analyzed. In (5) the evolution of time of VR is assessed with reference to earning, but in (6) comprehensive income is used.

In order to eliminate the effects of heteroscedasticity, standard errors were corrected using the White test (Verbeek, 2006). The intensity of the relationship between accounting values and market values is measured by R^2, which measures how much of the standard deviation of the firm market value (dependent variable) is explained by standard deviation of the accounting value (independent variable). VR studies are based on the principle that the higher R^2, the greater the variability of market value described by the accounting values, and therefore the higher are the usefulness of the financial reporting for investors.

The size and sign of coefficients of independent variables are also important. These coefficients measure the relationship between the dependant and the independent variable. This enables us to identify which of the independent variables has most influence on the dependant variable. In other words, analysis of coefficients (β_1 and β_2) shows which of the accounting values in the regression (*BVPS, EPS* or *CIPS*) has the most influence on market value, and thus which is most useful in terms of information for investors. The Chow test (Verbeek, 2006) of equality was used for comparison of the coefficients in different time periods.

Sample

Overall the main features of our sample in view of its purpose are the selection and number of firms; the number of observations; the selection of dates appropriate for measuring market variables. This research, as country-specific research focusing on India (Pavan and Paglietti, 2011; Cordazzo; 2008), analyzed the consolidated financial statements 2008-2015 of a sample of 114 companies listed on the Delhi Stock Exchange which accounted for approximately 81.37% of the entire stock market capitalization on 28 April 2016.

From the universe of listed companies (341), we excluded those companies:

- Listed after 31 December 2008 and/or no longer listed on 28 April 2016, to ensure availability of the figures for the entire period under observation ;
- With corporate address outside India, in order to avoid influence from contexts different from the Indian;
- Not providing a consolidated financial statement, to ensure homogeneity of the financial statements considered;
- Not closing financial statements on 31 December, to ensure homogeneity of the date of closure and of the relevant correlations with the stock market capitalizations;
- Not supplying all data necessary for the study, in order to ensure a constant number of firms in the sample for the entire time period under observation.

Among the remaining firms, we selected the 114 with highest capitalization on 28 April 2016. The sample was first analyzed as a whole, and was subsequently segmented into two sub-samples in order to show the particular characteristics in terms of the evolution of VR. The first subsample of 23 companies (hereafter "financial sector") consisted mainly of banks and insurance companies (88.99%). The second, residual, subsample comprised the remaining 91 companies (hereafter "industrial sector"). It consisted of approximately 78.42% companies other than banks and insurance companies. The data were taken directly from the financial statements of sample firms, rather than data banks. We examined 912 consolidated financial statements published in the period 2008 to 2015, from the 114 listed companies that make up the total sample. These financial statements show earning and equity of the holding company, as well as the OCI and the reclassification of the same company, as values required for the indirect determination of comprehensive income. The earning and equity taken from the consolidated financial statements refer to the holding company; in other words, we do not consider the earning and equity figures referring to the minority partners in the subsidiary companies.

The publication of comprehensive income was made mandatory by IAS 1 only from 1/1/2014 onwards. So until that date, comprehensive income had to be calculated indirectly as the sum of earning in the income statement, other comprehensive income and taking into account reclassification. In the period 2010-2013, other comprehensive income and reclassification were itemized in the statement of changes in equity. The number of shares necessary to determine the accounting value per share was taken directly from the notes of the consolidated financial statement. Share prices were taken directly from the Delhi Stock Exchange website. There is of course always a time lag before accounting information is incorporated into market prices, which means that there is a time lag between independent and dependent variables in our analysis. The date of recording the share price, the dependent variable, thus has to be chosen carefully. Given the regulations governing financial statements in India, the date 30 April was selected. It is assumed that on that date, capitalization provides a full reflection of the effects of the financial statement of the previous year.

RESULTS OF EMPIRICAL TESTS

Summary Statistics and Correlations

Table 1 presents descriptive statistics of the variables used in the study subdivided by time period. It shows that the average evolution is consistent with the different financial contexts which prevailed 2008-2015. Average market prices rose 2010-2012 compared to 2008-2009 as a result of favorable economic trends, but fell significantly in the last part of the period 2013-2015, because of the financial crisis. The other variables saw similar effects. For example, 2013-2015 saw a big fall in the average value of comprehensive income per share, which was equal to 0.082, compared to 0.678 in the previous period. Analysis of the standard deviation confirms higher volatility of the accounting and market information generated by IAS/IFRS. Because of the introduction of fair value, this particularly affected earning and comprehensive income.

Table 2 describes the Pearson correlation for some variables. The main finding is the fall in the level of correlation between accounting variables and market prices. Before the financial crisis this correlation was fairly significant, and was higher than 0.5. But from 2008 onwards, the correlation becomes much less significant, probably as a result of the effect on market prices of other variables rather than earning, comprehensive income and equity. The financial crisis in fact made markets more volatile, and less dependent on the ordinary flow of information issued by firms. This is a preliminary indication of the decline in the VR of earning and equity in 2013-2015.

Table 1. Descriptive statistics

General Sample	Mean	Median	Standard Deviation	Max	Min
Panel 2008-2009					
Price	7,772	4,485	9,544	59,520	0,060
BVPS	4,978	2,624	7,595	79,073	0,008
EPS	0,394	0,194	0,921	7,487	-1,982
Panel 2010-2012					
Price	10,882	6,725	13,141	94,010	0,124
BVPS	6,402	3,396	12,851	134,11	0,082
EPS	0,639	0,351	1,412	11,920	-12,292
CIPS	0,678	0,334	1,913	24,327	-12,468
Panel 2013-2015					
Price	6,357	3,578	9,822	89,620	0,080
BVPS	5,879	3,520	9,395	108,09	0,010
EPS	0,179	0,162	1,491	4,384	-21,909
CIPS	0,082	0,136	2,345	10,546	-30,728

Table 2. Pearson correlation matrix

General Sample	Price	BVPS	EPS	CIPS
Panel 2008-2009				
Price	1	0,705	0,699	-
BVPS		1	0,778	-
EPS			1	-
Panel 2010-2012				
Price	1	0,691	0,615	0,562
BVPS		1	0,766	0,704
EPS			1	0,855
CIPS				1
Panel 2013-2015				
Price	1	0,479	0,269	0,112
BVPS		1	0,145	-0,159
EPS			1	0,763
CIPS				1

Results

Tables 3 and 4 report the estimation results for equations used in the study. The following observations concern first the entire sample, and subsequently the two different sectors. In most cases, the Chow test is significant at the 1 per cent level. This suggests a structural break in the relationship between market price and the accounting measures. Only when referred to the comparison between 2009 pre-IAS/IFRS and 2009 post-IAS/IFRS does the Chow test not show statistically significant values.

Regarding the transition to International Accounting Standard (RQ1), the results indicate an increase in VR in 2009, when companies listed on the Milan Stock Exchange show an increase in R^2 adj. The increase is minimal for the industrial sector (R^2adj.: pre-IAS/IFRS 0.239, post-IAS/IFRS 0.287) and more marked for the financial sector (R^2adj.: pre-IAS/IFRS 0.610, post-IAS/IFRS 0.962). The estimation results for the coefficient also indicate that with the transition to IAS/IFRS the association between market price and BVPS decreases, while the association between market price and EPS increases in both sectors. The increase in VR in 2009 for the full sample is not confirmed by a comparison between the two periods 2008-2009 and 2010-2012, which finds a slight worsening of the R^2 adj. (for 2003-2004 R^2 adj. 0.628; for 2010-2012 R^2 adj. 0.617). The coefficient on BVPS is lower for the IAS/IFRS period, while the coefficient on EPS is higher. These results suggest a higher VR for earnings after the implementation of International Accounting Standards. For the industrial sector, the R^2adj. increases from 0.592 for the pre-IAS/IFRS period to 0.754 for the post-IAS/IFRS period with an increase of 27.36 per cent. This means that in the two years 2008-2009 the accounting measures describe 59.2% of the variability of the market prices, while the explanatory power increases to 75.4% in 2010-2012. For industrial companies too, the coefficient of EPS is higher and that of BVPS is lower, but the coefficient of BVPS increase in the post-IAS/IFRS period while the coefficient of EPS decreases. For the financial sector, on the other hand, there is a fall in the VR of accounting measures. In fact the R^2 adj. decreases from 0.929 to 0.687.

The comparison between 2008-2009 and 2010-2012 shows an increase in the coefficient on BVPS and a decrease in that on EPS for both sectors. This is probably because of the impact the transition to IAS/IFRS had on accounting measures. In fact, during the transition phase, (2009) the reclassifications were made on equity which underwent further variation at the beginning of 2010 as a result of the application of IAS 39 and 32. It is therefore consistent that in the transition towards IAS/IFRS it is equity which becomes more significant in information terms for investors.

Table 4 shows the effects of the financial crisis on the relation between market prices and accounting measures (RQ2). The reduction in R^2 adj. proves significant

Table 3. VR and transition to international accounting standards

Equation: $P_{it} = \beta_0 + \beta_1 BVS_{it} + \beta_2 EPS_{it} + \varepsilon_{it}$				
FULL SAMPLE				
	2009_{ITA}	$2009_{IAS/IFRS}$	$2008\text{-}2009_{ITA}$	$2010\text{-}2012_{IAS/IFRS}$
N	342	342	648	960
β_0	3,302 (3,815)***	2,861 (3,440)***	1,511 (3,366)***	0258 (1,069)
BVPS	0,476 (1,604)***	0,515 (2,260)**	0,975 (7,113)***	1,604 (14,27)***
EPS	7,741 (3,566)***	7,082 (3,743)***	6,513 (7,190)***	5,119 (8,330)***
R_2adj.	0,291	0,351	0,628	0,617
F-stat.	24,191	31,591	182,58	257,704
P-value (F-stat.)	0,000	0,000	0,000	0,000
Chow	-2,979		4,4098***	
INDUSTRIAL COMPANIES				
	2009_{ITA}	$2009_{IAS/IFRS}$	$2008\text{-}2009_{ITA}$	$2010\text{-}2012_{IAS/IFRS}$
N	273	273	510	792
β_0	3,249 (3,111)***	2,987 (2,910)***	1,159 (2,138)**	-0,245 (-1,519)
BVPS	0,677 (1,878)*	0,543 (1,582)	1,302 (7,528)***	2,118 (28,12)***
EPS	6,557 (2,491)**	7,681 (3,177)***	5,387 (5,444)***	4,464 (9,943)***
R_2adj.	0,239	0,287	0,592	0,754
F-stat.	15,12	19,197	123,969	404,089
P-value (F-stat.)	0,000	0,000	0,000	0,000
Chow	-7,321		18,521***	
FINANCIAL COMPANIES				
	2009_{ITA}	$2009_{IAS/IFRS}$	$2008\text{-}2009_{ITA}$	$2010\text{-}2012_{IAS/IFRS}$
N	69	69	138	168
β_0	2,786 (3,911)***	1,499 (3,237)***	1,282 (4,365)***	1,006 (2,449)**
BVPS	0,498 (1,677)	0,151 (2,261)**	0,452 (5,853)***	0,711 (3,873)***
EPS	4,634 (1,860)*	10,141 (7,422)***	9,005 (10,29)***	5,996 (3,846)***
R_2adj.	0,610	0,962	0,929	0,687
F-stat.	18,231	276,769	296,672	61,271
P-value (F-stat.)	0,000	0,000	0,000	0,000
Chow	1,117		2,707*	

P-value: *<0,1; **<0,05; ***<0,01

Table 4. VR, comprehensive income and financial crisis

Equation (A and C): $P_{it} = \beta_0 + \beta_1 BVS_{it} + \beta_2 EPS_{it} + \varepsilon_{it}$ Equation (B and D): $P_{it} = \beta_0 + \beta_1 BVS_{it} + \beta_2 CIPS_{it} + \varepsilon_{it}$				
FULL SAMPLE				
	A) EPS 2005-2007$_{IAS/IFRS}$	B) CIPS 2005-2007$_{IAS/IFRS}$	C) EPS 2008-2010$_{IAS/IFRS}$	D) CIPS 2008-2010$_{IAS/IFRS}$
N	960	960	948	948
β_0	0258 (1,069)	0,277 (1,130)	0,793 (2,878)***	0,551 (1,972)**
BVPS	1,604 (14,27)***	1,584 (13,78)***	0,737 (9,257)***	1,007 (7,869)***
EPS	5,119 (8,330)***		4,432 (6,723)***	
CIPS		5,191 (8,198)***		1,962 (3,351)***
R_2adj.	0,617	0,611	0,342	0,253
F-stat.	257,704	251,96	82,786	54,531
P-value (F-stat.)	0,000	0,000	0,000	0,000
Chow: A vs B C vs D A vs C B vs D	 0,171 8,940*** 31,786*** 26,624***			
INDUSTRIAL COMPANIES				
	A) EPS 2010-2012$_{IAS/IFRS}$	B) CIPS 2010-2012$_{IAS/IFRS}$	C) EPS 2013-2015$_{IAS/IFRS}$	D) CIPS 2013-2015$_{IAS/IFRS}$
N	792	792	765	765
β_0	-0,245 (-1,519)	-0,209 (-1,271)	0,520 (1,495)	0,253 (0,901)
BVPS	2,118 (28,12)***	2,113 (29,31)***	1,006 (6,312)***	1,254 (7,911)***
EPS	4,464 (9,943)***		3,563 (4,013)***	
CIPS		3,958 (8,617)***		1,427 (2,563)**
R_2adj.	0,754	0,765	0,309	0,229
F-stat.	404,089	429,676	57,918	38,744
P-value (F-stat.)	0,000	0,000	0,000	0,000
Chow: A vs B C vs D A vs C B vs D	 -2,684 11,487*** 27,025*** 15,647***			

continued on following page

Table 4. Continued

FINANCIAL COMPANIES				
	A) EPS 2010-2012$_{IAS/IFRS}$	B) CIPS 2010-2012$_{IAS/IFRS}$	C) EPS 2013-2015$_{IAS/IFRS}$	D) CIPS 2013-2015$_{IAS/IFRS}$
N	168	168	183	183
β_0	1,006 (2,449)**	0,937 (2,052)**	1,151 (3,655)***	1,303 (3,305)***
BVPS	0,711 (3,873)***	0,915 (7,564)***	0,279 (5,187)***	0,367 (5,564)***
EPS	5,996 (3,846)***		4,246 (4,274)***	
CIPS		4,809 (4,784)***		2,966 (3,543)***
R_2adj.	0,687	0,716	0,581	0,542
F-stat.	61,271	70,415	42,626	36,544
P-value (F-stat.)	0,000	0,000	0,000	0,000
Chow: A vs B C vs D A vs C B vs D	 1,095 5,694*** 21,363*** 25,133***			

P-value: *<0,1; **<0,05; ***<0,01

for the full sample as for each of the two sectors. There is also a fall in the coefficient on the independent variables (BVPS, EPS and CIPS). For the full sample, the R^2 adj. decreases from 0.617 (0.611 with CIPS) for the pre-crisis period to 0.342 (0.253 with CIPS) for 2013-2015. The reduction of the coefficient on EPS (or CIPS) is bigger than the reduction shown by the coefficient on BVPS. In fact, although the earnings coefficients remain higher than the BVPS coefficients even during financial crisis, the fall in earnings coefficients is more marked probably because of their greater volatility. The R^2 adj. for industrial companies decreases from 0.754 (0.765 with CIPS) to 0.309 (0.229 with CIPS), the coefficient on EPS decreases by 20.18 per cent (63,95 per cent for CIPS) and that of BVPS decreases by 52.50 per cent. For financial companies too, R^2 adj. and the coefficient on independent variables decrease.

A look at VR confirms the observations made on Table 2. In periods of financial crisis, accounting measures remain relatively significant for market price variability but they are less so than in periods of economic growth. This is probably because other variables have greater incidence on market prices during economic recession. The third research question (RQ3) asked whether EPS or the CIPS had greater VR in the period under observation. Of particular interest is the size of coefficient β_2

calculated with reference to earning per share or to comprehensive income per share. We found that EPS had greater VR than CIPS for the entire period (2010-2015). Although the coefficient of both variables falls during financial crisis (2013-2015), the β_2 relating to EPS remains higher than that relating to CIPS.

DISCUSSION

Quantitative methods of study such as VR are ideal for generalizing using the type of test that Karl Popper called "falsification" (Popper, 1963). This is one of the most rigorous tests to which a scientific proposition can be subjected; if just one observation does not fit with the proposition, the proposition is considered invalid and must be either revised or rejected. The principle that every "experiment" must be repeatable underpins scientific method and the possibility of falsifying a proposition. The consequence is that results can be generalized. Studies which use the same method on the same sample in a similar time period allow for a certain degree of generalization of results, taking account of differences where opportune. Comparison with findings by similar studies in fact is the more significant the more similarities there are. Different choices affected by researchers on the other hand can help to explain differences in results. In any case, the more marked the differences between studies, the less comparable are the findings and the less they can be generalized. This section discusses the potential uses and limitations of our findings, and compares them with previous studies.

This study finds an increase in combined VR resulting from the application of IAS/IFRS in the transition year, which confirms RQ1. But in a comparison between the period pre-IAS/IFRS and post-IAS/IFRS, VR does not rise. RQ1 is thus only partially confirmed. More precisely, this study confirms results of previous Indian studies (using the same equation) regarding the initial period post-IAS/IFRS, 2010-2012 (Pavan and Paglietti, 2011; Paglietti, 2009; Devalle, 2010). This is the only period for which there existed previous Indian VR studies that were similar in terms of variables, sample and number of observations recorded. For the period pre-IAS/IFRS (2003-2004) however our results cannot be compared with similar studies. Existing studies covered different time periods, quite apart from the fact that they reached conflicting conclusions, probably as a result of differences in time period and the number of observations (Pavan and Paglietti, 2011, p. 27; Devalle, 2010, p. 105). Devalle in fact makes a multi-country study on the pre-IAS/IFRS period, and presents far fewer observations on India than the present study or Paglietti. It is important to note that the "falsification" test in social science forms part of critical reflexivity. Deviant cases may result from different variables, or different samples.

Regarding levels of significance of the variables, this study has found that transition to IAS/IFRS led to an increase in VR of equity and a fall in VR of earning. This is consistent with the impact on equity of the first application of IAS 39 and 32. The finding appears to conflict with Paglietti's finding of a fall in relation to equity and an increase in relation to earning (Paglietti, 2009; Pavan & Paglietti, 2011), and also appears to conflict with Devalle's finding of a fall in relation to both these variables (Devalle et al., 2010, p. 105). But differences in the composition of the sample, particularly in terms of the division into sectors, are probably the reason for the differences in findings.

In the period of financial crisis, this study has found a deterioration of VR, thus confirming RQ2. This is consistent with the fact that accounting information can be less significant in times of financial crisis (Barth and Landsman, 2010; pp.404-405). This is because the speed of information is fundamental and market conditions tend not to reflect conditions of efficiency of the theoretical models (Modigliani and Miller, 1958). This study has found that financial crisis has greater incidence on the VR of earning. Moreover, comprehensive income becomes less significant than earning and this deterioration is greater for comprehensive income probably because of the impact of fair value. It is not possible to compare our findings for RQ2 with those of other studies, as our study is one of the very first to assess the effects of financial crisis on the relationship between market and accounting value.

Lastly, we found lower VR for comprehensive income than for earning, and RQ3 is not confirmed. Coefficients relating to equity and earning are found to be less significant. There is no India-specific study with which to compare findings, but the multi-country study by Ghoncarov & Hodgson on a sample of 6 countries including India found the same result (Ghoncarov & Hodgson, 2011, p. 44).

CONCLUSION

The importance of this chapter lies in the length of the period observed, which allows an assessment of VR of accounting information on one sample in periods that are economically diverse (economic growth and subsequent financial crisis), and covering the aspect of comprehensive income. The chapter thus makes a contribution to the furthering of VR research. Previous studies are only partially comparable in term of sample composition and time period, which are elements that in VR research, as in other fields, can lead to different results. VR studies may also use different premises or postulates, which also limit the generalizability of results. Discrepancies between results in fact offer food for thought on the incidence of the choice of variables. In social sciences, in fact, deviant cases or results and the falsifications they entail "are main sources of theory development, because they point to the development of new concepts, variables, and causal mechanisms, necessary in order to account for the deviant case and other cases like it" (Flyvbjerg, 2011, p. 305; David & Sutton, 2011). The fact that previous studies are partially falsified suggests that current theory is incomplete (Barth et al., 2001) rather than invalid (Holthausen & Watts, 2001). This incompleteness is a current limit on VR studies, but in future it should be overcome by further studies elucidating the contradictions brought to light by studies that are similar but not identical.

The discrepancies between the present study and previous work (i.e. RQ1) in fact suggest possible avenues for future research. For example, examination could be made of the impact of IAS 32 and 39 on the transition to International Accounting Standards, with particular reference to financial firms. The present chapter investigated the informational value of comprehensive income, and although findings of previous research are confirmed, more work is required to determine the reasons for this value. Future research could for example focus on individual OCIs. Lastly, the chapter confirms the hypothesis that in times of financial crisis the informational capacity of basic accounting values deteriorates, consistent with the theoretical underpinnings of VR (Barth et al., 2011). It thus answers the need voiced by Laux and Leuz regarding today's financial crisis: "One important step would be to show that prices were indeed distorted and deviated substantially from fundamental values, which is not an easy task either" (Laux & Leuz, 2009, p.20). Future research is required to identify those variables in various types of accounting information which retain VR times of financial crisis.

REFERENCES

Ball, R., & Brown, P. (1968, Autumn). An Empirical Evaluation of Accounting Income Numbers. *Journal of Accounting Research.*

Barth, M.E., Beaver, W.H., & Landsman, W.R. (2001). *The Relevance of the Value Relevance Literature for Financial Accounting Standard Setting: Another View. Journal of Accounting and Economics*, 31, 456-478.

Barth, M. E., & Clinch, G. (2009). Scale effects in capital markets-based accounting research. *Journal of Business Finance & Accounting*, *36*(3-4), 567–594. doi:10.1111/j.1468-5957.2009.02133.x

Barth, M. E., & Kallapur, S. (1996). The effects of cross-sectional scale differences on regression results in empirical accounting research. *Contemporary Accounting Research*, *13*(2), 234–265. doi:10.1111/j.1911-3846.1996.tb00514.x

Barth, M. E., & Landsman, W. R. (2010). How did financial reporting contribute to the financial crisis? *European Accounting Review*, *19*(3), 123–156. doi:10.1080/09638180.2010.498619

Barth, M. E., Landsman, W. R., & Lang, M. H. (2008). International Accounting Standards and Accounting Quality. *Journal of Accounting Research*, *46*(3), 234–265. doi:10.1111/j.1475-679X.2008.00287.x

Bartov, E., Goldberg, S. R., & Kim, M. (2005). Comparative value relevance among German, U.S., and International Accounting Standards: A German stock market perspective. *Journal of Accounting, Auditing & Finance*, *20*(2), 256–289.

Beaver, W. H. (1968). The information content of annual earnings announcements. *Journal of Accounting Research*, *6*(3), 325–367.

Beaver, W. H. (2002). Perspectives on Recent Capital Markets Research. *Accounting Review*, *77*(2), 459–473. doi:10.2308/accr.2002.77.2.453

Brown, S., Kin, L., & Lys, T. (1999). Use of R^2 in accounting research: Measuring changes in value relevance over the last four decades. *Journal of Accounting and Economics*, *2*(28), 567–597.

Callao, S., Jarne, J. J., & Lainez, J. A. (2007). Adoption of IFRS in Spain: Effect on the comparability and relevance of financial reporting. *Journal of International Accounting, Auditing & Taxation*, *16*(2), 356–375. doi:10.1016/j.intaccaudtax.2007.06.002

Collins, D. W., Maydew, E. L., & Weiss, I. S. (1997). Changes in the value-relevance of earnings and book values over the past forty years. *Journal of Accounting and Economics*, *24*(2), 345–375.

David, M., & Sutton, C. D. (2011). *Social Research: an introduction*. London: Sage.

Devalle, A. (2010). *Misurazione della performance nel bilancio IFRS. Comprehensive income, dibattito internazionale e value relevance*. Milano: Pearson Prentice Hall.

Devalle, A., Onali, E., & Magarini, R. (2010). Assessing the value relevance of accounting data after the introduction of IFRS in Europe. *Journal of International Financial Management Accounting*, *21*(2), 345–378. doi:10.1111/j.1467-646X.2010.01037.x

Dontoh, A., Radhakrishnan, S., & Ronen, J. (2004). The Declining Value-relevance of Accounting Information and Non-information-based Trading: An Empirical Analysis. *Contemporary Accounting Research*, *21*(2), 245–275.

Easton, P. D., & Sommers, G. A. (2003). Scale and the scale effect in market-based accounting research. *Journal of Business Finance & Accounting*, *31*(1-2), 435–476.

Entwistle, G. M., Feltham, G. D., & Mbagwu, C. (2010). The value relevance of alternative earnings measures: A comparison of pro-forma, GAAP and I/B/E/S earnings. *Journal of Accounting, Auditing & Finance*, *25*(2), 564–583.

Fama, E. F. (1970). Efficient Capital Markets: A review of the theory and empirical work. *The Journal of Finance*, *25*(2), 679–693. doi:10.2307/2325486

Feltham, G. A., & Ohlson, J. A. (1995). Valuation and Clean Surplus Accounting for Operating and Financial Activities. *Contemporary Accounting Research*, *11*(2), 768–795. doi:10.1111/j.1911-3846.1995.tb00462.x

Flyvbjerg, B. (2011). Case Study. In N. K. Denzin and Y. S. Lincoln (eds.), The Sage of Handbook of Qualitative Research (4th ed., Ch. 17, pp. 301-316). Thousand Oaks, CA: Sage.

Francis, J., & Schipper, K. (1999). Have Financial Statements Lost Their Relevance? *Journal of Accounting Research*, *37*(1), 123–146.

Goncharov, I., & Hodgson, A. (2011). Measuring and reporting income in Europe. *Journal of International Accounting Research*, *10*(1), 234–246. doi:10.2308/jiar.2011.10.1.27

Gu, Z. (2007). Across-sample incomparability of R2s and additional evidence on value relevance changes over time. *Journal of Business Finance & Accounting*, *37*(7-8), 324–356.

Hellström, K. (2006). The value relevance of financial accounting information in a transitional economy: The case of the Czech Republic. *European Accounting Review*, *15*(2), 354–377.

Holthausen, R. W., & Watts, R. L. (2001). The Relevance of the Value-Relevance Literature for Financial Accounting Standard Setting. *Journal of Accounting and Economics*, *31*(1), 356–387.

Jermakowicz, E. K., Prather-Kinsey, J., & Wulf, I. (2007). The Value Relevance of Accounting Income Reported by DAX-30 German Companies. *Journal of International Financial Management & Accounting*, *18*(3), 345–376. doi:10.1111/j.1467-646X.2007.01011.x

Kim, M., & Kross, W. (2006). The Ability of Earnings to Predict Future Operating Cash Flows Has Been Increasing - Not Decreasing. *CFA Digest*, *36*(2), 324–365.

Kothari, S. P. (2001). Capital Markets Research in Accounting. *Journal of Accounting and Economics*, *31*(1), 567–580.

Kothari, S. P., & Zimmerman, J. L. (1995). Price and return models. *Journal of Accounting and Economics*, *20*(2), 456–476. doi:10.1016/0165-4101(95)00399-4

Landsman, W. R., & Magliolo, J. (1988). Cross-Sectional Capital Market Research and Model Specification. *Accounting Review*, *63*(4), 423–456.

Lev, B., & Zarowin, P. (1999). The Boundaries of Financial Reporting and How to Extend Them. *Journal of Accounting Research*, *37*(2), 435–467. doi:10.2307/2491413

Modigliani, F., & Miller, M. (1958). The cost of capital, corporation finance and the theory of investment. *The American Economic Review*, (48), 453–478.

Ohlson, J. A. (1995). Earnings, Book Values and Dividends in Security Valuation. *Contemporary Accounting Research*, *11*(2), 345–367. doi:10.1111/j.1911-3846.1995.tb00461.x

Popper, K. (1963). *Conjectures and Refutations*. London: Routledge and Keagan Paul.

Schiebel, A. (2007). Empirical Value Relevance of German Gaap and IFRS. *Journal of Economics and Financial Sciences*, *1*(2), 321–352.

Schipper, K. (2005). The introduction of accounting standards in Europe: Implications for international convergence. *European Accounting Review*, *14*(1), 324–367. doi:10.1080/0963818042000338013

Soderstrom, N. S., & Sun, K. J. (2007). IFRS Adoption and Accounting Quality: A review. *European Accounting Review*, *16*(4), 245–267. doi:10.1080/09638180701706732

Subramanyam, K. R., & Hung, M. (2007). Financial statement effects of adopting international accounting standards: The case of Germany. *Review of Accounting Studies*, *12*(4), 456–482.

Veltri S. and Silvestri A. (2011), *La value relevance dei valori contabili dopo la crisi finanziaria: un'applicazione al mercato italiano*, Rivista Italiana di Ragioneria e di Economia Aziendale, Rirea, Roma.

Verbeek, M. (2006). *Econometria*. Bologna: Zanichelli.

Watts, R., & Zimmerman, J. (1978). Towards a positive theory of the determination of accounting standards. *Accounting Review*, *53*, 568–589.

Watts, R., & Zimmerman, J. (1990). Positive Accounting Theory. A Ten Year Perspective. *Accounting Review*, *65*(1), 345–378.

Chapter 13
Investigating the Impact of Declining Oil Prices in Global Stock Markets:
Oil Exporting and Oil Importing Countries

Jose J. Haspa DeLarosiere
Universidad EAFIT, Colombia

ABSTRACT

As well as illustrating wider and interrelated repercussions of plunging oil prices on the global economy – and its impact on global financial markets, this chapter also re affirms the realization that the strong form of the Efficient Market Hypothesis appears to introduce less accountability than the weak and semi strong components. Even though it appears that fundamentals underlying previous Financial Crises and recent volatilities differ, recent evidence also provides interesting information about turbulences that currently plague global stock markets. Can previous historical records be relied upon (reasonably or otherwise) to predict future outcomes? Where predictability (redictive values) and confirmatory attributes (confirming values) constitute components of relevance in financial reporting, then it appears that certain historical reports, data and information based on the age and relevance of such data, still constitute relevant and reliable data given that such information is current, relevant and reliable in the sense that it can be predicted upon, confirmed and verified.

DOI: 10.4018/978-1-5225-1900-3.ch013

Copyright ©2017, IGI Global. Copying or distributing in print or electronic forms without written permission of IGI Global is prohibited.

INTRODUCTION

Even though it appears that fundamentals underlying previous Financial Crises and recent volatilities in global stock markets differ, evidence also lends support to salient commonalities between major and significant events which have heralded financial turbulences that currently plague global stock markets.

Based on World Bank reports (2015, p. 155), similarities and reminders can be drawn between recent plunges in oil prices and the collapse in oil prices in 1985-86. Further, it is highlighted that between 1984-2013, five other episodes of oil price declines of 30 percent or more in a six-month period occurred, coinciding with major changes in the global economy and oil markets (see page 155):

- An increase in the supply of oil and change in OPEC policy (1985-86); U.S. recessions (1990–91 and 2001); the Asian crisis (1997–98); and the global financial crisis (2007–09).

In view of the above correlations, can distinguishing features be identified – such as to delineate the present plunges in oil prices from previous episodes? Several remarks have also been made in relation to oil importers, particularly emerging market economies such as China and India, benefiting from the recent drops in oil prices – hence mitigating potentially devastating consequences which could result from a full blown and elevated global crisis. As highlighted in previous chapters relating to the impact of recent regulatory and financial reforms – as well as monetary policies – and the response of emerging market economies to such regulatory reforms, these economies have found it difficult to recover from the recent Financial Crisis partly in attribution to such reforms. Is it then realistic and optimistic to expect that they should weather the storms generated by the recent oil plunges – even if expected to profit from lower oil prices?

Various sources of evidence and reports not only indicate that the impact of lower oil prices on growth is expected to boost activity in China by 0.1-0.2 percent because oil accounts for only 18 percent of its energy consumption, but that the sustained low oil prices of 2015 are expected to widen the current account surplus by some 0.4-0.7 percentage points of GDP (World Bank, 2015, p. 161). Further reports (BBC, 2015) also indicate that Thailand, India, South Korea – and to an extent, China and Japan, should benefit from recent plunges in oil prices for the following reasons:

- Lower inflation.
- Lower costs for business.
- Higher spending power for households.
- Improved government finances.

- Central banks can keep interest rates lower.
- Smaller deficits in a country's international payments.

One reason attributed to a limitation on China and Japan's ability to profit from present oil price reductions, are considered to be related to the problem of deflation or falling overall price levels (BBC, 2015). Further, it is highlighted that Japan has had recurrent episodes since the mid-1990s whilst it appears that China is about to witness a similar fate. Having considered those countries which are likely to benefit from falling oil prices, the following section considers which countries are likely to bear the greatest impact of the oil price plunges. The section also considers developments which have resulted in the fall in global oil prices.

Background and Literature Review on the Impact of Falling Oil Prices

Frankel (2006, p. 2) comments on the impact of declining commodity prices in the 1980s – 1990s (late 1980s and the 1990s) - a period, which he observes as one where prices generally declined:

- Many of the victims of emerging market crises in the 1990s were oil producers that were suffering, among other things, from low oil prices (Mexico, Indonesia, Russia) or others suffering from low agricultural prices (Brazil and Argentina).

He also notes the high record levels reached in 2006 – particularly with respect to copper, platinum, nickel, zinc, lead, as well as crude oil. Even though, in his opinion, the initial reaction to such prices between 2003 – 2004, was marked by relative indifference, he adds that by 2005 and 2006, the prices had reached such a level that their impact was to significant to be ignored. Certain reasons cited as being contributory to the initial indifference to the prices in 2003 -2004 are as follows (2006, p. 2):

- Oil was no longer a large share of the economy, it was said; (2) Futures markets showed that the "spike" in prices was expected to be only temporary; and (3) Monetary policy need focus only on the core CPI inflation rate and can safely ignore the volatile food and energy component, unless or until it starts to get passed through into the core rate.

Bastourre et al find that: "reductions in international interest rates and global risk appetite; rises in quantitative global liquidity measures and equity returns;

and US dollar depreciations, tend to diminish spreads of emerging economies and strengthen commodity prices simultaneously."

Central arguments of Frankel's paper (2006) are as follows:

- High real commodity prices can be a signal that monetary policy is loose (p. 3).
- High interest rates reduce the demand for storable commodities (or increase the supply) (p. 5).
- Monetary policy, as reflected in real interest rates, is an important - and usually under-appreciated determinant of the real prices of oil and other mineral and agricultural products, while far from being the only determinant (p. 5).

In addition to those objectives highlighted under the introductory section, this chapter, also aims to address the following:

- Commodity price cycles and their impact in financial markets.
- Causes of rises and declines (particularly large fluctuations) in commodity prices (pre and post Financial Crisis).
- Inflation targeting.
- Relationship between interest rates and commodity prices.
- real commodity price and the real interest rate, equation (negative relationship).

Investigations into monetary policies being adapted in response to current market volatilities and commodity prices will also be considered – as well as whether they conform with Frankel's remarks (2006, p. 24):

- Few believe that the proper response for an oil-importing country in the event of a large increase in world oil prices is to tighten monetary policy and thereby appreciate the currency sufficiently to prevent an increase in the price of oil in terms of domestic currency. The usual defense of inflation targeting offered by its many proponents is that in the event of such a shock, the central bank can easily deviate from the CPI target and explain the circumstances to the public. But what can be the argument for making such derogations on an ad hoc basis, when it is possible to build them into a simple target rule in the first place? Certainly not a gain in transparency and credibility. This is not to suggest that this regime would be appropriate for all countries, only that it might have advantages for countries that experience large volatility in their terms of trade. But it has become apparent in this decade that terms of trade volatility are a more serious issue than was believed in the 1980s and 1990s.

Reasons Attributed to Falling Oil Prices

Even though the generally attributed reason for the recent developments with oil prices is related to increased supply across oil exporting regions, including the increased output resulting from shale oil production in the United States – as well as oil output in Canada and other major oil exporting regions (Russia, Iraq and Libya), a combination of factors can be cited as causes for the recent developments.

Based on several sources and authorities on the literature, the following are attributed to the current decline in oil prices (World Bank, 2015b, p. 4 and World Bank, 2015a, pp. 156-157):

- Significant shift in OPEC policy resulting from a change in Saudi Arabia's role as the cartel's traditional "swing producer" following a disagreement with OPEC in late November 2014, on production cuts.
- Unwinding of some geopolitical risks.
- And an appreciation of the U.S. dollar.

Iran's return to the international oil market, following the removal of sanctions which were lifted against it under an international agreement with major world powers, is also cited as being contributory to the current over supply of global oil output (see New York Times, 2016).

Figures 1 and 2 illustrate the degree to which the oil prices have plunged – with particular reference to 2014 - as well as the trends in oil prices since 2007. Figure 2 reflects how the plunge in oil prices coincides with the onset of the 2008 Financial Crisis.

Even though many consumers have benefited from the recent plunges in oil prices and even though the recent slowdown in growth across emerging market economies have probably downplayed the impact and repercussions of the current fall in oil prices, the figures and records resulting from the fall out is significant and can be highlighted as revealed from these reports from the New Times (2016):

- A decline in earnings for companies that made record profits in recent years, leading such companies to decommission more than two-thirds of their rigs and sharply cut investment in exploration and production.
- Several companies having gone bankrupt – with an estimated loss of 250,000 jobs for oil workers.

The non-profitability of oil rigs and projects is also evidenced by the decision of the United States on the 6th November 2015, to put off the planned Pipeline Project negotiations between itself and Canada – as the Project was considered not only

Figure 1.
Source: BBC (2016). "Falling oil prices: How are countries being affected?" 18 January 2016

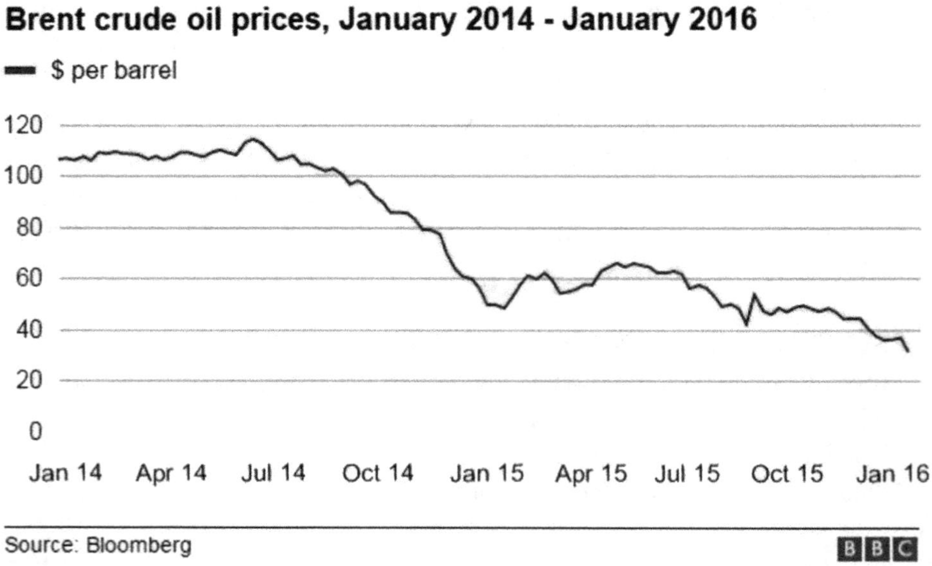

Figure 2.
Source: The New York Times (2016). http://www.nytimes.com/interactive/2016/business/energy-environment/oil-prices.html?_r=0

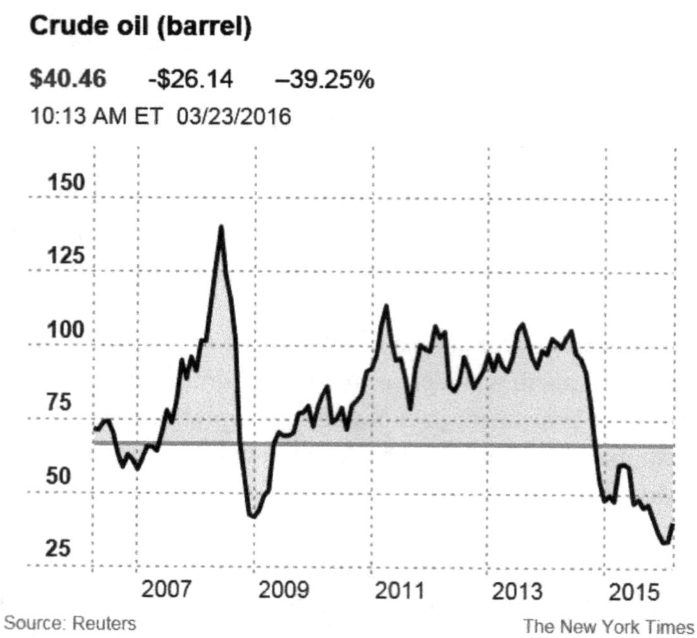

uneconomically profitable in matters of national interest, but also considered to generate adverse repercussions environmentally.

Whilst many states in the United States have benefited from the falling oil prices, other states such as Alaska, Texas, North Dakota, Oklahoma and Louisiana have been economically and negatively impacted by recent developments, that is the plunge in oil prices.

There are however positive signs of recovery – hopefully a speedy recovery. Having announced their intentions to cut back on oil outputs in February 2016, it is hoped that prominent OPEC members such as Saudi Arabia, Venezuela, Russia and Qatar will be able to sustain their agreement. Particularly in view of the fact that geopolitical tensions and conflicts have been triggered as a result of falling oil prices in several oil exporting regions. Furthermore, following increased supply from previously unexpected sources, this will necessitate greater global cooperation if cutbacks in oil supply and a meaningful effective agreement are to be realized.

MAIN FOCUS OF THE CHAPTER

Issues, Controversies, Problems

If benefits are expected from the recent plunges in oil prices – particularly in respect of oil importing countries, why are such benefits not being translated explicitly – as reflected by current global growth forecasts? Having touched lightly on such mitigating factors affecting the beneficial potential of current fall in oil prices, under the introductory section, it is also helpful to consider proposals aimed at translating and facilitating beneficial aspects of the falling oil prices.

Figure 3 illustrates the assertion by the IMF that policy responses to lower oil prices, which are still being formulated in many countries, will depend on a complex set of factors.

According to the IMF (2015, p. 34), policies of oil exporters should focus on fiscal adjustment, supported by stronger medium-term fiscal frameworks. It is also added that monetary policy should strike the right balance between the domestic cycle and the degree of vulnerabilities whilst countries exposed to potential financial strains would benefit from strengthening their macroprudential policy frameworks.

Further, in relation to oil exporting countries, the following observations are made (IMF, 2015, pp. 34-35):

- Countries outside of the Venn space, such as Norway, are able to adjust to lower oil prices gradually, and use their policy buffers to smooth the transition owing to comfortable fiscal and external buffers and limited policy risks.

Figure 3. Policy responses to lower oil prices

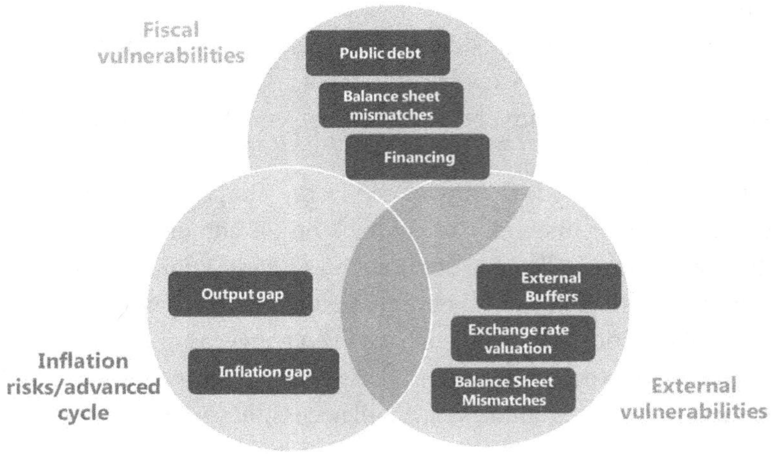

Figure 4. Annual impact of terms of trade by group

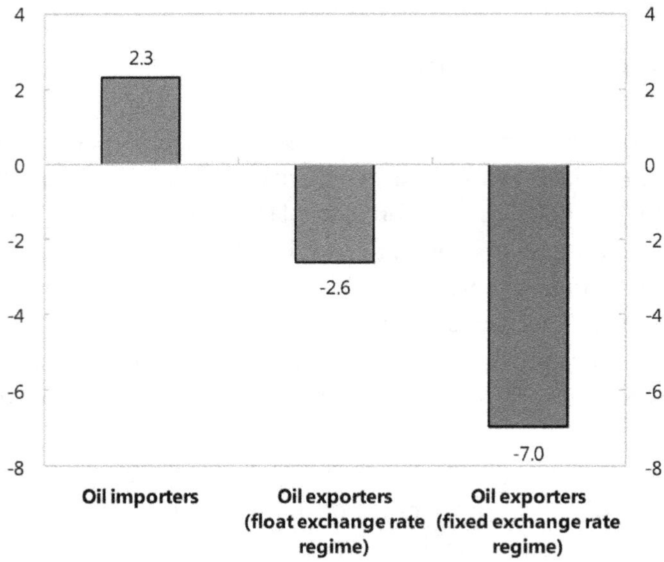

- At the other end, countries at the center of the Venn diagram (such as Venezuela) are better off adjusting policies at a swift pace immediately Also highlighted that policy changes vary depending on the exchange rate regime – for example, flexible exchange rate regime helps partly mitigate the external and fiscal impact of lower dollar oil prices, as long as there are no major foreign exchange balance sheet mismatches resulting.

Figure 5. Policy decision and responses (exporting oil countries)

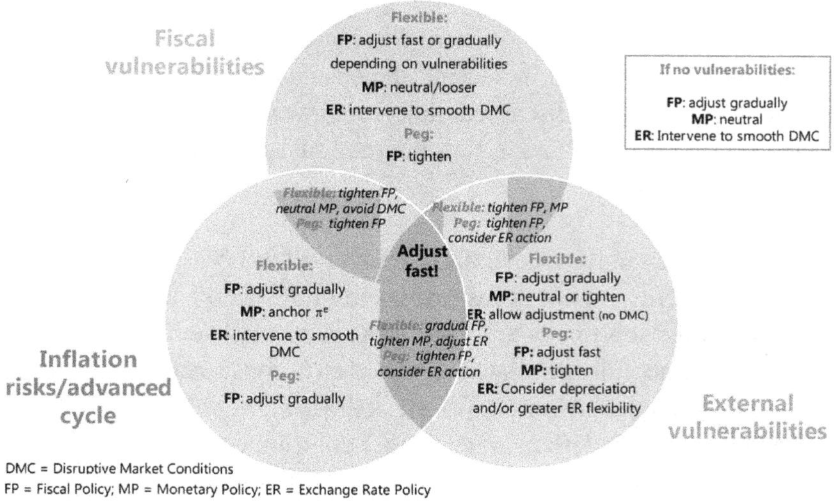

Figure 6. Policy decision and responses (importing oil countries)

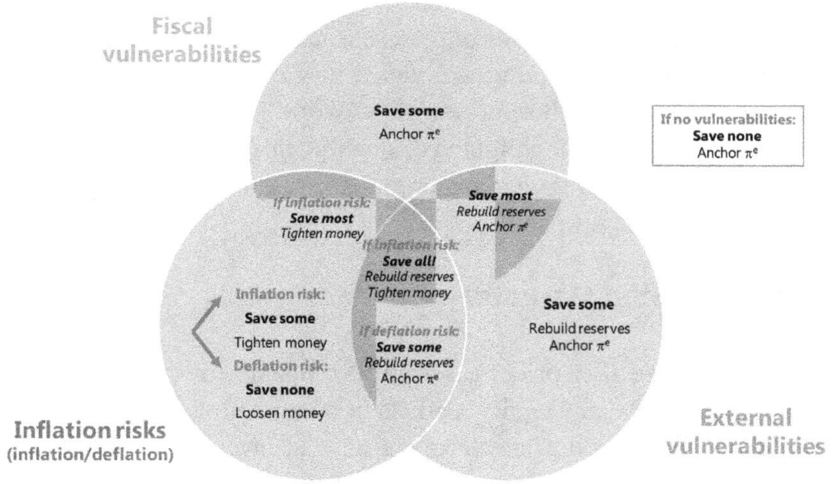

In relation to oil importing countries, the following observations are highlighted (see p. 36):

- Countries that are outside of the Venn space, and have a negative output gap, should implement policies which allow domestic demand to rise by the full amount of the windfall (in countries in this situation, but with a high degree of pass-through into retail prices such as the United States, there is no need for policy adjustment).

- For countries with fiscal and external vulnerabilities such as Egypt, priority should be given towards increasing the sustainability of fiscal and external positions by saving the fiscal windfall from lower energy subsidies, reducing public debt levels, and increasing international reserves as current account positions improve.

Given the complex multi-faceted factors involved, it is easy to understand why some expected benefits are not necessarily being translated by several countries – and in particular oil importing countries. This is particularly evident in cases where price reductions are not fully translated or passed on to consumers. Further priorities, such as the need to reduce deficits – as well as the lowering of energy subsidies, all aimed at reducing budget deficits, may further contribute to a mitigation of apparently intended price reductions across several jurisdictions.

Wider Repercussions of Oil Price Drops

According to the World Bank, a sharp recession in Russia would not only dampen growth in Central Asia, but also weaken external accounts in Venezuela or the Gulf Cooperation Council (GCC) countries - which may put at risk external financing support they provide to neighboring countries (World Bank, 2015, p. 161).

Further repercussions, as highlighted throughout this volume, relate to the present volatilities reverberating around major global stock markets – as well as panics which have triggered massive sell-offs.

Impact on Financial Markets

- The sharp decline in oil prices has been accompanied by substantial volatility in foreign exchange and equity markets of a number of emerging economies since October. Low oil prices have already led investors to reassess growth prospects of oil-exporting countries (World Bank, 2015, p. 162).

According to the IMF (2016, p. 124), several empirical studies have documented that certain unconventional monetary policies adopted in the aftermath of the Great Recession had significant impacts on inflation expectations or asset prices that convey information about these. References were made by the IMF to literature which have found "significant effects on break-even inflation rates" – such as those literature by (Guidolin and Neely, 2010; Krishnamurthy and Vissing-Jorgensen, 2011), literature on survey-based inflation expectations (Hofmann and Zhu, 2013), and firms' inflation expectations (Cloyne et al., 2016), as well as on interest rates and asset prices (Krishnamurthy and Vissing-Jorgensen, 2011; Swanson, 2016; Wright, 2012; Yu, 2016).

Furthermore, as added by the IMF (2016, p. 156):

- Risk-management approach to monetary policy seeks to avoid severe outcomes, including deflation. Policymakers do not worry about small deviations from desired outcomes but they attach an increasing marginal cost to inflation and output gap deviations as they grow larger. This implies prompt and aggressive actions to move the economy away from situations in which the risk of conventional policy instruments losing their effectiveness becomes larger—such as in a context of persistent economic slack and low inflation with the policy interest rate at the effective lower bound (ELB)."

SOLUTIONS AND RECOMMENDATIONS

From a consideration of challenges which have been encountered by many emerging economies since the wake of the recent Crisis, and particularly with respect to their macro prudential and regulatory frameworks, further efforts aimed at consolidating such frameworks – as well as challenges resulting from the implementation of recent regulatory reforms, which include the Basel III framework, reforms related Volcker's, Liikannen and Vicker's ring fencing rules and the separation of legal entities, need to be addressed.

The underlying causes of the 2007/08 Financial Crisis, as well as fundamentals can be distinguished from the recent causes of volatilities across major financial markets on the basis that several major flaws relating to the capital, liquidity framework are being addressed. However, it is also evident that many jurisdictions are still trying to recover as a result of the imposition of (apparently) burdensome capital, liquidity requirements, leverage ratios imposed as a result of such reforms. Central bank policy responses – particularly in major economies, will prove pivotal in the coming months if financial markets are to weather the current vulnerabilities which have recently been triggered in the wake of falling oil prices.

CONCLUSION

Central bank independence from political interference is advocated by many. The degree of independence is also to be considered since central bank monetary policy decisions cannot be implemented or realized effectively where such are made in the absolute absence and disregard of governmental and political considerations. Even though conspiracy theories have been put forward as regards the causes of recent plunges in oil prices, and even though these appear to be politically motivated, it is clear that many major economies are being affected as a result – hence it is questionable whether such theories have a credible basis.

Given wider and interrelated repercussions of plunging oil prices, as well as the apparent realization that the strong form of the Efficient Market Hypothesis appears to introduce less accountability than the weak and semi strong components, the need for public disclosure and transparency in financial reporting also constitutes a continual and vital area of focus. Where predictability (predictive values) and confirmatory attributes (confirming values) constitute components of relevance in financial reporting, then it appears that certain historical reports, data and information – based on the age and relevance of such data, still constitute relevant and reliable data – given that such information is current, relevant and reliable in the sense that it can be predicted upon, confirmed and verified.

As regards what constitutes current relevant information, this is always subject to judgment and debate – however it appears that information which is publicly available, less susceptible to manipulation, and upon which certain predictive and reliable values and judgment can be made, appear to be credible and relevant sources of information. How current or outdated or timely such information is will depend on the context and components of individual circumstances.

And as rightly added by the IMF (2016, p. 157), in relation to central bank policy responses, particularly the risk management approach to monetary policy, as discussed under the literature review section:

- Transparency is a key ingredient of this strategy (risk-management approach to monetary policy). Publishing the expected path of all the variables used at policy decision meetings, including the projected path for the policy interest rate, would help the central bank give a credible public account of its strategy. This would reinforce public confidence in the central bank's inflation objective and strengthen the transmission of policy actions to the economy: if the published path for policy interest rates is credible, the term structure of interest rates and asset prices, such as the exchange rate, will move in support of the policy objectives. In contrast, forecasting an overshooting of the inflation rate without communicating the whole breadth of the central bank's strategy might undermine confidence in the nominal anchor—it might look as though the central bank is doing "too little, too late" in terms of normalizing interest rates."

REFERENCES

Anzuini, A., Lombardi, M.J., & Pagano, P. (2013). The Impact of Monetary Policy Shocks on Commodity Prices. Banca d'Italia Bank for International Settlements.

Bastourre, D., Carrera, J., Ibarlucia, J., & Sardi, M. (2012, October). Common Drivers in Emerging Market Spreads and Commodity Prices (Working Paper). Central Bank of Argentina, Nacional University of La Plata Mariano Sardi Central Bank of Argentina.

BBC. (2016, January 18). Falling oil prices: How are countries being affected? 2016 http://www.bbc.co.uk/news/world-35345874

Belke, A., Bordon, I., & Hendricks, T. (2010). Global Liquidity and Commodity Prices—A Co-integrated VAR Approach for OECD Countries. *Applied Financial Economics*, *20*(3), 227–242. doi:10.1080/09603100903282713

Borensztein, E., & Reinhart, C. (1994). The Macroeconomic Determinants of Commodity Prices. *IMF Staff Papers*, *41*(2), 236–261. doi:10.2307/3867508

D'Amico, S., Kim, D.H., & Wei, M. (2014). Tips from TIPS: The Informational Content of Treasury Inflation-Protected Security Prices. US Federal Reserve Board.

Frankel, J.A. (2006, December). The Effect of Monetary Policy on Real Commodity Prices.

Guidolin, M., & Neely, C. J. (2010). *The Effects of Large-Scale Asset Purchases on TIPS Inflation Expectations. Economic Synopses 26*. Federal Reserve Bank of St. Louis.

Hofmann, B., & Feng Z. (2013). Central Bank Asset Purchases and Inflation Expectation. *BIS Quarterly Review*, March, 23–35.

IMF. (2015, July). Global Implications of Lower Oil Prices, IMF Staff Discussion Note.

International Monetary Fund. (2016, October). Global DisInflation in an Era of Constrained Monetary Policy.

Krauss, C. (2016, March 8). Oil Prices: What's Behind the Drop? Simple Economics. *New York Times*. Retrieved from http://www.nytimes.com/interactive/2016/business/energy-environment/oil-prices.html?_r=0

Krishnamurthy, A., & Vissing-Jorgenson, A. (2011). The Effects of Quantitative Easing on Interest Rates: Channels and Implications for Policy. *Brookings Papers on Economic Activity*, 2.

Poloz, S. S. (2014). *Integrating Uncertainty and Monetary Policy-Making: A Practitioner's Perspective.* Bank of Canada.

Swanson, E. T. (2016). Measuring the Effects of Federal Reserve Forward Guidance and Asset Purchases on Financial Markets. Economic Dynamics. Retrieved from https://www.economicdynamics.org/meetpapers/2016/paper_1222.pdf

Walker, A. (2015, February 26). Cheap oil: Asia's winners and losers. BBC News. Retrieved from http://www.bbc.co.uk/news/business-31444344

World Bank. (2015a, January). Understanding the Plunge in Oil Prices: Sources and Implications. Global Economic Prospects. Retrieved from https://www.worldbank.org/content/dam/Worldbank/GEP/GEP2015a/pdfs/GEP2015a_chapter4_report_oil.pdf

World Bank. (2015b, March). The Great Plunge in Oil Prices: Causes, Consequences, and Policy Responses. World Bank Group Policy Research Note.

Wright, J. H. (2012). What Does Monetary Policy Do to Long-Term Interest Rates at the Zero Lower Bound? *The Economic Journal, 122*(564), 447–466. doi:10.1111/j.1468-0297.2012.02556.x

Chapter 14
Information Uncertainty and Volatility in Financial Stock Markets:
Commodity Price Fluctuations and Business Cycles

Jose J Haspa DeLarosiere
Universidad EAFIT, Colombia

Soren Nielsen
Universidad EAFIT, Colombia

ABSTRACT

Rising oil prices, steel prices - as well as the stronger dollar certainly impacted the financial markets during the latter part of May 2016. So also, the expected announcement of higher interest rates in June 2016 by the Federal Reserve. As well as illustrating the impact of financial shocks for emerging economies, this chapter also illustrates the impact of financial shocks for smaller – as well as more advanced economies. Having highlighted through the entire volume, the macroeconomic consequences of the changes and fluctuations of commodity prices – as reflected through the recent global financial market volatilities. This chapter will also focus on the main channels through which commodities price fluctuations affect business cycles in EMEs.

DOI: 10.4018/978-1-5225-1900-3.ch014

Copyright ©2017, IGI Global. Copying or distributing in print or electronic forms without written permission of IGI Global is prohibited.

INTRODUCTION

The reaction of financial markets to announcements, as well as information uncertainty, has been clearly illustrated from results which have been revealed – most notably, during the months which ushered in 2016 – and particularly those preceding June 2016. As the EU Referendum looms on the 23rd of June 2016, there have been concerns relating primarily to information uncertainty – as well as forecasts which have dominated various sectors in relation to the impact on the UK economy in the event of a decision to leave the EU. During the month of May 2016, concerns were expressed by very prominent figures, including the Bank of England Governor, and the IMF Chief as regards the impact of leaving the Eurozone – as well as the resulting domino effects on other economies.

Whilst the Bank of England Governor and the IMF chief had clearly expressed the facts and concerns relating to the impact of information uncertainty – as a result of possible consequences of the UK leaving the European Union, it was the timing of their warnings that sparked outrage amongst the Brexit supporters – particularly with respect to Mark Carney, the Bank of England Governor, whose intervention in matters of such a political nature, was considered to be in contravention to the goals of the Monetary Policy Committee – in retaining central bank independence and abstaining from political intervention.

The events and controversial intervention, however, demonstrate serious concerns regarding the timing of the EU Referendum and the current state of the UK economy. Had the Referendum been held or scheduled to hold at a period where the UK and global economy were more economically robust, such warnings, it is highly likely, would have been more restrained.

Even though the manufacturing sector appeared to have stabilized in May 2016, recent reports highlighted trade deficits being at their highest levels since the Financial Crisis – with the recent Steel Crisis still being addressed. Hence the consequences of further uncertainty and Brexit were enough to warrant concerns such that the Bank of England had to take unprecedented steps in highlighting the dangers of leaving the European Union.

The impact of the EU Referendum had also been evident from stock market figures which reflected investment concerns – even where commodities such as oil prices played a significant role in impacting stock markets when price increases occurred - improving stock market values.

Rising oil prices, steel prices - as well as the stronger dollar certainly impacted the financial markets during the latter part of May 2016. So also, the expected announcement of higher interest rates in June 2016 by the Federal Reserve.

As well as illustrating the impact of financial shocks for emerging economies, this chapter also illustrates the impact of financial shocks for smaller – as well as more advanced economies. Having highlighted through the entire volume, the macroeconomic consequences of the changes and fluctuations of commodity prices – as reflected through the recent global financial market volatilities,

This chapter will also focus on the main channels through which commodities price fluctuations affect business cycles in EMEs.

LITERATURE REVIEW AND BACKGROUND TO THE STUDY

Bastourre et al (2012, p. 5) highlight the impact which commodity price increases has on the availability of external financing in emerging economies that rely strongly on commodities.

Furthermore, they argue that:

- The improvement in export prices of emerging economies brings about important consequences and that in addition to the relaxation of external restriction, there is a higher level of private expenditures and fiscal resources due to the expansionary effects on tax and non-tax revenues (for example, due to the existence of exports taxes or through public property of resources such as mines or oil camps). This in their opinion, is furthermore, related to a positive impact on economic activity and consumption levels in the short term and potentially to higher savings and investment levels in the long term.
- global liquidity and risk measures are the basic specification of push variables in econometric models available in the economic literature (page 8).
- That the macroeconomic aspects related to commodity dynamics have gone beyond the traditional channels linked to global demand and supply of primary goods and have focused on the effect of monetary and financial macroeconomic factors (page 11).

On the other hand, Frankel (2006, p. 5) affirms the argument that: "monetary policy, as reflected in real interest rates, is an important - and usually under-appreciated - determinant of the real prices of oil and other mineral and agricultural products, while far from being the only determinant."

The link between interest rates and commodity prices is also illustrated by Frankel (2006) whereby in consolidating his point, he highlights the fact that high interest rates reduce the demand for storable commodities, or increase the supply, through a variety of channels:

1. By increasing the incentive for extraction today rather than tomorrow (think of the rates at which oil is pumped, zinc is mined, forests logged, or livestock herds culled);
2. By decreasing firms' desire to carry inventories (think of oil inventories held in tanks) ;
3. By encouraging speculators to shift out of commodity contracts (especially spot contracts), and into treasury bills.

However it will be highlighted later on in the chapter, that even though theoretical based research indicates a correlation between interest rate and commodity prices, the same cannot be said in relation to empirical based research.

As well as investigating the causes of extreme fluctuations in commodity prices from 1990 to 2010, Cevik and Sedik (2011) find that macroeconomic factors comprise the main determinants of commodity prices. In so doing they bolster the argument by Bastourre et al in relation to the importance and impact of macroeconomic factors on commodity dynamics. In relation to the effects of demand and supply, they further conclude that although supply constraints have the expected effect, aggregate demand growth constitutes a key factor – with reference to empirical figures which they highlight as reflecting advanced economies accounting for more than half of global consumption and emerging economies accounting for the bulk of the incremental change in demand – hence, in their opinion, comprising a greater weight in commodity price formation.

In addition to seeking to address the questions relating to:

1. The macroeconomic consequences of the changes and fluctuations of commodity prices for small emerging market economies (EMEs) which export these goods; as well as
2. The main channels through which commodities price fluctuations affect business cycles in EMEs and how much impact they have in practice;

Fernandez, Gonzalez, and Rodriguez (2015, p. 5) also note that, EMEs, "often portrayed as being vulnerable to external forces and price takers in commodity markets, may have been subject to more macroeconomic volatility through these fluctuations in the prices of the commodity goods that they export."

Furthermore they conclude that (see page 35):

- The real effects generated by the fluctuations in the prices of these commodity goods can be amplified by the fact that they are often accompanied by movements in interest rates in opposite directions. And whilst most often movements in these relative prices have amplified the business cycle of

EMEs, there are instances where they have served as cushion devices against other forces.

In their paper "The Impact of Monetary Policy Shocks on Commodity Prices", Anzuini et al (2010, p. 140,141) conclude as their main finding that monetary policy shocks do affect commodity prices – even though the direct effect, in their opinion, is not significantly large. Further and with regard to oil, they also add that this conclusion is corroborated by the analysis of the impact of supply, inventories, and financial activity in futures, and that it should also be observed that "a stronger effect of monetary policy on commodity prices may pass through the indirect channels of expected economic growth and inflation". In this respect reference is made to Barsky and Kilian (2004).

MAIN FOCUS OF STUDY

Main channels through which commodities price fluctuations affect business cycles:

1. Channels of global demand and supply of primary goods.
2. Monetary and financial macroeconomic factors.

The impact of recent increased supply in oil production is evidenced by the fall and decline of oil prices – as reverberated through global financial markets – as well as constraints in revenues generated by many oil companies as a result of having generated low revenues. This has been discussed comprehensively in the preceding chapters to this volume. The impact of monetary policies on emerging economies – and their pace of recovery in the aftermath of the recent global Financial Crisis has also been discussed. Figure 1 depicts and illustrates those channels related to macroeconomic factors - though which price fluctuations of commodities impact business cycles.

In concluding that "financial shocks have become more relevant in explaining fluctuations in GDP during the recent economic slowdown in Brazil", Karpowicz, Lipinsky & Park (2016, p. 19), also make the following observations (see pages 16 and 17):

- The effect of financial shocks on real variables is non-negligible.
- While aggregate productivity shocks account for a large fraction of GDP and investment fluctuations, financial shocks also play an important role over the cycles.

Figure 1. Representation of the link between capital flows, commodity prices and common global factors in commodity exporters
Source: (Bastourre, Carrera, Ibarlucia, 2012)

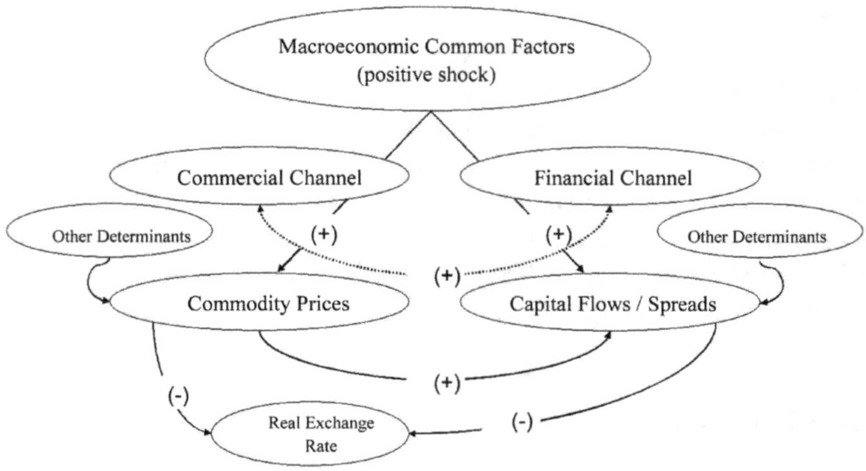

- For the longest part of the sample period, TFP shocks account for a large fraction of the consumption and investment fluctuations, and more prominently of GDP. However, the role of financial shocks becomes increasingly important during the recent economic downturn.

Jermann and Quadrini (2012, p. 30) propose a model that "incorporates explicitly the financial flows associated with firms' debt and equity financing." Based on the model they illustrate that:

- Shocks to firms' ability to borrow, combined with some rigidities in the adjustment of their financial structure, play an important role in generating business cycle movements, especially for labor.

Further, they investigate the effects of financial shocks using two alternative approaches (2012, p. 30):

- The first approach based on the use of model restrictions and observable variables to construct series of financial shocks – an approach which they describe as being "reminiscent of the Solow residual methodology for the construction of productivity shocks."
- The second approach is based on the estimation of the structural model using Bayesian methods.

In their view, both approaches suggest that financial shocks are important driving forces of the business cycle. In applying the model to interpret recent economic events, they contend and conclude that the tightening of firms' financing conditions has contributed significantly (although not exclusively) to the sharp downturn in GDP and labor starting in the second half of 2008.

Referring back to the previous chapter, in which Frankel's following comments were highlighted (2006, p. 24), namely:

- Few believe that the proper response for an oil-importing country in the event of a large increase in world oil prices is to tighten monetary policy and thereby appreciate the currency sufficiently to prevent an increase in the price of oil in terms of domestic currency. The usual defense of inflation targeting offered by its many proponents is that in the event of such a shock, the central bank can easily deviate from the CPI target and explain the circumstances to the public. But what can be the argument for making such derogations on an ad hoc basis, when it is possible to build them into a simple target rule in the first place? Certainly not a gain in transparency and credibility. This is not to suggest that this regime would be appropriate for all countries, only that it might have advantages for countries that experience large volatility in their terms of trade. But it has become apparent in this decade that terms of trade volatility is a more serious issue than was believed in the 1980s and 1990s.

Is there reason to be concerned about the Federal Reserve's decision to leave interest rates unchanged – particularly given the present financial market conditions, and view of previously anticipated rate hikes?

In the present climate of considerable uncertainty, it could very well be argued that leaving such rates unchanged, could be adjudged the most optimal monetary policy response - given complex prevailing factors in operation - which have been considered under this chapter.

Further, inconclusiveness in matters relating to interest rates is accentuated in the next section.

RECOMMENDATIONS AND SUGGESTIONS FOR FUTURE RESEARCH

References to the literature highlight the fact that the interest rate shock only accounts for a small portion of its price variability (Bastourre et al, 2012, p. 12). Given such inconclusiveness, as well "the difficulty in upholding that interest rates adequately summarize the liquidity stance, especially at times of financial stress",

Further research in this area, is encouraged. In this regard, Bastourre et al (2012, p. 11) also refer to evidence whereby even though theoretical based research indicates a correlation between interest rate and commodity prices – with reference to Hotelling's 1931 article, empirical based research, in their opinion, do not provide conclusive evidence about the hypothesis of a negative correlation between the international real interest rate and the real price of primary goods.

CONCLUSION

Economic effects of an exit (by the UK) from the European Union, according to the IMF (2016, p. 10,13), are as follows:

- A vote for exit would be followed by a long process with uncertain outcomes.
- A protracted period of uncertainty could weigh on confidence and investment and increase financial market volatility.
- On balance, the net economic costs of an exit are likely negative and substantial, though there is significant uncertainty about their precise magnitude.

The IMF (2016) also highlights that "in a baseline scenario in which the UK remains in the EU, growth is expected to recover in late 2016, as referendum-related effects wane, and to average around 2.2 percent over the medium term. Inflation is expected to rise gradually from its current low level (0.3 percent as of May 2016), as disinflationary effects from past commodity price falls dissipate and as tighter labor markets and minimum wage hikes help push up wages."

However, in its publication, "IMF Executive Board Concludes 2016 Article IV Consultation with the United Kingdom", it also accentuates those risks which persist – to which such positive baseline scenario is subject, namely:

1. Those related to the referendum;
2. The current account deficit, which reached a record high in 2015;
3. Uncertainty about the degree to which productivity growth, which has been low since the crisis, will recover; and
4. Vulnerabilities associated with property markets, which have been buoyant in recent years.

As reflected in the preceding section, it cannot be conclusively said that monetary policy, as represented through real interest rates, constitutes an important determinant of the real prices of oil – nor a decisive factor and correlation between interest rates and commodity prices be concluded. However, it is also evident that

1. Channels of global demand and supply of primary goods; as well as
2. Monetary and financial macroeconomic factors,

Constitute main channels through which commodities price fluctuations affect business cycles. This chapter has sought to illustrate and highlight the impact of financial shocks for smaller – as well as more advanced economies.

The chapter has also highlighted the main channels through which commodities price fluctuations affect business cycles in EMEs and advanced economies – drawing attention to areas in need of further redress in the literature.

Interest rates remained unchanged in June 2016, following indications by the Federal Reserve that its decision was also delayed by the EU Referendum in Britain, whose results it was acknowledged, would have definite repercussions for the global economy – and particularly in the event of an exit. In addition to the unexpected decision relating to the anticipated rate hike (which did not take place), the Federal Reserve also indicated that fewer rate hikes were to be expected in the near future. This decision not only capped off a week characterized by very volatile financial environment and market conditions, but was also impacted by other external factors such as those relating to Apple (its intellectual property rights and the sale of certain brands of iPhones in China) and the EU Referendum.

Interest rates remained unchanged by the Federal Reserve - even up till after the 2016 United States Presidential elections in November 2016. An atmosphere of considerable uncertainty followed however during the week beginning 14th November 2016 - whereby a lot of bond sell-outs took place - owing partly to i) uncertainties which related to the inflation measures and steps that would be undertaken by the incoming Trump administration, as well as ii)the strength of the dollar - which remained high following the Presidential elections, and (iii) prices of oil which were at a three month low level.

There were also higher yields for bond stocks over the long term period - consequential with higher returns - even though their values, presently, may not be as high.

Whilst the dollar remained strong post the 2016 U.S elections and generated uncertainty and possibilities of interest rate hikes by the Federal Reserve - with resulting anticipation and uncertainties for bond markets and sell-offs around global financial markets, Post Brexit impacts resulting from the value of the pound were also taking place in the United Kingdom.

This was principally felt in the airlines industry where on the 15th November 2016, it was reported that since airlines such as Easy jet reported in pounds - however paying for fuel in dollars, resulted in greater costs for the industry. Further, traffic costs which were also paid for in Euros, contributed to lower profits.

Against this backdrop and at the same time, the Yuan also fell to lowest levels in eight years against the dollar (6.85 to the dollar) - particularly as a result of the anticipation of higher interest rates by the Federal Reserve) - and this has also pushed up the value of the dollar.

It will be interesting to see what measures the Trump administration will take in 2017 - particularly amidst allegations and uncertainties relating to free trade agreements such as the North American Free Trade Agreement (NAFTA), the Trans Pacific Partnership, as well certain climate agreements. Previously, allegations had also been made in relation to the deliberate devaluation of the Yuan against the dollar - it will there be interesting how these issues are addressed and whether renegotiation will take place in respect of already negotiated free trade agreements - as well as those yet to be ratified. In view of the uncertainty, the value of gold also rose by 5%.

Providing the Financial Markets with Greater Certainty

Concerns over the Bank of England Governor, Mark Carney, would fulfil his eight-year term – as is usually the case with Bank of England Governors, had initially raised some uncertainties. Since the current Governor resumed office in June 2013, it was expected that if he stayed till 2021, this would be better for markets in terms of providing greater certainty. It is now known that the Governor will be staying till at least 2018 – generating greater certainty at this particularly uncertain time for global financial markets.

Table 1. Correlations between the spreads common factor and the first common factor of commodity prices with global determinants (from 1991-12 to 2011-2)

	Real EEs Spreads (Common Factor)		Real Commodities Prices (First Common Factor)	
	Correlation	p-Value	Correlation	p-Value
Variables				
Real Global Liquidity	-0.78	0	0.75	0
International Real Interest Rate (1 Year)	0.37	0	-0.32	0
International Real Interest Rate (3 Years)	0.47	0	-0.43	0
International Real Interest Rate (5 Years)	0.52	0	-0.48	0
Real S&P 500 Index	-0.43	0	0.23	0
Real Dow Jones Index	-0.53	0	0.31	0
VIX Volatility Index	0.09	0.18	-0.24	0
US Real Exchange Rate	0.16	0.02	-0.39	0

Source: (Bastourre, Carrera, Ibarlucia, 2012, p. 25)

Political risks and currency risks resulting from Brexit – as well as the United States Presidential elections in 2016 have also contributed to huge uncertainty in the financial markets.

Given the present climate of uncertainty and financial market volatilities, appropriate monetary policy responses – as well as the timeliness of such responses cannot be over emphasized – particularly in respect of those actions taken by oil importing and oil exporting countries whose actions are likely to significantly impact the activities and economy of major players, as well as the global economy.

REFERENCES

Aguiar, M., & Gopinath, G. (2007). Emerging Market Business Cycles: The Cycle is the Trend. *Journal of Political Economy*, *115*(1), 69–102. doi:10.1086/511283

Akinci, O. (2013). Global Financial Conditions, Country Spreads and Macroeconomic Fluctuations in Emerging Economies. *Journal of International Economics*, *91*(2), 358–371. doi:10.1016/j.jinteco.2013.07.005

Anzuini, A., Pagano, P., & Pisani, M. (2007). Oil Supply News in a VAR: Information from Financial Markets. Banca d'Italia.

Barsky, R. B., & Kilian, L. (2002). Do We Really Know That Oil Caused the Great Stagflation? A Monetary Alternative. Journal of Economic Perspectives, 18(4), 115–34.

Bastourre, D., Carrera, J., Ibarlucia, J., & Sardi, M. (2012, October). Common Drivers in Emerging Market Spreads and Commodity Prices (Working Paper).

Belke, A., Bordon, I., & Hendricks, T. (2010). Global Liquidity and Commodity Prices—A Co-integrated VAR Approach for OECD Countries. *Applied Financial Economics*, *20*(3), 227–242. doi:10.1080/09603100903282713

Bernanke, B., Boivin, J., & Eliasz, P. (2005). Measuring the Effects of Monetary Policy: A Factor-Augmented Vector Autoregressive (FAVAR) Approach. *The Quarterly Journal of Economics*, *120*, 387–422.

Byrne, J. P., Fazio, G., & Fiess, N. (2013). Primary commodity prices: Co-movements, common factors and fundamentals. *Journal of Development Economics, Elsevier*, *101*(C), 16–26. doi:10.1016/j.jdeveco.2012.09.002

Cevik, S., & Saadi, T. (2011, January). A Barrel of Oil or a Bottle of Wine: How Do Global Growth Dynamics Affect Commodity Prices? IMF Working Paper.

Chang, R., & Fernandez, A. (2013, November). On the Sources of Fluctuations in Emerging Economies. *International Economic Review*, *54*(4), 1267–1295. doi:10.1111/iere.12036

Dasgupta, D., & Ratha, D. (2000). What Factors Appear to Drive Private Capital Flows to Developing Countries? And How Does Official Lending Respond? Banco Mundial, Policy Research Working Papers.

Fernandez, A., Gonzalez, A. & Rodriguez, D. (2015). Sharing a ride on the commodities roller coaster: common factors in business cycles of emerging economies. IMF.

Fernandez, A., & Gulan, A. (2015). Interest Rates, Leverage, and Business Cycles in Emerging Economies: The Role of Financial Frictions, forthcoming. *American Economic Journal. Macroeconomics*, *7*(3), 153–188. doi:10.1257/mac.20120141

Frankel, J. (2006). The Effect of Monetary Policy on Real Commodity Prices. NBER Working Papers. Retrieved from http://www.nber.org/papers/w12713.pdf

Frankel, J., & Hardouvelis, G. (1985). Commodity Prices, Money Surprises, and Fed Credibility. *Journal of Money, Credit and Banking*, 17(4), 427-438.

Frankel, J. A., & Rose, A. K. (2010). Determinants of Agricultural and Mineral Commodity Prices. In R. Fry, C. Jones, & C. Kent (Eds.), Inflation in an Era of Relative Price Shocks. Reserve Bank of Australia.

González Rozada, M., & Levy Yeyati, E. (2006). Global Factors and Emerging Market Spreads. Banco Interamericano de Desarrollo Working Paper.

Hotelling, H. (1931). The Economics of Exhaustible Resources. *Journal of Political Economy*, *39*(2), 137–175. doi:10.1086/254195

IMF. (2016, June 17). United Kingdom: 2016 Article IV Consultation Press Release and Staff Report. Retrieved from http://www.imf.org/external/pubs/ft/scr/2016/cr16168.pdf

Jermann, U., & Quadrini, V. (2012). Macroeconomic Effects of Financial Shocks. *The American Economic Review*, *102*(1), 238–271. doi:10.1257/aer.102.1.238 PMID:25067842

Karpowicz, I., Lipinsky, F., & Park, J. (2016). A Closer Look at Sectoral Financial Linkages in Brazil I: Corporations' Financial Statements. IMF Working Paper.

Kasperkevic, J. (2016). Interest rates could rise as soon as June, federal reserve suggests. *The Guardian*. Retrieved from https://www.theguardian.com/business/2016/may/18/interest-rates-increase-federal-reserve-economy-brexit-china

Kilian, L., & Lewis, L. (2011). Does the Fed Respond to Oil Price Shocks? *The Economic Journal*, *121*(555), 1047–1072. doi:10.1111/j.1468-0297.2011.02437.x

Kilian, L., & Vega, C. (2011). Do Energy Prices Respond to U.S. Macroeconomic News? A Test of the Hypothesis of Predetermined Energy Prices. *The Review of Economics and Statistics*, *93*(2), 660–671. doi:10.1162/REST_a_00086

Kose, A., Otrok, C., & Whiteman, C. (2003). International Business Cycles: World, Region, and Country-specific factors. *The American Economic Review*, *93*(4), 1216–1239. doi:10.1257/000282803769206278

Lagarde, C. (2016, June 17). Unity in Diversity: The Case for Europe. Finance in Dialogue, Vienna. Retrieved from http://www.imf.org/external/np/speeches/2016/061716.htm

Neumeyer, P. A., & Perri, F. (2005). Business cycles in emerging economies: The role of interest rates. *Journal of Monetary Economics*, *52*(2), 345–380. doi:10.1016/j.jmoneco.2004.04.011

Reuters. (2016, June 15). Fed Keeps Interest Rates Unchanged, Signals Fewer Future Hikes. Retrieved from http://www.reuters.com/article/us-usa-fed-idUSKCN0Z10DI

Scrimgeour, D. (2010). Commodity Price Responses to Monetary Policy Surprises (Working Paper). Colgate University.

Smets, F., & Wouters, R. (2007). Shocks and Frictions in US Business Cycles: A Bayesian DSGE Approach. *The American Economic Review*, *97*(3), 586–606. doi:10.1257/aer.97.3.586

Uribe, M., & Yue, V. (2006). Country Spreads and Emerging Countries: Who Drives Whom? *Journal of International Economics*, *69*(1), 6–36. doi:10.1016/j.jinteco.2005.04.003

Vansteenkiste, I. (2009). How Important Are Common Factors in Driving Non-Fuel Commodity Prices? A Dynamic Factor Analysis. European Central Bank Working Paper.

Chapter 15
The Value Relevance of Financial and Non-Financial Information:
Evidence from Recent Academic Literature

Amitav Saha
The University of Notre Dame Australia, Australia

Sudipta Bose
The University of Newcastle, Australia

ABSTRACT

Value-relevance research is an important domain of modern capital market research. Accounting researchers have used the value-relevance research framework in many ways with the aim of measuring whether accounting information has a predicted association with equity market values. One of the most widely used models in value-relevance research is a modification of the Ohlson (1995) market valuation model in which the market value of a firm's equity is presumed to be a function of its book value of equity and abnormal earnings. Furthermore, using the Ohlson (1995) model, accounting researchers have documented the value relevance of different types of financial and non-financial information. Drawing on a selected number of recently published studies that have documented the value relevance of different types of financial and non-financial information, this chapter reviews and integrates recent findings, highlighting challenges and providing future directions for further research in this area.

DOI: 10.4018/978-1-5225-1900-3.ch015

Copyright ©2017, IGI Global. Copying or distributing in print or electronic forms without written permission of IGI Global is prohibited.

INTRODUCTION

Over the last four decades, value-relevance research has played an important role in understanding the valuation impact of various types of financial information. If any accounting information has a predicted association with equity market values, it is referred to as value relevant (Barth, Beaver, & Landsman, 2001); that is, value relevance is the ability of accounting numbers to explain the underlying differences in stock prices in capital markets. The seminal studies of Ball and Brown (1968) and Beaver (1968), in which they documented accounting income numbers as being informative for valuation, mark the beginning of capital market-related valuation research in accounting. Since then, many studies have documented the various valuation impacts of financial information. The valuation implications of non-financial information also originated a long time ago. Prior research includes studies examining the customer market penetration in the wireless communication industry (Amir & Lev, 1996); the citations of the patent application in the science and technology-based firms (Deng, Lev, & Narin, 1999); web usage in the valuation of internet stocks (Rajgopal, Venkatachalam, & Kotha, 2003); non-financial performance in the airline industry (Behn & Riley, 1999); and environmental performance (Barth and McNichols, 1994; Hughes, 2000; Johnston, Sefcik, & Soderstrom, 2008). According to Barth et al. (2001), the 'value relevance' terminology was first used by Amir, Harris, and Venuti (1993), with this followed by a formal valuation model developed by Ohlson (1995) which, to date, is the model predominantly used for value-relevance research.

This chapter uses an integrative approach to discuss the findings of recent value-relevance studies on financial and non-financial information and highlights the importance of integration between financial and non-financial information in valuation research. Prior survey articles have mainly focused on analyzing valuation research in different time periods focusing on either financial or non-financial information. An integrated discussion on the valuation implications of both financial and non-financial information is important as the business world has witnessed a proliferation of non-financial disclosures. Furthermore, the traditional form of reporting is also being challenged as new forms of reporting emerge (e.g., integrated reporting and the use of extensible business reporting language [XBRL]). Although an alternative form of reporting[1] has been introduced as mandatory in some countries, the traditional form is followed by the majority of countries. In consideration of this changing environment, this chapter reviews the recent value-relevance academic literature as the basis for responding to the key question of how the usefulness of financial and non-financial information could be increased.

Value-relevance research provides important evidence about the type of information that is related to the firm's market value. Despite an extensive amount of research having been conducted on the value relevance of financial and non-financial information, a very limited number of studies have reviewed the impact of this research. The objective of this chapter is to shed light on the importance of financial and non-financial information in the context of the capital market by drawing from recent value-relevance studies that have used the Ohlson (1995) model to examine the value relevance of financial or non-financial information. We are aware that the value-relevance literature is extensive; therefore, we have only focused on a selected number of financial and non-financial value-relevance studies published in reputed accounting journals for the period 2010–2016. These years have been selected as other researchers have provided a comprehensive summary of the published value-relevance research before this period (e.g., see Beisland (2009) for the value relevance of financial information and Clarkson (2012) for the value relevance of environmental performance, a specific component of non-financial information). We also acknowledge that we have reviewed papers based on this chapter's theme and that our review and discussion in the chapter are based on the recent value-relevance literature.

The remainder of this chapter is structured as follows. The following section explains the background of the value-relevance research with this followed by a literature review of the recent financial and non-financial value-relevance research. The chapter then uses an integrative approach to discuss the findings of the literature review, after which some challenges in the value-relevance research are considered. Finally, the chapter outlines some future research directions, with this followed by a conclusion.

BACKGROUND

Academic researchers have used various financial and non-financial information to assess the value relevance of such information. In doing so, the researchers have used different types of valuation models, such as the price model and the return model. Many variations of the price and return models have been used to examine the valuation implications. Several survey articles have discussed the various impacts of different types of valuation models (e.g., Holthausen & Watts, 2001; Richardson & Tinaikar, 2004). In this chapter, we focus on the valuation model developed by Ohlson (1995) in which the market value of a firm's equity is considered to be a function of its book value of equity and abnormal earnings. Many of the value-relevance studies have been conducted using the Ohlson (1995) model which is based on three important assumptions. First, the market value of the firm is equivalent to the present value of all future expected dividends, that is, the dividend discount model. Second, the accounting data and dividends satisfy the clean surplus relationship. Finally, a linear model frames the stochastic time-series behavior of abnormal earnings (Ohlson, 1995). Based on the three assumptions above, Ohlson (1995) developed the following model:

$$MV_t = BV_t + \alpha_1 AE_t + \alpha_2 v_t \quad (1)$$

where MV_t is the market value of the firm's equity at time t; BV_t is the book value of the firm's equity at the end of the year t; AE_t is abnormal earnings (the difference between net income and the book value of equity at the beginning of the period multiplied by the required rate of return) for the period t; and v_t is other financial and non-financial value-relevant information.

The Ohlson (1995) model is widely used in valuation research in a modified form. Capital market researchers often add additional explanatory variables to the Ohlson (1995) model to answer specific research questions (Barth & Clinch, 2009). Despite the popularity of the Ohlson (1995) model in valuation research, many researchers have identified various issues with this model. For the purpose of this chapter, we regard the Ohlson (1995) model as an acceptable and widely used market valuation model for examining the valuation implications of both financial and non-financial information. However, we highlight some challenges of the application of this model in more contemporary value-relevance research.

LITERATURE REVIEW

This chapter draws from the two dominant bodies of literature: first, studies that document the value relevance of financial information; and second, studies that document the value relevance of non-financial information. The amount of extant literature is vast in both areas so our focus is to identify information clearly denoted as value relevant. We have reviewed studies that used the Ohlson (1995) model and the modified Ohlson model and which were published between 2010 and 2016 in reputed accounting journals.

Value Relevance of Financial Information

We have reviewed a selected number of recent value-relevance studies that examined various valuation impacts of financial information. The recent studies on the value relevance of financial information fall under four broad categories, namely:

1. Studies that examined the valuation impact of the adoption of the International Financial Reporting Standards (IFRS);

2. Studies that examined the valuation impact of the alternative earnings measure and loss making firms;
3. Studies that examined the valuation implications of tax; and
4. A group of specialized value-relevance studies that addressed the valuation impact of other types of financial information.

Some additional details (i.e., country investigated, sample year(s) and sample size and journal name) are provided for each paper we reviewed in Appendix 1.

Valuation Implications of IFRS Adoption

Since the rapid adoption of IFRS from 2005 onwards, the extant literature has included a plethora of studies documenting its various effects (i.e., the impact on accounting quality and cost of capital, and other capital market-related valuation impacts), with the literature including a large number of value-relevance studies. When a country moves from local standards and adopts IFRS, it is pertinent to know whether the new set of standards would lead to higher information quality. Many studies have documented this effect by comparing IFRS with a country's local Generally Accepted Accounting Principles (GAAP). For example, Russia is one of the recent adopters of IFRS and completed the adoption in 2015, with Kim (2013) examining whether IFRS adoption produced more value-relevant information in Russia. The author examined a sample of Russian firms listed on the London Stock Exchange (i.e., that were required to prepare reports under IFRS) and a sample of locally listed Russian firms (i.e., that prepared reports using the Russian GAAP). Results showing a higher R-squared (R^2) regression value were perceived to have higher value relevance than those with a lower R-squared (R^2) regression value. Based on that premise, the author found that the adjusted R-squared (R^2) value was higher for firms listed on the London Stock Exchange than for Russian firms listed locally and concluded that IFRS-reporting firms had greater value relevance than Russian firms listed locally. Hence, the inference was that IFRS adoption in Russia would improve the information quality of locally listed Russian firms.

In contrast, Tsalavoutas, André, and Evans (2012) found that IFRS adoption did not improve accounting quality in Greece. The authors investigated a large sample of Greek companies to examine the relationship between market value and the book value of equity and net income figures before and after IFRS adoption in Greece. The authors found that both pre- and post-IFRS adoption, the reported figures of the book value of equity and net income were value relevant. Furthermore, as the authors did not find a higher R-squared (R^2) value after IFRS adoption, they concluded that IFRS adoption did not particularly improve Greek companies' accounting quality. In addition, the authors tested the value relevance of IFRS reconciliations between the Greek GAAP and IFRS for the 2004 figures and documented that this information was incrementally value relevant which is also consistent with prior literature.

Furthermore, Clacher, Ricquebourg, and Hodgson (2013) investigated whether there was a change in the value relevance of direct cash flow statements following IFRS adoption in Australia. The authors found that the direct cash flow statements were value relevant for firms from both industrial and extractive industries before and after IFRS adoption. In addition, they noted that, for industrial firms, value relevance significantly increased after IFRS adoption. The impact of IFRS adoption in an emerging economy was documented by Alali and Foote (2012): the authors examined firms in the United Arab Emirates (UAE) and showed that accounting information reported under IFRS was value relevant (i.e., information was value relevant for the period 2000–2004, although the value relevance actually declined for the years 2005–2006). Many IFRS-related value-relevance studies have focused on the effects of the transitory reconciliation statement which firms are required to produce upon IFRS adoption. More recently, Barth, Landsman, Young, and Zhuang (2014) examined the value relevance of net income adjustment from the mandatory IFRS reconciliation statement for a sample of 15 European countries and found that the aggregated net income adjustment of 11 standards was value relevant for both financial and non-financial firms. In addition, the authors documented that the net income adjustment of individual standards was incrementally value relevant for both financial and non-financial firms. Similarly, Horton and Serafeim (2010) examined the value relevance of IFRS reconciliation statements, reporting that the reconciliation adjustments related to impairment of goodwill, share-based payments, and deferred tax information were value relevant.

Valuation Implications of Alternative Earnings Measure and Loss-Making Firms

The literature shows that widely varied ways are used to calculate earnings as various factors are often depicted. In the United States (US), Standard & Poor (S&P) introduced a uniform earnings metric referred to as 'core earnings' in 2002 for the improvement of financial reporting. Wieland, Dawkins, and Dugan (2013) examined the core earnings and GAAP earnings of a large sample of US firms from 2001–2009 and found that core earnings were more value relevant than the US GAAP earnings. The authors showed that even higher value relevance resulted when they added stock option expenses back to core earnings. Similarly, Entwistle, Feltham, and Mbagwu (2010) examined the valuation impact of three alternative earning measures, namely: pro forma earnings, GAAP earnings, and Institutional Brokers' Estimate System (I/B/E/S) earnings to understand which measure had the highest value relevance. They found that all three measures of earnings were value relevant, also showing that pro forma earnings were the most value relevant followed by I/B/E/S earnings and GAAP earnings. In addition, Kang and Zhao (2010) investigated the valuation implications of another type of alternative earnings figure known as ‘funds from operations’ (FFO) compared with GAAP net income for a sample of US real estate investment trusts (REITs) and non-REITs. For the REIT industry, FFO is a unique performance measure with the main reconciliation item of FFO and GAAP net income being depreciation; therefore, the authors examined accumulated depreciation which they found to be value relevant for the REIT industry and less value relevant for the capital-intensive non-REIT industries.

Furthermore, the concept of alternative forms of earnings is also evident in South Africa where firms are required to disclose two sets of earnings figures, namely, GAAP earnings and headline earnings. Venter, Emanuel, and Cahan (2014) examined the value relevance of headline earnings and GAAP earnings and found that non-GAAP earnings (headline earnings) had higher value relevance than GAAP earnings. It is evident that there is considerable interest in examining the valuation implications of different types of earnings. Similarly, the valuation implications of loss-making firms are also documented in the recent value-relevance research. For example, Wu, Fargher, and Wright (2010) examined the role of exploration costs in the resource-based economy for the valuation of loss-making firms, finding that, in this type of economy, there was a relationship between exploration costs and the valuation of loss-making firms. Furthermore, the authors documented that both the value of capitalized exploration and development costs and the current period expenditures provided incremental information for the valuation of loss-making firms. In addition, Jiang and Stark (2013) extended prior research on the valuation impact of accounting information from loss-making firms by showing that the book value had a lower valuation impact for both high research and development-intensive and dividend-paying loss-making firms compared to other firms. In addition, when these authors allowed the coefficient of the book value to vary across loss-making firms, they found that the dividend was generally value relevant.

Valuation Implications of Tax

The valuation implications of tax accounting, tax planning, and tax information have been documented in recent value-relevance research. Australia’s adoption of IFRS has seen the income statement approach to accounting for income tax replaced with the balance sheet approach. In 2005, the transition year, companies were required to report deferred tax figures using both pre-IFRS income tax standards and post-IFRS income tax standards. Hanlon, Navissi, and Soepriyanto (2014) examined the incremental value relevance of deferred tax figures that resulted from asset revaluation under both income statement and balance sheet approaches. The deferred tax balances resulting from the balance sheet approach were found by the authors to be more value relevant than the income statement items. In addition, the authors showed that this result is driven by deferred taxes resulting from revaluation of property, plant, and equipment, and equity-accounted investments. Similarly, prior to IFRS adoption in New Zealand, companies were allowed to choose between comprehensive versus partial allocation methods for recognition of deferred tax liability. Wong, Wong, and Naiker (2011) examined value relevance by comparing the partial allocation method with the comprehensive allocation method, finding the partial allocation method to be value relevant whereas this was not the case for the comprehensive allocation method. However, the authors found the comprehensive allocation method to be value relevant for a subset of low asset growth firms.

In addition, Wahab and Holland (2012) investigated the valuation implications of tax planning activities in the context of UK firms. They found that there is a negative relationship between tax planning activities and the market value of a firm. In addition, the authors documented that tax planning activities actually reduced the firm's market value. An individual analysis of tax planning activities showed that the reason for this negative relationship was the permanent difference between taxable income and the accounting measure.

Valuation Implications of Other Financial Information

Academic researchers continue to document different types of other financial information as being value relevant. Beisland (2009) summarized some of the earlier studies that examined other specific financial information. In this chapter, we review some of the recent specialized value-relevance research whereas these studies investigated recognized information, recognized information versus disclosed information, and only disclosures. Oliveira, Rodrigues, and Craig (2010) investigated the valuation implications of other intangible assets and recognized goodwill in financial statements in Portugal. Both reported goodwill and other intangible assets were found by the authors to be value relevant. The other intangible assets included start-up costs, intangible assets in development, prepayments for purchases of identifiable intangible assets, and residual identifiable intangible assets. On the other hand, Callahan, Smith, and Spencer (2013) examined the valuation implications of the synthetic lease arrangement in the US context to distinguish the valuation implications of recognized information versus disclosed information. Since 2003, the Financial Accounting Standards Board (FASB)'s interpretation of FIN 46 has required many lessee firms to recognize consolidated synthetic leases in the balance sheet: before that date, only limited disclosures were required. This provided the authors with an opportunity to examine the valuation implications of disclosed versus recognized synthetic lease information. The authors identified and examined 125 US synthetic leasing firms, finding that the market placed greater weight on lease obligations disclosed in the actual financial statement than it did on synthetic lease liabilities disclosed in the notes to the accounts.

On the other hand, a group of recent studies examined the value relevance of information disclosed in the notes to the accounts. Based on firms from the US, Chen, Martin, Mashruwala, and Mashruwala (2014) examined the valuation implications of an underfunded multi-employer defined-benefit pension plan. The authors found that the underfunding of the multi-employer pension plan was value relevant for the 2011–2012 sample period. However, the valuation implications were different in their 2000–2010 sample period as they found that the underfunding of the multi-employer defined-benefit pension plan was negatively associated with share price. The authors suggested that the difference in result could be due to the incorporation of the multi-employer defined-benefit plan standard in 2011.

Furthermore, Kohlbeck and Mayhew (2010) investigated the market valuation impact of firms' disclosure and non-disclosure of related party information. In the US, since 2002, the Sarbanes–Oxley Act has banned related party loans. Using related party transaction disclosures from 2001, the authors showed that firms with related party transactions had a lower market valuation. In addition, in the US, three levels of information are used to measure fair value (FAS No. 157). Song, Thomas, and Yi (2010) examined whether these three levels have a differential value relevance, finding that all three levels were value relevant, but that value relevance was greater for Level 1 and Level 2 fair values than for Level 3 fair values. Finally, Gu and Li (2010) examined the value relevance of advertising expenditures from the pharmaceutical industry perspective. The authors found that advertising expenditures by pharmaceutical firms enhanced their market value. Moreover, advertising expenditures had a higher association with pharmaceutical firms than with non-pharmaceutical firms.

There is still a large number of value-relevance studies that have examined different financial accounting information and that have been published in reputed accounting journals. Studies have either provided new evidence on an existing line of research or have introduced a new line of research. Many value-relevance studies continue to be conducted in the US context.

Value Relevance of Non-Financial Information

While accounting information is generally value relevant, some of its value relevance has been lost over the years (Collins, Maydew, & Weiss, 1997). One of the reasons for this decline is the inability of current accounting systems to recognize the entirety of modern firms' resources. One important aspect not fully captured relates to non-financial information. It is argued that the value relevance of financial information could be increased if non-financial information is also considered. The general conclusion drawn from these studies is that accounting information cannot solely explain the variation in stock prices and returns, and that non-financial information augments the ability of users to evaluate and predict future performance (Bose, 2014). As with the value relevance of financial information, we have reviewed a selected number of recent value-relevance studies in the field of non-financial information which includes environmental performance/disclosures, carbon emissions, corporate social responsibility (CSR) disclosures, and other types of non-financial information. The same criteria were used for reviewing non-financial information as were used for the value relevance of financial information, that is, studies published between 2010 and 2016 in reputed accounting journals. The objective of this section of the chapter is to investigate the capital market implications of non-financial information disclosed by firms. In other words, to what extent does the capital market react in respect to a firm's disclosure of non-financial information (e.g., environmental performance/disclosures, carbon emissions, CSR disclosures, or other types of non-financial information)? Some additional details (i.e., country investigated, sample year(s) and sample size and journal name) are provided for each paper we reviewed in Appendix 2.

Valuation Implications of Environmental Performance/Disclosures

The debate on how environmental performance influences the market value of firms is basically divided into two schools of thought. The cost-concerned school argues that environmental investments and high environmental performance represent only increased cost, resulting in decreased earnings and lower market values and ultimately negatively affecting the market value of a firm. Conversely, the value creation school represents environmental efforts as a new way to increase competitive advantage and improve financial returns to investors and, consequently, to positively affect the market value of a firm (Hassel, Nilsson, & Nyquist, 2005). As revealed in prior literature, researchers have used a variety of measures for environmental performance, for example, pollution control information, pollution levels, Council on Economic Priorities (CEP) ratings, adoption of stringent global environmental standards, etc.

Recently, Clarkson, Fang, Li, and Richardson (2013), using Toxics Release Inventory (TRI) data from the US, examined the valuation relevance of voluntary environmental disclosures and environmental performance. The authors concluded that voluntary environmental disclosures were incrementally value relevant to the information provided by TRI data. The authors reported that each category of voluntary environmental disclosure was value relevant for investors. Furthermore, Middleton (2015) investigated the value relevance of environmental disclosures based on Russia. The author used the Russian Independent Ecological Rating Agency (NERA) as a measure of the firm's integral environmental performance. The results indicated that investors in Russia considered environmental performance as value-relevant information. Similarly, Plumlee, Brown, Hayes, and Marshall (2015) reinvestigated the association between environmental disclosure quality and firm value based on a sample of US firms across five industries. The authors reported that voluntary environmental disclosure quality was associated with firm value through both cash flow and the cost of equity components. The authors argued that both the type and nature of environmental disclosures were informative and documented the association between environmental disclosure quality and firm value.

Valuation Implications of Carbon Emissions

Prior studies in accounting have generally concluded that the capital market negatively assesses firms with poor environmental performance using different theoretical constructs of environmental performance (e.g., Superfund liability, water pollution, sulfur dioxide (SO_2) emission, Toxics Release Inventory (TRI), toxic waste). However, an emerging and newly raised environmental risk, carbon dioxide (CO_2) emissions, has recently created heightened interest among investors, regulators, and other stakeholders worldwide due to its negative and long-term economic consequences in terms of increasing both physical and financial risks (Bose, 2014). In response, empirical researchers have focused their research on the emerging area of the value relevance of carbon dioxide emissions. For example, Chapple, Clarkson, and Gold (2011) examined the impact of carbon dioxide emissions on the market value of equity for 58 Australian-listed firms for 2007. The authors used an event study consisting of five separate information events which were expected to impact on firms' market value. They also used a modified version of the Ohlson (1995) model to assess the value relevance of carbon dioxide emissions. The authors covered only firms with available greenhouse gases (GHG) emissions data: it was expected that these firms would be affected by a national Emissions Trading Scheme (ETS) anticipated at that time to start in 2011. The results indicated that the capital market penalized the most carbon-intensive firms relative to other firms in the sample by between 7 percent and 10 percent of market capitalization. This study focused on a very small number of firms that were more carbon-intensive, and also less profitable and more risky, in comparison to the less carbon-intensive firms in the sample.

Furthermore, Matsumura, Prakash, and Vera-Muñoz (2014) investigated the capital market impact of carbon dioxide emissions for US S&P 500 firms from 2006–2008. They used firms that voluntarily reported their GHG emissions information to the Carbon Disclosure Project (CDP). The authors found that carbon dioxide emissions negatively affected the market value of a firm. The results indicated that, for every additional thousand metric tonnes of carbon dioxide emissions, a reduction in market value of US$212,000 occurred. Moreover, as the authors concluded, firms with carbon dioxide emissions disclosures to the CDP had a higher median value (approximately US$2.3 billion) compared to similar firms with carbon dioxide emissions non-disclosures. Although Matsumura et al. (2014) employed the balance sheet approach in their baseline regression model, they also used the Ohlson (1995) model in the sensitivity analyses and reported that both models showed consistent results. Likewise, Clarkson, Li, Pinnuck, and Richardson (2015) investigated the capital market impact of carbon dioxide emissions under the European Union Carbon Emissions Trading Scheme (EU ETS). The study covered 843 firm-year observations in the 21 countries operating in the EU ETS from 2006–2009. The authors reported that firms' carbon dioxide allowances were not value-relevant information to investors; however, carbon dioxide allocation shortfalls negatively related to market value. In addition, the authors concluded that the value relevance of carbon dioxide emissions varied across firms and industries.

Valuation Implications of Corporate Social Responsibility Performance/Disclosures

Furthermore, several researchers have examined the value relevance of corporate social responsibility (CSR) performance/disclosures. de Villiers and Marques (2016) examined the different levels of CSR disclosures in the context of large European firms. Higher levels of disclosures were found by the authors to be positively associated with higher share prices. In addition, as they documented, lower levels of CSR disclosures in sensitive industries were negatively associated with share prices. The authors concluded that the positive impact of CSR disclosures on share prices is more pronounced in countries with more democracy, more government effectiveness, better regulatory quality, and more press freedom. Similarly, Gregory, Whittaker, and Yan (2016) examined the value relevance of corporate social performance (CSP) based on US firms. The study found that corporate social performance (CSP) was value relevant: it was also associated with a higher coefficient on earnings. The authors argued that the documented association between market value and CSP depended on either a lower cost of equity or greater earnings persistence.

Valuation Implications of Other Non-Financial Information

Several studies have examined the value relevance of different types of non-financial information including subsidies, the quality of management, and relations with investors. For example, using Chinese-listed firms, Lee, Walker, and Zeng (2014) investigated the value relevance of government subsidies. The authors found that subsidies were positively associated with firm value; however, for distressed firms and subsidies granted through non-tax channels, the positive impact was reduced. Agarwal, Taffler, and Brown (2011) investigated the value relevance of management quality over a 17-year period based on *Management Today* magazine's annual survey database, *Britain's Most Admired Companies*. The results indicated the quality of management to be value relevant. Furthermore, Agarwal, Taffler, Bellotti, and Nash (2015) argued that there is a lack of empirical studies showing the valuation impact of investor relations activities undertaken by firms and that the available evidence is conflicting. Consequently, the authors sought to provide some empirical evidence by examining a large US sample: as a result, they reported that effective investor relations activities by firms incrementally impacted on firm value.

INTEGRATED DISCUSSION

A considerable number of recent valuation studies have used the Ohlson (1995) model and the modified Ohlson (1995) model to observe the valuation impact of different types of financial information. Studies have continued to provide evidence that the IFRS produce value-relevant (Barth et al., 2014; Kim, 2013) and incrementally value-relevant (Horton & Serafeim, 2010) accounting information. In addition, one of our reviewed studies documented IFRS information as value relevant, although value relevance was declined during a bearish market period (Alali & Foote, 2012). Other studies have found both pre- and post-IFRS adoption accounting information to be value relevant (Clacher et al., 2013; Tsalavoutas et al., 2012), while IFRS reconciliation adjustments information has been proven to be value-relevant information (Barth et al., 2014; Horton & Serafeim, 2010; Tsalavoutas et al., 2012).

Furthermore, our review of recent value-relevance literature has shown that alternative earnings figures are documented as more value relevant than GAAP earnings, with alternative earnings including the concepts of core earnings (Wieland et al., 2013); pro forma earnings; and I/B/E/S earnings (Entwistle et al., 2010) in the US; and headline earnings in South Africa (Venter et al., 2014). In addition, researchers have documented some valuation implications of loss-making firms. One of our reviewed studies reported that, in a resource-based economy, the exploration costs of loss-making firms are incrementally value relevant (Wu et al., 2010), whereas another study reported that, dividend is generally value relevant when they allow coefficient of book value to vary across loss making firms (Jiang & Stark, 2013). Mixed findings were revealed in the value-relevance literature about the valuation implications of tax information. Some recent work on deferred tax has also shed light on the valuation implications of how deferred tax is accounted and allocated. One study has shown that deferred tax balances based on the balance sheet approach are more value relevant than when using the income statement approach (Hanlon et al.,

2014), whereas the partial approach to deferred tax allocation has been documented as more value relevant than the comprehensive approach, with some exceptions (Wong et al., 2011). Moreover, tax planning activities were found to have a negative relationship with firm value and also reduce firm value (Wahab & Holland, 2012).

In our review, we observed that, increasingly, more financial information is disclosed in the notes to the accounts than is recognized in the actual financial statements due to factors such as specific requirements from standard setters, materiality, and aggregation. Therefore, it is imperative to know the valuation implications of disclosed information versus information recognized in the financial statements. Some recent evidence has shown that recorded goodwill is value relevant (Oliveira et al., 2010): one study documented that the market placed greater weight on lease obligations disclosed in the actual financial statement compared to synthetic lease liabilities disclosed in the notes to the accounts (Callahan et al., 2013). On the other hand, a number of recent studies have documented different types of value-relevant disclosures, for example: firms with related party disclosures have a lower market valuation (Kohlbeck & Mayhew, 2010); all three levels of fair value information are value relevant (Song et al., 2010); advertising expenditure is value relevant from the pharmaceutical industry perspective (Gu & Li, 2010); and underfunding of a multi-employer defined-benefit pension plan was value relevant for the period 2011–2012 (Chen et al., 2014).

It appears that different types of accounting information are continuously being documented as value relevant, while this is also making an incremental contribution in a specific line of research. The usefulness of the value-relevance literature thus needs to be considered in greater depth. These findings can inform standard setters in drafting and amending new standards on various issues (this is further discussed in the challenges section). Furthermore, financial statement users would be able to see that there is an association between the type of information and the share price.

It has been argued that financial information alone is not able to capture the variation in stock prices; however, if non-financial information is considered along with financial information, the value relevance of financial information can be increased. As a result, a number of researchers have started to investigate the value relevance of non-financial information. As was the case with financial information, researchers have assessed the value relevance of different types of non-financial information, for example: carbon dioxide emissions (Chapple et al., 2011; Clarkson et al., 2014; Matsumura et al., 2014); Toxics Release Inventory (TRI) (Clarkson et al., 2013); environmental disclosures (Clarkson et al., 2013; Middleton, 2015); CSR disclosures (de Villiers & Marques, 2016; Gregory et al., 2016); subsidies (Lee et al., 2014); management quality (Agarwal et al., 2011); and investor relations (Agarwal et al., 2015). It is noteworthy that accounting researchers have, for a long time, shown interest in assessing the value relevance of environmental performance. It is also evident that researchers, using different types of theoretical constructs such as TRI emissions and carbon dioxide emissions, have consistently documented the negative impact of poor environmental performance on the firm's market value (Chapple et al., 2011; Clarkson et al., 2013; Clarkson et al., 2014; Matsumura et al., 2014).

However, these constructs have also been criticized due to their inability to reflect actual performance across the industry and country. Furthermore, it is argued that these constructs, with the exception of carbon dioxide emissions, reflect historical performance. Clarkson (2012) argued that "other information" in the Ohlson (1995) model focuses on prospective information, reflecting information which is useful for forecasting future abnormal earnings beyond what is achievable with the knowledge gained from current abnormal earnings. Based on this argument, it is considered that carbon dioxide emissions are an appropriate measure of environmental performance for the Ohlson (1995) model as this information represents a firm's future environmental liability by reflecting future litigation costs and abatement expenditures (Clarkson, 2012). Overall, the extant literature has documented that non-financial information disclosed by a firm is generally value-relevant information.

CHALLENGES OF VALUE-RELEVANCE RESEARCH

Like any other line of research, value-relevance research has many challenges. The Ohlson (1995) valuation model was developed on the premise that market value is a function of the book value of equity and abnormal earnings (alternative form of earnings commonly used as a substitute for abnormal earnings). In this model, other information is often tested as a test variable to understand whether that information is value relevant. However, over the years, we have found conflicting evidence about the main variables in the Ohlson (1995) model. While Collins et al. (1997) found that the value relevance of the book value of equity increased for US firms over a 40-year period (1953–1993), Francis and Schipper (1999) documented that the value relevance of earnings information declined for the 1952–1994 period for US firms. Similarly, Lev and Zarowin (1999), using a sample of US firms, found that the value relevance of reported earnings, cash flow, and book value declined from 1979–1996. In addition, Core, Guay, and Van Buskirk (2003) documented that the value relevance of accounting information has declined over time. More recently, Hail (2013) documented that reported earnings figures are becoming less useful for the purpose of valuation based on a large international sample and multiple valuation models.

Given that researchers are documenting the declining value relevance of the core components of the Ohlson (1995)-type valuation model, it is important to understand what factors are contributing to these conflicting results. One potential reason in this context could be the increasing number of loss-making firms over time (Givoly & Hayn, 2000; Hayn, 1995; Klein & Marquardt, 2006). Given that loss-making firms are less informative than profit-making firms, the effect could be to lower the goodness of fit for the regression model (Balachandran & Mohanram, 2011). Furthermore, using a sample from 1975–2004, Balachandran and Mohanram (2011) examined whether the decline in value relevance of general accounting information was driven by increased conservatism but did not find any association; however, they documented that firms had the most significant decline in value relevance in cases in which conservatism did not increase.

Another notable issue in value-relevance research is the role played by the scaling of variables used in the research model. Easton and Sommers (2003) found evidence that the coefficients in the price model could be driven by the largest market-capitalized firms which could result in issues like heteroscedasticity and coefficient bias. In order to overcome the scaling issue, Easton and Sommers (2003) suggested market capitalization should be used as a deflator in the price level regressions. Furthermore, Barth and Clinch (2009) comprehensively examined multiple scaling-related issues: multiplicative and additive scale effects, scale-varying valuation parameters, survivorship effects, and scale-related heteroscedasticity. They concluded that, regardless of the type of scale effect, share-deflated and undeflated specifications work the best for market value regression on earnings and book value. However, Jiang and Shen (2009) questioned the generalizability of the findings of Barth and Clinch (2009) to other jurisdictions given that their simulation was carried out using US data. Our review of recent value-relevance literature has shown the application of both scaled and unscaled models in market value regression on earnings and book value, suggesting that, to date, there is no uniform approach to scaling.

The other challenge of value-relevance research is whether the findings of this line of research play any role in standard setting. Some early studies provided conflicting evidence on whether value-relevance research would be relevant for setting international standards. Holthausen and Watts (2001) documented that value-relevance research provided limited or no insight for standard setting. In contrast, Barth et al. (2001) concluded that value-relevance literature would be useful for standard setting. We support the view of Barth et al. (2001) and believe that value-relevance research has the potential to contribute to standard setting. In particular, value-relevance research has a role to play in guiding the development of future standards and the amendment of existing standards as studies have clearly documented which type of information is value relevant and which is not value relevant. If the role of accounting standards is to contribute to the development of efficient capital markets then specific requirements that produce value-relevant information should be considered. Perhaps the main challenge is to build up an effective communication channel which may help the standard setters to utilize academic research findings, and also assist academic researchers to understand where further research is needed. In this regard, some recent initiatives from the Financial Accounting Standards Board (FASB) and the International Accounting Standards Board (IASB) are laudable. More collabora-tive approaches are needed for greater utilization of valuation research.

FUTURE RESEARCH DIRECTIONS

Many further opportunities for value-relevance research were identified in our review. In the review findings, we documented a large number of value-relevance studies that were conducted in a single country context and predominantly in the US context. It could be worthwhile to re-examine some of the issues in the context of a different country or in multi-country settings. Each country is different and may have differ-ences in its legal system, culture, institutional and accounting systems, and GAAP, and firms' operations may also be affected by social, political, and economic factors. Furthermore, a large number of countries adopted IFRS around 2005; therefore, with at least 10 years of IFRS adoption data available, some longitudinal studies can be designed to observe the incremental value relevance of IFRS information. In addition, our review has shown that relatively fewer studies have examined the value relevance of non-financial information compared to those that have studied financial information. We find that an increasing amount of non-financial informa-tion is gradually emerging, thus providing further opportunities for researchers to investigate the value relevance of this type of information.

CONCLUSION

In this chapter, we organized recent value-relevance literature into two main groups of information, namely, financial and non-financial, with researchers having used the Ohlson (1995) model to examine their research questions. We attempted to integrate the recent value-relevance research on a number of topic areas, and also sought to provide an integrated discussion on the overall valuation research on financial and non-financial information. Our review showed that the value-relevance research framework is still popular: many studies are continuing to use the Ohlson (1995) model and the modified Ohlson model to examine the valuation implications of different types of financial and non-financial information. However, we found the accounting literature was lacking recent academic research which has reviewed the findings of recent value-relevance research, and especially research which has integrated financial and non-financial information. In that regard, our chapter attempts to review the findings of value-relevance research published in reputed accounting journals for a selected time period. Our chapter sheds light on the new types of information that have been proven to be value relevant and on incremental contributions made by researchers in other areas. The value relevance research findings have potential to be used by regulators and standard setters to increase the usefulness of financial and non-financial information.

REFERENCES

Agarwal, V., Taffler, R., & Brown, M. (2011). Is management quality value relevant? *Journal of Business Finance & Accounting*, *38*(9-10), 1184–1208. doi:10.1111/j.1468-5957.2011.02267.x

Agarwal, V., Taffler, R. J., Bellotti, X., & Nash, E. A. (2015). Investor relations, information asymmetry and market value. in *Accounting and Business Research*, 46(1), 31-50. doi:10.1080/00014788.2015.1025254.

Alali, F. A., & Foote, P. S. (2012). The value relevance of international financial reporting standards: Empirical evidence in an emerging market. *The International Journal of Accounting*, *47*(1), 85–108. doi:10.1016/j.intacc.2011.12.005

Amir, E., Harris, T. S., & Venuti, E. K. (1993). A comparison of the value-relevance of US versus non-US GAAP accounting measures using form 20-F reconciliations. *Journal of Accounting Research*, *31*, 230–264. doi:10.2307/2491172

Amir, E., & Lev, B. (1996). Value relevance of nonfinancial information: The wireless communications industry. *Journal of Accounting and Economics*, *22*(1-3), 3–30. doi:10.1016/S0165-4101(96)00430-2

Balachandran, S., & Mohanram, P. (2011). Is the decline in the value relevance of accounting driven by increased conservatism? *Review of Accounting Studies*, *16*(2), 272–301. doi:10.1007/s11142-010-9137-0

Ball, R., & Brown, P. (1968). An empirical evaluation of accounting income numbers. *Journal of Accounting Research*, *6*(2), 159–178. doi:10.2307/2490232

Barth, M. E., Beaver, W. H., & Landsman, W. R. (2001). The relevance of the value relevance literature for financial accounting standard setting: Another view. *Journal of Accounting and Economics*, *31*(1-3), 77–104. doi:10.1016/S0165-4101(01)00019-2

Barth, M. E., & Clinch, G. (2009). Scale effects in capital markets-based accounting research. *Journal of Business Finance & Accounting*, *36*(3-4), 253–288. doi:10.1111/j.1468-5957.2009.02133.x

Barth, M. E., Landsman, W. R., Young, D., & Zhuang, Z. (2014). Relevance of differences between net income based on IFRS and domestic standards for European firms. *Journal of Business Finance & Accounting*, *41*(3-4), 297–327. doi:10.1111/jbfa.12067

Barth, M. E., & McNichols, M. (1994). Estimation and market valuation of environmental liabilities relating to superfund sites. *Journal of Accounting Research*, *32*, 177–209. doi:10.2307/2491446

Beaver, W. H. (1968). The information content of annual earnings announcements. *Journal of Accounting Research*, *6*, 67–92. doi:10.2307/2490070

Behn, B. K., & Riley, R. A. (1999). Using nonfinancial information to predict financial performance: The case of the US airline industry. *Journal of Accounting, Auditing & Finance*, *14*(1), 29–56.

Beisland, L. A. (2009). A review of the value relevance literature. *The Open Business Journal*, *2*(1), 7–27. doi:10.2174/1874915100902010007

Bose, S. (2014). *Capital market impact of the disclosure, assurance and management of Greenhouse Gas (GHG) Emissions: An international study* (Unpublished doctoral dissertation). UNSW Australia, Sydney, Australia.

Callahan, C. M., Smith, R. E., & Spencer, A. W. (2013). The valuation and reliability implications of FIN 46 for synthetic lease liabilities. *Journal of Accounting and Public Policy*, *32*(4), 271–291. doi:10.1016/j.jaccpubpol.2013.04.002

Chapple, L., Clarkson, P. M., & Gold, D. L. (2011). The cost of carbon: Capital market effects of the proposed emission trading scheme (ETS). *Abacus*, *49*(1), 1–33. doi:10.1111/abac.12006

Chen, T., Martin, X., Mashruwala, C. A., & Mashruwala, S. D. (2014). The value and credit relevance of multiemployer pension plan obligations. *Accounting Review*, *90*(5), 1907–1938. doi:10.2308/accr-51010

Clacher, I., Ricquebourg, A. D., & Hodgson, A. (2013). The value relevance of direct cash flows under International Financial Reporting Standards. *Abacus*, *49*(3), 367–395. doi:10.1111/abac.12010

Clarkson, P. M. (2012). The valuation relevance of environmental performance: Evidence from the academic literature. In S. Jones & J. Ratnatunga (Eds.), *Contemporary issues in sustainability accounting, assurance and reporting* (pp. 11–42). Bingley, UK: Emerald Group Publishing.

Clarkson, P. M., Fang, X., Li, Y., & Richardson, G. D. (2013). The relevance of environmental disclosures: Are such disclosures incrementally informative? *Journal of Accounting and Public Policy, 32*(5), 410–431. doi:10.1016/j.jaccpubpol.2013.06.008

Clarkson, P. M., Li, Y., Pinnuck, M., & Richardson, G. (2015). The value relevance of greenhouse gas emissions under the European Union carbon emissions trading scheme. *European Accounting Review, 24*(3), 551–580. doi:10.1080/09638180.2014.927782

Collins, D. W., Maydew, E. L., & Weiss, I. S. (1997). Changes in the value relevance of earnings and book values over the past forty years. *Journal of Accounting and Economics, 24*(1), 39–67. doi:10.1016/S0165-4101(97)00015-3

Core, J. E., Guay, W. R., & Van Buskirk, A. (2003). Market valuations in the new economy: An investigation of what has changed. *Journal of Accounting and Economics, 34*(1), 43–67. doi:10.1016/S0165-4101(02)00087-3

de Villiers, C., & Marques, A. (2016). Corporate social responsibility, country-level predispositions, and the consequences of choosing a level of disclosure. *Accounting and Business Review, 46*(2), 167–195. doi:10.1080/00014788.2015.1039476

Deng, Z., Lev, B., & Narin, F. (1999). Science and technology as predictors of stock performance. *Financial Analysts Journal, 55*(3), 20–32. doi:10.2469/faj.v55.n3.2269

Easton, P. D., & Sommers, G. A. (2003). Scale and the scale effect in market-based accounting research. *Journal of Business Finance & Accounting, 30*(1-2), 25–56. doi:10.1111/1468-5957.00482

Entwistle, G. M., Feltham, G. D., & Mbagwu, C. (2010). The value relevance of alternative earnings measures: A comparison of pro forma, GAAP, and I/B/E/S Earnings. *Journal of Accounting, Auditing & Finance, 25*(2), 261–288.

Francis, J., & Schipper, K. (1999). Have financial statements lost their relevance? *Journal of Accounting Research, 37*(2), 319–352. doi:10.2307/2491412

Givoly, D., & Hayn, C. (2000). The changing time-series properties of earnings, cash flows and accruals: Has financial reporting become more conservative? *Journal of Accounting and Economics, 29*(3), 287–320. doi:10.1016/S0165-4101(00)00024-0

Gregory, A., Whittaker, J., & Yan, X. (2016). Corporate social performance, competitive advantage, earnings persistence and firm value. *Journal of Business Finance & Accounting, 43*(1-2), 3–30. doi:10.1111/jbfa.12182

Gu, F., & Li, J. Q. (2010). The value-relevance of advertising: Evidence from pharmaceutical industry. *Journal of Accounting, Auditing & Finance, 25*(1), 85–120.

Hail, L. (2013). Financial reporting and firm valuation: Relevance lost or relevance regained? *Accounting and Business Review, 43*(4), 329–358. doi:10.1080/00014788.2013.799402

Hanlon, D., Navissi, F., & Soepriyanto, G. (2014). The value relevance of deferred tax attributed to asset revaluations. *Journal of Contemporary Accounting & Economics, 10*(2), 87–99. doi:10.1016/j.jcae.2014.03.001

Hassel, L., Nilsson, H., & Nyquist, S. (2005). The value relevance of environmental performance. *European Accounting Review, 14*(1), 41–61. doi:10.1080/0963818042000279722

Hayn, C. (1995). The information content of losses. *Journal of Accounting and Economics, 20*(2), 125–153. doi:10.1016/0165-4101(95)00397-2

Holthausen, R. W., & Watts, R. L. (2001). The relevance of the value-relevance literature for financial accounting standard setting. *Journal of Accounting and Economics, 31*(1-3), 3–75. doi:10.1016/S0165-4101(01)00029-5

Horton, J., & Serafeim, G. (2010). Market reaction to and valuation of IFRS reconciliation adjustments: First evidence from the UK. *Review of Accounting Studies, 15*(4), 725–751. doi:10.1007/s11142-009-9108-5

Hughes, K. E. II. (2000). The value relevance of non-financial measures of air pollution in the electric utility industry. *Accounting Review, 75*(2), 209–228. doi:10.2308/accr.2000.75.2.209

Jiang, W., & Shen, Y. (2009). Discussion of scale effects in capital markets-based accounting research. *Journal of Business Finance & Accounting, 36*(3/4), 289–296. doi:10.1111/j.1468-5957.2009.02146.x

Jiang, W., & Stark, A. W. (2013). Dividends, research and development expenditures, and the value relevance of book value for UK loss-making firms. *The British Accounting Review, 45*(2), 112–124. doi:10.1016/j.bar.2013.03.003

Johnston, D. M., Sefcik, S. E., & Soderstrom, N. S. (2008). The value relevance of greenhouse gas emissions allowances: An exploratory study in the related United States SO2 market. *European Accounting Review*, *17*(4), 747–764. doi:10.1080/09638180802481615

Kang, S.-H., & Zhao, Y. (2010). Information content and value relevance of depreciation: A cross-industry analysis. *Accounting Review*, *85*(1), 227–260. doi:10.2308/accr.2010.85.1.227

Kim, O. (2013). Russian accounting system: Value relevance of reported information and the IFRS adoption perspective. *The International Journal of Accounting*, *48*(4), 525–547. doi:10.1016/j.intacc.2013.10.007

Klein, A., & Marquardt, C. A. (2006). Fundamentals of accounting losses. *Accounting Review*, *81*(1), 179–206. doi:10.2308/accr.2006.81.1.179

Kohlbeck, M., & Mayhew, B. W. (2010). Valuation of firms that disclose related party transactions. *Journal of Accounting and Public Policy*, *29*(2), 115–137. doi:10.1016/j.jaccpubpol.2009.10.006

KPMG. (2011). Integrated Reporting in practice: The South African story. Retrieved from https://www.kpmg.com/Global/en/topics/corporate-reporting/better-reporting/Documents/the-south-african-story.pdf

Lee, E., Walker, M., & Zeng, C. (2014). Do Chinese government subsidies affect firm value? *Accounting, Organizations and Society*, *39*(3), 149–169. doi:10.1016/j.aos.2014.02.002

Lev, B., & Zarowin, P. (1999). The boundaries of financial reporting and how to extend them. *Journal of Accounting Research*, *37*(2), 353–385. doi:10.2307/2491413

Matsumura, E. M., Prakash, R., & Vera-Muñoz, S. C. (2014). Firm-value effects of carbon emissions and carbon disclosures. *Accounting Review*, *89*(2), 695–724. doi:10.2308/accr-50629

Middleton, A. (2015). Value relevance of firms integral environmental performance: Evidence from Russia. *Journal of Accounting and Public Policy*, *34*(2), 204–211. doi:10.1016/j.jaccpubpol.2014.12.001

Ohlson, J. A. (1995). Earnings, book values, and dividends in equity valuation. *Contemporary Accounting Research*, *11*(2), 661–687. doi:10.1111/j.1911-3846.1995.tb00461.x

Oliveira, L., Rodrigues, L. L., & Craig, R. (2010). Intangible assets and value relevance: Evidence from the Portuguese stock exchange. *The British Accounting Review*, *42*(4), 241–252. doi:10.1016/j.bar.2010.08.001

Plumlee, M., Brown, D., Hayes, R. M., & Marshall, R. S. (2015). Voluntary environmental disclosure quality and firm value: Further evidence. *Journal of Accounting and Public Policy*, *34*(4), 336–361. doi:10.1016/j.jaccpubpol.2015.04.004

Rajgopal, S., Venkatachalam, M., & Kotha, S. (2003). The value relevance of network advantages: The case of e-commerce firms. *Journal of Accounting Research*, *41*(1), 135–162. doi:10.1111/1475-679X.00099

Richardson, G., & Tinaikar, S. (2004). Accounting based valuation models: What have we learned? *Accounting and Finance*, *44*(2), 223–255. doi:10.1111/j.1467-629X.2004.00109.x

Song, C. J., Thomas, W. B., & Yi, H. (2010). Value relevance of FAS No. 157 fair value hierarchy information and the impact of corporate governance mechanisms. *Accounting Review*, *85*(4), 1375–1410. doi:10.2308/accr.2010.85.4.1375

Tsalavoutas, I., André, P., & Evans, L. (2012). The transition to IFRS and the value relevance of financial statements in Greece. *The British Accounting Review*, *44*(4), 262–277. doi:10.1016/j.bar.2012.09.004

Venter, E. R., Emanuel, D., & Cahan, S. F. (2014). The value relevance of mandatory non-GAAP earnings. *Abacus*, *50*(1), 1–24. doi:10.1111/abac.12020

Wahab, N. S. A., & Holland, K. (2012). Tax planning, corporate governance and equity value. *The British Accounting Review*, *44*(2), 111–124. doi:10.1016/j.bar.2012.03.005

Wieland, M. M., Dawkins, M. C., & Dugan, M. T. (2013). The differential value relevance of S&Ps core earnings versus GAAP earnings: The role of stock option expense. *Journal of Business Finance & Accounting*, *40*(1-2), 55–81. doi:10.1111/jbfa.12013

Wong, J., Wong, N., & Naiker, V. (2011). Comprehensive versus partial deferred tax liabilities and equity market values. *Accounting and Finance*, *51*(4), 1087–1106. doi:10.1111/j.1467-629X.2011.00430.x

Wu, H., Fargher, N., & Wright, S. (2010). Accounting for investments and the relevance of losses to firm value. *The International Journal of Accounting*, *45*(1), 104–127. doi:10.1016/j.intacc.2010.01.005

KEY TERMS AND DEFINITIONS

Financial Information: Any accounting information that is reported in the financial statements or in the notes to the accounts including numbers calculated using accounting information.

Non-Financial Information: Any information that is not part of the financial statements and the notes to the accounts but rather arises from corporate social responsibility (CSR) disclosures, environmental disclosures, government subsidies, management quality, investor relations, etc.

ENDNOTE

1 South Africa mandated integrated reporting for firms listed on the Johannesburg Securities Exchange (JSE) from the years commencing on or after 1 March 2010 (KPMG, 2011).

APPENDIX 1

Table 1. Studies examined value relevance of financial information (2010-2016)

Author(s)	Country	Sample Year(s)	Sample Size	Journal
Chen, Martin, Mashruwala, & Mashruwala (2015)	US	2000-2012	1465 firm-years	The Accounting Review
Barth, Landsman, Young, & Zhuang (2014)	15 Countries	2005	1201 firms	Journal of Business Finance & Accounting
Hanlon, Navissi, & Soepriyanto (2014)	Australia	2005	291 firm-year	Journal of Contemporary Accounting & Economics
Venter, Emanuel, & Cahan (2014)	South Africa	2002-2009	2042 firm-years	Abacus
Wieland, Dawkins, & Dugan (2013)	US	2001-2009	33661firms-years	Journal of Business Finance & Accounting
Callahan, Smith, & Spencer (2013)	US	2004	125 firm-year	Journal of Accounting and Public Policy
Jiang & Stark (2013)	UK	1991-2010	3931 firm-years	The British Accounting Review
Clacher, Ricquebourg, & Hodgson (2013)	Australia	2000-2010	3381 firm-years	Abacus
Kim (2012)	Russia	1995-2010	324 firm-years	The International Journal of Accounting
Alali & Foote (2012)	UAE	2000-2006	1934 firm-months	The International Journal of Accounting
Tsalavoutas, Andre, & Evans (2012)	Greece	2001-2008	1861 firm-years	The British Accounting Review
Wahab & Holland (2012)	UK	2005-2007	444 firm-years	The British Accounting Review
Wong, Wong, & Naiker (2011)	NZ	2000-2004	411 firm-years	Accounting & Finance
Kang & Zhao (2010)	US	2000-2005	468 firm-years	The Accounting Review
Song, Thomas, & Yi (2010)	US	2008	1260 firm-quarters	The Accounting Review
Kohlbeck & Mayhew (2010)	US	2001	1194 firm-year	Journal of Accounting and Public Policy
Wu, Fargher, & Wright (2010)	Australia	1993-2006	6799 firm-years	The International Journal of Accounting
Oliveira, Rodrigues, & Craig (2010)	Portugal	1998-2008	354 firm-years	The British Accounting Review
Gu & Li (2010)	US	1995-2004	4966 firm-years	Journal of Accounting, Auditing & Finance
Entwistle, Feltham, & Mbagwu (2010)	US	2000-2004	1493 firm-years	Journal of Accounting, Auditing & Finance
Horton & Serafeim (2010)	UK	2006	297 firm-year	Review of Accounting Studies

APPENDIX 2

Table 2. Studies examined value relevance of non-financial information (2010-2016)

Author(s)	Country	Sample Year(s)	Sample Size	Journal
Gregory, Whittaker, & Yan (2016)	US	1991-2008	12,584 firm-years	Journal of Business Finance & Accounting
de Villiers & Marques (2016)	22 European Countries	2007-2010	1,227 firm-years	Accounting and Business Research
Agarwal, Taffler, Bellotti, & Nash (2015)	US	2000-2002	13,415 firm-cases	Accounting and Business Research
Middleton (2015)	Russia	2005-2007	152 firm-years	Journal of Accounting and Public Policy
Plumlee, Brown, Hayes, & Marshall (2015)	US	2000-2005	474 firm-years	Journal of Accounting and Public Policy
Lee, Walker, & Zeng (2014)	China	2002-2008	4,898 firm-years	Accounting, Organizations and Society
Matsumura, Prakash, & Vera-Muñoz (2014)	US	2006-2008	970 firm-years	The Accounting Review
Clarkson, Li, Pinnuck, & Richardson (2014)	EU ETS Countries	2006-2009	843 firm-years	European Accounting Review
Clarkson, Fang, Li, & Richardson (2013)	US	2003 and 2006	195 firm-years	Journal of Accounting and Public Policy
Agarwal, Taffler, & Brown (2011)	UK	1990-2007 ex. 1993	3,850 firm-years	Journal of Business Finance & Accounting
Chapple, Clarkson, & Gold (2011)	Australia	2007	58 firms	Abacus

Chapter 16
Information Asymmetries in the Context of Restatement Announcements

Pierangelo Rosati
Irish Centre for Cloud Computing and Commerce (IC4), Dublin City University, Ireland

Pietro Mazzola
SDA Bocconi School of Management, Italy

Riccardo Palumbo
University "G. d'Annunzio" of Chieti-Pescara, European Capital Markets CRC, Italy

ABSTRACT

This chapter presents the results of an empirical investigation on stock trading activity in the context of restatement announcements. The aim is to explore whether sophisticated investors may anticipate accounting restatements, and which factors lead their trading strategies. The empirical analysis shows that sophisticated investors sell before and buy after the announcement. Moreover sophisticated investors trade more when information asymmetry and event-related risk are higher, and do not care about stock's recent performance. In contrast, unsophisticated investors do not follow a particular trading strategy before or after the announcement, stay away from trading when the information gap (risk) is too wide (high), but trade more on stock with positive past performance. Results suggest that sophisticated investors are able to anticipate restatements and exploit their information advantage to speculate.

DOI: 10.4018/978-1-5225-1900-3.ch016

Copyright ©2017, IGI Global. Copying or distributing in print or electronic forms without written permission of IGI Global is prohibited.

INTRODUCTION

The Financial Accounting Standards Board (FASB) defines a restatement as a revision of a previously issued financial statement to correct a material error. Restatements have gathered a considerable interest from researchers, regulators and investors due to the significant impact they have on issuers' value. A consistent portion of research investigates market reaction to accounting restatements. Several studies document large negative reaction with a loss in equity value of 10 percent, or even higher (Hribar & Jenkins, 2004; Palmrose, Richardson, & Scholz, 2004). Part of this reaction is due to revisions in firm's expected performance and part to a reduction in management capabilities and financial statements reliability (Badertscher, Hribar, & Jenkins, 2011). A recent strand of the literature focuses on the relation between information flow among investors and the market response to restatement announcements. Hribar et al. (2010) show that institutional investors tend to quit from restatement companies one quarter before the announcement. Badertscher et al. (2011) demonstrate that insider trading and company's share repurchase before a restatement announcements have a signaling effect for investors.

This chapter aims to extend this literature by investigating the difference between sophisticated and unsophisticated investors trading strategies in the context of restatement announcement. Previous studies adopt ownership data to discriminate investors. Differently, we adopt a microstructure approach and classify investors based on their trading behaviors. This allows us to document the trading strategies implemented by each investor's type on a daily basis.

This chapter explores four hypotheses about the difference between sophisticated and unsophisticated trading. The first hypothesis is that sophisticated investors are able to anticipate accounting restatement and sell before the event's disclosure. By comparing abnormal buy and sell trading volumes, it emerges that sophisticated investors tend to sell until the day before the announcement, whereas unsophisticated investors do not change their strategy in the same period. The second hypothesis is that, given that the information advantage rests on the side of sophisticated investors, they trade more when information asymmetry is higher. The results show a positive impact of information asymmetry on sophisticated investors trading volume. On the contrary, such an impact is negative for unsophisticated investors. The third hypothesis is that sophisticated investors trade more when the risk related to the impact of the announcement on the stock price is higher. Results are coherent with the expectations and show that an increase in uncertainty has a positive impact of sophisticated investors trading. Unsophisticated investors, instead, tend to stay away from too risky stocks. The fourth and last hypothesis is that sophisticated investors do not consider stock's recent performance in their decision process, while unsophisticated do. Results show no impact of stock performance on sophisticated strategy and a positive effect on both buy and sell volumes of unsophisticated investors.

LITERATURE REVIEW AND HYPOTHESES

Recent accounting scandals have raised both regulators and financial community interest on accounting restatements. Unsurprisingly, the literature in this field has grown significantly in the last decade (Hribar & Jenkins, 2004; Badertscher et al., 2011).

Existing studies agree on negative consequences of restatements and deeply investigated their causes and consequences. Using a relatively small sample (73 US restating companies from 1976 to 1985), Kinney and McDaniel (1989) showed that restating companies present lower returns and higher leverage; subsequently lots of effort has been dedicated to measure the market reaction and to identify event's features which could amplify or mitigate such an impact. Change in equity value is typically quantified in terms of abnormal returns in order to avoid the influence of market trend; previous studies show that restating companies lose about 10 percent of their market value within two days following a restatement announcement (Dechow, Sloan, & Sweeney, 1996; GAO, 2003; Wilson, 2008; Kravet & Shevlin, 2010; Burks, 2011). Furthermore, some characteristics of restatements may exacerbate such a negative reaction. If a restatement:

1. Involves multiple and core account revisions (e.g.: revenues and cost of sales),
2. Has large impact on net income,
3. Is deemed fraudulent, or
4. Is auditor-initiated, the loss in market value can be as high as 20 percent (Anderson & Yohn, 2002; Palmrose et al., 2004; Hennes, Leone, & Miller, 2008).

A second branch of the literature investigates the relation between corporate governance and restatements. Companies could adopt adequate measures in order to prevent restatements to occur or repeat over time. Aier, Comprix, Gunlock and Lee (2005) show that CFO financial expertise is negatively associated with restatements. Carcello, Neal, Palmrose and Scholz (2011) find the same effect for audit committee independence and expertise. Adopting more conservative financial reporting strategy may represent a wise option as well, however Moore and Pfeiffer (2004) report that restating firms do not appear to change their strategy after a restatement. Finally, top executives and audit committee members may decide to not engage in 'arguable' accounting practices in order to avoid possible reputational damages.

Restatements turn to be very costly for them in terms of compensation, reputation and job loss (Srinivasan, 2005; Desai, Hogan, & Wilkins, 2006; Cheng & Farber, 2008; D. Collins, Masli, Reitenga, & Sanchez, 2009).

Overall, previous studies suggest that part of the market reaction is due to revisions in expected future earnings and financial statement reliability, and part is due to the increase in uncertainty about management credibility (Badertscher et al., 2011).

Financial studies investigate the difference between informed and uniformed investors. Two types of investors are assumed to be informed: insiders, since they possess private information, and institutional investors, since they are reasonably supposed to be more sophisticated and have more resources to spend in information mining. In this chapter, we refer to informed investors as sophisticated investors; on the opposite, we refer to uninformed investors as unsophisticated investors.

Beneish (1999), Li and Zhang (2006), Agrawal and Cooper (2008), and Badertscher et al. (2011) provide evidence of insiders' strategic trading before restatement announcements. Drake, Myers, Scholz and Sharp (2015) provide evidence of abnormal short selling behavior surrounding, but not before, restatement announcements. Despite the large number of studies investigating the informational advantage of institutional investors (D. W. Collins, Gong, & Hribar, 2003; Ke & Petroni, 2004; Ke & Ramalingegowda, 2005; Ke, Petroni, & Yu, 2008), to the extent of our knowledge, only one paper (Hribar et al., 2010) which investigates institutional investors' behavior in relation to restatement announcements. Hribar et al. (2010) argue that institutional investors act as they partially anticipate potential accounting irregularities. Institutional investors adjust their holdings downward prior to the restatement announcements and their information advantage is mainly due to their higher ability in information processing. However, it is plausible that not all sophisticated investors decide to quit so long time in advance. Some of them might not be able so get alerts so early or might simply decide to monitor the situation if the irregularities are not likely to be disclosed.

This chapter addresses this gap in the literature by deepening in sophisticated investors' behavior and by analyzing their daily trading behaviors in the context of restatement announcements.

Accounting restatements are complex information, and investors should not be able to anticipate it. Either managers or third parties (e.g. external auditors, SEC) might discover irregularities and this makes the information timing unpredictable. Even if they were company-initiated, managers would be unwilling to share this information with outsiders. Consequently, investors' reaction to such events mostly relies on their ability (and speed) in processing information. It is possible that part of sophisticated investors fails to detect signals of a forthcoming restatement as early as predicted by Hribar et al. (2010), or they might decide to wait until the restatement is about to be announced. If this happens, abnormal trading activity coming from sophisticated investors should arise right before the announcement. This discussion leads to the first research hypothesis.

H1: Sophisticated investors sell before a restatement announcement, while unsophisticated do not.

If H1 is true, then sophisticated and sophisticated investors carry on different trading strategies, which are based on the information available. Sophisticated investors typically have higher information quality (Barron, Byard, & Kim, 2002; Barron, Harris, & Stanford, 2005; Bushee & Goodman, 2007; Hribar et al., 2010). This means that information asymmetry rests on their side. On the other hand, unsophisticated investors can adapt their trading strategies only after the information disclosure. Therefore sophisticated (unsophisticated) investors might (might not) be willing to trade in case of high information asymmetry. This leads to the second research hypothesis.

H2: Sophisticated (unsophisticated) investors trade more (less) before restatement announcements because of the increase in information asymmetry.

Unsophisticated investors typically have stricter wealth constraints compared than sophisticated investor. Consequently, unsophisticated investors are more reluctant to face risk compared with sophisticated investors (Hirshleifer, 2001; Kaniel, Liu, Saar, & Titman, 2012). When announcing a restatement, managers typically are not able to provide reliable estimation about the impact that the restatement is going to have on net income. The market appears to impose less severe losses to firms which are able to provide information about the effect of restatement quickly (Hirschey, Smith, & Wilson, 2015; BenYoussef & Khan, 2016). However, a restatement triggers a long and complex process and managers need time to assess the real impact. This situation causes an increase in information uncertainty and risk for investors. This discussion leads us to the third research hypothesis.

H3: Sophisticated (unsophisticated) investors trade more (less) when information uncertainty is higher.

Another important factor, which is likely to influence traders' buying and selling decisions, is stock's recent performance. As Grinblatt and Keloharju (2001) note, "*the impact of past returns on the buy versus sell decision is complicated by equilibrium constraints*"; furthermore, existing studies (Odean, 1998; Choe, Kho, & Stulz, 1999; Grinblatt & Keloharju, 2000) report some heterogeneity among countries. As we know from the literature present above, sophisticated investors are able to better process complex information (such as restatement) and have less wealth constraint compared to unsophisticated investors. Therefore they should be able to make better forecast of restatement consequences and decide to buy, hold or sell a stock regardless stock's past performance. This leads us to the fourth research hypothesis.

H4: Past stock returns have lower impact on buy/sell decision of sophisticated than unsophisticated investors.

METHODOLOGY AND EMPIRICAL RESULTS

Data

This paper focuses on accounting restatement announcements, which are typical non-recurring and unscheduled events. There is no specific period of time when they are more likely to be disclosed. Both annual and interim reports can be affected by errors, and these errors can be discovered even long time after the original filling. With such characteristics, accounting restatement are extremely interesting from a research point of view because of their significant impact and heterogeneity, but also time-consuming from a data collection perspective. Most of the existing studies rely on a database compiled by the U.S. Government Accountability Office (GAO), which is public available. Such a database covers (in two subsequent issues) a 10-year period starting from January 1997 and provides company name, disclosure date and causes for each restatement. However, it starts to become out of the date, since regulatory and technological innovations might have modified the speed and magnitude of investors' reaction to restatement announcements. To the extent of our knowledge the only database, which goes beyond the period covered by GAO, is Audit Analytics, but it has some event overlap issues (Karpoff, Koester, Lee, & Martin, 2012). Being aware of the potential biases these two sources might introduce, we replicated the GAO methodology and built our dataset from scratch. We adopted the Power Search tool as provided by Lexis-Nexis Academic and searched for the following keywords: "restate", "restatement", "restates", "restated" or "restating" within fifty words of "financial statement" or "earnings" and variations such as "adjust", "amend" and "revise" within fifty words of "financial statement" or 'earnings". Our search included all English news and SEC filings in order to find the date when the information firstly became public. We collected all the documents announcing a restatement from 1st January 2007 to 31st December 2013. The initial sample included 6,500 events. Table 1 summarizes the number of events collected for each year.

Table 1. Events by year

Year	No. of Events
2007	1,367
2008	949
2009	762
2010	858
2011	855
2012	856
2013	853
No. of events	**6,500**

This table reports the number of events for each year as detected in Lexis-Nexis Academic database. The search was performed using the Power Search tool with the following keywords: "restate", "restatement", "restates", "restated", "restating", "adjust", "amend" or "revise" within fifty words of "financial statement" or "earnings".

From the initial sample we selected companies listed on New York Stock Exchange, NASDAQ and Amex. We deleted 142 events due to clerical errors or omissions and further 3,857 events because of market data availability. For the remaining 2,501 we retrieved trades and quotes data, as well as changes in shares outstanding, from Thomson Reuters Tickhistory Database (TRTH). In order to be included in the final sample we require companies to have market data available for at least 60 trading days before and after the announcement, and at least 50 percent of the non-zero daily trading volume in the estimation period (-60;-21). This was necessary to avoid companies delisted right after the restatement and illiquid stocks. These restrictions led us to delete further 1,499 events. Finally, we deleted 478 events because of overlapping. In other words if a company had multiple restatement announcements within 61 trading days we kept the only the first one. Table 2 summarizes all the filters applied. The final sample consists of 524 restatements occurred to 455 firms.

In order to identify trades involving sophisticated and unsophisticated investors, we classified all transactions as follows. A trade was assigned to sophisticated investors if its volume was higher than 10,000 shares or its market value was higher than 200,000 dollars[1]. Previous studies show that trading size is highly effective in separating institutional and individual investors activities (LaPlante & Muscarella, 1997; C. Lee & Radhakrishna, 2000). We also classified transaction as buyer or seller-initiated according to Lee and Ready's (1991) algorithm paying attention to combining trades which occurred at the same time-stamp in order to avoid biases due to order fragmentation.

Table 2. Data sets and applied filters

	No. of restatement
Events from Lexis-Nexis	6,500
Filter for restatement due to errors or omissions	(142)
Filter for market and data availability on TRTH	(3,857)
Filter for number of trading days	(1,499)
Filter for overlapping	(478)
Final sample	524
No. of firms	455

This table summarizes the sampling process. The restatement announced by US companies between 2007 and 2013 were extracted from the Lexis-Nexis database. Stocks in the final sample has to be listed in NYSE, NASDAQ or AMEX, have market data available for a 121-day period centered on the annoucnement day (-60;+60) and this time interval must not overlap with other restatements or corporate events for the same company.

To detect differences in sophisticated and unsophisticated investors' behavior, we considered the daily trading volume of each investor type. There is a wide literature which shows that trading volume is more effective than stock price in separating sophisticated and unsophisticated investors' trades (Bamber, Barron, & Stevens, 2011). We adopted log turnover as a measure for trading volume. Raw turnover is defined as the trading volume divided by outstanding shares. Turnover has a major benefit, it corrects for the number of outstanding shares; therefore it provides a cleaner interpretation of the results compared to absolute volume (i.e. number of shares traded). However, the distribution of raw turnover is highly skewed and this might bias statistical tests and regression coefficient estimators. See Table 3 for summary statistics. Skewness and kurtosis show a clear divergence from normality so we applied a log transformation in order to normalize the distribution (Chae, 2005). Table 3 shows that, after applying the logarithm, our measure of trading volume is very close to normality.

Unless otherwise noted, any following reference to volume, trading volume and turnover refers to log turnover as defined in Equation (1). Equation (2) shows how we estimated the abnormal trading volume, which is the difference between the trading volume of stock *i* in day *t* minus the median value $\left(\overline{LogTurnover_i}\right)$ of trading volume in the estimation period for the same stock[2].

$$LogTurnover = log\left(\frac{TradingVolume_{i,t}}{Outstanding_{i,t}}\right) \quad (1)$$

Table 3. Turnover descriptive statistics

Sample	Mean	SD	Kurtosis	Skewness
	Daily Turnover (%)			
Sophisticated-Buy	0.122	0.060	8.571	2.635
Unsophisticated-Buy	1.373	0.272	0.178	0.957
Sophisticated-Sel	0.140	0.164	47.208	6.540
Unsophisticated-Sell	1.379	0.295	2.492	1.637
Full sample	3.439	0.692	0.562	1.119
	Log Daily Turnover			
Sophisticated-Buy	-2.933	0.152	-0.447	-0.143
Unsophisticated-Buy	-6.449	0.044	-0.545	0.221
Sophisticated-Sel	-2.939	0.128	0.557	-0.322
Unsophisticated-Sell	-6.432	0.044	-0.325	0.326
Full sample	-5.515	0.045	-0.433	0.311

This table reports the summary statistics of daily turnover for a 41-day period centered on the announcement day (-20;+20). The summary statistics include mean, standard deviation, skewness and kurtosis. The daily turnover is defined as daily trading volume divided by outstanding shares.

$$AbnormalTurnover\left(\varepsilon_{i,t}\right) = LogTurnover_{i,t} - \overline{LogTurnover_{i}} \tag{2}$$

Figure 1 provides a graphical representation of the change in trading volume from day -20 to day +20. Chae (2005) shows that abnormal trading volume increases prior to unscheduled announcement. A restatement represents a typical unscheduled announcement thus we expect to find a similar pattern in our data. The graph shows the expected increase in trading volume. Interestingly, Chae (2005) find a similar trend before merger and acquisition (M&A) announcements. M&As are usually anticipated by rumors (Aspris, Foley, & Frino, 2014; Siganos & Papa, 2015), therefore the similarity in volume pattern with restatements might be a signal of a possible investors' anticipation.

Palmrose et al. (2004), among others, provide evidence of negative market reaction to restatement announcements. Figure 2 plots the cumulative abnormal stock returns for a 21-day period starting 10 days before the restatement announcement (day 0). The time series shows a clear downward trend, which is coherent with previous studies.

Figure 1. Cumulative abnormal volume (-20; +20)

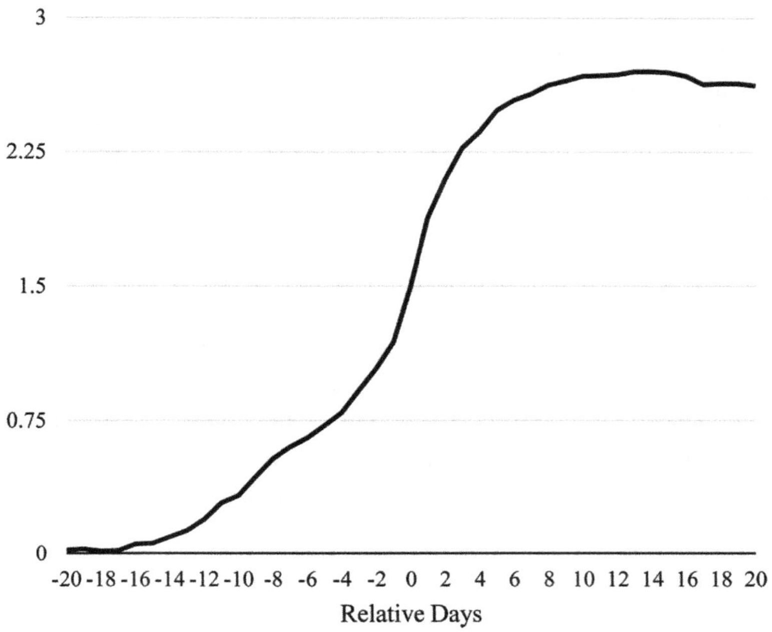

Figure 2. Cumulative abnormal returns (-20;+20)

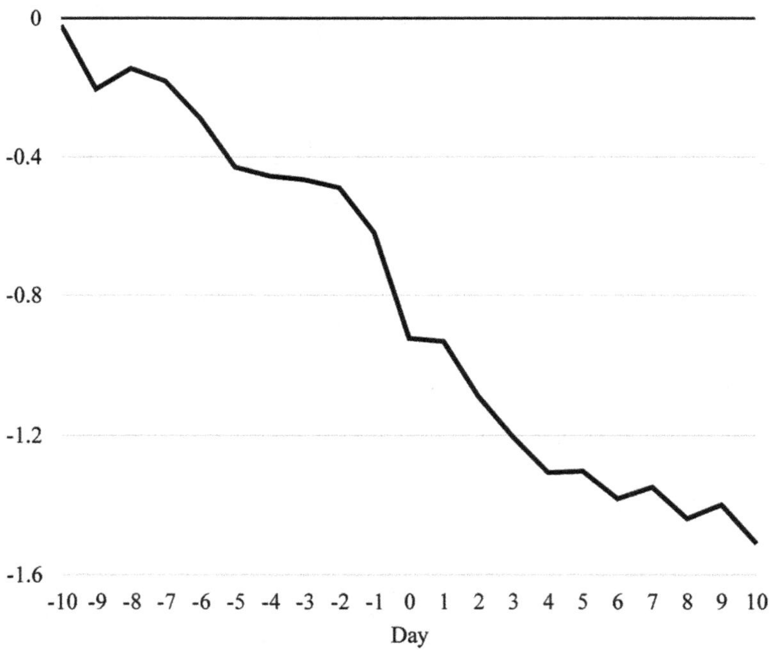

Univariate Analysis

Using the variables described above, we report the cross-sectional average abnormal turnover for all four subsamples from day -7 to +7 in Table 4. This table shows that the abnormal volume due to sophisticated investors is significantly larger than the abnormal volume generated by unsophisticated investors, and that the difference between the two groups is statistically significant.

We also analyze the difference in net selling activity between sophisticated and unsophisticated investors. Based on the assumption that more informed traders would leave companies before the announcement, we estimated investors' net activity on the sell side, i.e. the difference the difference between abnormal sell and abnormal buy volumes (Hribar et al., 2010). Figure 3 provides a graphical representation of the cross sectional abnormal net selling activity for each investor type. When the line is above (below) zero, investors are net seller (buyer). The graph shows that sophisticated investors tend to be net buyers from day -7 to day -4 and

Table 4. Daily abnormal turnover around the restatement announcement

	Buy				Sell			
Day	**Block**	**Non-Block**	***t*-statistics**		**Block**	**Non-Block**	***t*-statistics**	
-7	5.240	0.050	-28.48	***	5.2544	0.0669	-27.95	***
-6	5.313	0.028	-29.26	***	5.156	0.031	-27.8	***
-5	5.252	0.047	-28.26	***	5.063	0.062	-27.21	***
-4	5.191	0.067	-28.03	***	5.195	0.045	-27.65	***
-3	4.911	0.117	-26.58	***	5.056	0.102	-27.07	***
-2	5.004	0.119	-26.72	***	5.242	0.104	-28.06	***
-1	4.845	0.117	-25.98	***	5.060	0.132	-26.68	***
0	5.096	0.290	-27.12	***	4.940	0.291	-25.71	***
1	4.581	0.350	-23.24	***	4.732	0.373	-24.08	***
2	4.879	0.227	-25.68	***	5.040	0.185	-26.52	***
3	4.904	0.146	-25.59	***	5.013	0.145	-26.37	***
4	4.986	0.058	-25.56	***	5.107	0.078	-27.18	***
5	5.085	0.100	-27.28	***	5.159	0.093	-27.94	***
6	5.304	0.031	-28.88	***	5.088	0.063	-27.49	***
7	5.174	0.028	-28.12	***	5.214	0.010	-28.49	***

This table reports the cross sectional daily abnormal turnover for a 15-day period centered on the announcement day (-7;+7) and for each investor and trade types. Abnormal turnover is reported as the difference between log turnover and the median value of log turnover estimated from 60 to 21 day before the announcement, where turnover is trading volume divided by shares outstanding. ***, ** and * denote that the *t*- statistics are significant at one, five or ten percent level respectively.

Figure 3. Net abnormal selling (-7; +7)

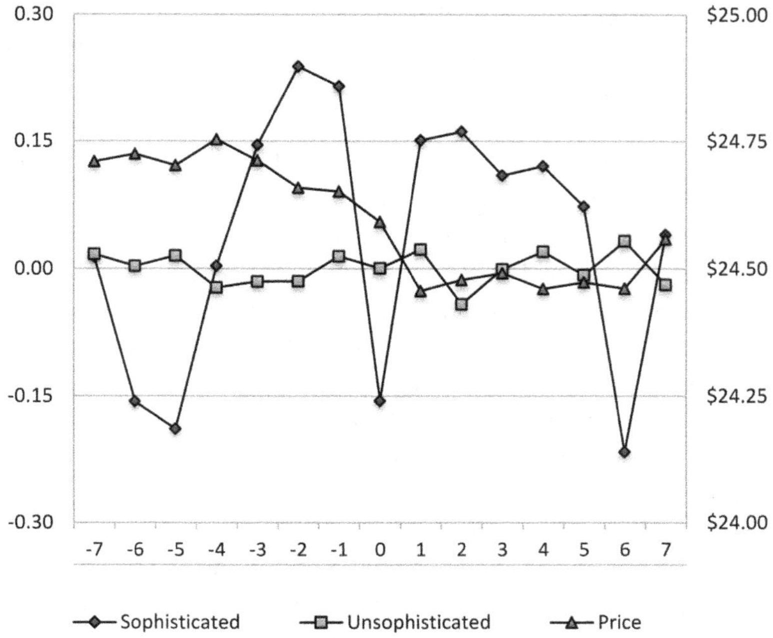

net sellers from day -3 to day -1. On the other hand, unsophisticated investors' activity is quite constant over time. Looking also at the change in stock price, sophisticated investors show a clear speculative behavior since they sell just before the price drop suggesting that they are able to anticipate the announcement. These results lead us to accept H1.

Multivariate Analysis

This paragraph presents the regression analysis implemented in order to test the hypotheses H2-H4. The aim is to show whether sophisticated and unsophisticated investors rely on different factors in shaping their trading strategies.

In building the regression model we followed Chae (2005). We run the regression on four subsamples i.e. sophisticated-buy, sophisticated-sell, unsophisticated-buy and unsophisticated-sell. Differences in significance and magnitude of the regression coefficients across subsamples lead us to our results.

Equation 3 presents the regression model.

$$\varepsilon_{i,s} = \beta_0 + \beta_1 InfoAsym_i + \beta_2 Risk_i + \beta_3 PrcChg_i + \beta Year_{i,s} + \epsilon_{i,s} \qquad (3)$$

The notation $\varepsilon_{i,s}$ is the cumulative abnormal trading volume for stock *i* in subsample *s* over a 5-day period centered on the announcement day (-2;+2); $InfoAsym_i$ is a proxy for information asymmetry before the announcement (-60;-20); $Risk_i$ is a proxy for event-related risk; $PrcChg_i$ represents the difference between average absolute return of stock *i* and average absolute value-weighted market index return[3] from day -10 day to day -3. $Year_{i,t}$ are dummy variables to check for year fix effect.

The bid-ask spread, calculated as the difference between ask and bid prices divided by the quoted midpoint, is our proxy for information asymmetry. Copeland and Galai (1983), Glosten and Milgrom (1985) and Venkatesh and Chiang (1986), among others, show that market makers widen their bid-ask spreads when information asymmetry arises in order to protect themselves from trading with informed traders. Since high bid-ask spread is associated with higher information asymmetry, and being information asymmetry on the side of sophisticated investors, we expect to find a positive (negative) relation between sophisticated (unsophisticated) buy and sell activities (H2).

Choosing a proxy for event-related risk is a bit more complex since the literature does not provide a generally recognized measure. Following Chae (2005), we adopted the absolute price change on the announcement day, which, in spite of possible endogeneity problems, provides a clear idea of the surprise and the direct impact caused by the announcements. As noted above, sophisticated investors have access to higher quality information and are able to process complex information quickly; moreover they have less severe wealth constraints and can face riskier trading strategies compared to unsophisticated investors. This means that sophisticated investors might decide to trade more when the risk is higher in order to seek higher profit. On the other hand, unsophisticated investors need to be more careful about what they buy or sell because of their limited resources and information disadvantage. Following H3, we expect to find a positive (negative) relation between sophisticated (unsophisticated) trading volume and risk.

PrcChg is a measure of stock performance compared to the market index. Since sophisticated investors typically have high analytics skills, they could decide to not follow stock's past performance in designing their strategies. Unsophisticated investors usually do not have many resources dedicated to performance forecasting, so in defining their strategies they can rely only on past performance. Agreeing with these considerations, H4 implies that recent stock performance does not have any impact on sophisticated investors trading behavior, while it is positively related with unsophisticated trading.

In order to check for possible multicollinearity problems caused by strong correlations between the variables included in the regression model, we performed a correlation analysis. Table 5 reports the Pearson correlation coefficients[4] among

Table 5. Correlation matrix

Variables	CAVBS		CAVBU		CAVSS		CAVSU		InfoAsy		Risk	PrcChg
CAVBS	1.000											
CAVBU	0.793	***	1.000									
CAVSS	-0.270	***	-0.259	***	1.000							
CAVSU	-0.263	***	-0.263	***	0.899	***	1.000					
InfoAsy	0.108	**	0.093	**	-0.106	**	-0.084	*	1.000			
Risk	0.152	***	0.136	***	-0.089	**	-0.076	*	-0.004		1.000	
PrcChg	-0.010		-0.022		0.133	***	0.118	***	0.163	***	0.056	1.000

This table reports the Pearson correlation coefficients among variables in our final sample. *CAVBS* and *CAVSS* are the cumulative abnormal volume over a 5-day period centered on the Announcement day (-2,+2) for buy and sell of sophisticated investors. *CAVBU* and *CAVSU* are the cumulative abnormal volume over a 5-day period centered on the Announcement day (-2, +2) for buy and sell of unsophisticated investors. *InfoAsy* is the average percentage bid-ask spread from day -60 to day -20. *Risk* is the absolute price change in the event day. *PrcChg* is the difference between the average absolute return of the stock and the average absolute value-weighted market index return from day -10 to day -3. ***, ** and * denote that the correlation coefficients are statistically significant at one, five or ten percent respectively.

variables in Equation (3). A strong positive correlation exists only between buy and sell trading volumes of the two types of investors signaling that unsophisticated investors tend to follow sophisticated investors' activity. Interestingly, the coefficients between information asymmetry, risk and stock performance and volumes have all the same sign. This means that there is no single factor, which causes the differences in investors' behavior.

Table 6 summarizes the results of the OLS regression. Results show that information asymmetry has positive impact on both buy (Panel A) and sell (Panel B) volumes of sophisticated investors. In other words, they trade more when information asymmetry is higher. The sell-side coefficient is larger then the buy-side one, suggesting that sophisticated investors tend to be net seller when information asymmetry arises. On the other hand, Panel B and Panel D show that higher level of information asymmetry induces unsophisticated investors to trade less on both buy and sell sides. A restatement announcement triggers a downward price revision, therefore this evidence leads us to conclude that sophisticated investors exploit their information advantage to avoid losses and therefore to accept H2.

Looking at the proxy for risk, Table 6 shows that unsophisticated investors buy and sell less when the risk increases. On the opposite side, risk triggers an increase in sophisticated investors' trading. There is a well-known positive link between risk and returns, thus it is plausible that sophisticated investors attempt to speculate from the turmoil restatement-induced. This evidence leads us to accept H3.

Table 6. Regression analysis

Independent Variables												
Intercept	InfoAsy	Risk	PrcChg	Y2008	Y2009	Y2010	Y2011	Y2012	Y2013	R-squared	F-Value	N
Panel A: Sophisticated-Buy												
21.087	2.961	50.951	-45.151	1.503	3.462	1.441	4.587	3.657	3.464	0.046	2.75	524
(-13.66)	(-2.43)	(-3.6)	(-0.86)	(-0.64)	(-1.29)	(-0.57)	(-1.17)	(-1.72)	(-1.81)			
Panel B: Unsophisticated-Buy												
1.531	-0.813	-6.586	39.164	-0.197	0.141	0.104	-1.780	-0.809	0.125	0.066	4.05	524
(-4.92)	(-3.31)	(-2.31)	(-3.72)	(-0.42)	(-0.26)	(-0.2)	(-2.25)	(-1.89)	(-0.32)			
Panel C: Sophisticated-Sell												
22.610	2.998	46.908	-58.090	-0.822	0.914	0.263	1.607	3.919	2.608	0.041	2.46	524
(14.37)	(2.41)	(3.25)	(-1.09)	(-0.35)	(0.33)	(0.10)	(0.40)	(1.81)	(1.34)			
Panel D: Unsophisticated-Sell												
1.472	-0.619	-5.468	32.814	-0.209	-0.115	0.265	-1.675	-0.758	0.038	0.053	3.16	524
(4.91)	(-2.61)	(-1.99)	(3.23)	(-0.46)	(-0.22)	(0.54)	(-2.20)	(-1.84)	(0.10)			

This table reports the results of regressing cumulative abnormal trading volume on proxies for information asymmetry, risk and stock's recent performance for each combination of investor and trade type. The dependent variable in Panel A is the cumulative abnormal buying volume for sophisticated investors from day -2 to day +2. The dependent variable in Panel B is the cumulative abnormal buying volume for unsophisticated investors from day -2 to day +2. The dependent variable in Panel C is the cumulative abnormal selling volume for sophisticated investors from day -2 to day +2. The dependent variable in Panel D is the cumulative abnormal selling volume for unsophisticated investors from day -2 to day +2. *InfoAsy* is the average percentage bid-ask spread for each stock from day -60 to day -20. *Risk* is the absolute price change in the event day. *PrcChg* is the difference between the average absolute return of the stock and the average absolute value-weighted market index return from day -10 to day -3. The t-statistics of regression coefficients are given in parentheses below their corresponding figures.

The results of the regression analysis also show that recent stock performance does not have a significant impact on sophisticated investors trading. However, its effect turns to be positive and significant for unsophisticated investors. The evidence suggests that unsophisticated investors trade more in stocks with positive past performance. These results lead us accept H4.

Robustness Test

In our analysis we adopt the bid-ask spread as a proxy for information asymmetry. However, it embeds two components, namely adverse selection and transaction costs (Glosten & Harris, 1988; Huang & Stoll, 1997). This means that the positive relations between trading volumes and information asymmetry described above might be driven by a change in transaction costs instead of in information asymmetry. In order to test the robustness of our results, we run the regression model presented in Equation (3) using the probability of information-based trading (PIN) as proxy for information asymmetry (Easley, Kiefer, & O'Hara, 1997; Easley, Hvidkjaer, & O'hara, 2002) Table 7 reports the results of the OLS regression.

Table 7. Robustness test

Independent Variables												
Intercept	PIN	Risk	PrcChg	Y2008	Y2009	Y2010	Y2011	Y2012	Y2013	R-squared	F-Value	N
Panel A: Buy-Block												
17.619	23.738	48.532	-31.170	2.441	2.441	5.062	5.369	3.877	3.454	0.066	4.02	524
(9.76)	(4.11)	(3.60)	(-0.61)	(1.06)	(1.97)	(1.00)	(1.38)	(1.84)	(1.83)			
Panel B: Buy-NonBlock												
1.672	-1.789	-6.366	34.024	-0.340	-0.297	-0.107	-1.863	-0.827	0.075	0.051	3.04	524
(4.51)	(-1.51)	(-2.21)	(3.24)	(-0.72)	(-0.56)	(-0.21)	(-2.34)	(-1.91)	(0.19)			
Panel C: Sell-Block												
19.185	23.536	44.506	-43.800	0.115	2.533	1.329	2.385	4.137	2.603	0.060	3.63	524
(10.43)	(3.99)	(3.11)	(-0.84)	(0.05)	(0.97)	(0.52)	(0.60)	(1.93)	(1.35)			
Panel D: Sell-NonBlock												
1.555	-1.221	-5.313	28.862	-0.314	-0.448	0.107	-1.734	-0.770	-0.002	0.042	2.51	524
(4.37)	(-1.07)	(-1.92)	(2.86)	(-0.69)	(-0.88)	(0.22)	(-2.26)	(-1.86)	(-0.00)			

This table reports the results of regressing cumulative abnormal trading volume on proxies for information asymmetry, risk and stock's recent performance for each combination of investor and trade type. The dependent variable in Panel A is the cumulative abnormal buying volume for sophisticated investors from day -2 to day +2. The dependent variable in Panel B is the cumulative abnormal buying volume for unsophisticated investors from day -2 to day +2. The dependent variable in Panel C is the cumulative abnormal selling volume for sophisticated investors from day -2 to day +2. The dependent variable in Panel D is the cumulative abnormal selling volume for unsophisticated investors from day -2 to day +2. *PIN* is the average probability of information-based trading for each stock from day -60 to day -20. *Risk* is the absolute price change in the event day. *PrcChg* is the difference between the average absolute return of the stock and the average absolute value-weighted market index return from day -10 to day -3. Y20XX are dummies for single year of the announcement date. The *t*-statistics of regression coefficients are given in parentheses below their corresponding figures.

Signs and significance of the regression coefficients are all confirmed, except for the significance of the new proxy for Panel B and Panel D. However, it does not affect our main conclusions. We can conclude that our results are robust to different information asymmetry measures.

FUTURE RESEARCH DIRECTIONS

Our results are coherent with evidence on insider and informed trading around company events in general and provide further evidence in this field. However, some interesting questions are still open.

First, why do sophisticated investors start buying at the event day? Collecting the time of the announcements might be painful, but an intraday analysis might provide new valuable insights.

Second, is there any difference in market response if the announcements are released during trading or non-trading hours? For example, if a restatement were announced during the weekend, both sophisticated and unsophisticated investors would have time to evaluate possible consequences and define appropriate trading strategies.

Third, does information advantage of sophisticated investors rise from their analytical power or from other information sources? Studies investigating this dimension would provide significant contributions to the insider trading literature.

CONCLUSION

This chapter provides empirical evidence on investors' response to restatement announcements. Using a dataset of 524 restatements announced by 455 US public companies from 2007 to 2013, the results show that sophisticated investors may anticipate restatement announcements and trade in advance of sophisticated investors in order to avoid losses. Sophisticated investors increase their abnormal buying activity until four days before the announcement, and then they implement an intensive selling activity until one day before the announcement. On the other side unsophisticated investors do not appear to follow any particular strategy before restatement announcements suggesting that they are not able to predict them.

The results also show that some specific determinants influence buy and sell choices of sophisticated and unsophisticated investors in matters relating to restatement announcements. First of all, information asymmetry makes sophisticated (unsophisticated) investors trade more (less). Information advantage rests on the side of sophisticated investors so they speculate on it as long as they can. Stock's risk also encourages sophisticated trading. From higher risk they can gain higher profit. Finally, our results show that sophisticated investors are not influenced by recent stock returns; indeed they typically have high analytics skills so they can rely on better predictions about companies' future performance to define their trading strategy. On the other hand, unsophisticated investors are positively and significantly influenced by recent performance.

Overall our results suggests that unsophisticated investors mostly rely on accounting and other public information in deciding their trading strategies while sophisticated investors integrate accounting information with other sources which allow them to better predict firm's future performance and detect the non-reliability of accounting information. Furthermore, the negative stock price reaction, which follows a restatement announcement, is partly due to the revision of accounting information and partly to a decrease in trust in management capabilities and in the accounting information they provide.

ACKNOWLEDGMENT

The research work described in this chapter was supported by the Irish Centre for Cloud Computing and Commerce, an Irish national Technology Centre funded by Enterprise Ireland and the Irish Industrial Development Authority, and by the European Capital Market CRC.

REFERENCES

Agrawal, A., & Cooper, T. (2008). *Insider trading before accounting scandals*. EFA.

Aier, J. K., Comprix, J., Gunlock, M. T., & Lee, D. (2005). The financial expertise of CFOs and accounting restatements. *Accounting Horizons*, *19*(3), 123–135. doi:10.2308/acch.2005.19.3.123

Anderson, K. L., & Yohn, T. L. (2002, September). The effect of 10K restatements on firm value, information asymmetries, and investors' reliance on earnings. In *Information Asymmetries, and Investors' Reliance on Earnings*.

Aspris, A., Foley, S., & Frino, A. (2014). Does insider trading explain price run-up ahead of takeover announcements? *Accounting and Finance*, *54*(1), 25–45. doi:10.1111/acfi.12003

Badertscher, B. A., Hribar, S. P., & Jenkins, N. T. (2011). Informed trading and the market reaction to accounting restatements. *Accounting Review*, *86*(5), 1519–1547. doi:10.2308/accr-10093

Bamber, L. S., Barron, O. E., & Stevens, D. E. (2011). Trading volume around earnings announcements and other financial reports: Theory, research design, empirical evidence, and directions for future research*. *Contemporary Accounting Research*, *28*(2), 431–471. doi:10.1111/j.1911-3846.2010.01061.x

Barron, O. E., Byard, D., & Kim, O. (2002). Changes in analysts information around earnings announcements. *Accounting Review*, *77*(4), 821–846. doi:10.2308/accr.2002.77.4.821

Barron, O. E., Harris, D. G., & Stanford, M. (2005). Evidence that investors trade on private event-period information around earnings announcements. *Accounting Review*, *80*(2), 403–421. doi:10.2308/accr.2005.80.2.403

Beneish, M. D. (1999). The detection of earnings manipulation. *Financial Analysts Journal*, *55*(5), 24–36. doi:10.2469/faj.v55.n5.2296

BenYoussef, N., & Khan, S. (2016). Timing of earnings restatements: CEO equity compensation and market reaction. *Accounting and Finance*. doi:10.1111/acfi.12220

Burks, J. J. (2011). Are investors confused by restatements after Sarbanes-Oxley? *Accounting Review*, *86*(2), 507–539. doi:10.2308/accr.00000017

Bushee, B. J., & Goodman, T. H. (2007). Which Institutional Investors Trade Based on Private Information About Earnings and Returns? *Journal of Accounting Research*, *45*(2), 289–321. doi:10.1111/j.1475-679X.2007.00234.x

Carcello, J. V., Neal, T. L., Palmrose, Z. V., & Scholz, S. (2011). CEO Involvement in Selecting Board Members, Audit Committee Effectiveness, and Restatements*. *Contemporary Accounting Research*, *28*(2), 396–430. doi:10.1111/j.1911-3846.2010.01052.x

Chae, J. (2005). Trading volume, information asymmetry, and timing information. *The Journal of Finance*, *60*(1), 413–442. doi:10.1111/j.1540-6261.2005.00734.x

Cheng, Q., & Farber, D. B. (2008). Earnings restatements, changes in CEO compensation, and firm performance. *Accounting Review*, *83*(5), 1217–1250. doi:10.2308/accr.2008.83.5.1217

Choe, H., Kho, B.-C., & Stulz, R. M. (1999). Do foreign investors destabilize stock markets? The Korean experience in 1997. *Journal of Financial Economics*, *54*(2), 227–264. doi:10.1016/S0304-405X(99)00037-9

Collins, D., Masli, A., Reitenga, A. L., & Sanchez, J. M. (2009). Earnings restatements, the Sarbanes-Oxley Act, and the disciplining of chief financial officers. *Journal of Accounting, Auditing & Finance*, *24*(1), 1–34.

Collins, D. W., Gong, G., & Hribar, P. (2003). Investor sophistication and the mispricing of accruals. *Review of Accounting Studies*, *8*(2-3), 251–276. doi:10.1023/A:1024417513085

Copeland, T. E., & Galai, D. (1983). Information effects on the bid-ask spread. *The Journal of Finance*, *38*(5), 1457–1469. doi:10.1111/j.1540-6261.1983.tb03834.x

Dechow, P. M., Sloan, R. G., & Sweeney, A. P. (1996). Causes and consequences of earnings manipulation: An analysis of firms subject to enforcement actions by the sec. *Contemporary Accounting Research*, *13*(1), 1–36. doi:10.1111/j.1911-3846.1996.tb00489.x

Desai, H., Hogan, C. E., & Wilkins, M. S. (2006). The reputational penalty for aggressive accounting: Earnings restatements and management turnover. *Accounting Review*, *81*(1), 83–112. doi:10.2308/accr.2006.81.1.83

Drake, M. S., Myers, L. A., Scholz, S., & Sharp, N. Y. (2015). Short Selling Around Restatement Announcements When Do Bears Pounce? *Journal of Accounting, Auditing & Finance*.

Easley, D., Hvidkjaer, S., & Ohara, M. (2002). Is information risk a determinant of asset returns? *The Journal of Finance*, *57*(5), 2185–2221. doi:10.1111/1540-6261.00493

Easley, D., Kiefer, N. M., & OHara, M. (1997). One day in the life of a very common stock. *Review of Financial Studies*, *10*(3), 805–835. doi:10.1093/rfs/10.3.805

GAO. (2003). *GAO-03-395R. Financial Statement Restatement Database*.

Glosten, L. R., & Milgrom, P. R. (1985). Bid, ask and transaction prices in a specialist market with heterogeneously informed traders. *Journal of Financial Economics*, *14*(1), 71–100. doi:10.1016/0304-405X(85)90044-3

Glosten, L. R., & Harris, L. E. (1988). Estimating the components of the bid/ask spread. *Journal of Financial Economics*, *21*(1), 123–142.

Grinblatt, M., & Keloharju, M. (2000). The investment behavior and performance of various investor types: A study of Finland's unique data set. *Journal of Financial Economics*, *55*(1), 43–67. doi:10.1016/S0304-405X(99)00044-6

Grinblatt, M., & Keloharju, M. (2001). What makes investors trade? *The Journal of Finance*, *56*(2), 589–616. doi:10.1111/0022-1082.00338

Hennes, K. M., Leone, A. J., & Miller, B. P. (2008). The importance of distinguishing errors from irregularities in restatement research: The case of restatements and CEO/CFO turnover. *Accounting Review*, *83*(6), 1487–1519. doi:10.2308/accr.2008.83.6.1487

Hirschey, M., Smith, K. R., & Wilson, W. M. (2015). The Timeliness of Restatement Disclosures and Financial Reporting Credibility. *Journal of Business Finance & Accounting*, *42*(7-8), 826–859. doi:10.1111/jbfa.12125

Hirshleifer, D. (2001). Investor psychology and asset pricing. *The Journal of Finance*, *56*(4), 1533–1597. doi:10.1111/0022-1082.00379

Hribar, P., Jenkins, N., & Wang, J. (2010). Institutional investor and accounting restatement. *Asian Journal of Finance & Accounting*, *1*(2). doi:10.5296/ajfa.v1i2.194

Hribar, P., & Jenkins, N. T. (2004). The effect of accounting restatements on earnings revisions and the estimated cost of capital. *Review of Accounting Studies*, *9*(2-3), 337–356. doi:10.1023/B:RAST.0000028194.11371.42

Huang, R. D., & Stoll, H. R. (1997). The components of the bid-ask spread: A general approach. *Review of Financial Studies, 10*(4), 995–1034. doi:10.1093/rfs/10.4.995

Kaniel, R., Liu, S., Saar, G., & Titman, S. (2012). Individual investor trading and return patterns around earnings announcements. *The Journal of Finance, 67*(2), 639–680. doi:10.1111/j.1540-6261.2012.01727.x

Karpoff, J. M., Koester, A., Lee, D. S., & Martin, G. S. (2012). A critical analysis of databases used in financial misconduct research. Mays Business School Research Paper.

Ke, B., & Petroni, K. (2004). How informed are actively trading institutional investors? Evidence from their trading behavior before a break in a string of consecutive earnings increases. *Journal of Accounting Research, 42*(5), 895–927. doi:10.1111/j.1475-679X.2004.00160.x

Ke, B., Petroni, K. R., & Yu, Y. (2008). The effect of regulation FD on transient institutional investors trading behavior. *Journal of Accounting Research, 46*(4), 853–883. doi:10.1111/j.1475-679X.2008.00296.x

Ke, B., & Ramalingegowda, S. (2005). Do institutional investors exploit the post-earnings announcement drift? *Journal of Accounting and Economics, 39*(1), 25–53. doi:10.1016/j.jacceco.2004.02.002

Kinney, W. R. Jr, & McDaniel, L. S. (1989). Characteristics of firms correcting previously reported quarterly earnings. *Journal of Accounting and Economics, 11*(1), 71–93. doi:10.1016/0165-4101(89)90014-1

Kravet, T., & Shevlin, T. (2010). Accounting restatements and information risk. *Review of Accounting Studies, 15*(2), 264–294. doi:10.1007/s11142-009-9103-x

LaPlante, M., & Muscarella, C. J. (1997). Do institutions receive comparable execution in the NYSE and Nasdaq markets? A transaction study of block trades. *Journal of Financial Economics, 45*(1), 97–134. doi:10.1016/S0304-405X(97)81614-5

Lee, C., & Radhakrishna, B. (2000). Inferring investor behavior: Evidence from TORQ data. *Journal of Financial Markets, 3*(2), 83–111. doi:10.1016/S1386-4181(00)00002-1

Lee, C. M. C., & Ready, M. J. (1991). Inferring Trade Direction from Intraday Data. *The Journal of Finance, 46*(2), 733–746. doi:10.1111/j.1540-6261.1991.tb02683.x

Li, O. Z., & Zhang, Y. (2006). Financial restatement announcements and insider trading.

Moore, E. A., & Pfeiffer, R. J. (2004). The effect of financial statement restatements on firms' financial reporting strategies.

Odean, T. (1998). Are investors reluctant to realize their losses? *The Journal of Finance*, *53*(5), 1775–1798. doi:10.1111/0022-1082.00072

Palmrose, Z.-V., Richardson, V. J., & Scholz, S. (2004). Determinants of market reactions to restatement announcements. *Journal of Accounting and Economics*, *37*(1), 59–89. doi:10.1016/j.jacceco.2003.06.003

Siganos, A., & Papa, M. (2015). FT coverage and UK target price run-ups. *European Journal of Finance*, *21*(12), 1070–1089. doi:10.1080/1351847X.2014.924077

Srinivasan, S. (2005). Consequences of financial reporting failure for outside directors: Evidence from accounting restatements and audit committee members. *Journal of Accounting Research*, *43*(2), 291–334. doi:10.1111/j.1475-679x.2005.00172.x

Venkatesh, P., & Chiang, R. (1986). Information Asymmetry and the Dealers Bid-Ask Spread: A Case Study of Earnings and Dividend Announcements. *The Journal of Finance*, *41*(5), 1089–1102. doi:10.1111/j.1540-6261.1986.tb02532.x

Wilson, W. M. (2008). An empirical analysis of the decline in the information content of earnings following restatements. *Accounting Review*, *83*(2), 519–548. doi:10.2308/accr.2008.83.2.519

ENDNOTES

1. These parameters are coherent with the classification of block trades for NYSE, NASDAQ and Amex.
2. See Bamber et al. (2011) for reasons for choosing median, instead of mean, value as measure for normal trading volume.
3. Since stocks in our sample are listed in different markets, each stock has been associated with its respective market index.
4. An absolute value of the coefficient lower than 0.3 (higher than 0.7) denotes a weak (strong) correlation.

Chapter 17

"Volcker/Vickers Hybrid"? The Liikanen Report and Justifications for Ring Fencing and Separate Legal Entities

Marianne Ojo
George Mason University, USA

ABSTRACT

Whilst some valid and justified arguments have been put forward in favor of ring fencing, that is, constructing a fire-wall between consumer and investment banks, and that such activities can be achieved without restructuring banks into separate legal entities, the Liikanen Report highlights why there is need for such re-structuring. As well as considering the merits of ring fencing and the establishment of separate legal activities and entities, this chapter aims to highlight why a suitable model aimed at mitigating risks of contagion can to a large extent, be justified on a cost-benefit analysis basis. Furthermore, the chapter ultimately concludes that even though a greater degree of separation of legal entities and activities persist with the model which is referred to as "total separation", a certain degree of independence between bank activities would also be necessary under ring fencing if its purposes and objectives are to be fulfilled.

DOI: 10.4018/978-1-5225-1900-3.ch017

Copyright ©2017, IGI Global. Copying or distributing in print or electronic forms without written permission of IGI Global is prohibited.

INTRODUCTION

In the Final Report of "The High-Level Expert Group on Reforming the Structure of the EU Banking Sector, chaired by Erkki Liikanen,[1] the need for re-structuring banks into separate legal activities is highlighted. In assessing such a need, two considerations were given due attention (See page i of the Report):

The important role of recovery and resolution plans – whereby the decision on possible separation of bank entities was to be conditionally based on the assessment of such plans; The mandatory separation of banks' proprietary trading and other risky activities.

The Liikanen Review was established in November 2011 by EU commissioner, Michel Barnier, to conduct a full scale analysis of Europe's lending sector and recommend banking reforms for the region." (Varriale, 2012).

The mandatory separation of banks' proprietary trading and other risky activities could be distinguished from the case which exists with Volcker's Rule in that an outright ban or prohibition on proprietary trading (all forms of risky investment practices) and certain relationships with hedge funds and private equity funds is not implied under such mandatory separation.

The "Volcker Rule" which can be found under Section 619[2] of Title VI of the Dodd Frank Act states that:

1. ***Prohibition:*** *Unless otherwise provided in this section, a banking entity shall not*
    a. *Engage in proprietary trading; or*
    b. *Acquire or retain any equity, partnership, or other ownership interest in or sponsor a hedge fund or a private equity fund.*
2. ***Nonbank Financial Companies Supervised by the Board:*** *Any nonbank financial company supervised by the Board that engages in proprietary trading or takes or retains any equity, partnership, or other ownership interest in or sponsors a hedge fund or a private equity fund shall be subject, by rule, as provided in subsection (b)(2), to additional capital requirements for and additional quantitative limits with regards to such proprietary trading and taking or retaining any equity.*

Whilst the Volcker Rule is considered by some commentators as being parallel to a separation of banking activities and entities, it is more draconian in the sense that the model allows for less scope and flexibility than the "hybrid" model which is being considered under the Liikanen Review. Those arguments which increasingly favor a more flexible model and which is directed in favor of ring fencing, arise from the inherent difficulties in the definitions attributed to financial and non-bank financial companies. Since such definitions present some ambiguities, is it really possible to effectively establish "completely" separate legal entities and activities? As the case, has always been, ambiguities with legal definitions will always provide a leeway for financial institutions (whether non-bank financial or financial institutions) to manipulate the rules. Furthermore, other complexities arise from corporate ownership structures of banking groups across various jurisdictions – particularly where such groups operate across various jurisdictions with huge differences in legal definitions and operating activities.

The Vicker's Report also adds that prohibiting only those activities caught by the Volcker rule would not achieve all the objectives of ring-fencing (ICB, 2011, p. 45).

It is interesting to note that the Liikanen Report also highlights that "in the discussions within the Group, some members expressed a preference for a combination of measures: imposing a non-risk- weighted capital buffer for trading activities and leaving the separation of activities conditional on supervisory approval of a recovery and resolution plan, rather than a mandatory separation of banking activities." (page ii of the Liikanen Report):

In the spirit of transparency both basic alternatives and their motivation" were presented in the report - however, the option was made to recommend "mandatory separation of certain trading activities.

As stated earlier, the mandatory separation of banks' proprietary trading and other risky activities, such as that opted for under the Liikanen Report, could be distinguished from the case which exists under Volcker's Rule and could be considered a hybrid in the sense that it does not impose such stringent requirements as those applicable under Volcker's Rule whilst not being as "watered down"[6] as the ring fencing recommendations in the Vickers Report.

Whilst a hybrid model for European banks may appear to have its merits, it will be demonstrated that risks are inherent in both models – whether these relate to complete separation of legal entities or whether these are based on ring fencing alone. The distinction between what could be considered risky bank trading activities and less risky ones and whether the goals to be achieved through such a distinction could effectively be realized through the restructuring of banks into separate legal entities, as well as cost considerations involved in undertaking such restructuring will be discussed in subsequent sections of this chapter.

Objectives of the Legal Separation of Financial Activities and Banking Entities and Arguments in Favor of Ring Fencing

In concluding that "it is necessary to require legal separation of certain particularly risky financial activities from deposit-taking banks within a banking group," the High Level Expert Group highlighted the "central objectives" of such a separation, which are as follows:[3]

- To make banking groups – particularly their socially most vital parts safer and less connected to high risk trading activities.
- To limit the implicit or explicit stake of tax payer in the trading parts of banking groups.

Further objectives could be the Group's opinions that (see page ii of the Liikanen Report.):

- Separation of such activities (between high risk and less riskier ones) into separate legal entities is the "most direct way of tackling banks' complexity and interconnectedness and that as such, separation would make banking groups simpler and more transparent; as well as facilitate market discipline and supervision and, ultimately, recovery and resolution.

As re iterated earlier, those not in favor of a mandatory separation of banking activities, whose objectives are listed above, opted for a "preference for a combination of measures which consists of imposing a non-risk weighted capital buffer for trading activities and leaving the separation of activities conditional on supervisory approval of a recovery and resolution plan."

Whilst such objectives of a mandatory separation of banking activities are justified, proponents of ring fencing, namely those opting for ring fencing rather than a complete separation of retail banking from riskier investment banking divisions, have put forward several arguments in favour of ring fencing activities.

The following sub section considers the purpose of ring fencing as well as arguments in favor of ring fencing.

According to Vickers Report, the purpose of ring fencing is "to isolate those banking activities where continuous provision of service is vital to the economy and to a bank's customers in order to ensure, first, that this provision is not threatened as a result of activities which are incidental to it and, second, that such provision can be maintained in the event of the bank's failure without government solvency support (see page 35, for further information on the location of the ring fence, see page 36)." Furthermore, it was added in the Report that in achieving the purposes of ring fencing, that retail banking activities should have economic independence,[4] as well as the requirement of measures for independent governance which is aimed at enforcing "the arm's length relationship" (see page 12).

Arguments in favor of ring fencing are as follows (see ICB, 2011, p. 12, 26, 59, 65)

- Ring fencing should generate "significantly lower economic costs" than full separation.
- Ring fencing would secure principal benefits such as guarding against certain contagion risks.
- The fact that challenges encountered by ring fencing are manageable and not materially greater than those of full separation.
- Legal impediments which exist with full separation.
- It is not certain whether total separation would necessarily facilitate greater financial stability.[5]
- That total separation is harder to enforce under European Union Law since universal banks in other member states remain entitled to own UK retail banking operations.
- The "workability" and "practicability" of ring fencing and the fact that ring fenced banks would be easier to monitor, supervise and manage than universal banks "other things being equal."
- The argument that it can be "robustly" implemented within the current EU framework and the difficulty in securing changes to relevant EU Law.
- Legal obstacles which persist with "full separation" particularly since European Law places constraints on the degree to which ownership of companies can be controlled.
- That ring-fenced banks should be able to engage in effective risk management."

Ring fencing, hence, obviously has immense benefits attached to its implementation – however prominent proponents of complete legal separation, include Mr. Volcker who adds that "even though the Vickers Report (John Vickers) and himself have the same concerns in mind, the logic would be to separate the two parts of banking, not to keep them within the same institution" (see Daily Telegraph). Furthermore, he adds that it was unclear how the two parts of banking could be entirely independent when under ring fencing they would be subordinated to the holding company.

Whilst the Financial Services Authority Prudential chief, Bailey, has publicly supported the need for a separation of trading activities into separate legal entities (see Varriale, 2012), the former Bank of England Governor, Mervyn King, also expressed his disappointment over the decision to opt for ring fencing rather than total separation (Daily Telegraph).

Vickers Report also acknowledges those advantages inherent in the separation of legal entities (ICB, 2011, p. 63):

1. Argument that common ownership increases contagion from the rest of the financial system to retail banks through increased reputational links.
2. Argument that it is not possible to implement effective rules governing economic links between banks unless they are in separate corporate groups."

The Report however adds that "the risk that the rest of the group could bring down a ring-fenced bank could be managed by insisting that the ring-fenced bank is not dependent for its solvency, liquidity or continued operations on the rest of the group."[6] In bolstering arguments which favour ring fencing, the Report also adds that even though arguments persist in favour of complete separation, namely, that:

1. By removing difficult to resolve wholesale/investment banking activities from ring-fenced banks, the problem is transferred elsewhere but not solved,
2. That in a world of ring-fencing, governments would continue to bail out non-ring- fenced banks (ICB, 2011:46),

that reforms introduced in the aftermath of Crises such as that of Lehman Brothers including greater use of central counterparties and proposals included in Chapter 4 of the Report (Vickers Report) ensure that creditors are appropriately exposed to losses.

Having considered both models, it (ultimately) has to be said that both involve some degree of separation of legal entities or banking activities. The difference between both lies in the extent of such a separation. Whilst achieving the purposes of ring fencing would require some degree of economic independence for retail banking activities, a greater degree of independence, is certainly characteristic of a complete separation of banking activities or legal entities within the group.

CONCLUSION

This chapter has considered the merits, objectives and cost-benefit attributes of respective models associated with the Vickers Report, Liikanen Report and Volckers Rule – by way of reference to the degree of separation of legal entities or banking activities involved, as well as whether an outright ban or prohibition on proprietary trading is involved.

Given the risks and benefits inherent under both models of ring fencing and complete legal separation, it appears that the more favorable model will largely be decided on a cost analysis basis. It is most certain and apparent that no model could ever completely eliminate risks and that a complete and total separation of legal activities or entities also, would practically be impossible or not feasible.

"Significant differences in the ownership structure and corporate governance arrangements between different banks" as well as "significant diversity in bank business models across the EU and across EU Member States, numerous labels which exist to classify banks and their business models",[7] would also present immense challenges for the model being proposed under the Liikanen Report.

Potential legal impediments and leeway for banks in manipulating rules owing to existing definitions of financial institutions also persist – particularly with the option involving a "complete" separation of legal entities and activities.[8] While cost arguments have been advanced in favor of ring fencing, the same arguments are considered to be instrumental in compelling some universal banks to consider the option of complete separation.

REFERENCES

Ebrahimi, H. (2012). Paul Volcker: Ring-fencing Banks is Not Enough. *Telegraph.co.uk*. Retrieved from http://www.telegraph.co.uk/finance/newsbysector/banksandfinance/9561624/Paul-Volcker-ring-fencing-banks-is-not-enough.html

International Financial Law Review. (2013). Banking Sector Reforms. Retrieved from http://www.iflr.com/Article/3107360/Banking-sector-reform-a-definitive-quide-to-the-latest-developments.html?LS=EMS763204

Myles, D. (2012, November 6). Why Kay, Volcker Are Wrong About Ring Fencing. *International Financial Law Review*. Retrieved from http://www.iflr.com/Article/3113446/Banking/Why-Kay-Volcker-are-wrong-about-ringfencing.html

Independent Commission on Banking. (2011, September). Vickers Report ICB Final Report Recommendations.

The Final Report of The High-Level Expert Group on Reforming the Structure of the EU Banking Sector. (n. d.).

The Independent Commission on Banking (ICB). (2011, September). Final Report Recommendations. Retrieved from http://webarchive.nationalarchives.gov.uk/20131003105424/https:/hmt-sanctions.s3.amazonaws.com/ICB%20final%20report/ICB%2520Final%2520Report[1].pdf

The Liikanen Report (Final Report). (2012, October 2).

Varriale, G. (2012, September 18). Liikanen Poll: Volcker/Vickers Hybrid Wrong For Europe's Banks. Retrieved from http://www.iflr.com/Article/3090682/Liikanen-poll-VolckerVickers-hybrid-wrong-for-Europes-banks.html

Varriale, G. (2012, November 7). FSA Prudential Chief: Why Banks Must Be Ring Fenced. *International Financial Law Review*. Retrieved from http://www.iflr.com/Article/3114533/EU/FSA-prudential-chief-why-banks-must-be- ringfenced.html

ENDNOTES

1 Hereinafter referred to as the Liikanen Report (Final Report, 2nd October 2012).

2 SEC. 619. Prohibitions on proprietary trading and certain relationships with hedge funds and private equity funds.

3 See page i of the Liikanen Report. "The Group's recommendations regarding separation concern businesses which are considered to represent the riskiest parts of trading activities and where risk positions can change most rapidly."

4 Economic independence, it is added "requires firstly, that the UK retail subsidiary of a wider banking group should meet regulatory requirements for capital, liquidity, funding and large exposures on a standalone basis, and secondly, that the permitted extent of its relationships with other parts of the group should be no greater than regulators generally allow with third parties and should be conducted on an arm's length basis."

5 "It would remove a channel of contagion risk from investment banking to retail banking (and vice versa) but preclude support for troubled retail banks from elsewhere in banking groups."

6 "Full separation has risks as well as benefits. Reputational links mean that it is likely that a ring-fenced bank would if possible be saved from failure by the rest of its corporate group if it got into difficulty. When domestic retail banking is suffering losses but the rest of the banking system is doing well, more retail banks would fail under full separation than under ring-fencing."

7 "These labels typically focus only on one or two of the numerous dimensions along which different bank business models may differ. The labels may conceal that, for example, some of today's universal banks operate quite differently from how they operated 30 years ago. In general, bank business models can be characterised in terms of several key dimensions or attributes: (i) size; (ii) activities, as evident from a bank's customer base, asset structure and income model; (iii) capital and funding structure; (iv) ownership and governance;

(v) corporate and legal structure; and (vi) geographic scope, including how cross-border operations are legally and operationally structured. " See pages 32 and 50 of the Liikanen Report.

8 In respect of definitions see pg 58 of Vicker's Report and also http://circa.europa.eu/irc/dsis/nfaccount/info/data/esa95/en/een00074.htm. Financial institutions are considered to be "all corporations and quasi-corporations which are principally engaged in financial intermediation and/or in auxiliary financial activities". Financial intermediation is in turn, defined as the activity in which an institutional unit acquires financial assets and liabilities on its own account by engaging in financial transactions in the market."

Chapter 18
Ring Fencing Volcker's Rule?
Justifications for Ring Fencing and Separate Legal Entities Revisited

Marianne Ojo
George Mason University, USA

ABSTRACT

This chapter is aimed at highlighting why ring fencing not only presents a more feasible and cost effective option to other models, but also why its degree of flexibility provides the more appropriate balance in a financial environment whose trend is increasingly inclined towards conglomeration. Whilst the Liikanen Report highlights why there is need for re-structuring of banks into separate legal entities – as a means of achieving ring fencing activities, the mandatory separation of banks' proprietary trading and other risky activities, such as that opted for under the Liikanen Report could be distinguished from the position under Volcker's Rule in the sense that it does not impose such stringent requirements as those applicable under Volcker's Rule – whilst not being as flexible as ring fencing recommendations proposed in the Vickers Report.

DOI: 10.4018/978-1-5225-1900-3.ch018

Copyright ©2017, IGI Global. Copying or distributing in print or electronic forms without written permission of IGI Global is prohibited.

INTRODUCTION

In assessing the need for re-structuring banks into separate legal activities, two considerations which have been given due attention are (Liikanen Report, 2012, p. 1):

- The important role of recovery and resolution plans – whereby the decision on possible separation of bank entities was to be conditionally based on the assessment of such plans;
- The mandatory separation of banks' proprietary trading and other risky activities.

The first of these considerations is justifiable on the basis of the lessons learned from Northern Rock. Northern Rock highlighted the important role of recovery and resolution plans and illustrates a situation where the Bank of England was unable to act as effectively to perform its traditional role as lender of last resort without such a role being made public. The Northern Rock crisis also highlighted problems which were inherent in the tripartite arrangement between the Treasury, the Financial Services Authority and the Bank of England for dealing with financial stability - which includes amongst others, the inability of the Bank to act as lender of last resort for a limited time without such a role being made public.

The rationale for the second consideration, that is, the mandatory separation of banks' proprietary trading and other risky activities, however, appears less convincing given the challenges attributed to shadow banking activities, as well as the corresponding difficulties in achieving what could effectively be regarded as a separation of banks' proprietary trading and other risky activities.

As indicated in the predecessor paper to this paper, arguments which increasingly favor a more flexible model and which are directed in favor of ring fencing, arise from the inherent difficulties in the definitions attributed to financial and non-bank financial companies – as well as certain ambiguities presented through these definitions. Furthermore, the extent to which "completely" separate legal entities and activities can be achieved, as well as cost implications involved, provide greater justifications for the adoption of a more flexible model directed at ring fencing.

Justifications for Ring Fencing

Why should jurisdictions which have invested so much in restructuring their regulatory systems to cope with particular risks (for instance, cross sector services risks associated with conglomeration), be compelled into imposing further laws aimed at facilitating the restructuring of the legal entities of their banks? If further restructuring were to occur, should the rules governing such restructuring be so draconian such that they allow for little scope and flexibility – a situation which appears to be similar to that presented under the Volcker Rule model? Whilst the Volcker Rule model certainly has its merits, it has been argued by many that a number of ring fencing objectives might not be achieved if the mere prohibition of just certain activities under the Volcker rule were only taken into consideration.

According to Vickers Report (pages 35, 36), the purpose of ring fencing is "to isolate those banking activities where continuous provision of service is vital to the economy and to a bank's customers in order to ensure, first, that this provision is not threatened as a result of activities which are incidental to it, and second, that such provision can be maintained in the event of the bank's failure without government solvency support."

Arguments in favor of the adoption of the Ring Fencing Model, as highlighted in the predecessor paper are as follows (ICB, 2011, p. 12, 26, 59, 65):

- Ring fencing should generate "significantly lower economic costs" than full separation.
- Ring fencing would secure principal benefits such as guarding against certain contagion risks.
- The fact that challenges encountered by ring fencing are manageable and not materially greater than those of full separation.
- Legal impediments which exist with full separation.
- It is not certain whether total separation would necessarily facilitate greater financial stability.
- That total separation is harder to enforce under European Union Law since universal banks in other member states remain entitled to own UK retail banking operations.
- The "workability" and "practicability" of ring-fencing and the fact that ring-fenced banks would be easier to monitor, supervise and manage than universal banks "other things being equal."
- The argument that it can be "robustly" implemented within the current EU framework the difficulty in securing changes to relevant EU Law.
- Legal obstacles which persist with "full separation" particularly since European Law places constraints on the degree to which ownership of companies can be controlled.
- That ring-fenced banks should be able to engage in effective risk management.

The Liikanen Review considered a "hybrid" model which embraces features of models presented by Volcker's Rule and the Vicker's Report. In so doing, it does not impose such stringent requirements as those applicable under Volcker's Rule whilst not being as flexible as the ring fencing recommendations in the Vicker's Report.

Preference for a combination of measures which consists of imposing a non-risk weighted capital buffer for trading activities and the operation of the separation of activities conditional on supervisory approval of a recovery and resolution plan, rather than a mandatory separation of banking activities, under the Liikanen Report, also appears to offer a more flexible route - even though this is still not as flexible as the model under the Vicker's Report. Such a flexible preference appears more feasible than a mandatory separation of banking activities given:

- The costs associated with mandatory separation of banking activities.
- The difficulties of achieving what is reasonably considered to be an effective and acceptable degree of separation of banking – owing to the rise of the conglomeration over the years.

In view of the above mentioned attributes of ring fencing and given the need to consider the increased trend towards conglomeration, ring fencing would appear to be the most economic, appropriate and more time-relevant model to adopt.

Whilst commending Volcker's Rule, some flaws identified by Sheel and Ganguly as being associated with the Rule are as follows:

1. The fact that Volcker's Rule "merely prohibits an entity that accepts public deposits from undertaking certain types of trades – and that even as it prohibits, proprietary trading, it allows hedging and market making."
2. The inability of efforts aimed at separating banking (from trading activities) to guarantee that commercial banking is more immune from risky lending practices.

In addressing Sheel and Ganguly's question in regards whether Glass-Steagall would have prevented the global financial melt-down of 2008, it needs to be remembered that the financial environment has evolved over the years. More complex forms of risks have evolved over the years and the firewall which existed with Glass-Steagall could not reasonably be expected to cope with the less advanced and less complex risks which existed some decades ago. Credit risk is certainly a major risk to be addressed – however so are counter party risks.

Furthermore, other numerous types of risks have manifested themselves in recent years. Other risks emanating from complex OTC derivatives trading and shadow banking further complicate the problem.

Ultimately, the distinction between commercial banking, insurance and securities sectors has become more blurred as a result of the rise of conglomerates. Hence the Glass-Steagall Act would not have effectively addressed these developments – as well as the more complex forms of risks which have resulted from OTC derivatives trading and other cross services sector risks – for which the adoption of integrated regulation (single financial services regulation) in many Scandinavian countries, Germany and the UK has been commended.

CONCLUSION

Whilst the Liikanen Report highlights why there is need for re-structuring of banks into separate legal entities – as a means of achieving ring fencing activities, the mandatory separation of banks' proprietary trading and other risky activities, such as that opted for under the Liikanen Report could be distinguished from the position under Volcker's Rule in the sense that it does not impose such stringent requirements as those applicable under Volcker's Rule – whilst not being as flexible as ring fencing recommendations proposed in the Vickers Report.

However the level of flexibility – such as that offered in the Vickers Report recommendations, or the second option under the Liikanen Report consisting of a preference for a combination of measures – leaving the separation of activities conditional on supervisory approval of a recovery and resolution plan, is to a large extent, necessary given the cost-benefit considerations involved in facilitating a mandatory separation.

Having regard to the need to manage cross sector services' risks, the extent to which conglomeration has assumed control over the structure of many bank entities and enterprises, justifications for consolidated regulation of financial services' sectors, as well as the questioning of the logic to reverse efforts aimed at effectively managing evolving risks within the financial environment, ring fencing appears to be the most favorable, more feasible and cost-effective option.

To what extent can financial statements and in particular, accounting information, which are supposed to present a picture of the state of a firm's financial position and affairs, be reasonably relied upon – given such volatilities across financial markets?

According to Sindreu (2016):

One reliable measure of Brexit's impact on the United Kingdom has been the gap between the stock price of medium sized companies and large ones... and it is widening again...

He then adds that "even though Britain's FTSE 100 and FTSE 250 stock indices have been flying high, is this a sign that all is fine in post Brexit world?" In confirming his opinion that it was unlikely that all was fine post Brexit, he bolsters this by stating that the growing gap between both indexes could signal that concerns were rising – given the fact and his explanation that "stocks tend to rise when the currency in which they are denominated drops – because a lot of corporations' income is made abroad, in foreign currencies."

With Brexit's impact and particularly the impact of the pound's devaluation still being felt in markets abroad, the impact of the uncertainty generated in response to the outcome of the U.S Presidential election results were even much evident – as illustrated by the above figures which confirm the well known saying that "when Wall Street sneezes, the other financial markets catch a cold."

In terms of financial markets' reaction, such was the certainty in the United Kingdom that the "Remain" voters would be triumphant in the aftermath of the EU Referendum that it was rumored on the night before the release of the results, that the UKIP leader, Nigel Farage had conceded. Further, the financial markets soared to very high levels – with the value of the pound also reaching all-time highs on the night before the 24th June.

Having predicted the results of the EU Referendum wrongly, the 24th June, a day after (during which it had been revealed that the Remain voters had lost by a margin of about 4%), witnessed the value of the pound dropping to historically low levels. The impact of the Referendum on the pound has not only resulted in lower export prices, higher import prices, but also higher inflation levels. Further, the FTSE 100 closed the day – as well as the week ending, the 24th June at about -200. Other major indices such as the Nikkei 225 and the Dow Industrial closed in extremely negative regions of -1286.33 and – 610.32 respectively. Even though volatilities are still being experienced across the markets, a huge degree of stability has occurred Post Brexit.

Higher inflation levels attributed to the value of the pound and initial panics and volatilities across the market were responded to swiftly by the Governor of the Bank of England through a cut in interest rates to 0.25% – during the first week of August 2016. Quantitative easing measures were also introduced in a bid to add some monetary stimulus to the levels of economic activity. Interestingly it was not the reaction of the Bank that was later criticized but the emphasis of "Project Fear" whereby many claimed that undue fears and uncertainty had been instilled into the general public in the build up to the EU Referendum – as regards possible detrimen-

Table 1. Global stock markets at the close of the week (week closing 4th November 2016) – prior to the U.S elections

Dow Industrial	-17,888.28	-42.39
FTSE 100	-6,693.26	-97.25
Nikkei 225	-16,905.36	-307.72
Hang Seng		-337

tal consequences for the UK economy - should it leave the European Union. This particularly being the case Post Brexit – when markets appear to have recovered and the country weathering all the storms of Brexit reasonably well.

Just as the Brexit results were wrongly predicted and it was demonstrated that markets cannot be relied upon, the same scenario was echoed during the days culminating to the November 8th 2016 US Presidential elections. In response to announcements that the FBI had cleared Hilary Clinton of any alleged mishandling and criminal investigations relating to her Emails, markets soared in the anticipation that a Clinton victory, one which was seen to favor certainty, was inevitable. The financial markets were also considered to be anti-Trump – not only given the levels of uncertainty which a President-elect Trump was viewed as generating, but also in respect of his alleged approaches of protectionism in trade matters.

Even before the election results had been confirmed on the morning of the 9th November 2016, with 137 electoral college votes being declared for Trump, and just 104 for Clinton, and more significantly with the 270 magic target having not even been confirmed, the Dow Futures had already dropped by 500 points. Further, the Mexican Peso dropped to record lows against the dollar – and most stocks in Asia down 1-2%. In view of risk aversion, transfers were witnessed with movements to safer haven stocks. The Mexican Peso which had been performing well the day before – based on anticipations of a Clinton victory, was now reacting to possible consequences of a Trump victory – namely, higher trade tariffs, taxes on cars and the building of "the Wall".

At this stage, the markets were already clearly reacting to a shock and historically low and volatile levels were understandable following confirmation of the Presidential results. The value of the dollar also dropped to low levels. However, in contrast to Brexit – during which stock markets remained volatile for a longer period, the shock appeared to be temporary and shares rallied throughout the day. The Brexit effect, it appears, has greater consequences – not just in respect of initial inflation levels – which prompted the central bank governor to take inflationary targeting measures, but also other possible repercussions which have necessitated the Government to take those fiscal initiatives of taxation of high earners and a focus on long term investment - all aimed reducing the current Government deficit. Such initiatives and post Brexit developments, it appears, will impact UK and global trade relations.

Whilst stock market reactions across the globe, in response to the US Presidential election results, were clearly attributable to uncertainty, it appears that markets are now reacting and adjusting well to news of a Trump Presidency – following initial shocks. And whilst it is clear that financial markets dislike uncertainty, it is also evident from Brexit and the US Presidential result experiences, that markets can and do over react to certain announcements.

REFERENCES

Ebrahimi, H. (2012). Paul Volcker: Ring-fencing Banks is Not Enough. *Telegraph. co.uk*. Retrieved from http://www.telegraph.co.uk/finance/newsbysector/banksand-finance/9561624/Paul-Volcker- ringfencing-banks-is-not-enough.html

International Financial Law Review. (2013). Banking Sector Reforms. Retrieved from http://www.iflr.com/Article/3107360/Banking-sector-reform-a-definitive-guide-to-the-latest-developments.html?LS=EMS763204

Myles, D. (2012, November 6). Why Kay, Volcker Are Wrong About Ring Fencing. *International Financial Law Review*. Retrieved from http://www.iflr.com/Article/3113446/Banking/Why-Kay-Volcker-are-wrong-aboutringfencing.html

Sheel, A., & Ganguly, M. (2013). Ring Fencing Wall Street. *Indian Express*. Retrieved from http://www.indianexpress.com/news/ringfencing-wall-street/1210651/0

The Final Report of The High-Level Expert Group on Reforming the Structure of the EU Banking Sector The Liikanen Report (Final Report). (2012, October 2).

The Independent Commission on Banking. (2011, September). Vickers Report Recommendations (Final Report). Retrieved from http://webarchive.nationalarchives.gov.uk/20131003105424/https:/hmt-sanctions.s3.amazonaws.com/ICB%20final%20 report/ICB%2520Final%2520Report[1].pdf

The Independent Commission on Banking (ICB). (2011, September). Final Report Recommendations. Retrieved from http://webarchive.nationalarchives.gov.uk/20131003105424/https:/hmt-sanctions.s3.amazonaws.com/ICB%20final%20 report/ICB%2520Final%2520Report[1].pdf

The Volcker Rule, Section 619 of Title VI of the Dodd Frank Act. (n. d.).

Varriale, G. (2012). FSA Prudential Chief: Why Banks Must Be Ring Fenced *International Financial Law Review*. Retrieved from http://www.iflr.com/Article/3114533/EU/FSA-prudential-chief-why-banks-must- beringfenced.html

Varriale, G. (2012, September). Liikanen Poll: Volcker/Vickers hybrid wrong for Europe's Banks. *International Financial Law Review*. Retrieved from http://www.iflr.com/Article/3090682/Liikanen-poll-VolckerVickers-hybrid-wrong-for-Europes-banks.html

Appendix

STATEMENT REGARDING THE SUPERVISORY CAPITAL ASSESSMENT PROGRAM

"This afternoon marks the culmination of the Supervisory Capital Assessment Program. Three independent federal banking supervisory agencies--the Federal Reserve, the Office of the Comptroller of the Currency, and the Federal Deposit Insurance Corporation--have worked closely and collaboratively since late February to simultaneously assess the financial conditions of the 19 largest bank holding companies in the United States. These institutions play a vital role in our economy, holding among them two-thirds of the assets and more than one-half of the loans in the U.S. banking system. More than 150 examiners, economists, accountants, and other specialists conducted a rigorous and comprehensive review of these firms, one unprecedented in scale and scope.

These examinations were not tests of solvency; we knew already that all these institutions meet regulatory capital standards. Rather, the assessment program was a forward-looking, "what-if" exercise intended to help supervisors gauge the extent of the additional capital buffer necessary to keep these institutions strongly capitalized and lending, even if the economy performs worse than expected between now and the end of next year.

The results released today should provide considerable comfort to investors and the public. The examiners found that nearly all the banks that were evaluated have enough Tier 1 capital to absorb the higher losses envisioned under the hypothetical adverse scenario. Roughly half the firms, though, need to enhance their capital structure to put greater emphasis on common equity, which provides institutions the best protection during periods of stress. Many of the institutions have already taken actions to bolster their capital buffers and are well-positioned to raise capital from private sources over the next six months. However, our government, through the Treasury Department, stands ready to provide whatever additional capital may be necessary to ensure that our banking system is able to navigate a challenging economic downturn.

The capital assessment results we are reporting today are just one important element of the government's broader and ongoing efforts to strengthen the financial system and the economy. The current crisis has been one of the most challenging financial and economic episodes in modern history, but we face no problems that cannot be overcome with insight, patience, and persistence. The Federal Reserve, through its independent actions and in collaboration with the other agencies represented here, will certainly do its part in our common effort to restore stability and prosperity."

Statement by Chairman Ben S. Bernanke
May 7, 2009

Compilation of References

The Independent Commission on Banking. (2011, September). Vickers Report Recommendations (Final Report). Retrieved from http://webarchive.nationalarchives.gov.uk/20131003105424/https:/hmt-sanctions.s3.amazonaws.com/ICB%20final%20report/ICB%2520Final%2520Report[1].pdf

Aaker, D. A. (1996). Measuring brand equity across products and markets. *California Management Review*, *38*(3), 102–120. doi:10.2307/41165845

Aaker, D. A., & Joachimsthaler, E. (2000). *Brand Leadership*. New York: The Free Press.

Abernethy, M., Bianchi, P., Labory, S., Lev, S., Wyatt, A., & Zambon, S. (2003). *Study on the Measurement and Reporting of Intangible Assets and Associated Reporting Practices*. Commission of the European Communities.

Acharya, V., & Naqvi, H. (2012). The seeds of a crisis: A theory of bank liquidity and risk-taking over the business cycle. *Journal of Financial Economics*, *106*(2), 345–366. doi:10.1016/j.jfineco.2012.05.014

Adrian, T., & Shin, H.S. (2010). Prices and quantities in the monetary policy transmission mechanism. Federal Reserve Bank of New York Staff Report.

Agarwal, V., Taffler, R. J., Bellotti, X., & Nash, E. A. (2015). Investor relations, information asymmetry and market value. in *Accounting and Business Research*, 46(1), 31-50. doi:10.1080/00014788.2015.1025254.

Agarwal, V., Taffler, R., & Brown, M. (2011). Is management quality value relevant? *Journal of Business Finance & Accounting*, *38*(9-10), 1184–1208. doi:10.1111/j.1468-5957.2011.02267.x

Agrawal, A., & Cooper, T. (2008). *Insider trading before accounting scandals*. EFA.

Aguiar, M., & Gopinath, G. (2007). Emerging Market Business Cycles: The Cycle is the Trend. *Journal of Political Economy*, *115*(1), 69–102. doi:10.1086/511283

Aharony, J., Lee, C. J., & Wang, T. J. (2000). Financial packaging of IPO firms in China. *Journal of Accounting Research*, *38*(1), 103–126. doi:10.2307/2672924

Ahlawat, S.S., & Lowe. (2004). An Examination of Internal Auditor Objectivity: In-House versus Outsourcing. *Auditing: A Journal of Practice & Theory*, *23*(2), 147-58.

Aier, J. K., Comprix, J., Gunlock, M. T., & Lee, D. (2005). The financial expertise of CFOs and accounting restatements. *Accounting Horizons*, *19*(3), 123–135. doi:10.2308/acch.2005.19.3.123

Ailawadi, K., & Keller, K. L. (2004). Understanding retail branding: Conceptual insights and research priorities. *Journal of Retailing*, *80*(4), 331–342. doi:10.1016/j.jretai.2004.10.008

Akinci, O. (2013). Global Financial Conditions, Country Spreads and Macroeconomic Fluctuations in Emerging Economies. *Journal of International Economics*, *91*(2), 358–371. doi:10.1016/j.jinteco.2013.07.005

Alali, F. A., & Foote, P. S. (2012). The value relevance of international financial reporting standards: Empirical evidence in an emerging market. *The International Journal of Accounting*, *47*(1), 85–108. doi:10.1016/j.intacc.2011.12.005

Aldhizer, G. R. III, Cashell, J. D., & Martin, D. R. (2003). Internal Audit Outsourcing. *The CPA Journal*, *8*(3), 30–25.

Alexander, D., & Nobes, C. (2013). Financial Accounting: An International Introduction (5th ed.).

Alexander, S. S. (1964). Price Movements in Speculative Markets: Trends or Random Walks Bank for International Settlements.

Al-Harshani, M. (2003). *The Effect of Inherent Risk, Knowledge Spillover, and Litigation Risk on External Auditors' Reliance on Client's Internal Audit Functions* [Dissertation]. University of Arkansas. Retrieved from http://www.frc.org.uk/Our-Work/Publications/APB/ES-1-(Revised)-Integrity,-objectivity-and-inde-(1).aspx

Ali, A., & Hwang, L.-S. (1999). Country-Specific Factors Related to Financial Reporting and the Value Relevance of Accounting Data. *Journal of Accounting Research*, *38*(1), 1–21. doi:10.2307/2672920

Aljifri, K., & Hussainey, K. (2007). The determinants of forward-looking information in annual reports of UAE companies. *Managerial Auditing Journal*, *22*(9), 881–894. doi:10.1108/02686900710829390

Aljifri, K., & Khasharmeh, H. (2006). An investigation into the suitability of the international accounting standards to the United Arab Emirates environment. *International Business Review*, *15*(5), 505–526. doi:10.1016/j.ibusrev.2006.05.009

Amador, J., Gómez-Gonzalez, J., & Murcia, A. (2013). Loan growth and bank risk: New evidence. *Financial Markets and Portfolio Management*, *27*(4), 365–379. doi:10.1007/s11408-013-0217-6

Amihud, Y.; Mendelson, H. & Pedersen, L. (2005). *Liquidity and Asset Prices*.

Amihud, Y.; Mendelson, H. & Pedersen, L. (2005). Liquidity and Asset Prices. *Foundations and Trends in Finance*, 1(4), 269-364.

Amihud, Y.; Mendelson, H. & Pedersen, L., (2005). *Liquidity and Asset Prices*. Foundations and Trends in Finance.

Amir, E., Harris, T., & Lev, B. (1996). Value-relevance of nonfinancial information: The wireless communications industry. *Journal of Accounting and Economics*, *22*(1-3), 3–30. doi:10.1016/S0165-4101(96)00430-2

Amir, E., Harris, T., & Venuti, E. (1993). A comparison of the value-relevance of US versus non-US gap accounting measures using form 20-f reconciliations. *Journal of Accounting Research*, *31*(Suppl.), 230–264. doi:10.2307/2491172

Anderson, K. L., & Yohn, T. L. (2002, September). The effect of 10K restatements on firm value, information asymmetries, and investors' reliance on earnings. In *Information Asymmetries, and Investors' Reliance on Earnings*.

Anson, W. (2008). *The intangible assets handbook: maximizing value from intangible assets*. Washington, DC: American Bar Association, Section of Business Law.

Anzuini, A., Lombardi, M.J., & Pagano, P. (2013). The Impact of Monetary Policy Shocks on Commodity Prices. Banca d'Italia Bank for International Settlements.

Anzuini, A., Pagano, P., & Pisani, M. (2007). Oil Supply News in a VAR: Information from Financial Markets. Banca d'Italia.

Aspris, A., Foley, S., & Frino, A. (2014). Does insider trading explain price run-up ahead of takeover announcements? *Accounting and Finance*, *54*(1), 25–45. doi:10.1111/acfi.12003

Bacidore, J. (1997). The Impact of Decimalization on Market Quality: An Empirical Investigation of the Toronto Stock Exchange. *Journal of Financial Intermediation*, *6*(2), 92–120. doi:10.1006/jfin.1997.0213

Badertscher, B. A., Hribar, S. P., & Jenkins, N. T. (2011). Informed trading and the market reaction to accounting restatements. *Accounting Review*, *86*(5), 1519–1547. doi:10.2308/accr-10093

Balachandran, S., & Mohanram, P. (2011). Is the decline in the value relevance of accounting driven by increased conservatism? *Review of Accounting Studies*, *16*(2), 272–301. doi:10.1007/s11142-010-9137-0

Ball, R., & Brown, P. (1968, Autumn). An Empirical Evaluation of Accounting Income Numbers. *Journal of Accounting Research*.

Ball, R., & Brown, P. (1968). An empirical evaluation of accounting income numbers. *Journal of Accounting Research*, *6*(2), 159–178. doi:10.2307/2490232

Bamber, L. S., Barron, O. E., & Stevens, D. E. (2011). Trading volume around earnings announcements and other financial reports: Theory, research design, empirical evidence, and directions for future research*. *Contemporary Accounting Research*, *28*(2), 431–471. doi:10.1111/j.1911-3846.2010.01061.x

Bank for International Settlements. (2007). Evolving banking systems in Latin America and the Caribbean: challenges and implications for monetary policy and financial stability.

Bank for International Settlements. (2008). Transmission mechanisms for monetary policy in emerging market economies. BIS Papers.

Bank for International Settlements. (2014). 84th Annual Report.

Bank for International Settlements. (2014). The transmission of unconventional monetary policy to the emerging markets. BIS Papers.

Bank for International Settlements. (2015). CGFS Papers No 54 Regulatory change and monetary policy.

Bank for International Settlements. (2015). CGFS Papers No 54 Regulatory change and monetary policy. Committee on the Global Financial System and the Markets Committee.

Bank for International Settlements. (2015). What do new forms of finance mean for EM central banks? BIS Papers.

Bank for International Settlements. (2015, December). Uneasy calm awaiting lift-off. BIS Quarterly Review.

Bao, B. H., & L. Chow. (1999). The usefulness of earnings and book value for equity valuation in emerging capital markets: evidence from listed companies in the People's Republic of China. *Journal of International Financial Management and Accounting*, 10(2), 85–104.

Barclay, M., Christie, W., Harris, J., Kandel, E., & Schultz, P. (1999). Effects of Market Reform on the Trading Costs and Depths of NASDAQ Stocks. *The Journal of Finance*, *54*(1), 1–34. doi:10.1111/0022-1082.00097

Barclay, M., Hendershott, T., & McCormick, T. (2003). Competition Among Trading Venues: Information and Trading on Electronic Communications Networks. *The Journal of Finance*, *58*(6), 2637–2666. doi:10.1046/j.1540-6261.2003.00618.x

Barron, O. E., Byard, D., & Kim, O. (2002). Changes in analysts information around earnings announcements. *Accounting Review*, *77*(4), 821–846. doi:10.2308/accr.2002.77.4.821

Barron, O. E., Harris, D. G., & Stanford, M. (2005). Evidence that investors trade on private event-period information around earnings announcements. *Accounting Review*, *80*(2), 403–421. doi:10.2308/accr.2005.80.2.403

Barsky, R. B., & Kilian, L. (2002). Do We Really Know That Oil Caused the Great Stagflation? A Monetary Alternative. Journal of Economic Perspectives, 18(4), 115–34.

Barth, M.E., Beaver, W.H., & Landsman, W.R. (2001). *The Relevance of the Value Relevance Literature for Financial Accounting Standard Setting: Another View. Journal of Accounting and Economics*, 31, 456-478.

Barth, M. E., Beaver, W. H., Hand, J. R. M., & Landsman, W. R. (1999). Accruals, Cash Flows and Equity Values. *Review of Accounting Studies*, *3*(3/4), 205–229. doi:10.1023/A:1009630100586

Barth, M. E., Beaver, W. H., & Landsman, W. R. (2001). The relevance of the Value Relevance Literature for Financial Accounting Standard Setting: Another View. *Journal of Accounting and Economics*, *31*(1-3), 77–104. doi:10.1016/S0165-4101(01)00019-2

Barth, M. E., Beaver, W. H., & Landsman, W. R. (2001). The Relevance of the Value Relevance Literature for Financial Accounting Standard Setting: Another View. *Journal of Accounting and Economics*, 31.

Barth, M. E., & Clinch, G. (2009). Scale Effects in Capital Market-Based Accounting Research. *Journal of Business Finance & Accounting*, *36*(3-4), 253–288. doi:10.1111/j.1468-5957.2009.02133.x

Barth, M. E., & Kallapur, S. (1996). The effects of cross-sectional scale differences on regression results in empirical accounting research. *Contemporary Accounting Research*, *13*(2), 234–265. doi:10.1111/j.1911-3846.1996.tb00514.x

Barth, M. E., & Landsman, W. R. (2010). How did financial reporting contribute to the financial crisis? *European Accounting Review*, *19*(3), 123–156. doi:10.1080/09638180.2010.498619

Barth, M. E., Landsman, W. R., & Lang, M. H. (2008). International Accounting Standards and Accounting Quality. *Journal of Accounting Research*, *46*(3), 234–265. doi:10.1111/j.1475-679X.2008.00287.x

Barth, M. E., Landsman, W. R., Young, D., & Zhuang, Z. (2014). Relevance of differences between net income based on IFRS and domestic standards for European firms. *Journal of Business Finance & Accounting*, *41*(3-4), 297–327. doi:10.1111/jbfa.12067

Barth, M. E., & McNichols, M. (1994). Estimation and market valuation of environmental liabilities relating to superfund sites. *Journal of Accounting Research*, *32*, 177–209. doi:10.2307/2491446

Bartov, E., Goldberg, S. R., & Kim, M. (2005). Comparative value relevance among German, U.S., and International Accounting Standards: A German stock market perspective. *Journal of Accounting, Auditing & Finance*, *20*(2), 256–289.

Bartov, E., Goldberg, S. R., & Kim, M. S. (2001). The Valuation-Relevance of Earnings and Cash Flows: An International Perspective. *Journal of International Financial Management and Accounting*, *12*(2), 103–176. doi:10.1111/1467-646X.00068

Basel Committee on Banking Supervision. (2012). *The Internal Audit Function in Banks*. Retrieved from www.bis.org/publ/bcbs223.pdf

Basel Committee on Banking Supervision. (2013, October). The Regulatory Framework: Balancing Risk Sensitivity, Simplicity and Comparability.

Bastourre, D., Carrera, J., Ibarlucia, J., & Sardi, M. (2012, October). Common Drivers in Emerging Market Spreads and Commodity Prices (Working Paper).

Bastourre, D., Carrera, J., Ibarlucia, J., & Sardi, M. (2012, October). Common Drivers in Emerging Market Spreads and Commodity Prices (Working Paper). Central Bank of Argentina, Nacional University of La Plata Mariano Sardi Central Bank of Argentina.

Baumol, J.W. (1960). The Stock Market and Economic Efficiency. New York: Furham University Press.

BBC. (2016, January 18). Falling oil prices: How are countries being affected? 2016 http://www.bbc.co.uk/news/world-35345874

Beattie, V., Fearnley, S., & Brandt, R. (2001). *Behind Closed Doors: What Company Audit Is Really About*. Institute of Chartered Accountants in England and Wales. doi:10.1057/9780230599413

Beatty, A., & Weber, J. (2006). Accounting Discretion in Fair Value Estimates: An Examination of SFAS 142 Brand image and reputation Impairments. *Journal of Accounting Research*, *44*(2), 257–288. doi:10.1111/j.1475-679X.2006.00200.x

Beaver, W. H. (1968). The information content of annual earnings announcements. *Journal of Accounting Research*, *6*(3), 325–367.

Beaver, W. H. (1968). The information content of annual earnings announcements. *Journal of Accounting Research*, *6*, 67–92. doi:10.2307/2490070

Beaver, W. H. (2002). Perspectives on Recent Capital Markets Research. *Accounting Review*, *77*(2), 459–473. doi:10.2308/accr.2002.77.2.453

Behn, B. K., & Riley, R. A. (1999). Using nonfinancial information to predict financial performance: The case of the US airline industry. *Journal of Accounting, Auditing & Finance*, *14*(1), 29–56.

Beisland, L. A. (2009). A review of the value relevance literature. *The Open Business Journal*, *2*(1), 7–27. doi:10.2174/1874915100902010007

Belke, A., Bordon, I., & Hendricks, T. (2010). Global Liquidity and Commodity Prices—A Co-integrated VAR Approach for OECD Countries. *Applied Financial Economics*, *20*(3), 227–242. doi:10.1080/09603100903282713

Beneish, M. D. (1999). The detection of earnings manipulation. *Financial Analysts Journal*, *55*(5), 24–36. doi:10.2469/faj.v55.n5.2296

BenYoussef, N., & Khan, S. (2016). Timing of earnings restatements: CEO equity compensation and market reaction. *Accounting and Finance*. doi:10.1111/acfi.12220

Bernanke, B., Boivin, J., & Eliasz, P. (2005). Measuring the Effects of Monetary Policy: A Factor-Augmented Vector Autoregressive (FAVAR) Approach. *The Quarterly Journal of Economics*, *120*, 387–422.

Bhattacharya, U., & Spiegel, M. (1998). Anatomy of a Market Failure: NYSE Trading Suspensions (1974-1988). *Journal of Business & Economic Statistics*, *16*, 216–222.

Bikker, J., & Metzemakers, P. (2005). Bank provisioning behavior and procyclicality. *Journal of International Financial Markets, Institutions and Money*, *15*(2), 141–157. doi:10.1016/j.intfin.2004.03.004

Blackett, T. (2003). Brands and brand strategies (R. Clifton and J. Simmons Eds.). Princeton, NJ: Bloomberg Press.

Borensztein, E., & Reinhart, C. (1994). The Macroeconomic Determinants of Commodity Prices. *IMF Staff Papers*, *41*(2), 236–261. doi:10.2307/3867508

Borio, C, McCauley, R., & McGuire, P. (2011, September). Global credit and domestic credit booms. BIS Quarterly Review.

Bose, S. (2014). *Capital market impact of the disclosure, assurance and management of Greenhouse Gas (GHG) Emissions: An international study* (Unpublished doctoral dissertation). UNSW Australia, Sydney, Australia.

Bouvatier, V., & Lepetit, L. (2008). Banks pro cyclical behavior: Does provisioning matter? *Journal of International Financial Markets, Institutions and Money*, *18*(5), 513–526. doi:10.1016/j.intfin.2007.07.004

Bouvatier, V., & Lepetit, L. (2012). Provisioning rules and bank lending: A theoretical model. *Journal of Financial Stability*, *8*(1), 25–31. doi:10.1016/j.jfs.2011.04.001

Braam, G., & Nijssen, E.J. (2001). *Antecedents of the Adoption of the Balanced Scorecard* (Working Paper). University of Nijmegen.

Brown, R. E. (1962). Changing Audit Objectives and Techniques. *Accounting Review*, *37*(4), 696.

Brown, S., Kin, L., & Lys, T. (1999). Use of R^2 in accounting research: Measuring changes in value relevance over the last four decades. *Journal of Accounting and Economics*, *2*(28), 567–597.

Burks, J. J. (2011). Are investors confused by restatements after Sarbanes-Oxley? *Accounting Review*, *86*(2), 507–539. doi:10.2308/accr.00000017

Bushee, B. J., & Goodman, T. H. (2007). Which Institutional Investors Trade Based on Private Information About Earnings and Returns? *Journal of Accounting Research*, *45*(2), 289–321. doi:10.1111/j.1475-679X.2007.00234.x

Byrne, J. P., Fazio, G., & Fiess, N. (2013). Primary commodity prices: Co-movements, common factors and fundamentals. *Journal of Development Economics, Elsevier*, *101*(C), 16–26. doi:10.1016/j.jdeveco.2012.09.002

Callahan, C. M., Smith, R. E., & Spencer, A. W. (2013). The valuation and reliability implications of FIN 46 for synthetic lease liabilities. *Journal of Accounting and Public Policy*, *32*(4), 271–291. doi:10.1016/j.jaccpubpol.2013.04.002

Callao, S., Jarne, J. J., & Lainez, J. A. (2007). Adoption of IFRS in Spain: Effect on the comparability and relevance of financial reporting. *Journal of International Accounting, Auditing & Taxation*, *16*(2), 356–375. doi:10.1016/j.intaccaudtax.2007.06.002

Camodeca, R., Almici, A. & Brivio, A.R. (2014). The value relevance of accounting information in the Italian and UK stock markets. *Problems and Perspectives in Management*, 12(4).

Campisi, D. (2006). The measurement of intangible assets: a method to assess knowledge productivity. *Proceedings of the 2006 Business & Economics Society International Conference*, Florence.

Carcello, J. V., Neal, T. L., Palmrose, Z. V., & Scholz, S. (2011). CEO Involvement in Selecting Board Members, Audit Committee Effectiveness, and Restatements*. *Contemporary Accounting Research*, *28*(2), 396–430. doi:10.1111/j.1911-3846.2010.01052.x

Cashin, P., Cespedes, L. F., & Sahay, R. (2004). Commodity Currencies and the Real Exchange Rate. *Journal of Development Economics*, *75*(1), 239–268. doi:10.1016/j.jdeveco.2003.08.005

Cavallo, M., & Majnoni, G. (2002). Do banks provision for bad loans in good times? Empirical evidence and policy implications. In R. Levich, G. Majnoni, & C. Reinhart (Eds.), *Ratings, rating agencies and the global financial system*. Kluwer Academic Publishers. doi:10.1007/978-1-4615-0999-8_19

Cevik, S., & Saadi, T. (2011, January). A Barrel of Oil or a Bottle of Wine: How Do Global Growth Dynamics Affect Commodity Prices? IMF Working Paper.

Chae, J. (2005). Trading volume, information asymmetry, and timing information. *The Journal of Finance*, *60*(1), 413–442. doi:10.1111/j.1540-6261.2005.00734.x

Chandler, R. A., Edwards, J. R., & Anderson, M. (1993). Changing Perceptions of the Role of the Company Auditor: 1840 – 1940. In Accounting and Business Research, 23.

Chang, R., & Fernandez, A. (2013, November). On the Sources of Fluctuations in Emerging Economies. *International Economic Review*, *54*(4), 1267–1295. doi:10.1111/iere.12036

Chapple, L., Clarkson, P. M., & Gold, D. L. (2011). The cost of carbon: Capital market effects of the proposed emission trading scheme (ETS). *Abacus*, *49*(1), 1–33. doi:10.1111/abac.12006

Chen, C. J. P., Chen, S., & Su, X. (2001). S, Chen & S, Su (2001). Is accounting information value-relevant in the emerging Chinese stock market? *Journal of International Accounting, Auditing & Taxation*, *10*(1), 1–22. doi:10.1016/S1061-9518(01)00033-7

Cheng, Q., & Farber, D. B. (2008). Earnings restatements, changes in CEO compensation, and firm performance. *Accounting Review*, *83*(5), 1217–1250. doi:10.2308/accr.2008.83.5.1217

Chen, T., Martin, X., Mashruwala, C. A., & Mashruwala, S. D. (2014). The value and credit relevance of multiemployer pension plan obligations. *Accounting Review*, *90*(5), 1907–1938. doi:10.2308/accr-51010

Chen, Y., & Rogoff, K. (2003). Commodity Currencies and Empirical Exchange Rate Puzzles. *Journal of International Economics*, *60*(1), 133–160. doi:10.1016/S0022-1996(02)00072-7

Choe, H., Kho, B.-C., & Stulz, R. M. (1999). Do foreign investors destabilize stock markets? The Korean experience in 1997. *Journal of Financial Economics*, *54*(2), 227–264. doi:10.1016/S0304-405X(99)00037-9

Chordia, T., Sarkar, A., & Subrahmanyam, A. (2001). Common Determinants of Bond and Stock Market Liquidity: The Impact of Financial Crises, Monetary Policy, and Mutual Fund Flows.

Chordia, T., Sarkar, A., & Subrahmanyam, A. (2001). Common Determinants of Bond and Stock Market Liquidity: The Impact of Financial Crises.

Chordia, T., Sarkar, A., & Subrahmanyam, A. (2001, December 11). Common Determinants of Bond and Stock Market Liquidity: The Impact of Financial Crises. Monetary Policy, and Mutual Fund Flows.

Chordia, T., & Ball, C. (2001). True Spreads and Equilibrium Prices. *The Journal of Finance*, *56*(5), 1801–1836. doi:10.1111/0022-1082.00390

Chordia, T., Roll, R., & Subrahmanyam, A. (2000). Commonality in Liquidity. *Journal of Financial Economics*, *56*(1), 3–28. doi:10.1016/S0304-405X(99)00057-4

Chui, M., Kuruc, E., & Turner, P. (2016). *Emerging market companies: currency mismatches, leverage and profitability*. Mimeo.

Clacher, I., Ricquebourg, A. D., & Hodgson, A. (2013). The value relevance of direct cash flows under International Financial Reporting Standards. *Abacus*, *49*(3), 367–395. doi:10.1111/abac.12010

Clarke, J., Jandik, T., & Mandelker, G. (2001). The Efficient Markets Hypothesis. Retrieved from http://m.e-m-h.org/ClJM.pdf

Clarkson, P. M. (2012). The valuation relevance of environmental performance: Evidence from the academic literature. In S. Jones & J. Ratnatunga (Eds.), *Contemporary issues in sustainability accounting, assurance and reporting* (pp. 11–42). Bingley, UK: Emerald Group Publishing.

Clarkson, P. M., Fang, X., Li, Y., & Richardson, G. D. (2013). The relevance of environmental disclosures: Are such disclosures incrementally informative? *Journal of Accounting and Public Policy*, *32*(5), 410–431. doi:10.1016/j.jaccpubpol.2013.06.008

Clarkson, P. M., Li, Y., Pinnuck, M., & Richardson, G. (2015). The value relevance of greenhouse gas emissions under the European Union carbon emissions trading scheme. *European Accounting Review*, *24*(3), 551–580. doi:10.1080/09638180.2014.927782

Collins, D. W., Gong, G., & Hribar, P. (2003). Investor sophistication and the mispricing of accruals. *Review of Accounting Studies*, *8*(2-3), 251–276. doi:10.1023/A:1024417513085

Collins, D. W., Maydew, E. L., & Weiss, I. S. (1997). Changes in the value relevance of earnings and book values over the past forty years. *Journal of Accounting and Economics*, *24*(1), 39–67. doi:10.1016/S0165-4101(97)00015-3

Collins, D. W., Maydew, E. L., & Weiss, I. S. (1997). Changes in the value-relevance of earnings and book values over the past forty years. *Journal of Accounting and Economics*, *24*(2), 345–375.

Collins, D., Masli, A., Reitenga, A. L., & Sanchez, J. M. (2009). Earnings restatements, the Sarbanes-Oxley Act, and the disciplining of chief financial officers. *Journal of Accounting, Auditing & Finance*, *24*(1), 1–34.

Cooper, G. (2008). *The Origin of Financial Crises: Central Banks, Credit Bubbles and the Efficient Market Fallacy*. New York: Vintage Books.

Copeland, T. E., & Galai, D. (1983). Information effects on the bid-ask spread. *The Journal of Finance*, *38*(5), 1457–1469. doi:10.1111/j.1540-6261.1983.tb03834.x

Core, J. E., Guay, W. R., & Van Buskirk, A. (2003). Market valuations in the new economy: An investigation of what has changed. *Journal of Accounting and Economics*, *34*(1), 43–67. doi:10.1016/S0165-4101(02)00087-3

Cravera, A., Maglione, M., & Ruggieri, R. (2001). *The Valuation of Intellectual Capital.*

Cunningham, L. (2006). *Too Big to Fail: Moral Hazard in Auditing and the Need to Restructure the Industry Before it Unravels*. Boston College Law School Faculty Papers.

Curran, J. (1994). China's investment boom. *Fortune*, (March 7), 116–122.

D'Amico, S., Kim, D.H., & Wei, M. (2014). Tips from TIPS: The Informational Content of Treasury Inflation-Protected Security Prices. US Federal Reserve Board.

Dasgupta, D., & Ratha, D. (2000). What Factors Appear to Drive Private Capital Flows to Developing Countries? And How Does Official Lending Respond? Banco Mundial, Policy Research Working Papers.

David, M., & Sutton, C. D. (2011). *Social Research: an introduction*. London: Sage.

de Villiers, C., & Marques, A. (2016). Corporate social responsibility, country-level predispositions, and the consequences of choosing a level of disclosure. *Accounting and Business Review*, *46*(2), 167–195. doi:10.1080/00014788.2015.1039476

Dechow, P. M., Sloan, R. G., & Sweeney, A. P. (1996). Causes and consequences of earnings manipulation: An analysis of firms subject to enforcement actions by the sec. *Contemporary Accounting Research*, *13*(1), 1–36. doi:10.1111/j.1911-3846.1996.tb00489.x

Demirguc-Kunt, A., & Levine, R. (1996). Stock Markets, Corporate Finance and Economic Growth: An Overview. *The World Bank Economic Review*, *10*(2), 223–239. doi:10.1093/wber/10.2.223

Deng, Z., Lev, B., & Narin, F. (1999). Science and technology as predictors of stock performance. *Financial Analysts Journal*, *55*(3), 20–32. doi:10.2469/faj.v55.n3.2269

Desai, H., Hogan, C. E., & Wilkins, M. S. (2006). The reputational penalty for aggressive accounting: Earnings restatements and management turnover. *Accounting Review*, *81*(1), 83–112. doi:10.2308/accr.2006.81.1.83

Devalle, A. (2010). *Misurazione della performance nel bilancio IFRS. Comprehensive income, dibattito internazionale e value relevance*. Milano: Pearson Prentice Hall.

Devalle, A., Onali, E., & Magarini, R. (2010). Assessing the value relevance of accounting data after the introduction of IFRS in Europe. *Journal of International Financial Management Accounting, 21*(2), 345–378. doi:10.1111/j.1467-646X.2010.01037.x

Dewing, P., & Russell, P. O. (2005). *The Role of Auditors, Reporting Accountants and Skilled Persons in UK Financial Services Supervision Institute of Chartered Accountants of Scotland.* The Institute of Chartered Accountants of Scotland. Retrieved from https://www.icas.com/__data/assets/pdf_file/0016/10582/63-The-Role-of-Auditors-Reporting-Accountants-And-Skilled-Persons-In-UK-FInancial-Services-Supervision-ICAS.pdf

DeZoort, , Houston, R. W., & Peters, M. F. (2001, Summer). The Impact of Internal Auditor Compensation and Role on External Auditors Planning Judgments and Decisions. *Contemporary Accounting Research, 18*(2), 257–281. doi:10.1506/7ERQ-LD54-BTQV-TUVE

Dicksee, L. (1892). Auditing: A Practical Manual for Auditors. Retrieved from https://archive.org/details/auditingpractica00dickuoft

DiGabriele J. A. (2012). Narrative Inquiry of the Inchoate Ethical Risks of Forensic Accounting Experts under Amended Rule 26 Communications. *Ethics & Critical Thinking Journal*, (1).

DiGabriele, J. A. (2011). An Observation of Differences in the Transparent Objectivity of Forensic Accounting Expert Witnesses. *Journal of Forensic & Investigative Accounting, 3*(2).

Dontoh, A., Radhakrishnan, S., & Ronen, J. (2004). The Declining Value-relevance of Accounting Information and Non-information-based Trading: An Empirical Analysis. *Contemporary Accounting Research, 21*(2), 245–275.

Drake, M. S., Myers, L. A., Scholz, S., & Sharp, N. Y. (2015). Short Selling Around Restatement Announcements When Do Bears Pounce? *Journal of Accounting, Auditing & Finance.*

Easley, D., Hvidkjaer, S., & Ohara, M. (2002). Is information risk a determinant of asset returns? *The Journal of Finance, 57*(5), 2185–2221. doi:10.1111/1540-6261.00493

Easley, D., Kiefer, N. M., & OHara, M. (1997). One day in the life of a very common stock. *Review of Financial Studies, 10*(3), 805–835. doi:10.1093/rfs/10.3.805

Easton, P. D., & Sommers, G. A. (2003). Scale and the scale effect in market-based accounting research. *Journal of Business Finance & Accounting, 31*(1-2), 435–476.

Easton, P. D., & Sommers, G. A. (2003). Scale and the scale effect in market-based accounting research. *Journal of Business Finance & Accounting, 30*(1-2), 25–56. doi:10.1111/1468-5957.00482

Ebrahimi, H. (2012). Paul Volcker: Ring-fencing Banks is Not Enough. *Telegraph.co.uk*. Retrieved from http://www.telegraph.co.uk/finance/newsbysector/banksandfinance/9561624/Paul-Volcker-ringfencing-banks-is-not-enough.html

Ebrahimi, H. (2012). Paul Volcker: Ring-fencing Banks is Not Enough. *Telegraph.co.uk*. Retrieved from http://www.telegraph.co.uk/finance/newsbysector/banksandfinance/9561624/Paul-Volcker-ring-fencing-banks-is-not-enough.html

Ehlers, T., & Villar, A. (2015). The role of banks. BIS Papers.

Eichengreen, B. (2002). Can emerging markets float? Should they inflation target? Banco Central do Brasil Working Papers Series.

Eichengreen, B. (2002). Can emerging markets float? Should they inflation target? *Banco Central do Brasil Working Papers*.

El-Erian, M., & Kumar, M. S. (1995, February 16–17). Emerging Stock Markets in Middle Eastern Countries. *Paper presented at theWorld Bank Conference on Stock Markets, Corporate Finance and Economic Growth*, Washington DC.

Engel, C., & West, K. D. (2005). Exchange rates and fundamentals. *Journal of Political Economy*, *113*(3), 485–517. doi:10.1086/429137

Entwistle, G. M., Feltham, G. D., & Mbagwu, C. (2010). The value relevance of alternative earnings measures: A comparison of pro forma, GAAP, and I/B/E/S Earnings. *Journal of Accounting, Auditing & Finance*, *25*(2), 261–288.

Entwistle, G. M., Feltham, G. D., & Mbagwu, C. (2010). The value relevance of alternative earnings measures: A comparison of pro-forma, GAAP and I/B/E/S earnings. *Journal of Accounting, Auditing & Finance*, *25*(2), 564–583.

Ernst & Young. (2006). *Trends in Australian and New Zealand Internal Auditing, Third Annual Benchmarking Survey 2006*. Australia: Ernst & Young.

Ernst & Young. (2014). *Applying IFRS IFRS 15 Revenue from Contracts with Customers: A closer look at the new revenue recognition standard June 2014*. Retrieved from http://www.ey.com/Publication/vwLUAssets/Applying_IFRS:_A_closer_look_at_the_new_revenue_recognition_standard_(June_2014)/%24FILE/Applying-Rev-June2014.pdf

Eu Jin, T., & Cobbin, P. (2005, July). A Re Visitation of the Audit Expectations Gap: Judicial and Practitioner Views on the Role of the Auditor in late- Victorian England. *Sage. Accounting History*, *10*(2), 35–66. doi:10.1177/103237320501000203

European Commission. (2009). Paragraph 10 International Accounting Standard 8 Accounting Policies, Changes in Accounting Estimates and Errors Financial Stability Board. Retrieved from http://www.financialstabilityboard.org/2014/09/pr_140918

European Commission. (2009). *Paragraph 10 International Accounting Standard 8 Accounting Policies*. Changes in Accounting Estimates and Errors.

Executive Office of the President of the United States. (2015, July). Long-term interest rates: a survey.

Fama, E.F. (1965). Random Walks in Stock Market Prices Selected Papers. University of Chicago. Retrieved from https://www.chicagobooth.edu/~/media/34F68FFD9CC04EF1A76901F6C61C0A76.PDF

Fama, E. (1970). Efficient Capital Markets: A Review of Theory and Empirical Work. *The Journal of Finance*, *25*(2), 383. doi:10.2307/2325486

Fama, E. F., & Miller, M. H. (1971). *Theory of Finance Dryden Press*. Hinsdale, Illinois.

Farquhar, P. H. (1989). Managing brand equity. *Marketing Research*, *1*(September), 24–33.

Feltham, G. A., & Ohlson, J. A. (1995). Valuation and Clean Surplus Accounting for Operating and Financial Activities. *Contemporary Accounting Research*, *11*(2), 689–732. doi:10.1111/j.1911-3846.1995.tb00462.x

Fernandez, A., Gonzalez, A. & Rodriguez, D. (2015). Sharing a ride on the commodities roller coaster: common factors in business cycles of emerging economies. IMF.

Fernandez, A., & Gulan, A. (2015). Interest Rates, Leverage, and Business Cycles in Emerging Economies: The Role of Financial Frictions, forthcoming. *American Economic Journal. Macroeconomics*, *7*(3), 153–188. doi:10.1257/mac.20120141

Ferraro, D., Rogoff, K., & Rossi, B. (2015). Can Oil prices Forecast Exchange Rates? *Journal of International Money and Finance*, *54*, 116–141. doi:10.1016/j.jimonfin.2015.03.001

Financial Accounting Foundation. (2014). *FASB Accounting Standards Codification about the Codification (v 4.9)*.

Financial Services and Markets Act 2000 (2000). Retrieved from: http://www.legislation.gov.uk/ukpga/2000/8/contents

Financial Stability Board. (2012). Identifying the Effects of Regulatory Reforms on Emerging Market and Developing Economies: A Review of Potential Unintended Consequences.

Financial Stability Board. (2012). Identifying the Effects of Regulatory Reforms on Emerging Market and Developing Economies: A Review of Potential Unintended Consequences. Report to the G20 Finance Ministers and Central Bank Governors.

Financial Stability Board. (2012). Identifying the Effects of Regulatory Reforms on Emerging Market and Developing Economies: A Review of Potential Unintended Consequences. Report to the G20 Finance Ministers and Central Bank Governors. *Financial Stability Board in coordination with Staff of the International Monetary Fund and the World Bank.*

Financial Stability Board. (2014). FSB Plenary meets in Cairns, Australia. Retrieved from http://www.financialstabilityboard.org/2014/09/pr_140918

Flyvbjerg, B. (2011). Case Study. In N. K. Denzin and Y. S. Lincoln (eds.), The Sage of Handbook of Qualitative Research (4th ed., Ch. 17, pp. 301-316). Thousand Oaks, CA: Sage.

Francis, J., & Schipper, K. (1999). Have Financial Statements Lost Their Relevance? *Journal of Accounting Research*, *37*(Suppl. 2), 319–352. doi:10.2307/2491412

Francis, J., Schipper, K., & Vincent, L. (2002). Expanded disclosures and increased usefulness of earnings announcements. *Accounting Review*, *77*(3), 515–546. doi:10.2308/accr.2002.77.3.515

Frankel, J. (2006). The Effect of Monetary Policy on Real Commodity Prices. NBER Working Papers. Retrieved from http://www.nber.org/papers/w12713.pdf

Frankel, J. A., & Rose, A. K. (2010). Determinants of Agricultural and Mineral Commodity Prices. In R. Fry, C. Jones, & C. Kent (Eds.), Inflation in an Era of Relative Price Shocks. Reserve Bank of Australia.

Frankel, J., & Hardouvelis, G. (1985). Commodity Prices, Money Surprises, and Fed Credibility. *Journal of Money, Credit and Banking*, 17(4), 427-438.

Frankel, J.A. (2006, December). The Effect of Monetary Policy on Real Commodity Prices.

FRC. (2004). Ethical Statement: Integrity, Objectivity and Independence. Retrieved from https://www.frc.org.uk/Our-Work/Publications/APB/ES-1-Integrity,-objectivity-and-independence-2004.pdf

FRC. (2006). Financial Reporting Council Annual Report 2005/2006. Retrieved from https://www.frc.org.uk/FRC-Documents/FRC/Annual-Report-2005-06.pdf

G20 Finance Ministers and Central Bank Governors. (2012). Leaders declaration. Retrieved from http://g20watch.edu.au/g20-leaders-declaration-loscabos-2012

G20 Finance Ministers and Central Bank Governors. (2012). Retrieved from http://g20watch.edu.au/g20-leaders-declaration-loscabos-2012

Gali, J., & Monacelli, T. (2005). Monetary policy and exchange rate volatility in a small open economy. *The Review of Economic Studies*, *72*(3), 707–734. doi:10.1111/j.1467-937X.2005.00349.x

GAO. (2003). *GAO-03-395R. Financial Statement Restatement Database*.

Garcia, F. V., & Liu, L. (1999). Macroeconomic Determinants of Stock Market Development. *Journal of Applied Econometrics*, *2*(1), 29–59.

Garrett, A. (2012). The Role of Internal Audits in External Audits. *CAE Conference*, Abu Dhabi, UAE.

Geiger, M., Jordan Lowe, D., & Pany, K. (2002). Outsourced Internal Audit Services and The Perception of Auditor Independence. *The CPA Journal*. Retrieved from http://www.nysscpa.org/cpajournal/2002/0402/features/f042002.htm

Genberg, H. (2008). The changing nature of financial intermediation and its implications for monetary policy. BIS Working Papers.

Givoly, D., & Hayn, C. (2000). The changing time-series properties of earnings, cash flows and accruals: Has financial reporting become more conservative? *Journal of Accounting and Economics*, *29*(3), 287–320. doi:10.1016/S0165-4101(00)00024-0

Glosten, L. R., & Harris, L. E. (1988). Estimating the components of the bid/ask spread. *Journal of Financial Economics*, *21*(1), 123–142.

Glosten, L. R., & Milgrom, P. R. (1985). Bid, ask and transaction prices in a specialist market with heterogeneously informed traders. *Journal of Financial Economics*, *14*(1), 71–100. doi:10.1016/0304-405X(85)90044-3

Goncharov, I., & Hodgson, A. (2011). Measuring and reporting income in Europe. *Journal of International Accounting Research*, *10*(1), 234–246. doi:10.2308/jiar.2011.10.1.27

González Rozada, M., & Levy Yeyati, E. (2006). Global Factors and Emerging Market Spreads. Banco Interamericano de Desarrollo Working Paper.

Göttsche, M., & Schauer, M. (2011). The value relevance of accounting figures in the European market reconsidered, European Accounting Association (EAA). *Proceedings of the34th Annual Congress*, Roma.

Gregory, A., Whittaker, J., & Yan, X. (2016). Corporate social performance, competitive advantage, earnings persistence and firm value. *Journal of Business Finance & Accounting*, *43*(1-2), 3–30. doi:10.1111/jbfa.12182

Grinblatt, M., & Keloharju, M. (2000). The investment behavior and performance of various investor types: A study of Finland's unique data set. *Journal of Financial Economics*, *55*(1), 43–67. doi:10.1016/S0304-405X(99)00044-6

Grinblatt, M., & Keloharju, M. (2001). What makes investors trade? *The Journal of Finance*, *56*(2), 589–616. doi:10.1111/0022-1082.00338

Grossman, S. J., & Stiglitz, J. E. (1980, June). On the Impossibility of Informationally Efficient Markets. *The American Economic Review*, *70*(3), 393–408.

Gu, F., & Li, J. Q. (2010). The value-relevance of advertising: Evidence from pharmaceutical industry. *Journal of Accounting, Auditing & Finance*, *25*(1), 85–120.

Guidolin, M., & Neely, C. J. (2010). *The Effects of Large-Scale Asset Purchases on TIPS Inflation Expectations. Economic Synopses 26*. Federal Reserve Bank of St. Louis.

Gu, Z. (2007). Across-sample incomparability of R2s and additional evidence on value relevance changes over time. *Journal of Business Finance & Accounting*, *37*(7-8), 324–356.

Hail, L. (2013). Financial reporting and firm valuation: Relevance lost or relevance regained? *Accounting and Business Review*, *43*(4), 329–358. doi:10.1080/00014788.2013.799402

Hanlon, D., Navissi, F., & Soepriyanto, G. (2014). The value relevance of deferred tax attributed to asset revaluations. *Journal of Contemporary Accounting & Economics*, *10*(2), 87–99. doi:10.1016/j.jcae.2014.03.001

Hassel, L., Nilsson, H., & Nyquist, S. (2005). The value relevance of environmental performance. *European Accounting Review*, *14*(1), 41–61. doi:10.1080/0963818042000279722

Haw, I. M., Qi, D., & Wu, W. (1998a). Value-relevance of financial reporting disclosures in an emerging capital market: the case of B-shares and H-shares in China (Working paper). The Chinese University of Hong Kong.

Haw, I. M., Qi, D., & Zhang, W. G. 1998b earnings management of listed firms in response to security regulations in China's emerging capital market (Working paper). The Chinese University of Hong Kong.

Hayn, C. (1995). The information content of losses. *Journal of Accounting and Economics*, *20*(2), 125–153. doi:10.1016/0165-4101(95)00397-2

Hayn, C., & Hughes, P. (2006). Leading Indicators of Brand image and reputation Impairment. *Journal of Accounting, Auditing & Finance*, *21*(3), 223–265.

Hellström, K. (2006). The value relevance of financial accounting information in a transitional economy: The case of the Czech Republic. *European Accounting Review*, *15*(2), 354–377.

Hennes, K. M., Leone, A. J., & Miller, B. P. (2008). The importance of distinguishing errors from irregularities in restatement research: The case of restatements and CEO/CFO turnover. *Accounting Review*, *83*(6), 1487–1519. doi:10.2308/accr.2008.83.6.1487

Hirschey, M., Smith, K. R., & Wilson, W. M. (2015). The Timeliness of Restatement Disclosures and Financial Reporting Credibility. *Journal of Business Finance & Accounting*, *42*(7-8), 826–859. doi:10.1111/jbfa.12125

Hirshleifer, D. (2001). Investor psychology and asset pricing. *The Journal of Finance*, *56*(4), 1533–1597. doi:10.1111/0022-1082.00379

Hitchins, J., Hogg, M., & Mallet, D. (2001). *Banking: A Regulatory Accounting and Auditing Guide*. Institute of Chartered Accountants England and Wales HM Treasury "Cooperation Between Internal and External Auditors", A Good Practice Guide. Retrieved from http://www.hm-treasury.gov.uk/d/auditors_190105.pdf

Hofmann, B., & Feng Z. (2013). Central Bank Asset Purchases and Inflation Expectation. *BIS Quarterly Review*, March, 23–35.

Holthausen, R. W., & Watts, R. L. (2001). The Relevance of the Value-Relevance Literature for Financial Accounting Standard Setting. *Journal of Accounting and Economics*, *31*(1), 356–387.

Holthausen, R. W., & Watts, R. L. (2001). The Relevance of Value Relevance Literature for Financial Accounting Standard Setting. *Journal of Accounting and Economics*, *31*(1-3), 3–75. doi:10.1016/S0165-4101(01)00029-5

Horton, J., & Serafeim, G. (2010). Market reaction to and valuation of IFRS reconciliation adjustments: First evidence from the UK. *Review of Accounting Studies*, *15*(4), 725–751. doi:10.1007/s11142-009-9108-5

Hotelling, H. (1931). The Economics of Exhaustible Resources. *Journal of Political Economy*, *39*(2), 137–175. doi:10.1086/254195

Hribar, P., & Jenkins, N. T. (2004). The effect of accounting restatements on earnings revisions and the estimated cost of capital. *Review of Accounting Studies*, *9*(2-3), 337–356. doi:10.1023/B:RAST.0000028194.11371.42

Hribar, P., Jenkins, N., & Wang, J. (2010). Institutional investor and accounting restatement. *Asian Journal of Finance & Accounting*, *1*(2). doi:10.5296/ajfa.v1i2.194

Huang, R. D., & Stoll, H. R. (1997). The components of the bid-ask spread: A general approach. *Review of Financial Studies*, *10*(4), 995–1034. doi:10.1093/rfs/10.4.995

Huepkes, E. H. G. (2005). The External Auditor and the Bank Supervisor: Sherlock Holmes and Doctor Watson? *Journal of Banking Regulation*, *7*(1-2), 145–159. doi:10.1057/palgrave.jbr.2340010

Hughes, K. E. II. (2000). The value relevance of non-financial measures of air pollution in the electric utility industry. *Accounting Review*, *75*(2), 209–228. doi:10.2308/accr.2000.75.2.209

Humphrey, C. (1997). Debating Audit Expectations. In M. Sherer & S. Turley (Eds.), Current Issues in Auditing (3rd ed.). London: Paul Chapman.

Humphrey, C. P., Turley, S., Moizer, P. (1993). Protection Against Detection: The Case of Auditors and Fraud. *Accounting, Auditing & Accountability Journal*, *6*(1).

IAS 8 Accounting Policies, Changes in Accounting Estimates and Errors. (2009).

IAS. (n. d.). 8 Accounting Policies, Changes in Accounting Estimates and Errors.

IASplus. (n.d.). IAS 8 Accounting Policies, Changes in Accounting Estimates and Errors. Retrieved from http://www.iasplus.com/en/standards/ias/ias8

IFAC. (n. d.). *Basis for Conclusions on ISA 610 and ISA 315*. Prepared by the Staff of the IAASB.

IFRS, (2015). Financial Reporting Standards for the World Economy June 2015.

IFRS. (2014). Fairness of Reporting, Acceptable Accounting Risk and the IASB's Conceptual Framework Review: Insights from the Enron Trial.

IFRS. (2014). *IFRS 9 Financial Instruments*.

IFRS. (2015, June). Financial Reporting Standards for the World Economy 2015 IOSCO. Retrieved from http://www.iosco.org/library/pubdocs/pdf/IOSCOPD282.pdf

IFRS. (2015, June). Financial Reporting Standards for the World Economy.

IFRS. (2016). *IFRS 16 Leases, Project Summary and Feedback Statement*.

IMF. (2015, July). Global Implications of Lower Oil Prices, IMF Staff Discussion Note.

IMF. (2016, June 17). United Kingdom: 2016 Article IV Consultation Press Release and Staff Report. Retrieved from http://www.imf.org/external/pubs/ft/scr/2016/cr16168.pdf

Impey, A. (n. d.). *Understanding IFRS*. PwC. Retrieved from: http://www.pwc.com/ng/en/publications/understanding-ifrs.html

Independent Commission on Banking. (2011, September). Vickers Report ICB Final Report Recommendations.

Institute of Internal Auditors (IIA). (2009). *The Role of Internal Auditing in Resourcing the Internal Audit Activity*. IIA Position Paper. Retrieved from https://na.theiia.org/standards- guidance/Public %20Documents/IPPF_PP_Role_of_IA_in_Resourcing_the_IAA_01- 09.pdf

International Financial Law Review. (2013). Banking Sector Reforms. Retrieved from http://www.iflr.com/Article/3107360/Banking-sector-reform-a-definitive-guide-to-the-latest-developments.html?LS=EMS763204

International Financial Law Review. (2013). Banking Sector Reforms. Retrieved from http://www.iflr.com/Article/3107360/Banking-sector-reform-a-definitive-quide-to-the-latest-developments.html?LS=EMS763204

International Monetary Fund. (2016, October). Global DisInflation in an Era of Constrained Monetary Policy.

IOSCO. (2008). Letter to Chairman, Financial Stability Forum. Retrieved from http://www.iosco.org/library/pubdocs/pdf/IOSCOPD282.pdf

ISA (UK and Ireland). (n. d.). 250 Section B: Material significance. Retrieved from https://www.frc.org.uk/Our-Work/Publications/APB/ISA-250B-The-auditor-s-right-and-duty-to-report-to.pdf

ISA (UK and Ireland). (n. d.). 320 Retrieved from https://www.frc.org.uk/Our-Work/Publications/APB/ISA-320-Materiality-in-planning-and-performing-an.aspx

ISA (UK and Ireland). (n. d.). The Auditor's Responsibility to Consider Fraud in an Audit of Financial Statements. Retrieved from https://www.frc.org.uk/Our-Work/Publications/APB/240-The-auditor-s-responsibility-to-consider-fraud.pdf

Jermakowicz, E. K., Prather-Kinsey, J., & Wulf, I. (2007). The Value Relevance of Accounting Income Reported by DAX-30 German Companies. *Journal of International Financial Management & Accounting, 18*(3), 345–376. doi:10.1111/j.1467-646X.2007.01011.x

Jermann, U., & Quadrini, V. (2012). Macroeconomic Effects of Financial Shocks. *The American Economic Review, 102*(1), 238–271. doi:10.1257/aer.102.1.238 PMID:25067842

Jiang, W., & Shen, Y. (2009). Discussion of scale effects in capital markets-based accounting research. *Journal of Business Finance & Accounting, 36*(3/4), 289–296. doi:10.1111/j.1468-5957.2009.02146.x

Jiang, W., & Stark, A. W. (2013). Dividends, research and development expenditures, and the value relevance of book value for UK loss-making firms. *The British Accounting Review, 45*(2), 112–124. doi:10.1016/j.bar.2013.03.003

Johnston, D. M., Sefcik, S. E., & Soderstrom, N. S. (2008). The value relevance of greenhouse gas emissions allowances: An exploratory study in the related United States SO2 market. *European Accounting Review*, *17*(4), 747–764. doi:10.1080/09638180802481615

Kang, S.-H., & Zhao, Y. (2010). Information content and value relevance of depreciation: A cross-industry analysis. *Accounting Review*, *85*(1), 227–260. doi:10.2308/accr.2010.85.1.227

Kaniel, R., Liu, S., Saar, G., & Titman, S. (2012). Individual investor trading and return patterns around earnings announcements. *The Journal of Finance*, *67*(2), 639–680. doi:10.1111/j.1540-6261.2012.01727.x

Kaplan, R.S., & Norton, D.P. (1992). The Balanced Scorecard – Measures that Drive Performances. *Harvard Business Review*, 1992, 71 – 79.

Karpoff, J. M., Koester, A., Lee, D. S., & Martin, G. S. (2012). A critical analysis of databases used in financial misconduct research. Mays Business School Research Paper.

Karpowicz, I., Lipinsky, F., & Park, J. (2016). A Closer Look at Sectoral Financial Linkages in Brazil I: Corporations' Financial Statements. IMF Working Paper.

Kasperkevic, J. (2016). Interest rates could rise as soon as June, federal reserve suggests. *The Guardian.* Retrieved from https://www.theguardian.com/business/2016/may/18/interest-rates-increase-federal-reserve-economy-brexit-china

Ke, B., & Petroni, K. (2004). How informed are actively trading institutional investors? Evidence from their trading behavior before a break in a string of consecutive earnings increases. *Journal of Accounting Research*, *42*(5), 895–927. doi:10.1111/j.1475-679X.2004.00160.x

Ke, B., Petroni, K. R., & Yu, Y. (2008). The effect of regulation FD on transient institutional investors trading behavior. *Journal of Accounting Research*, *46*(4), 853–883. doi:10.1111/j.1475-679X.2008.00296.x

Ke, B., & Ramalingegowda, S. (2005). Do institutional investors exploit the post-earnings announcement drift? *Journal of Accounting and Economics*, *39*(1), 25–53. doi:10.1016/j.jacceco.2004.02.002

Keller, K. L. (2006). Building customer based brand equity: a blue print for creating strong brands. Marketing Science Institute Working Paper.

Keynes, J.M. (2000). A Tract on Monetary Reform, New York: Great Minds Series, Prometheus Books. (First published in 1924)

Khanagha, J. B. (2011). Value Relevance of Accounting Information in the United Arab Emirates. *International Journal of Economics and Financial Issues*, 1(2), 33-45.

Kilian, L., & Lewis, L. (2011). Does the Fed Respond to Oil Price Shocks? *The Economic Journal*, *121*(555), 1047–1072. doi:10.1111/j.1468-0297.2011.02437.x

Kilian, L., & Vega, C. (2011). Do Energy Prices Respond to U.S. Macroeconomic News? A Test of the Hypothesis of Predetermined Energy Prices. *The Review of Economics and Statistics*, *93*(2), 660–671. doi:10.1162/REST_a_00086

Kim, M., & Kross, W. (2006). The Ability of Earnings to Predict Future Operating Cash Flows Has Been Increasing - Not Decreasing. *CFA Digest*, *36*(2), 324–365.

Kim, O. (2013). Russian accounting system: Value relevance of reported information and the IFRS adoption perspective. *The International Journal of Accounting*, *48*(4), 525–547. doi:10.1016/j.intacc.2013.10.007

Kinney, W. R. Jr, & McDaniel, L. S. (1989). Characteristics of firms correcting previously reported quarterly earnings. *Journal of Accounting and Economics*, *11*(1), 71–93. doi:10.1016/0165-4101(89)90014-1

Klein, A., & Marquardt, C. A. (2006). Fundamentals of accounting losses. *Accounting Review*, *81*(1), 179–206. doi:10.2308/accr.2006.81.1.179

Kohlbeck, M., & Mayhew, B. W. (2010). Valuation of firms that disclose related party transactions. *Journal of Accounting and Public Policy*, *29*(2), 115–137. doi:10.1016/j.jaccpubpol.2009.10.006

Kohli, C., Harich, K., & Leuthesser, L. (2005). Creating brand identity: A study of evaluation of new brand names. *Journal of Business Research*, *58*(11), 1506–1515. doi:10.1016/j.jbusres.2004.07.007

Kohlscheen, E., & Miyajima, K. (2015). The transmission of monetary policy in EMEs in a changing financial environment: A longitudinal analysis. BIS Working Papers.

Kohlscheen, E., & Rungcharoenkitkul, P. (2015). Changing financial intermediation: implications for monetary policy transmission. BIS Papers.

Kohlscheen, E., Avalos, F. H., & Schrimpf, A. (2016, March). When the Walk is not Random: Commodity Prices and Exchange Rates. Bank for International Settlements Working Papers.

Kohlscheen, E. (2014). Long-run Determinants of the Brazilian Real: A Closer Look at Commodities. *International Journal of Finance & Economics*, *19*(4), 239–250. doi:10.1002/ijfe.1493

Kose, A., Otrok, C., & Whiteman, C. (2003). International Business Cycles: World, Region, and Country-specific factors. *The American Economic Review*, *93*(4), 1216–1239. doi:10.1257/000282803769206278

Kothari, S. P. (2001). Capital Markets Research in Accounting. *Journal of Accounting and Economics*, *31*(1), 567–580.

Kothari, S., & Zimmerman, J. (1995, September). Price and return models. *Journal of Accounting and Economics*, *20*(2), 155–1. doi:10.1016/0165-4101(95)00399-4

Kotler, P. (1994). *Principles of Marketing*. New Jersey: Prentice Hall.

KPMG. (2010). *Briefing Sheet Conceptual Framework for Financial Reporting*. KPMG.

KPMG. (2010, October). Briefing Sheet Conceptual Framework for Financial Reporting.

KPMG. (2010, October). Briefing Sheet Conceptual Framework for Financial Reporting.

KPMG. (2011). Integrated Reporting in practice: The South African story. Retrieved from https://www.kpmg.com/Global/en/topics/corporate-reporting/better-reporting/Documents/the-south-african-story.pdf

Krauss, C. (2016, March 8). Oil Prices: What's Behind the Drop? Simple Economics. *New York Times*. Retrieved from http://www.nytimes.com/interactive/2016/business/energy-environment/oil-prices.html?_r=0

Kravet, T., & Shevlin, T. (2010). Accounting restatements and information risk. *Review of Accounting Studies*, *15*(2), 264–294. doi:10.1007/s11142-009-9103-x

Krishnamurthy, A., & Vissing-Jorgenson, A. (2011). The Effects of Quantitative Easing on Interest Rates: Channels and Implications for Policy. *Brookings Papers on Economic Activity*, 2.

Kwansa, F. A., Mayo, C., & Demirciftci, T. (2008). The importance of intangible assets: trends and patterns. In *M.D. Olsen (Ed.), Handbook of hospitality strategic management* (pp. 181–202). Amsterdam: Butterworth-Heinemann. doi:10.1016/B978-0-08-045079-7.00008-9

La Porta, R., Lopez-de-Silanes, F., Shleifer, A. & Vishny, R. (1996). Law and Finance. *NBER*.

La Porta, R., Lopez-de-Silanes, F., Shleifer, A., & Vishny, R. (1996). Law and Finance. NBER.

Laffont, J., & Maskin, E. S. (1990, February). The Efficient Market Hypothesis and Insider Trading on the Stock Market. *Journal of Political Economy*, *98*(1), 70–93. doi:10.1086/261669

Lagarde, C. (2016, June 17). Unity in Diversity: The Case for Europe. Finance in Dialogue, Vienna. Retrieved from http://www.imf.org/external/np/speeches/2016/061716.htm

Landsman, W. R., & Magliolo, J. (1988). Cross-Sectional Capital Market Research and Model Specification. *Accounting Review*, *63*(4), 423–456.

LaPlante, M., & Muscarella, C. J. (1997). Do institutions receive comparable execution in the NYSE and Nasdaq markets? A transaction study of block trades. *Journal of Financial Economics*, *45*(1), 97–134. doi:10.1016/S0304-405X(97)81614-5

Lee, C. M. C., & Ready, M. J. (1991). Inferring Trade Direction from Intraday Data. *The Journal of Finance*, *46*(2), 733–746. doi:10.1111/j.1540-6261.1991.tb02683.x

Lee, C., & Radhakrishna, B. (2000). Inferring investor behavior: Evidence from TORQ data. *Journal of Financial Markets*, *3*(2), 83–111. doi:10.1016/S1386-4181(00)00002-1

Lee, E., Walker, M., & Zeng, C. (2014). Do Chinese government subsidies affect firm value? *Accounting, Organizations and Society*, *39*(3), 149–169. doi:10.1016/j.aos.2014.02.002

Lev, B. (2001). *Intangibles: Management, Measurement and Reporting*. Washington: Brookings Institute Press.

Lev, B., & Zarowin, P. (1999). The Boundaries of Financial Reporting and How to Extend Them. *Journal of Accounting Research*, *37*(2), 435–467. doi:10.2307/2491413

Li, O. Z., & Zhang, Y. (2006). Financial restatement announcements and insider trading.

Liggio, C.D. (1974). The Expectation Gap. *The Accountant's Waterloo Journal of Contemporary Business*, 3(3)

Lynn, L. E. (1999). *The Management of Intellectual Capital: The issues and the practice. In Management Accounting Issues Paper 16 Management Accounting Practices Handbook*. Hamilton, Ontario: Society of Management Accountants of Canada.

MacDonald, R., & Ricci, L. (2004). Estimation of the Equilibrium Real Exchange Rate for South Africa. *The South African Journal of Economics*, *72*(2), 282–304. doi:10.1111/j.1813-6982.2004.tb00113.x

Martory, B., & Verdier, F. (2000). *Comment traiter le goodwill? Pratique d'une theorie, theorie d'une pratique. In Comptabilite, Controle* (Vol. 6). Audit.

Matsumura, E. M., Prakash, R., & Vera-Muñoz, S. C. (2014). Firm-value effects of carbon emissions and carbon disclosures. *Accounting Review*, *89*(2), 695–724. doi:10.2308/accr-50629

Michaelson, W. M. (2005). Advocacy and the Expert Witness. *Expert Witnessing in Forensic Accounting.*, *1*(1), 63–70.

Middleton, A. (2015). Value relevance of firms integral environmental performance: Evidence from Russia. *Journal of Accounting and Public Policy*, *34*(2), 204–211. doi:10.1016/j.jaccpubpol.2014.12.001

Mihaljek, D., Scatigna, M. & Villar, A. (2002). Recent Trends in Bond Markets BIS Papers.

Modigliani, F., & Miller, M. (1958). The cost of capital, corporation finance and the theory of investment. *The American Economic Review*, (48), 453–478.

Modigliani, F., & Miller, M. (1959). The Cost of Capital Corporate Finance and the theory of Investment. *The American Economic Review*, *48*, 261–297.

Mohanty, M (2014). Market volatility and foreign exchange intervention in EMEs: what has changed? BIS Papers.

Mohanty, M. (2014). Market volatility and foreign exchange intervention in EMEs: what has changed? BIS Papers.

Mohanty, M. S., & Rishabh, K. (2016). Financial intermediation and monetary policy transmission in EMEs: What has changed post-2008 crisis? BIS Working Papers.

Mohanty, M.S., & Rishabh, K. (2016). Financial intermediation and monetary policy transmission in EMEs: What has changed post-2008 crisis? BIS Working Papers.

Mohanty, M., & Turner, P. (2008). *Monetary policy transmission in emerging market economies: what has changed?* BIS Papers.

Monsanto v. Tidball 2009 WL 2757047 (E.D. Mo.)

Moore, E. A., & Pfeiffer, R. J. (2004). The effect of financial statement restatements on firms' financial reporting strategies.

Mulenga, M. J. (2015). Value Relevance of Accounting Information of Listed Public Sector Banks in Bombay Stock Exchange. *Research Journal of Finance and Accounting*, 6(8).

Murcia, A., & Kohlscheen, E. (2016, March). Moving in tandem: bank provisioning in emerging market economies BIS Working Papers.

Murcia, A., & Kohlscheen, E. (2016, March). Moving in tandem: bank provisioning in emerging market economies. BIS Working Papers.

Myles, D. (2012, November 6). Why Kay, Volcker Are Wrong About Ring Fencing. *International Financial Law Review*. Retrieved from http://www.iflr.com/Article/3113446/Banking/Why-Kay-Volcker-are-wrong-aboutringfencing.html

Myles, D. (2012, November 6). Why Kay, Volcker Are Wrong About Ring Fencing. *International Financial Law Review*. Retrieved from http://www.iflr.com/Article/3113446/Banking/Why-Kay-Volcker-are-wrong-about-ringfencing.html

Nakaso, h. (2016, March 3). Japan's Economy and Monetary policy (Speech). Bank of Japan business leaders meeting, Okinawa.

Neumeyer, P. A., & Perri, F. (2005). Business cycles in emerging economies: The role of interest rates. *Journal of Monetary Economics*, *52*(2), 345–380. doi:10.1016/j.jmoneco.2004.04.011

Odean, T. (1998). Are investors reluctant to realize their losses? *The Journal of Finance*, *53*(5), 1775–1798. doi:10.1111/0022-1082.00072

Ohlson, J. (1995). Earnings, book values, and dividends in equity valuation. *Contemporary Accounting Research*, *11*(Spring), 661–687. doi:10.1111/j.1911-3846.1995.tb00461.x

Ojo, M. (2006). General Literature on the Audit Expectations Gap. *Journal of Forensic Accounting*, *8*(1-2).

Ojo, M. (2006, June 2). Auditor Independence - Its Importance to the External Auditor's Role in Banking Regulation and Supervision. *Paper presented at the 2006 Global Conference on Business and Finance*, San Jose, Costa Rica.

Ojo, M. (2014, October). The Basel Capital Adequacy and Regulatory Framework: Balancing Risk Sensitivity, Simplicity and Comparability. *Centre of Excellence for Scientific & Research Journalism*, *3*(4), 516–522.

Oliveira, L., Rodrigues, L. L., & Craig, R. (2010). Intangible assets and value relevance: Evidence from the Portuguese stock exchange. *The British Accounting Review*, *42*(4), 241–252. doi:10.1016/j.bar.2010.08.001

Olugbenga, A. A., & Oyerinde, A. A. (2014). Value Relevance of Financial Accounting Information of Quoted Companies in Nigeria: A Trend Analysis. *Research Journal of Finance and Accounting*, 5(8).

Oshodin and Chijoke. (2014). The comparative study of value relevance of financial information in the Nigeria banking and petroleum sectors. *Journal of Business Studies Quarterly*, *6*(1).

Paape, L. (2007). *Corporate Governance: The Impact on the Role, Position, and Scope of Services of the Internal Audit Function* (Unpublished PhD Dissertation). Erasmus Research Institute of Management, Erasmus University.

Pagano, M. (1993). Financial Markets and Growth: An Overview. *European Economic Review*, *37*(2-3), 613–622. doi:10.1016/0014-2921(93)90051-B

Palmrose, Z.-V., Richardson, V. J., & Scholz, S. (2004). Determinants of market reactions to restatement announcements. *Journal of Accounting and Economics*, *37*(1), 59–89. doi:10.1016/j.jacceco.2003.06.003

Park, C. W., Jaworski, B. J., & Maclnnis, D. J. (1986). Strategic brand concept-image management. *Journal of Marketing*, *50*(October), 135–145. doi:10.2307/1251291

Pathirawasam, C. (2010). Value relevance of accounting information: Evidence from Sri Lanka. *International Journal of research in commerce & management.*

Pedneault, S. (2009). *Fraud 101 Techniques and Strategies for Understanding Fraud.* Hoboken, NJ: John Wiley & Sons Inc.

Pesando, J. E. (1979, November). On the Random Walk Characteristics of Short- and Long-Term Interest Rates In an Efficient Market. *Journal of Money, Credit and Banking*, *11*(4), 457–466. doi:10.2307/1992047

Petersen, K. H. (2012). Risk and Modern Finance Theory: A Non-mathematical Analysis of Mathematical Models.

Peterson, K.H. (n.d.). Risk and modern finance theory: a non-mathematical analysis of mathematical models. Retrieved from http://ntu.ac.uk/nbs/document_uploads/108661.pdf

Petty, R., & Guthrie, J. (2000). *Journal of Intellectual Capital, 3.*

Pierce, B. & Kilcommins, M. (1996). The Audit Expectations Gap: The Role of Auditing Education. University Business School Research Papers, Dublin City.

Plumlee, M., Brown, D., Hayes, R. M., & Marshall, R. S. (2015). Voluntary environmental disclosure quality and firm value: Further evidence. *Journal of Accounting and Public Policy*, *34*(4), 336–361. doi:10.1016/j.jaccpubpol.2015.04.004

Poloz, S. S. (2014). *Integrating Uncertainty and Monetary Policy-Making: A Practitioner's Perspective.* Bank of Canada.

Popper, K. (1963). *Conjectures and Refutations.* London: Routledge and Keagan Paul.

Porter, B. (1993). An Empirical Study of the Audit Expectation. Performance Gap Accounting and Business Research, 24(93).

Poterba, J. M., & Summers, L. H. (1988). Mean Reversion in Stock Prices: Evidence and Implications. *Journal of Financial Economics, 22*(1), 27–59. doi:10.1016/0304-405X(88)90021-9

Power, M. (1999). The Audit Society: Rituals of Verification. Oxford University Press.

Prawitt, D.F., Sharp, & Wood. (2011). Internal Audit Outsourcing and the Risk of Misleading or Fraudulent Financial Reporting: Did Sarbanes-Oxley Get It Wrong? *Contemporary Accounting Research, 19*(11), 38-46.

PWC. (2015). Global Markets Liquidity Study August 2015

PWC. (2015, August). Global Markets Liquidity Study.

Raggio, R., & Leone, P. R. (2005). Separating Equity and Value. *Proceedings of theZIBS Brand Valuation Workshop*, Atlanta, GA, USA.

Rajgopal, S., Venkatachalam, M., & Kotha, S. (2003). The value relevance of network advantages: The case of e-commerce firms. *Journal of Accounting Research, 41*(1), 135–162. doi:10.1111/1475-679X.00099

Reuters. (2016, June 15). Fed Keeps Interest Rates Unchanged, Signals Fewer Future Hikes. Retrieved from http://www.reuters.com/article/us-usa-fed-idUSKCN0Z10DI

Richardson, G., & Tinaikar, S. (2004). Accounting based valuation models: What have we learned? *Accounting and Finance, 44*(2), 223–255. doi:10.1111/j.1467-629X.2004.00109.x

Roos, J., Roos, G., Dragonetti, N.C. & Edvinsson, L. (1997). *Intellectual Capital: Navigating in the New Business Landscape.* Houndsmills, Basingtoke: Macmillan.

Rossi, S. (2016). The launch of Solvency II – the implementation of the new regime: open issues, implications for business models, and effects on institutional and financial communication/ Keynote address by Mr Salvatore Rossi, Senior Deputy Governor of the Bank of Italy and President of IVASS (Istituto per la Vigilanza sulle Assicurazioni), at the IVASS Conference 2016, Rome, 3 March 2016.

Rossi, S. (2016, March 3). The launch of Solvency II – the implementation of the new regime: open issues, implications for business models, and effects on institutional and financial communication (Keynote address). *Proceedings of the IVASS Conference '16*, Rome.

Schiebel, A. (2007). Empirical Value Relevance of German Gaap and IFRS. *Journal of Economics and Financial Sciences, 1*(2), 321–352.

Schipper, K. (2005). The introduction of accounting standards in Europe: Implications for international convergence. *European Accounting Review*, *14*(1), 324–367. doi:10.1080/09638180420003338013

Scrimgeour, D. (2010). Commodity Price Responses to Monetary Policy Surprises (Working Paper). Colgate University.

Seiler, M. J., & Rom, W. (1997). A Historical Analysis of Market Efficiency: Do Historical Returns Follow a Random Walk? *Journal Of Financial And Strategic Decisions*, 10(2).

Sharma, A., Kumar, S., & Singh, R. (2012). Value Relevance of Financial Reporting and Its Impact on Stock Prices: Evidence from India. *South Asian Journal of Management*, *19*(2), 60–77.

Sharma, M. (2014). Value relevance of accounting information: A comparative study of public and private sector companies in India. *Asia Pacific Journal of Research, 1*(12).

Sheel, A., & Ganguly, M. (2013). Ring Fencing Wall Street. *Indian Express.* Retrieved from http://www.indianexpress.com/news/ringfencing-wall-street/1210651/0

Sheel, A., & Ganguly, M. (2016). Financial Regulatory Reforms – A Mid Term Assessment from an Emerging Market Perspective. In R. Kathuria, N.K. Nagpal, (Eds.), Global Economic Cooperation. Springer Verlag.

Sheel, A., & Ganguly, M. (2016). *Financial Regulatory Reforms – A Mid Term Assessment from an Emerging Market Perspective. In*R. Kathuria & N. K. Nagpa, (Eds.), *Global Economic Cooperation.* Springer Verlag.

Shin, H. S. (2012, November 7). The second phase of global liquidity and its impact on emerging economies (Keynote address). *Proceedings of the Asia Economic Policy Conference*, Federal Reserve Bank of San Francisco.

Shin, H. S., & Turner, P. (2015). What does the new face of international financial intermediation mean for emerging market economies?" *Bank of France Financial Stability Review*, 19.

Shin, H.S. (2012, November 7). The second phase of global liquidity and its impact on emerging economies (Keynote address). *Proceedings of the Asia Economic Policy Conference*, Federal Reserve Bank of San Francisco.

Shin, H.S., & Turner, P. (2015). What does the new face of international financial intermediation mean for emerging market economies? Bank of France Financial Stability Review.

Siganos, A., & Papa, M. (2015). FT coverage and UK target price run-ups. *European Journal of Finance*, *21*(12), 1070–1089. doi:10.1080/1351847X.2014.924077

Sikka, P., Puxty, A., Willmott, H., & Cooper, C. (2003). The Impossibility of Eliminating the Expectations Gap: Some Theory and Evidence. *Critical Explorations on Accounting*, *9*(3), 299–330. doi:10.1006/cpac.1997.0159

Singh, D. (2006). The Role of Third Parties in Banking Regulation and Supervision. *Journal of International Banking Regulation*, 4(3).

Singh, D. (2003). The Role of Third Parties in Banking Regulation and Supervision. *Journal of International Banking Regulation*, *4*(3).

Singh, K., & Kalirajan, K. (2007). Monetary transmission in post-reform India: An evaluation. *Journal of the Asia Pacific Economy*, *12*(2), 158–187. doi:10.1080/13547860701252371

Smets, F., & Wouters, R. (2007). Shocks and Frictions in US Business Cycles: A Bayesian DSGE Approach. *The American Economic Review*, *97*(3), 586–606. doi:10.1257/aer.97.3.586

Sobrun, J., & Turner, P. (2015a). Bond markets and monetary policy dilemmas for emerging market economies. BIS Working Papers.

Soderstrom, N. S., & Sun, K. J. (2007). IFRS Adoption and Accounting Quality: A review. *European Accounting Review*, *16*(4), 245–267. doi:10.1080/09638180701706732

Song, C. J., Thomas, W. B., & Yi, H. (2010). Value relevance of FAS No. 157 fair value hierarchy information and the impact of corporate governance mechanisms. *Accounting Review*, *85*(4), 1375–1410. doi:10.2308/accr.2010.85.4.1375

Srinivasan, S. (2005). Consequences of financial reporting failure for outside directors: Evidence from accounting restatements and audit committee members. *Journal of Accounting Research*, *43*(2), 291–334. doi:10.1111/j.1475-679x.2005.00172.x

Stewart, J., & Subramaniam, N. (2010). *Internal Audit Independence and Objectivity: Emerging Research Opportunities*. Academic Press.

Subramanyam, K. R., & Hung, M. (2007). Financial statement effects of adopting international accounting standards: The case of Germany. *Review of Accounting Studies*, *12*(4), 456–482.

Sundaresan, S. (2009). *Development of financial markets in Asia and the Pacific: the international financial crisis and policy challenges*. BIS Papers.

Sveiby, K.E. (n. d.). *Methods for Measuring Intangible Assets*. Retrieved from www.sveiby.com.au/Intangible Methods.htm

Swanson, E. T. (2016). Measuring the Effects of Federal Reserve Forward Guidance and Asset Purchases on Financial Markets. Economic Dynamics. Retrieved from https://www.economicdynamics.org/meetpapers/2016/paper_1222.pdf

The Final Report of The High-Level Expert Group on Reforming the Structure of the EU Banking Sector The Liikanen Report (Final Report). (2012, October 2).

The Final Report of The High-Level Expert Group on Reforming the Structure of the EU Banking Sector. (n. d.).

The Independent Commission on Banking (ICB). (2011, September). Final Report Recommendations. Retrieved from http://webarchive.nationalarchives.gov.uk/20131003105424/https:/hmt-sanctions.s3.amazonaws.com/ICB%20final%20report/ICB%2520Final%2520Report[1].pdf

The Liikanen Report (Final Report). (2012, October 2).

The Volcker Rule, Section 619 of Title VI of the Dodd Frank Act. (n. d.).

Thornton. (2010). Evaluating the Internal and External Audit Function. Wiley and Sons.

Tsalavoutas, I., André, P., & Evans, L. (2012). The transition to IFRS and the value relevance of financial statements in Greece. *The British Accounting Review*, *44*(4), 262–277. doi:10.1016/j.bar.2012.09.004

Turner, P. (2014). The long-term interest rate, financial risks and policy choices in EMEs. BIS Working Papers.

U.S Economy About. (2016). How does the stock market work? Retrieved from http://useconomy.about.com/od/themarkets/f/Stock_Market_Co.htm

U.S Economy About. (2016). Stock Market Correction. Retrieved from http://useconomy.about.com/od/glossary/g/Market_Correcti.htm

Upson, R. B. (1972). Random Walk and Forward Exchange Rates: A Spectral Analysis. *Journal of Financial and Quantitative Analysis*, *7*(4), 1897. doi:10.2307/2329624

Uribe, M., & Yue, V. (2006). Country Spreads and Emerging Countries: Who Drives Whom? *Journal of International Economics*, *69*(1), 6–36. doi:10.1016/j.jinteco.2005.04.003

Vansteenkiste, I. (2009). How Important Are Common Factors in Driving Non-Fuel Commodity Prices? A Dynamic Factor Analysis. European Central Bank Working Paper.

Varriale, G. (2012). FSA Prudential Chief: Why Banks Must Be Ring Fenced *International Financial Law Review*. Retrieved from http://www.iflr.com/Article/3114533/EU/FSA-prudential-chief-why-banks-must- beringfenced.html

Varriale, G. (2012, November 7). FSA Prudential Chief: Why Banks Must Be Ring Fenced. *International Financial Law Review*. Retrieved from http://www.iflr.com/Article/3114533/EU/FSA-prudential-chief-why-banks-must-be- ringfenced.html

Varriale, G. (2012, September 18). Liikanen Poll: Volcker/Vickers Hybrid Wrong For Europe's Banks. Retrieved from http://www.iflr.com/Article/3090682/Liikanen-poll-VolckerVickers-hybrid-wrong-for-Europes-banks.html

Varriale, G. (2012, September). Liikanen Poll: Volcker/Vickers hybrid wrong for Europe's Banks. *International Financial Law Review*. Retrieved from http://www.iflr.com/Article/3090682/Liikanen-poll-VolckerVickers-hybrid-wrong-for-Europes-banks.html

Veltri S. and Silvestri A. (2011), *La value relevance dei valori contabili dopo la crisi finanziaria: un'applicazione al mercato italiano*, Rivista Italiana di Ragioneria e di Economia Aziendale, Rirea, Roma.

Venkatesh, P., & Chiang, R. (1986). Information Asymmetry and the Dealers Bid-Ask Spread: A Case Study of Earnings and Dividend Announcements. *The Journal of Finance*, *41*(5), 1089–1102. doi:10.1111/j.1540-6261.1986.tb02532.x

Venter, E. R., Emanuel, D., & Cahan, S. F. (2014). The value relevance of mandatory non-GAAP earnings. *Abacus*, *50*(1), 1–24. doi:10.1111/abac.12020

Verbeek, M. (2006). *Econometria*. Bologna: Zanichelli.

Wahab, N. S. A., & Holland, K. (2012). Tax planning, corporate governance and equity value. *The British Accounting Review*, *44*(2), 111–124. doi:10.1016/j.bar.2012.03.005

Walker, A. (2015, February 26). Cheap oil: Asia's winners and losers. BBC News. Retrieved from http://www.bbc.co.uk/news/business-31444344

Watts, R., & Zimmerman, J. (1978). Towards a positive theory of the determination of accounting standards. *Accounting Review*, *53*, 568–589.

Watts, R., & Zimmerman, J. (1990). Positive Accounting Theory. A Ten Year Perspective. *Accounting Review*, *65*(1), 345–378.

Wieland, M. M., Dawkins, M. C., & Dugan, M. T. (2013). The differential value relevance of S&Ps core earnings versus GAAP earnings: The role of stock option expense. *Journal of Business Finance & Accounting*, *40*(1-2), 55–81. doi:10.1111/jbfa.12013

Wilson, W. M. (2008). An empirical analysis of the decline in the information content of earnings following restatements. *Accounting Review*, *83*(2), 519–548. doi:10.2308/accr.2008.83.2.519

Wong, J., Wong, N., & Naiker, V. (2011). Comprehensive versus partial deferred tax liabilities and equity market values. *Accounting and Finance*, *51*(4), 1087–1106. doi:10.1111/j.1467-629X.2011.00430.x

World Bank. (2015a, January). Understanding the Plunge in Oil Prices: Sources and Implications. Global Economic Prospects. Retrieved from https://www.worldbank.org/content/dam/Worldbank/GEP/GEP2015a/pdfs/GEP2015a_chapter4_report_oil.pdf

World Bank. (2015b, March). The Great Plunge in Oil Prices: Causes, Consequences, and Policy Responses. World Bank Group Policy Research Note.

Wright, J. H. (2012). What Does Monetary Policy Do to Long-Term Interest Rates at the Zero Lower Bound? *The Economic Journal*, *122*(564), 447–466. doi:10.1111/j.1468-0297.2012.02556.x

Wu, H., Fargher, N., & Wright, S. (2010). Accounting for investments and the relevance of losses to firm value. *The International Journal of Accounting*, *45*(1), 104–127. doi:10.1016/j.intacc.2010.01.005

Wuyts, G. (2007). Stock Market Liquidity. *Determinants and Implications Tijdschrift voor Economie en Management*, *LII*(2).

Xiang, B. (1998). Institutional factors influencing China's accounting reforms and standards. *Accounting Horizons*, (June), 105–119.

Yartey, C. A., (2008). The Determinants of Stock Market Development in Emerging Economies: Is South Africa Different? IMF.

Yartey, C.A. (2008). The Determinants of Stock Market Development in Emerging Economies: Is South Africa Different? *IMF*.

Yartey, C. A. (2007). Macroeconomic and Institutional Determinants of Stock Market Development in Africa. In J. Okpara (Ed.), *Management and Economic Development in Sub-Saharan Africa: Theoretical and Applied Perspectives*. London: Adonis and Abbey Publishers.

About the Contributors

Marianne Ojo has published a total of more than 80 internationally peer-reviewed books, ISI accredited journal articles, book chapters and conference proceedings papers. She currently works as Visiting Professor, post-doctoral researcher as well as university lecturer and Visiting Scholar and is currently also engaged in several projects at affiliated universities in the United States (George Mason University) as well as supervision of graduate and non-graduate students. Furthermore, she serves as a reviewer for various scientific and academic journals which have been accredited with highest credentials at international level. Her previous academic commitments include Insolvency and Research work at LTB, Frankfurt, Research Fellow at the Center for European Law, University of Bremen (2007 – 2010), Teaching Associate and Graduate Teaching Assistant at Oxford Brookes University (2004 – 2007). She has also collaborated with several other authors as well as contributed in several consultation and academic exercises with the Bank for International Settlements.

Sudipta Bose holds a PhD in Accounting from UNSW Australia and a Master of Business Administration (MBA). Currently, he works with the University of Newcastle. He is a Chartered Accountant (CA) and a Certified Management Accountant (CMA), and he has previously worked in the Finance division of a multinational telecommunication company (Telenor Group, Norway). His research interests include capital market, cost of equity capital, carbon emissions and assurance, sustainability reporting and assurance, integrated reporting and assurance and corporate governance. Recently, he has published in his scholarly article in the British Accounting Review (BAR) and the Journal of Banking and Finance Law and Practice (JBFLP). Sudipta is also a member of European Accounting Association (EAA) and Accounting and Finance Association of Australia and New Zealand (AFAANZ).

James A. DiGabriele, Ph.D./D.P.S., CPA/ABV/CFF: is a Professor of Accounting and Chair of the Department of Accounting Law & Taxation at Montclair State University. He is also the managing director of DiGabriele, McNulty, Campanella

& Co., LLC, in Fairfield, New Jersey; an accounting firm specializing in forensic/investigative accounting and litigation support. His articles have appeared in numerous academic and professional journals including, Accounting Horizons, Critical Perspectives on Accounting, Issues in Accounting Education, Journal of Legal Economics, Journal of Forensic Accounting. The CPA Journal and Journal of Accountancy, Journal of Business Valuation & Economic Loss Analysis and Issues in Accounting Education. He has qualified as an expert in forensic accounting in Federal and State courts.

J. DeLarosiere studied Economics as a major for his undergraduate studies – as well as completed his postgraduate universities in Brazil. Having worked as a lecturer for several years in the Faculty of Social Sciences in Rio de Janeiro, he decided to further his career in the area of Financial Economics – with a focus on the stock markets and government regulation and policies. He is also particularly interested in research related to the BRICS economies – as well as the impact of regulatory and economic reforms and policies on emerging economies.

Manoj Kumar received his PhD in Mechanical Engineering from the Indian Institute of Technology, Delhi, India. He is presently working as Director, International Engineering Services, New Delhi, India. He has authored or co-authored over 80 research papers in journals and conferences.

Sarah Newton wishes to consolidate on her PhD, with legal - as well as financial related research after having graduated with a BSc in Accounting and a Master's degree in Economics. She has worked as a lecturer and Visiting Scholar at several universities in the United Kingdom and hopes that greater focus on the research aspect of her work will broaden horizons and career possibilities globally.

Soren Nielsen is currently expanding on his research career in Economics and International Business with a focus on Financial Markets and Emerging Economies, having worked at the School of Business at Copenhagen University.

Ionica Oncioiu holds a Ph.D. in economy and accounting. Her research interests include the development of SMEs innovation, Project Management, Accounting Information Systems, Asset Management and E-Commerce Marketing. She had more than 10 years of experience in this area and has published 10 text books and more than 70 papers in scholarly peer reviewed international journals. She also authored eight books.

Riccardo Palumbo is Professor of Accounting and Finance at the University "G. d'Annunzio" of Chieti-Pescara. He holds a PhD from the University "Federico II" of Napoli. His research specialisation includes accounting and capital markets and accounting history. He has published a large number of monographs and articles in scholarly journals and has presented his work at a number of leading Universities in Europe and Australia.He has held a number of research positions including as a visiting scholar at the Capital Markets Cooperative Research Centre and visiting professor at the School of Business at the University of Sydney in Australia. He holds a number of academy, government and industry positions in Italy.He is member of the College of Auditors at the Italian Society of Teachers of Accounting (SIDREA - Società Italiana dei Docenti di Ragioneria e di Economia Aziendale); he is a member of the Committee which rates accounting journals in Italy [Commissione Triennale di Lavoro dell'Accademia Italiana di Economia Aziendale – AIDEA]; he has been consultant for the Italian Committee for Evaluation of Research [CIVR – Comitato di indirizzo per la valutazione della ricerca]; he also serves on the Board of Directors of MediaPharma srl (spin-off of University of Chieti-Pescara). He serves on a number of Committees at his University and is the Director of a Master programme in Business Innovation and the head of the Master of Science in Economics and Management.

Pierangelo Rosati is a post-doctoral researcher of the Irish Centre for Cloud Computing and Commerce (IC4) at Dublin City University Business School. Dr. Rosati holds a PhD in Management and Business Administration from the University "G. d'Annunzio" of Chieti-Pescara (Italy) and an MBA from the Alma Mater Studiorum University of Bologna (Italy). He was appointed visiting Ph.D. student at the Capital Markets Cooperative Research Center (CMCRC) in Sydney (Australia) and his research interests span from financial accounting to auditing, market microstructure, and accounting information systems. Dr. Rosati has also been involved in industry as a consultant as well as a board member.

James Rossi wishes to consolidate on the area of publications and research in complementary fields of law and accounting related research. Having gained undergraduate and postgraduate degrees in Economics, with a focus on teaching and lecturing in Economics, Dr Rossi also wishes to consolidate on present achievements with reputable global based research.

Amitav Saha holds a Master of Philosophy from the UNSW Australia and a Master of Commerce degree from Macquarie University. He serves as Head of Accounting at The University of Notre Dame Australia's Sydney School of Business. Amitav is a qualified Certified Practicing Accountant (CPA) and a Fellow of the

Institute of Public Accountants Australia (FIPA). Amitav has presented his research at scholarly conferences across Australia, Europe and the US. His research interests include capital market related valuation research, International Financial Reporting Standards (IFRS), corporate disclosures, and business education. Amitav is also a member of American Accounting Association and European Accounting Association.

Index

F

G

I

L

M

N

O

R

S

T

U

V

Purchase Print + Free E-Book or E-Book Only*

Purchase a print book through the IGI Global Online Bookstore and receive the e-book for free or purchase the e-book only! Shipping fees apply.

www.igi-global.com

Recommended Reference Books

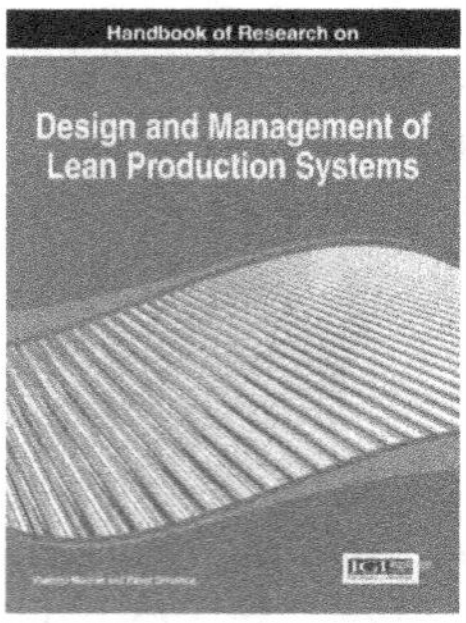

ISBN: 978-1-4666-5039-8
© 2014; 487 pp.
List Price: $260

ISBN: 978-1-4666-7476-9
© 2015; 508 pp.
List Price: $212

ISBN: 978-1-4666-6182-0
© 2014; 325 pp.
List Price: $180

ISBN: 978-1-4666-4474-8
© 2014; 735 pp.
List Price: $276

ISBN: 978-1-4666-5950-6
© 2014; 290 pp.
List Price: $156

ISBN: 978-1-4666-6595-8
© 2015; 406 pp.
List Price: $156

*IGI Global now offers the exclusive opportunity to receive a free e-book with the purchase of the publication in print, or purchase any e-book publication only. You choose the format that best suits your needs. This offer is only valid on purchases made directly through IGI Global's Online Bookstore and not intended for use by book distributors or wholesalers. Shipping fees will be applied for hardcover purchases during checkout if this option is selected.

Should a new edition of any given publication become available, access will not be extended on the new edition and will only be available for the purchased publication. If a new edition becomes available, you will not lose access, but you would no longer receive new content for that publication (i.e. updates). The free e-book is only available to single institutions that purchase printed publications through IGI Global. Sharing the free e-book is prohibited and will result in the termination of e-access.

Publishing Information Science and Technology Research Since 1988

IGI GLOBAL DISSEMINATOR OF KNOWLEDGE

www.igi-global.com Sign up at www.igi-global.com/newsletters facebook.com/igiglobal twitter.com/igiglobal

Stay Current on the Latest Emerging Research Developments

Become an IGI Global Reviewer for Authored Book Projects

The overall success of an authored book project is dependent on quality and timely reviews.

In this competitive age of scholarly publishing, constructive and timely feedback significantly decreases the turnaround time of manuscripts from submission to acceptance, allowing the publication and discovery of progressive research at a much more expeditious rate. Several IGI Global authored book projects are currently seeking highly qualified experts in the field to fill vacancies on their respective editorial review boards:

Applications may be sent to:
development@igi-global.com

Applicants must have a doctorate (or an equivalent degree) as well as publishing and reviewing experience. Reviewers are asked to write reviews in a timely, collegial, and constructive manner. All reviewers will begin their role on an ad-hoc basis for a period of one year, and upon successful completion of this term can be considered for full editorial review board status, with the potential for a subsequent promotion to Associate Editor.

If you have a colleague that may be interested in this opportunity, we encourage you to share this information with them.

www.igi-global.com

InfoSci®-Books

A Database for Progressive Information Science and Technology Research

Maximize Your Library's Book Collection!

Invest in IGI Global's InfoSci®-Books database and gain access to hundreds of reference books at a fraction of their individual list price.

The InfoSci®-Books database offers unlimited simultaneous users the ability to precisely return search results through more than 75,000 full-text chapters from nearly 3,400 reference books in the following academic research areas:

Business & Management Information Science & Technology • Computer Science & Information Technology
Educational Science & Technology • Engineering Science & Technology • Environmental Science & Technology
Government Science & Technology • Library Information Science & Technology • Media & Communication Science & Technology
Medical, Healthcare & Life Science & Technology • Security & Forensic Science & Technology • Social Sciences & Online Behavior

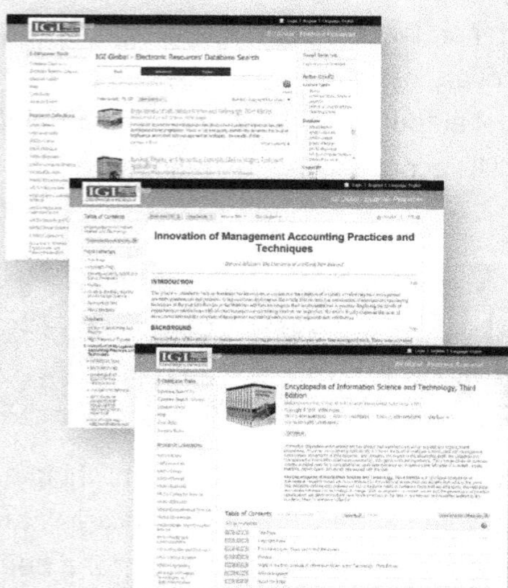

Peer-Reviewed Content:
- Cutting-edge research
- No embargoes
- Scholarly and professional
- Interdisciplinary

Award-Winning Platform:
- Unlimited simultaneous users
- Full-text in XML and PDF
- Advanced search engine
- No DRM

Librarian-Friendly:
- Free MARC records
- Discovery services
- COUNTER4/SUSHI compliant
- Training available

To find out more or request a free trial, visit:
www.igi-global.com/eresources

IGI Global
DISSEMINATOR OF KNOWLEDGE
www.igi-global.com

IGI Global
Proudly Partners with

eContent Pro

eContent Pro specializes in the following areas:

Academic Copy Editing
Our expert copy editors will conduct a full copy editing procedure on your manuscript and will also address your preferred reference style to make sure your paper meets the standards of the style of your choice.

Expert Translation
Our expert translators will work to ensure a clear cut and accurate translation of your document, ensuring that your research is flawlessly communicated to your audience.

Professional Proofreading
Our editors will conduct a comprehensive assessment of your content and address all shortcomings of the paper in terms of grammar, language structures, spelling, and formatting.

IGI Global Authors, Save 10% on eContent Pro's Services!

Scan the QR Code to Receive Your 10% Discount

The 10% discount is applied directly to your eContent Pro shopping cart when placing an order through IGI Global's referral link. Use the QR code to access this referral link. eContent Pro has the right to end or modify any promotion at any time.

Email: customerservice@econtentpro.com

econtentpro.com

www.ingramcontent.com/pod-product-compliance
Lightning Source LLC
LaVergne TN
LVHW080559300926
849162LV00005B/991